THE FABRICATION OF VIRTUE

English prison architecture, 1750–1840

The fabrication of virtue

English prison architecture, 1750-1840

ROBIN EVANS
Lecturer, Architectural Association, London

CAMBRIDGE UNIVERSITY PRESS

Cambridge
London   New York   New Rochelle
Melbourne   Sydney

Published by the Press Syndicate of the University of Cambridge
The Pitt Building, Trumpington Street, Cambridge CB2 1RP
32 East 57th Street, New York, NY 10022, USA
296 Beaconsfield Parade, Middle Park, Melbourne 3206, Australia

First published 1982

Printed in Great Britain at
the University Press, Cambridge

Library of Congress catalogue card number: 81-18105

British Library Cataloguing in Publication Data

Evans, Robin
The fabrication of virtue: English prison
architecture, 1750—1840.
1. Prisons — England — Construction — History
I. Title
725'.6   HV8829.G7

ISBN 0 521 23955 9

Contents

Illustrations

Acknowledgements

I began collecting material on prison architecture in 1969. In 1975 a dissertation on the subject was submitted to the University of Essex, the text of which forms the basis of this book, though it has been extensively revised and rewritten during the last three years. Over so long a period of gestation many persons and institutions have helped in many ways. It is therefore inevitable but regrettable that these brief acknowledgements record only the tip of the iceberg. I hope that omissions are not taken to signify lack of gratitude or recognition on my part, for I realize that nothing could have been accomplished without the invisible service provided by all those who go unmentioned.

With much gratitude I acknowledge the help and advice of Joseph Rykwert whose erudition illuminated many dark patches for me. His support and encouragement were crucial to my rather tentative early efforts while later, his careful reading of successive drafts led to the excision of superfluous material and the better consideration of what remained. I owe a good deal to Ian McIvor of the Scottish National Monument Record for information on eighteenth-century prisons in Edinburgh; to Theresa Ward for help with the Bentham Papers; to Dr J.R.S. Whiting for material on the Gloucester prisons, and to Rodney Mace, Dr John Bold and Brian Collinge for help with sources, illustrations and much else besides.

The discussions I had with Dr Heather Tomlinson and Dr Michael Ignatieff, both of whom were working on related subject matter, helped me clarify my position and plot the areas on which our agreements and disagreements were most pronounced. I should also thank Professor Stan Cohen and Raphael Samuel for their valuable criticism of parts of the thesis text.

I am very grateful indeed for the encouragement offered at various times by Massimo Scolari, Tony Vidler, John Bender, Sergio Lenci,

Adrian Forty, Georges Teyssot, Renzo Dubini, Chris Hale and Alvin Boyarsky.

To Professor J.H. Burns and Dr Robin Middleton I give special thanks; the former for generously telling me so much that I would never otherwise have found out about Bentham, the latter for all he has done, though he would be the last to admit it.

The greater part of the research was carried out at the British Library where a larger selection of eighteenth- and nineteenth-century tracts on prison reform, discipline and construction were to be found than in other archives. Material was also consulted in the National Library of Scotland, Edinburgh; the Guildhall Library, London; The Soane Museum, London; the Victoria and Albert Museum Library, London; the Royal Institute of British Architects Library and Drawings Collection, London; the Bentham Papers, University College London; the Institute of Criminology, Cambridge; and the Howard League Collection, University of Warwick. In all these libraries and collections the staff were courteous and helpful. In 1972 and 1979 I made the rounds of local record offices, trying the patience of archivists and staff, whose willingness to spend time and effort searching for plans or tracing records cannot be adequately repaid, but for which I am more than grateful. Particular mention should be made of the Corporation of London Record Office, and the County Record Offices for Gloucestershire, Wiltshire, and Essex, all of which contain extensive collections of germane architectural drawings and documents.

Attention should also be drawn to the kindness of individuals, companies and institutions in allowing reproduction of illustrations, drawings or photographs within their copyright. The photographic section of the British Library has been especially generous in this regard. Specific acknowledgements are given with the list of illustrations. Parts of the book have previously been published, though not in exactly the same form. Chapter 5 is based on an article, 'Bentham's Panopticon', that appeared in *Controspazio* (1970) and then in *Architectural Association Quarterly* (1971). Sections of chapter 2 and chapter 6 appeared in an article on prison labour in *Lotus 12* (1976). I am grateful to the editors of these journals for permission to reproduce. I should also like to thank Colonel Hayward of the Home Office for his help in arranging access to Pentonville and other prisons.

The Nuffield Foundation provided me with a fellowship for 1978/9 which, although for research on another subject, enabled me to draw more general conclusions than those of the original thesis. The final chapter is largely the result of work done during that year.

I would like to record my thanks also to William Davies of Cambridge University Press for his interest and good judgement, Elizabeth O'Beirne-Ranelagh, also of C.U.P., for her skilful editing and Sylvia Whitehouse for doing what she claimed she could not do, quickly producing a perfect typescript from a confusing and sometimes illegible draft. Finally I thank my wife Janet not just for all the typing, researching, reading, re-reading, correcting, comments and suggestions, but for generosity and patience that bordered on the indulgent.

R.E.
Finsbury Park, 1981

Prison offers the same sense of security to the convict as does a royal palace to a King's guest. They are the 2 buildings constructed with the most faith, those which give the greatest certainty of being what they are.

Jean Genet, *The Thief's Journal*

Introduction

The history of English prisons between 1750 and 1850 is also the history of the emergence of a new kind of architecture, associated with reform. The penal reforms of the late eighteenth and early nineteenth century not only regularized imprisonment and made it the centrepiece of the penal system but gave to it a moral purpose. During the same period the prison became a proper subject for architecture. This double novelty, the development of an institution and the application of architecture to its buildings, provided the ideal conditions for the perfecting of techniques that sought to make architecture the instigator of virtue.

A brief comparison may indicate the extent of the change brought about during the course of one century. In 1750, England's most notorious prison was Newgate. It had been reconstructed in 1667 on a site in the wall of London, where from Roman times a gate had stood. Since the thirteenth century, or perhaps earlier, the gate had housed a prison. But Newgate was not prison architecture in any sense we would now understand. Despite being the most recognizable and most infamous gaol in the country, it was to all appearances no more than it had always been — a city gate. Indeed it was almost identical to another of London's gates, Cripplegate, which had been rebuilt in 1663 to accommodate the Water Bailiff of London and his household (Fig. 14). The only external signs of Newgate's use as a gaol were the three emblematic figures of Truth, Justice and Mercy that stood in niches over the centre portal facing the street. Internally, the unexceptional layout was hard to distinguish from any other variety of building. Thus the nature of the prison was neither manifest in the facades nor could it be easily identified from the evidence of the plan (Fig. 15).

There can be no doubt, however, that the nature of eighteenth-century imprisonment was amply demonstrated in this same place by the occasional arrival of chained gangs of prisoners from other gaols; their departure for transportation; the exit of others in the tumbril for

1

WD

execution; the noise of inmates soliciting alms from the begging grate into the main thoroughfare of Newgate Street; the glimpse of many more through the open windows into the congested wards above, giving a hint of the immense concentration of low life within a single habitation (the prison was often host to over 300). A rich traffic between gaol and city also made it possible for many outsiders to penetrate the interior and witness the exploitative machinations of the keeper and his deputies, the licentiousness, the overcrowding, the pervasiveness of mortal disease and moral contamination. Out of all this, together with what was rumoured and what was published, emerged a contemporary picture of Newgate as the home of vice, exemplifying the consequences of disorder and dissipation. Whatever life in Newgate was really like, it was repeatedly used to illustrate evil in its natural habitat as a mixture of unbridled crude pleasure, bestiality and filth. This, though, was hardly the gaol's explicit judicial function, which was still generally limited to the attendant task of holding prisoners before trial and before execution of sentence.

Mid-eighteenth-century Newgate certainly expressed the nature of imprisonment, but architecture was not the means of expression. The facade provided the scene of exposition for a perverse *tableau vivant*, but was not itself conceived as a significant medium for propagating the meaning of imprisonment (Fig. 1). Nor indeed was the interior arrangement calculated to give specific shape to prison life. This does not mean that there was no relationship between the form of the building and the events that took place within it — as is pointed out in chapter 1, such a relationship did exist, but it was not one that established the prison as distinct from other buildings, neither was it likely to have been the product of conscious design.

By 1850, England's most famous prison was Pentonville, the Model Prison and the antithesis of Newgate, marking the end of the movement for penal reform as Newgate had marked its beginning. At Pentonville imprisonment, by now the major legal sanction, was both a penalty and a course of treatment. Joshua Jebb, the first Surveyor General of Prisons, had supervised its design and construction himself. Everything about it had been conceived with forethought, care and precision for the purpose of amending the criminal mind, a process referred to as reformation of character. On the one hand walls were raised of ever greater solidity, at an ever increasing frequency and with ever more cunning to

1. The London Rairey Shows. A satirical print showing Jack Sheppard and Jonathan Wilde at Newgate, 1750.

compartmentalize and separate inmates; the cell became all important (Fig. 187). On the other hand great tunnels of space lined with a dense network of sophisticated services were stretched throughout the prison to give all 520 cells an exactly equal status, to maintain their solitude and to reunify them under the gaze of the governor who occupied the very centre (Fig. 183). The entire prison was under his scrutiny and jurisdiction, yet the convicts within their cells, though they could be spied on locally by warders, or interrogated by the chaplain, were removed from view. The surveillance that was such a strong forming agency of the plan was not a surveillance of the inmates as it had been in the Panopticon and in certain American penitentiaries; it was surveillance of the silent space that separated them.

This vast institution, with its centrifugal vistas, its overwhelming repetition of units, its gadgets and machinery, contained no accidents. Everything was arranged to prevent the genesis and spread of vice. In Newgate corruption and profanity were concentrated into one place and incidentally exhibited as a parody of evil: in Pentonville they were to be erased from the character of the convict with the aid of what J.T. Burt, Assistant Chaplain, confidently described as 'moral science', an effective hybrid of piety and rationalism that sought the salvation of man in the condition of his soul but understood the soul to be a product of this world. Thus Pentonville, in so far as it was an agency of reformation, was a vast and complex piece of engineering aimed not at the conquest of nature, but at the conquest of human nature.

If the model cells were hermetic within the prison, the prison was hermetic within the world at large. Yet Pentonville was unmistakably a penal institution, in the first place because the portcullis entrance added by Sir Charles Barry made play of the commonplace association between ancient dungeon incarceration and contemporary imprisonment (more insipidly than most, as it happens), and secondly, because Jebb's radial cell blocks, which henceforth would form the skyline of every new prison, became a direct and powerful evocation in their own right, though he had not regarded their appearance as a matter of any importance in designing them (Fig. 200). All else was hidden. Few signs of life could be seen from the outside, so architecture, good, bad, or indifferent, by intention or by accident, was now the sole medium transmitting the character of the prison to the public.

The contrast between Newgate and Pentonville does little more than measure the distance from a relic of ancient practice to an advanced technical achievement. Still, if it suggests that between the beginning and end points of this study a truly remarkable change took place in prison architecture as well as in imprisonment, then it will have served its purpose. Between the demolition of old Newgate in 1767 and the completion of Pentonville in 1842 nearly every gaol and house of correction in the land had been rebuilt or closed. In the ensuing decades the same process of demolition and re-establishment was to be repeated, this time spawning copies and minor variants of the Pentonville model from Bodmin to Newcastle, so that by 1880 what was by then the national prison system had undergone two radical reappraisals and two thorough reconstructions, both dictated by the imperatives of penal reform. These two waves of building indicate a profound belief in the transforming powers of architecture. At the very least, new prisons were expected to stem the tide of mutual corruption between prisoners. Perhaps, by supplying the precondition of solitude, they would also work on the mind, the character, the soul, subduing temper and raising the spirit. The following chapters describe how the model prisons came about and, in relating events against the background of earlier practice, seek to define the links that were thought to attach architecture to moral science.

The entire generation of Victorian prisons based on Pentonville are now often interpreted by the authorities as an unpalatable method of exacting vengeance, and were characteristically described in one official publication as 'built . . . to carry out a system of brutal deterrence'. But until very recently an exactly opposite interpretation was to be found in scholarly literature, where they were seen as the products of benevolence. This proposition can be demonstrated with reference to contemporary sources, for it reflects the opinion held by reformers and experts in penal matters about their own endeavours; they wrote the books and drafted the reports. But during the last 20 years, and especially since the publication of David Rothman's *Birth of the Asylum* (1971), Michel Foucault's *Surveiller et Punir* (1975) and Michael Ignatieff's *A Just Measure of Pain* (1978), the essential ambivalence of the reformed prisons has been better recognized. Reflection on their humanity or inhumanity served to deflect attention away from their being, first and foremost, the location for a process that had nothing directly to do with kindness or severity.

It appears that the exacting architecture of nineteenth-century prisons stemmed from two ideas, the one but a step beyond the other. The first was to be found neither in architecture nor in penal theory but, curiously enough, in a patriarchal conception of psychology; it was that 'evil communication corrupts', a common phrase frequently quoted by reformers, lifted from St Paul's Epistle to the Corinthians. The second idea was to draw this dismal picture of social intercourse into the structure, form and content of our surroundings. There had been an endless reiteration of complaints that evil communication was destroying innocence and corrupting good manners in towns, suburbs, and the country, in taverns, brothels and prisons from the sixteenth century onwards. Remedies had been sought in the strengthening of family discipline, the more effective execution of the laws or the exculpation of venery. Only in the late eighteenth century, and then as if with a blinding flash of insight, was architecture discovered to be a serviceable weapon in this continuing war of attrition against vice. For a variety of reasons reformers and architects alike were able to suggest an instrumental relationship between architecture and morality quite different from the familiar theory that buildings could represent virtue in their visible form.

Whereas for a long time architecture had been considered as an element in the armoury of civilization, as part of a defensive strategy against depredation, or as an emblem of political order writ large, the new institutions — reformed gaols, houses of correction and penitentiaries — maintained this princely logic of defence and display only on their outer surface, where they touched the rest of the world. The formation of the interior subscribed to another set of principles, neither defensive nor emblematic but causal. These buildings, with their proliferating components and patterned plans, were to map the location of staff and inmates, guide their movements and mediate the transactions between them. Grouped or solitary, moving or at rest, under instruction or at work, unseen, seeing or being seen, heard or unheard, nearby or at a distance, it was always architecture that fixed the shape of experience. This is what made the reformed prisons and model prisons into far more than places of punishment, providing sites for the development of an architecture that would, for the first time, take full advantage of its latent powers. A new role had been found for it as a vessel of conscience and as pattern giver to society, extending its boundaries way beyond the limits customarily ascribed to it either as an art or as a prosaic utility.

Could it be, then, that the study of this relatively lowly building type hovering between conventional architecture and engineering exposes a dark side of architecture that was turned briefly into the light during the period of reform? At the present time few theorists, critics or practitioners would allow architecture more than a very modest influence. They would rather see all such claims as evidence of a misguided utopianism tied to the inflated rhetoric of modern movement pioneers, point to the failure of their aspirations and consider the matter closed. It is also true that the prisons of the eighteenth and nineteenth centuries were declared failures. As soon as constructed they were found wanting. They never proved capable of delivering quite what was expected of them: they did not manufacture goodness in quantity. Yet all along, the philanthropists, architects and administrators responsible for their establishment felt themselves in possession of a kind of knowledge — what John Howard described as 'the more rational plan for softening the mind in order to its amendment ' — that would subdue the animal in man more surely than other agencies and would do so by investing power in places rather than persons. They believed that by removing a large portion of the authority concentrated till then in the unreliable hands of gaolers, and redistributing it throughout the inert and seemingly passive body of the prison building, they would be able to reduce the violence of authority and increase its scope at one and the same time. This claim may have been exaggerated; it may have provided an uncertain foundation on which to erect so extensive a superstructure. Perhaps it was regarded as a useful fiction fostered by philanthropists eager to believe in a method perfectly tailored to the requirements of reform, by administrators eager to vindicate the untried, and by architects eager to establish their professional usefulness in the new world of committee patronage. Illusions there certainly were — about the tractability of the criminal mind, about the benevolence of the new kinds of imprisonment, about the certitude of results, about the mechanical facility of it all. But the reader will have to decide from what follows whether it is altogether an illusion that architecture can silently preside over us.

Whatever the insights or illusions, they gave rise to a new kind of architecture; of that there can be no doubt. The techniques of isolation, sanitation, pacification and observation described in the central chapters of this book soon spread to cover other kinds of abnormality in hospitals, lunatic asylums and workhouses. These techniques spread wider too, becoming diluted into the commonplaces of a profession that made increasing claim to serve society's needs. Later in the nineteenth century, in schools, housing and town planning a similar sort of design, which conceived society at a great distance but touched it intimately, was more hesitantly applied to the central task of fabricating normality, rather than the peripheral task of rectifying abnormality. Still, it was in the prisons that these techniques achieved their most perfect, elaborate and unrelenting expression, there that the connection between the building and its intended effects were stated most clearly and unequivocally, and there that its actual effects were observed most meticulously. For these reasons alone the present study seemed worth undertaking.

1   Another world, yet the same

It is easy enough to see that architecture fixed the shape of experience in the nineteenth-century prison. But surely this is what architecture does in any case; perhaps more gently, in more familiar scenery, with more commonplace elements, yet just as insistently. So, did the architects whose work this book describes develop something new, or did they bring a hidden but intrinsic aspect of architecture into the light for the first time? Either way, what difference did their discovery make to the prison or to architecture in general? Such questions could better be contemplated if more were known about early prisons, particularly about prison buildings and prison conditions preceding the reforms which were set in motion after 1779. Unfortunately, the contemporary documents that have survived, as well as more recent studies based on them, are, with few exceptions, short of information about buildings and their use. So this chapter can only make a provisional reconstruction from more or less isolated fragments. In doing so it may at least suggest the degree of correlation between the structure of prison buildings and the nature of prison life in seventeenth- and eighteenth-century England.

The reformers themselves provide the most vivid and the most detailed accounts of unreformed prisons. This is because they recognized that unreformed prison buildings were intimately bound up with persistent customs and practices which they were determined to suppress. It is not therefore surprising that we see the old gaols, bridewells and sponging houses largely through their eyes. The reformers do not present us with one picture, however, but two. The first and the most familiar belongs to a rhetoric of rostrum and pamphlet: tortured bodies wasting in dungeons; debauchery and rebellion under stinking vaults; unredeeming hells full of vermin and cruelty; dank, crowded hives. These were the spectres raised by men with an urgent mission when reform became an active political issue. They translated easily into historical opinion after the event and, for some time, stood in the way of any other

9

perception of the past. W.L. Clay, writing in 1861, could despatch the period in a single sentence: 'Before Howard's time the state of English prisons was horrible and disgusting.'[1]

The second is a very different picture; more an itemization than a characterization, put together painstakingly, piece by piece, prison by prison, circuit by circuit; a compilation of facts — though still tinctured with indignation — that would provide an essential datum from which any improvement could be measured. John Howard was the originator of this approach.

Chosen as Sheriff of Bedfordshire in 1773, Howard visited the County Gaol and found it iniquitous. He proposed that fees be paid by the County rather than by the prisoners. His fellow magistrates asked for precedents. Howard sought them in the neighbouring gaols of Huntingdon and Cambridge, found none and travelled further. Soon he had visited every gaol and then every house of correction and bridewell in England and Wales. All of this produced not one precedent, but by now his odyssey had turned into a more general quest for knowledge. In all he was to make four English prison tours and seven tours abroad.

In 1777 the information he had collected was mustered together and published in Warrington as *The State of the Prisons*; a work with no literary pretensions, yet a classic. In 1792 the fourth and most complete edition went to press. Particulars of each prison were presented, as in the following examples:[2]

Beccles Bridewell, Suffolk.
A room on the ground floor called the *ward*, a chamber for women called the *upper ward*, a day room with a fire place; and a dungeon seven steps underground. In the *ward* is a window to the street which is highly improper, as I have always seen numbers of idle persons crowding about it. No proper separation of men and women. Only one court. The keeper has a large garden — Salary, £11.10s.0d. Licence for beer (a riotouse alehouse). Clauses against spiritous liquors not hung up. Fees, 6s.8d. Allowance, a two-penny loaf a day (weight, July 9th, 1782, 20 oz.). 30 shillings a year for straw. £5 a year for coals. When prisoners work they have half the profit.
1776   Feb. 6,   prisoners 3
1779   April 2,   prisoners 9
1782   July 8,   prisoners 15
[Table of fees also reproduced in the original.]

Reading County Bridewell, Berkshire.
This is the town bridewell. It was formerly a church, and is a spacious room, with 4 dark suffocating huts on one side for night rooms, one for men 16 feet by 10½

and 6½ high: aperture in the door 8" × 5": straw worn to dust, not changed for many months; one for women 15 foot 8" × 19 foot 9"; aperture in the door 7" × 5": the 2 other rooms less — the county pays rent to the corporation — it is dirty and out of repair. Men and women are together in daytime. No court: no water: allowance to felons 3*d* a day; and to petty offenders, 2 pint loaves each every sunday and one every week-day. Keeper's salary £18. from the county; £2 from the town; fees 4*s*.4*d*. No table: licence for beer: half the profit of the prisoners' work: £2 a year to find them straw. Clauses against spiritous liquor hung up: and there were, on a board, some orders to be observed, approved . . .

April 28th 1778

1776	Jan. 1,	prisoners 6
1776	Nov. 1,	prisoners 6
1779	April 21,	prisoners 7
1782	March 5,	prisoners 13

Accommodation was detailed, the fees were recorded, as were the staff and their emoluments, the number of prisoners, where they slept, where they worked and under what conditions. Peculiarities were noted.

With the publication of Howard's findings the nation's prisons passed from the unknown to the known. All the vaguely apprehended truths and extravagant generalizations were now underwritten with a body of facts. Methodical, without a great intellect, a campaigner but no visionary, Howard was neither well-educated nor a good writer. It was to some extent his consciousness of these defects which led to his originality. 'Enough of the declamatory kind has been written by others', he said. His talent was not for elaborate digressions on morality nor for invective and so he would confine himself to the 'narration of facts'.[3]

Similar surveys were later made by Dr Alexander Smith, J.C. Lettsome, James Neild, T.F. Buxton, the Society for the Improvement of Prison Discipline, several Parliamentary Commissions and, eventually, the Home Department in a continuous revision of Howard's achievement, but as a technique its greatest influence over events was at its inception. *The State of the Prisons* was the first effective instrument forged in the cause of rebuilding — many would say the decisive instrument — and it is significant that it was hardly about new prisons at all, but about the old ones, showing that conditions in them throughout the country were surprisingly uniform, but uniformly bad. Most prisons were in need of repair, many required extensive remodelling, many more would have to be entirely rebuilt. All needed drastic reform of rules and finance. It was an unflattering picture from life, but there was nothing spectacular about it. Only occasionally were situations of bestial nastiness encountered, or genuine dungeons discovered, although both semi-basements and cellars were described as 'dungeons' by Howard.[4] Yet in spite of this darkening of the view, and despite the episodes of misconduct, impropriety, misappropriation and ill-treatment peppered amongst the listings and tabulations, the impression is not of unusual cruelty so much as of banality; of a despicable humanity in a commonplace setting.

From the surveys of Howard (1774–88) and Neild (1800–6)[5] it can be seen that the majority of prisons were very small and were found in a limited variety of situations. Characteristically they would be towards the edge of a town or city, occasionally at its centre. Sometimes they would be associated with or incorporated into other public buildings. Some were lodged within the gatehouses of city walls (as were London Newgate, Ludgate, Exeter Southgate Prison, Scarborough Gaol, Southampton Town Gaol, Newcastle County Gaol, the City of Hereford Gaol and Bridewell, Chester Northgate Gaol, Canterbury City Gaol, Carmarthen Borough Gaol, Chichester City Gaol and Bridewell, Stamford Town Gaol, Abingdon Town Gaol, Newport Town Gaol, Bristol Newgate and Carlisle City Gaol), or located on the site of a gate (like the old Dorchester County Gaol, St Peter's Gaol, York, Lincoln City and County Gaol and Stafford County Bridewell), or within castle keeps (Tower of London, Colchester Prison, Dover Gaol, Cambridge County Gaol and Bridewell, Norwich County Gaol, Windsor Debtors' Prison, Lincoln Castle Prison, Oxford County Gaol, Worcester County Gaol and Bridewell, Shrewsbury Town Gaol and Bridewell, Hereford Bridewell, Gloucester County Gaol, St Brievell's Debtors' Prison, Launceston County Gaol, York Castle County Gaol, Knaresborough Debtors' Prison, Lancaster County Gaol, Chester County Gaol and Haverfordwest Prison).[6] There were two prisons on the sites of old priories (Hereford County Gaol and Preston County Bridewell), two in palaces (London Bridewell and the Savoy Prison), some within old mansions (like the 'majestik, queer ruin' of Bury St Edmunds Town Bridewell, and the Liverpool Borough Gaol in the Earl of Derby's castellated villa), four in disused chapels (Nottingham Town House of Correction, Usk County Bridewell, Carnarvon County Gaol and Tiverton Town Bridewell), one under a chapel apparently still in use (Kendal) Town Gaol), one in a disused church (Reading Bridewell), one in a disused synagogue (Bury Bridewell), several in town or guild halls

(Nottingham Town Gaol, Dolgelly Bridewell, Coventry Bridewell, Coventry City Bridewell, Cardiff Town Gaol, Brackley Gaol, Berwick Town and City Gaol, Walsall Town Gaol, Tiverton Town Gaol, Knaresborough Town Gaol, Sheffield Town Gaol, Penryn Borough Gaol and Aldborough Gaol), seven amalgamated with poorhouses or workhouses (Wrexham County Bridewell, Newport Isle of Wight Bridewell and Town Gaol, Yarmouth Bridewell, Thame Bridewell, Ludlow Town Bridewell, Liverpool Bridewell and Warrington Town Bridewell), one in stables (Penrith Prison), others under courtrooms or council chambers (Rochester County Gaol, Deal Gaol, East Grinstead Prison, Wallingford Town Gaol), and eight within taverns (Reading Town Compter, Tower Hamlets Gaol, West Wycomb Prison, Kettering Prison, Basingstoke Prison, Halifax Prison, Nantwich Prison, Newport Pagnell Prison and Bradford Debtors' Prison). Practically all the remaining 200 or so institutions recorded by Howard between 1773 and 1777 were nothing more or less than rooms, cottages or lodging houses, hardly distinguishable from the buildings around them and betraying no sign of their special function.

Because of this inscrutability of purpose, the few surviving plans of buildings untouched by reform cannot easily be read as architectural drawings. The most informative of them are like little maps that intimate a pattern of occupation (Fig. 2); they have a geography, but they do not have a geometry, and the difference is a critical one. The larger prisons had generally been erected over a period of decades or even centuries — aggregations of improvements and remodellings undertaken by carpenters and artisans with no purpose but to provide more room and a degree of security, and security was in any case more easily supplied by the purchase of ironmongery than by building. An inventory of Clerkenwell House of Correction taken in 1765, in which bars on windows, gratings, bolts, chains, locks and keys for doors and spikes on walls, together with 26 pairs of double irons, 4 pairs of handcuffs, 10 pairs of single irons and one pair of shackles constitute the greater part of the list, indicates the reliance on these items to hold the prison population in place.[7] This meant that the one thing peculiar to the prison, the need to prevent escape, did not greatly affect its internal distribution or disturb the elevation of its buildings, except in the frequent but by no means universal provision of a boundary wall mounted with *chevaux-de-frise*.

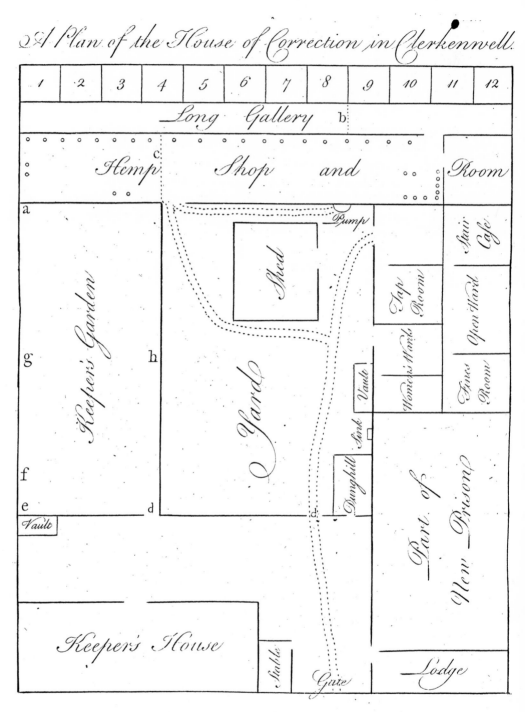

2. Clerkenwell House of Correction, plan drawn by Jacob Ilive, 1757.

3. Norwich Castle County Gaol in 1786. The building to the right of the keep was the County Courthouse. To the left was the gaoler's house.

15

Old castles, like Norwich, sprouted a jumble of hovels outside as well as inside the fractured curtain wall of the keep (felons accommodated within, debtors and misdemeanants without) (Figs. 3, 4); the Southwark Counter (Borough Compter) was arranged as a small lodging house, with a parlour, kitchen and dormitory on the ground floor and more select chambers above;[8] Marlborough Bridewell, an eight room dwelling, was enlarged by the addition of a terrace of simple cottage-like shells as late as 1786 (Fig. 5).[9] The unencumbered floor space of Devizes Bridewell and Town Gaol, a lath and plaster building remodelled by Esau Reynolds between 1771 and 1775, resembled nothing so much as a workshop, though Howard reported that no employment was provided there (Fig. 6);[10] the Marshalsea, conforming to the local pattern of development, lined a small urban court off the Borough High Street (Fig. 7); Ludgate extended along the sides of a blind alley, and the principal ranges of building in the Fleet Prison and King's Bench were substantial tenements which the inhabitants ruefully referred to as colleges (Figs. 8, 11).

Hovel, cottage, house, workshop, lodging house, terrace, alley, court and tenement, the most commonplace types of accommodation in towns and cities, were the identifiable forms in the construction and layout of early eighteenth-century prisons.

The physical likeness between the prison and other secular buildings is perhaps hardly surprising, since most buildings were then modelled on dwellings of one kind or another: palaces, villas, mansions and so forth. Even so, the prison took patterns of so varied a character yet of such fundamental ordinariness that it could not be said to constitute a specific building type at all.

In contrast, prison literature, particularly in the seventeenth century, portrayed imprisonment not as a replica of daily life but as its opposite; as another world, a crowded but uncharted realm whose moral flavour was devoid of any relation to decent life. The theme was derived from Thomas Dekker,[11] but was expressed tenaciously enough to suggest more than the reiteration of a literary device. Geffray Mynshull for example, writing from King's Bench in 1617 to try and secure his own release, returned again and again to the 'otherness' of the prison. Despite its being in the heart of a familiar city, it might as well have been on the other side of the earth. It was 'a microcosmos, a little world of woe, . . . a mappe of misery', a famous city with every trade, a little Commonwealth within which a citizen suffered exile, a banishing, a pilgrimage to Jerusalem through a desert, a labyrinth full of blind meanders. It was a tour of the secret villanies of mankind. You needed a guide through prison as you would on a passage through Africa.[12]

Towards the middle of the eighteenth century the piles of metaphors and similes fall away, but the image at the core remains. Jacob Ilive, on his arrival at Clerkenwell House of Correction, declared himself 'as utter a stranger as if I had been born in some distant region'; a French traveller in 1790 referred to King's Bench again as an independent republic with its own gardens, shops and taverns.[13]

To find out of what this otherness consisted, and how the prison, to all appearances so ordinary, sustained it, an attempt will have to be made to find the points of correspondence between what is known of prison life and what is known of prison building. An undue emphasis

4. Norwich Castle County Gaol. A section of the keep made in 1826 showing remains of the early eighteenth-century felons' prison.

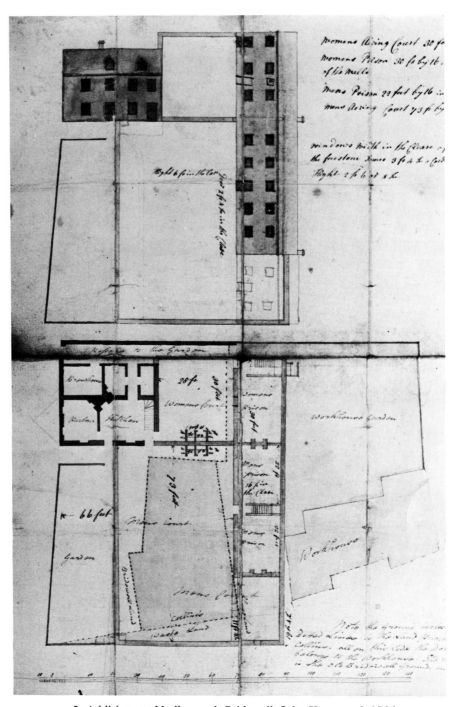

5. Additions to Marlborough Bridewell, John Hammond, 1786.

will have to be placed on London prisons, as there is so much more recorded information concerning them. If the account is partial for this reason, the effect is to some extent (but only to some extent) cancelled out by the greater emphasis laid on these very prisons — especially the Fleet and Newgate — in the literature of reform.

Some general points first. There were in the eighteenth century three kinds of imprisonment: for debtors, mostly importunate tradesmen and householders, who comprised roughly half the prison population; for felons awaiting assize trial or execution of sentence, very occasionally committed to a specific term of imprisonment; and for misdemeanants and petty offenders sent for corrective discipline, mostly apprentices, servants, prostitutes and vagabonds. These were distinguishable types of imprisonment, but they were hardly distinct.[14] Although debtors often enjoyed greater liberties, misdemeanants were sometimes put to work, and felons were frequently chained, no practice was exclusive to any one category. Although there were independent institutions catering for each condition — debtors' prisons, felons' gaols and houses of correction or bridewells — there were many mixed prisons too in which the situation was virtually the same for all. In the most general terms, it was

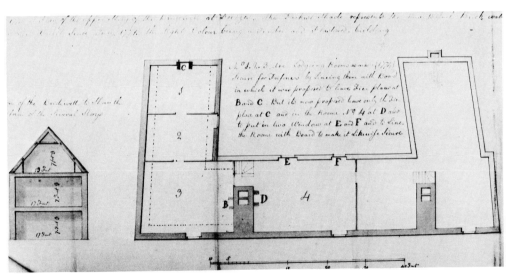

6. Alterations to Devizes Bridewell and Town Gaol, Esau Reynolds. 1771–5.

7. The Marshalsea, London, from a survey taken in 1773.

20

true that felons suffered the worst conditions, misdemeanants received the most discipline, and debtors paid the highest prices, yet these differences were to be observed within a relatively narrow spectrum.

The view commonly expressed by eighteenth-century jurists that imprisonment, except in the bridewells, was not in itself a penalty, has sometimes been taken as representative of the climate of opinion, but was not really so. All kinds of imprisonment were understood to be punishments, and were a recognized part of the machinery of suffering, if infrequently prescribed as such. But it was suffering of an odd sort, indirectly applied, unregistered, not quite within the purview of justice, a condition rather than an event. Nor was it any longer violent in quite the old sense. The relentless flagellations, brandings, mutilations, pillorying and carting which haunted the gaols and bridewells from the sixteenth century to the beginning of the eighteenth were abating. A margin of judicial savagery still existed either side of the prison, for those sentenced to be pilloried or whipped before imprisonment or for those awaiting execution, and private floggings were still carried out in the bridewells as part of a sentence; but sanguinary penalties were less in evidence after 1720.[15] And as the calculated legal inflictions of bodily pain decreased, an insidious violence generated from within the prison was more clearly exposed; a violence partly commercial, partly domestic in character, flourishing on legal procedures without being an acknowledged part of them.

The salient feature of eighteenth-century prison life for all debtors, felons and certain bridewell prisoners was its cost. Fees were levied for every kind of provision and for every variety of privilege. The beneficiaries in these transactions were the keepers or their servants. Keepers would generally be appointed by the local magistrates and aldermen more or less as contractors undertaking to prevent escapes, in return for which they were permitted to charge prisoners for services incidentally rendered. Their office was an unassailable monopoly and so was coveted as a limited form of tax farming, particularly in the larger metropolitan prisons (one of the great scandals unearthed by a Commons Committee in 1729 was the recent sale of the warder's office at the Fleet for £5,000),[16] but also in less lucrative situations (as at Bedford County Gaol where descendants of the Howard/Richardson families held the gaolership in almost unbroken succession between 1711 and 1814).[17] Because of this prisons were run as exploitative hostels, something nicely illustrated by a dispute that arose in 1716 between the woman gaoler and some prisoners at Shrewsbury County Gaol, which could easily be construed as a squabble between landlady and lodgers. The gaoler, a widow by the name of Joan Crumpton, complained to the Quarter Sessions that certain of her prisoners:

Frequently send for strong liquors out of the town into the gaol, sitt up late, gett drunk, and very often insult and abuse the said gaoler and her servants, and disturb other prisoners. And doe pretend that the garretts and several of the other rooms (if ye prisoners find their own beds) are free from paying anything to the said gaoler, and has thrown out the gaoler's beds out of some of the rooms and have put in some of their own bedds, and doe refuse to pay anything for the same, and doe

8. View of the Fleet, from Rowlandson and Pugin, *The Microcosm of London*, 1808.

lock up the doors and keep the gaoler out of severale of the rooms pretending they have a right so to doe.[18]

Incidents such as this tell something of the day to day relationship between gaoler and gaoled in unreformed prisons. Stories of the rapacity of gaolers were countless and well founded, since prisoners were delivered into their hands as assets to be stripped. Yet while it was possible for gaolers to rule their little dominions as tyrants, it was more usual for them to live as peaceably as was consistent with raking a substantial profit from inmates. Their power was in fact limited by the uncomfortable relationship which they were obliged to maintain with prisoners, the unwilling source of their wealth; not, as after the reforms, by the relationship they were obliged to maintain with the magistrates. Theirs was, more than anything else, a power exerted over a prisoner's circumstances, not aimed directly at his conduct. Rules were less in evidence than tables of fees, and where written rules were to be found, they regulated the domestic routine of the wards rather than personal behaviour. At Ludgate — the extreme example — these rules amounted to a democratic constitution under which a prisoner elected as steward had charge of the entire 'domestic government' from the distribution of alms and charities to the washing of floors.[19] Similar rules were instituted at Newgate in 1633.[20] In both cases the prisoners' rights were soon eroded but, characteristically, so as to procure further monetary advantage for the keeper.

The fundamental cruelty of seventeenth- and eighteenth-century imprisonment was therefore the cruelty of extortion. Thus events illustrated in *The Cry of the Oppressed*, purporting to describe the Fleet in 1693, mostly hinged around the gaolers' gratifying themselves and lining their pockets at the expense of the prisoners (Fig. 9). The effects of extortion were various: it could lead to starvation, coercive brutality, illness, destitution and also contributed to the 'otherness' of the prison, but was not in itself evident in the format of prison buildings, or at least not directly. There were, however, two aspects of prison life, stemming from the basic fact of the gaoler's monopoly, which left evidence in plans: the grading of accommodation and the provision of supplies.

The passage of goods, persons and information in and out of the prison was a major source of profit and so efforts were always made to keep control of such lucrative traffic without greatly discouraging it.

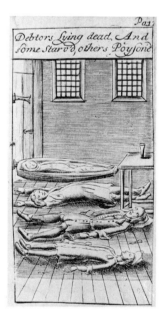

9. Ten illustrations from *The Cry of the Oppressed*, 1693.

P. 7.

A Debtor drag'd in a Hurdle Call'd the Goalers Coach.

P. 27.

A Goaler knocking a Woman in the Head with his Keys

P.

Debtors in a Dungion 9 foot under Ground.

Debtors and Hoggs togeather the Hoggs feeding on Beasts Inwards

There was rarely more than one entrance to a prison and often the gaoler's house, if separate, stood between the outer gate and the inner prison as at Fisherton Anger, Ruthin County Gaol, Macclesfield Town Bridewell, Cockermouth Bridewell, Batley Gaol, Truro Town Gaol, Birmingham Town Gaol, the Fleet, King's Bench[21] and at Clerkenwell House of Correction, where Jacob Ilive, sentenced to three years' hard labour in 1754, detailed the numerous extortions that the gaoler, Henry Wallbank, was able to levy. For instance, numbers 3 and 8 in the recently constructed block of cells called the long gallery (a fore-shadowing of later practice) were alleged to be 'bawdy houses' to which prisoners, on payment of 6*d.* to the underkeeper, could resort with wives and prostitutes (Fig. 2). Female prisoners of easy virtue were frequently entertained in the taproom by customers solicited from out-side before purchasing access to the cells, thereby furnishing the keeper with yet more profit. On the other hand Ilive could procure books and materials to learn Arabic, to write copiously and to earn money with printing work brought to him by friends, when not employed at beating hemp for hard labour.[22] Indeed there is much to suggest that little con-trol was exerted over either quantity or quality of goods or persons in or out of prisons as long as the gaoler partook of the transactions. Allegations regarding the sale of sexual favours from prisoners, to prisoners and between prisoners with the connivance of the gaoler are rife from the sixteenth century onwards. Newgate regulations banished dogs in 1792, and pigs, geese and poultry in 1814.[23] One day in 1702 William Fuller, the imposter, was intrigued to find, among the spectators admitted to Bridewell, a woman and her niece who had travelled from Northampton just to see him beat hemp.[24] A party of customs officials seized quantities of smuggled tea, coffee, chocolate and lace valued at £1,500 in the Fleet Prison during 1778.[25]

The list could go on indefinitely, but it is not only scandals and curiosities that illustrate the permeability of the old prisons. A useful adjunct to the gaol economy was the begging grate to provide for poor prisoners unable to obtain money from relatives or patrons (Fig. 10). Ludgate prisoners successfully petitioned the Mayor of London in 1698/9 for permission to knock a second begging hole through the prison walls so cryers could solicit from both at once to prevent passers-by from escaping their pleas. In 1759 Marmaduke Johnson estimated that £60 p.a. (which he regarded as trifling) was collected in this way.[26]

At Newgate a grated door, 'the gigger' as it was called, faced onto Newgate Street. It was used for begging, as an assembly point for acquaintances and for the purchase of supplies from an adjoining shop, with the shopkeeper's servant as messenger. Access to it cost 1s.6d. in 1724.[27] The same purpose might be served by an ordinary window as at

FLEET PRISON — POOR DEBTORS' CELL.

10. The Fleet. Begging grate onto Fleet Market, early nineteenth century.

Beccles Bridewell, or by the boot on a string always left dangling from the upper stories of Exeter Southgate Gaol, or even by fettered prisoners being released into the street with a bowl, or shackled to the outside of the prison wall.[28] But the characteristic arrangement was the grate and this was one of the few situations in which the building was used to frame human relationships. It marked, after all, the highly sensitive point where the interior of the prison extended directly onto the street.

The street extended more easily into the prison in the form of taverns, shops, coffee houses, stalls and vendors. A survey of the Marshalsea in 1773 shows a chandler's shop, a taproom for the sale of wine and beer and drinking rooms for their consumption within the walls (Fig. 7). Likewise at Newgate in the early eighteenth century there were at least three distinct places for the purchase of consumables: the cellar, run by a prisoner, the 'cellarman', supplying wine, brandy, beer, tobacco, candles and other requisites to better off felons; the taphouse, selling the same range of goods to poorer felons; and the lodge, providing for debtors. The taphouse and lodge were leased by the gaoler to external proprietors.[29] But the greatest diversity of services were to be found in the two largest debtors' prisons, the Fleet and King's Bench.

At King's Bench (Fig. 11), untouched by the reforms even in 1828 because of its anomolous status, there were, in the dark, smelly area between the tenement and the north-east wall, the following: oyster stalls, green shops, brokers' repositories and carpenters' benches; 'here piano-fortes have been manufactured and boots soled and heeled; here is also a shop for the sale of everything, not forgetting the pawn-brokers' duplicates. Here the taylors goose runs piping on his board — Shave for 1*d*., hair cut for 2*d*., and dressed for 3*d*., hatters, bell hangers, washerwomen and children taken in to nurse.'[30] Such was the prisoners' section. The kitchen was let to a cook who would supply inmates and outsiders too. There were two taprooms, one at each end of the tenement terrace. In one of the 'houses', number 8, there was a hot mutton pie shop at the foot of the stairs, at number 9 a meat shop. There were also 'private' dining rooms, breakfast rooms, a coffee house for the better class of prisoner (as at the Fleet) and a market set up inside the prison at the south-east end of the court by the kitchens, where street vendors came to sell fish, poultry, fruit and vegetables.

Like the run of indulgent descriptions of London street life in the late eighteenth and early nineteenth century, the *Description of the*

11. View of the King's Bench, from Rowlandson and Pugin, *The Microcosm of London*, 1808.

29

King's Bench cited above points to the diverse trades and activities spilling out of buildings as indicator of a kind of urbanity in low life. Their existence within the walls of a prison, even as large as King's Bench which could comfortably house 400, was something of a triumph for commerce, yet such flourishing trade would have been the pride of any gaoler as long as he presided over it. So the key position from which to guard the prison, as far as he was concerned, was not the centre but if anything the edge, at the point of egress and entry, where he could monitor traffic to and from prisoners rather than monitor the transactions between prisoners, which were not customarily subject to fees. Thus, when prisoners and keepers occupied the same house, the prisoners would be in the garrets or cellar with the gaoler living between the front and back doors. At Cirencester Bridewell the prison was reached via stairs in a shop selling garden seeds run by the gaoler.[31]

These, the only correspondences that can be made out by comparing the evidence of architecture with contemporary descriptions of the relationship between gaoler and prisoners, affected the periphery of the gaol. Inside, various kinds of division can be discerned from plans, or to be more precise from their annotation, which describe the relationships between prisoners. The most basic of all were between men and women and between felons and debtors (in some two room prisons the sexual division was made, in others the legal division). The next step was to distinguish between the 'common side' and the 'masters' side', the latter with more comfortable and less crowded accommodation for higher fees. This arrangement was found in almost all county gaols and metropolitan prisons during the eighteenth century, and seems to have been the vestige of an earlier practice, the object of which was to fit accommodation to rank.

In the Fleet Prison the principle had been extended into a reproduction of social gradations in the world at large, perhaps because the Fleet had received both the vulgar and the exalted brought before the Star Chamber before its abolition in 1641, and also large numbers of gentry and nobility committed as recusants in the late sixteenth century.[32] For these same reasons successive warders found it expedient to build 'messuages' — chambers like those at the inns of court — on land adjacent to the prison which they held as freeholders. A prisoner purchased a suite of rooms, a room, or part of a room and held the key. The warden trespassed if he forced entry.[33] Sir Frances Englefield took three chambers in which, according to Harris the warden, he received as many as 60 visitors a day. Lady Amy Blount was provided with an inner and an outer chamber (two rooms, one reached through the other), the latter for her servants.[34] Below the level of gentry, prisoners were expected to share beds. Common prisoners slept in large communal wards. A table of fees for 1619 divided the Fleet prisoners into seven estates as follows: (1) An Archbishop, a Duke, a Duchess; (2) a Marquess, a Marquesse, an Earle, a Countesse, a Vicomtesse; (3) a Lord spiritual or temporal, a Lady the wife of a Baron or Lord; (4) a Knight, a Lady the wife of a Knight, a Doctor of Divinity or Law and others of like calling; (5) an Esquire, a gentleman or gentlewoman that shall sit at the Parlour Commons, or any other person under that degree that shall be at the Parlour Commons; (6) a Yeoman, or any other that shall be at the Hall Commons, man or woman; (7) a poor man of the wards that hath his part at the box (i.e. money received from the grate).[35] There were seven corresponding lists of charges from £24.6s.8d. to 2s.4d. exclusive of lodging and ordinary consumables. Only six years later another table divided the prisoners into 13 ranks, which may indicate that the arrangement was more fluid than it appears but which also translated gradations of status, which were to be maintained within the prison in the same way as outside it, into distinctions of consumption, expense and accommodation.[36]

The frequently expressed fastidiousness about mixing, about a 40s. debtor urinating with a £5 debtor, about residing in prisons where 'without distinction, intermixed is seen / A squire dirty, a mechanick clean' (Fig. 9b),[37] suggests that prison society was by no means always a reflection of recognized relationships of degree and was easily reduced to a simple index of purchasing power. Certainly this was the situation in the late eighteenth century, by which time the attempt to match accommodation to status was only recognizable in the names of certain rooms and wards: duke's chambers, masters' wards, common side, rookery. In the 1730s, a graded sequence of accommodation at different prices was apparently made available to all prisoners in the Fleet whatever their social standing. Simon Wood complained of having to put up with the common side which, he said, was deliberately 'made dismal and neglected, in order to invite as many as possible to the masters' side, who are not admitted till they can raise £1.8s.8d.'[38] The masters' side — judged the most commodious prison in the land — had spacious rooms, glazed windows and an attractive garden; the common side had paltry rooms with no glazing, in fact with hardly a window. It was, he lamented, a sad thing to be evicted from the masters' to the common side for non-payment of rent, but worse, as befell him, to be evicted from the common side and have to 'walk the prison' in all weathers.

It has to be admitted that the two parallels between architectural distribution and social organization discussed above — the peripheral position of the gaoler and the internal division of the prison into inferior and superior accommodation — apply not as general rules, but as the most distinct relationships that can be made out. They have to be searched for in plans which are, on the whole, heterogeneous in detail (no room is likely to be exactly the same as the next) but homogeneous overall. Clearly, these plans did not issue from any consistent idea of relative position or size or of relative accessibility, one part to another. By themselves they are indecipherable, unlike nineteenth-century prison plans, and it is only annotations and descriptive accounts that allow interpretations to be plotted into the fabric of the prison at all. At best, the building was only a partial and indistinct reflection of the character of prison life and, as the gatehouses, churches, poorhouses, guild halls, priories, public houses, mansions, villas and cottages which were turned into prisons suggest, buildings were colonized as more or less passive receptacles for the purpose of confinement. Decisions taken by the gaoler about where to locate this or that were likely to be a more potent organizing force than the pre-existing arrangement of the building. Such decisions were not always entirely unrelated to the building as found — with common siders often relegated to the most decayed parts (Marshalsea, Fleet); with debtors in garrets, felons in vaulted cellars, and so forth — but these tended to be fortuitous alignments rather than planned correlations. In many cases the designations of the rooms could be juggled at random without substantially affecting the nature of the institution.

It would appear, then, that the social reality of prison life was moulded less from bricks and mortar than from relationships created directly between the keeper, his servants and their prisoners and maintained by custom. There was one crucial exception to this rule which is not just discernible but typical, and which derived from the very homogeneity of prison building.

The grading of wards was an attempt to localize the most conspicuous and yet most ambiguous characteristic of life in the larger prisons: its concentrated gregariousness. In 1561 Henry Ellis had said of bridewell prisoners that 'no facultye will be contynued among such people if any skope of passage be had',[39] expressing the simple idea that a group of prisoners were the antithesis of a community, since they always sought to escape. It would be difficult to find any similar statement made during the seventeenth or eighteenth centuries. The tendency to escape was evidently counterbalanced by a tendency to form a peculiar sort of community within the confines of the prison; a community that was described in a number of ways — sometimes as an affliction:

As in Hell, it is thought the Devills are the lesse tormentors: so here our fellow prisoners lie heaviest upon us, and are to a new commoner worse than flies to a sore leg.   (Edmund Gayton, 1655)[40]

A ward for 50 prisoners . . . to be and lie constantly in, dress and eat their meat in, and for all other necessary occasions and offices, which caused great annoyances contagions and yearly mortality among them.
                                    (Humphrey Gyfford, Poultry Compter, 1670)[41]

Sometimes it was described as a source of solace:

The company one with the other is but a vying of complaints, and the causes they have to rail on fortune . . . and there is a great deal of good fellowship in this.
                                                          (John Earle, 1629)[42]

Society is the string at which the life of man hangs . . . men of all conditions are forced into a prison as all sorts of rivers fall into the sea . . . my counsel then is, that thou be sociable to all, acquainted with few, trust not any, or if any . . . not above one.   (Thomas Dekker, 1617)[43]

or as a source of diversion:

My imprisonment was no great suffering to me for I had an honest jailer who showed me all the kindness he could. I had a large room and liberty to walk in a fair garden, and my wife was never so cheerful a companion to me as in prison, and was very much against my seeking to be released; and she brought me so many necessaries that we kept house as contentedly and comfortably as at home though in a narrower room; and I had a sight of more friends in one day than I had at home in half a year.   (Richard Baxter, Clerkenwell House of Correction, 1684)[44]

As to their diversions, when they are not beating hemp, they chiefly turn upon, hunting the slipper, thread my needle nan, and prison and bars. The men play at chuck farthing, toffing up, leap frog, etc. They both take a particular delight in the fairy dance called rolly-powly, which is a very merry exercise but abominably obscene. In rainy weather they will sit in the shed and sing a chorus making a loud noise.   (Jacob Ilive, Clerkenwell House of Correction, 1757)[45]

The prison community was almost always described as a source of corruption (see ch. 2). At any rate, there can be no doubt that the experience of imprisonment for debtors, felons and minor offenders in cities or towns of any size entailed the unremitting company of others at close quarters (Fig. 12).

In 1724 *An Accurate Description of Newgate* was published by B.L. of Twickenham, who was probably one of the keeper's deputies. It was not a complete account but nevertheless gave a detailed record of certain parts of the prison. In 1767, as a preliminary to rebuilding, a committee of the Corporation of London had plans taken of old Newgate (Fig. 13).[46] These two sources, which tally quite closely despite the 40 years separating them, provide the best guide to the internal workings of a large unreformed gaol. As so happens, Newgate was the nation's most notorious prison, reputed to be an 'Abominable sink of beastliness', 'a Tower of Babel' and understood to be 'very badly contrived' even in the 1760s.[47] Vastly overcrowded at times, always verminous, often the harbinger of fever epidemics and the usual habitat of a quantity of infamous criminals, it proved to be an eloquent advertisement for reform.

Twice damaged by fires since its original construction as a prison by Richard Whittington in the fifteenth century, refronted in 1630/1, its most recent rebuilding had been in 1672, after the Great Fire of London. As pointed out in the Introduction, although it was the country's most recognizable prison, it was nearly identical to one of the other London gates, Cripplegate (rebuilt 1663) (Fig. 14), which contained living apartments for the Water Bailiff of London.[48] The 1767 survey shows the interior to have been both compact and labyrinthine (Fig. 15). The only organizing forces giving pattern to the distribution of rooms were four internal staircases climbing from the ground to the fourth floor. The chambers were generally grouped around the stair landings in insular clusters disconnected from adjacent apartments to form two or three separate territories on each floor. As a result, accommodation for the various kinds of prisoner tended to extend vertically in columns around a given staircase. The wards for male common side debtors, for example, stretched over three floors around one stair. In the earlier part of the eighteenth century master side felons occupied four floors in the same way.[49] Three of the staircases tied the parts of the prison together (the exception being a stair towards the centre of

12. Thomas Rowlandson, water colour sketch of the Marshalsea, 1825.

the building which existed solely to connect the Women's High Felon's Hall on the fourth floor with the entrance to the prison, landing at no intermediate point, if the 1767 survey is to be believed).

As one of the keeper's men, B.L. gave detailed descriptions of only the better sections of Newgate, in particular the master debtors' side; his purpose was apparently to attract a superior class of inmate. In relating the arrangements and itemizing the characteristics of various wards, however, he conveyed a good deal of information about how the rooms were occupied. In the Masters' Side Debtors' Hall ward, a modest room 24 foot by 16 foot and 14 foot high, directly above the lodge, there was a fireplace with cob-irons and hemp-jack for roasting meat, several benches, a table, and dishes and plate, for ''Tis generally agreed on, by the major part (and sometimes by all) of the prisoners of each ward, to dine together', though each to his own for breakfast and supper.[50] There was a shelf for scullery work and food preparation

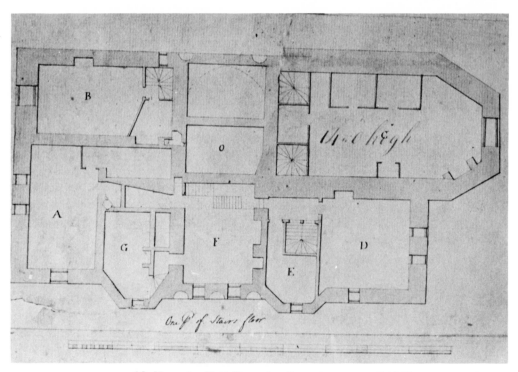

13. Newgate. First floor plan from the survey of 1767.

14. London City Gates, including Cripplegate (bottom left, 1663) and Newgate (bottom right, 1672).

38

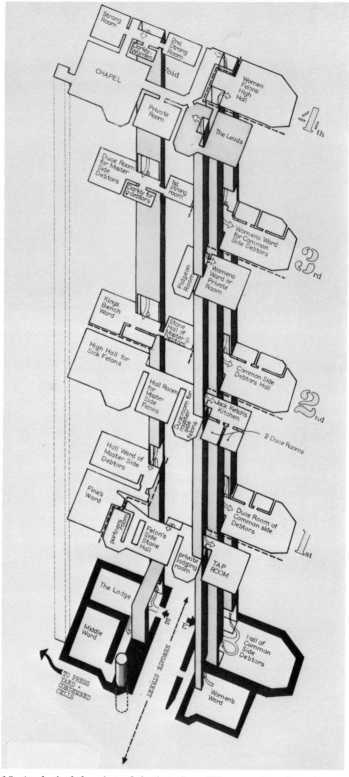

15. Analytical drawing of the interior of Newgate based on the survey of 1767.

performed by the poorest prisoner in lieu of fees for lodging and victualling. Around two sides of the room were timber galleries supported on posts, the upper part divided into five bed compartments, under which, the author grandly declared, occupants might walk at their pleasure. Given the prevalence of 'chumming' (sharing a bed to halve the price) the ward would normally hold up to ten prisoners. In one corner stood an open privy. Immediately outside, in a small room, was a lead water cistern for the exclusive use of master side debtors. At 8 a.m. the ward doors were unlocked, the window shutters opened and the room aired. Furniture was stacked and the ward washed by the last prisoner admitted. The turnkey locked the doors again at 9 p.m. Between these hours visitors were given unrestricted though sometimes costly access. All this was 3s. a week, or less when beds were shared.

The significant features of a good ward were the fireplace, the beds and the lower density of occupation. One ward, King's Bench, was regarded as slightly superior because it was less crowded and because the privy was outside the room; the rest were worse. Common side debtors had to put up with unglazed windows (Debtors' Hall), barrack beds (Women's Ward, Tangier Ward); common side felons with sleeping on wood or even stone floors, no fireplaces, no convenient water and rooms with no windows at all (Middle Ward, Stone Hold).

Each ward was a compacted little society thrown in on itself for most though not all of the time. 'Every ward here in', says B.L., 'hath generally a reciprocal conversation with each other; as in the morning, they interchangeably make visits.'[51] The difference between intercourse within and without the ward was that within it association was not interfered with by keeper and turnkeys. The four staircases which, as has already been pointed out, provided independent channels of movement up and down the building also gave the keeper an opportunity to intercept and restrict the 'reciprocal conversations' when he saw fit, in a way that would not have been possible with the circuits of interconnected rooms so familiar in seventeenth- and eighteenth-century planning. This, though, allowed a degree of control only over the larger social grouping of the entire gaol. Within the wards prisoners made their own society. Newgate was an aggregation of wards varying considerably in size and population but all as autarkic as the Master Side Debtors' Hall. Visiting the place a year after the publication of B.L.'s description, Bernard de Mandeville was shocked at the liberty he found there: 'They eat and drink what they can purchase, everybody has admittance to them, and they are debarred from nothing but going out. Their most serious hours they spend in mock tryals, and instructing one another in cross questions to confound witnesses.'[52] The domestic economy of the wards made prison society an assemblage of groups. Within this federal structure little room could be found for anything beyond the space of the wards themselves. A few rooms might allow for the possibility of sequestration as either penalty or privilege: two darklies, two private rooms and two small master side felons' Duce Rooms (in 1728 a condemned cell block was also added to the south in the Press Yard); a few might serve for larger associations: the lodge for debtors, the taphouse for common side felons, the cellar for master side felons, the High Hall for all felons, but only the chapel was accessible to the whole prison, and even then not all at once. No space was occupied by the keeper, who lived in a house nearby, so neither the institution as a whole nor individuals within it registered very strongly in this multiplicity of similar elements.

Bewildering as it may seem, the maze of 42 chambers in old Newgate was nonetheless subject to a coherent enough pattern of occupation. The same could be said of the Fleet as described by Alexander Harris, and Clerkenwell House of Correction as described by Jacob Ilive (though both of these had plenty of space for general assembly).[53] In other cases the relationship between the arrangement of prison buildings and their occupation is a matter of plausible inference rather than anything more substantial. Nevertheless, if a comparison were to be sought between the way divisions were made in reformed and unreformed prisons, the tendency to rely on adaption to the purpose at hand in unreformed prisons and the tendency to engrave relationships and differences decisively and indelibly into the figure of the plan in reformed prisons would have to be noticed. The peculiar structure of prison life was largely invisible before reform. The one legible characteristic was its permeability (presence of shops and trades, multiple occupation of wards, the begging grate, the taproom, shared privys, pumps and cisters, similarity to other kinds of building), but permeability was hardly a characteristic in contemporary terms, as it was also exhibited in slum backlands and country villas. It was a characteristic in terms of later developments, differing from reformed prisons as it differed from reformed housing or reformed hospitals. The essential distinction was not between one type of building and another, but between one way of laying out buildings and another. In terms of architecture the frequent references to the prison as a microcosm (at Newgate the prisoners' seal described it as such (Fig. 16))[54] expresses its character well enough: something in the world, distinct from it, but like it.

Signs of a change came just before the reforms. New gaols and houses of correction, substantially constructed and detached from other buildings, began to appear. They had pretensions to symmetry and employed the repertory of classical elements. The first prison edifice of this kind, as far as is known, was York Castle County Gaol (Fig. 17), completed in 1705, probably by a local mason, William Wakefield; a building in the baroque manner, with a giant order of pilasters raised on a rusticated platform, a central clock-tower and segmental pediments on the wings. It housed keeper, debtors and felons and was planned throughout in much the same way as were the secondary storeys (the servants' offices and bedrooms) of great houses, that is with a central corridor as sole access to rooms.[55] This extraordinary building remains unique, even anomalous, but in 1756 a county prison for Derby was erected at Nun's Green with a correct Palladian facade by William Hiorns. All accommodation was consolidated into a single range of building with four separate yards attached. The keeper's apartment was in the

16. Emblem of Newgate from *The Humble Petition of the Poor Distressed Prisoners*, 1676.

17. York Castle County Gaol, attributed to William Wakefield, 1705.

42

centre.[56] An 'elegant yet plain' bridewell with similar properties was built at Newport in Essex in 1775 by William Hillyer, who also built the County Gaol at Moulsham (1773–7) (Figs. 18, 19).[57] Also with distinctly architectural qualities were Wakefield House of Correction by John Carr and John Watson (1766–70), Bath Prison by Thomas Ware Atwood (1772–3), Hertford County Gaol by Robert Palmer (1774–6)[58] and of course, Dance's Newgate (1768–80).

It is around this time that the ordinary practice of architecture began to separate from the building trades. In 1753 Robert Brettingham, whose son was to attend the Royal Academy, tour Italy with Soane, and design three new prisons between 1789 and 1794,[59] announced in a Norfolk newspaper that: 'As the said Mr. Brettingham is leaving off the business of Mason, he intends to act in the character of an Architect,

18. Moulsham County Gaol, Chelmsford, William Hillyer, 1773–7, as it was in 1810. The House of Correction at the far end of what was, originally, a symmetrical facade was added by John Johnson in 1806.

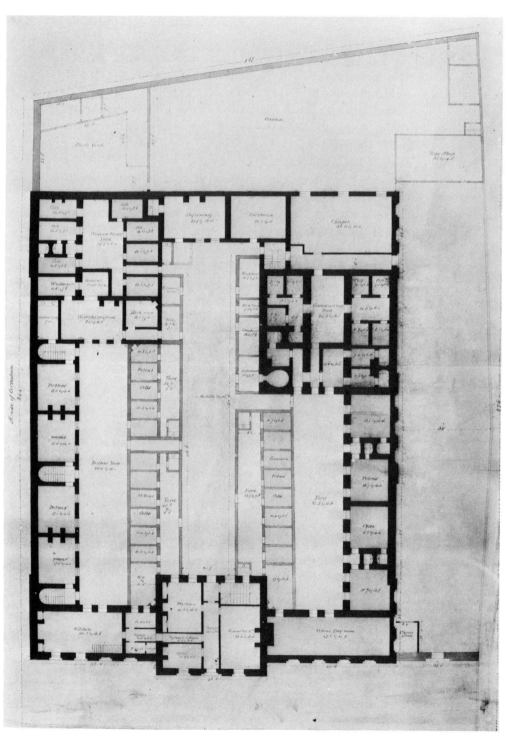

19. Moulsham County Gaol, ground plan, Hillyer's building in black.

in drawing plans & elevations, giving estimates, or putting out work, or measuring up any sort of building, for any gentleman in the County.'[60] Acting in the character of an architect meant the adoption of techniques which allowed a proposal to be laid forth for examination in the absence of the building itself, above all in the form of a drawing. Plans, sections and elevations — the principal tools of the profession — made it possible to see a building from a distance and yet to see its multifarious internal workings at a glance; to survey it from an abstracted, privileged vantage point as if it were a dissected body, and to see it so before the fact of its construction. With the introduction of architecture into the building of prisons at this critical moment, not only did they gain a separate identity as institutions — an appearance that would serve more and more to distinguish them from any other type of building — and not only were they made to follow the rigorous geometry of a plan, but decisions about internal arrangements were taken out of the hands of keepers and put into the hands of Justices of the Peace who were henceforth regarded as the architect's proper clients. It had not been uncommon for gaolers to maintain the fabric of their own prisons, even to rebuild them, as part of their contractual obligation. At Bedford in 1724 John Oakley was granted the gaolership for life on undertaking to tile the thatched part of the roof and maintain the prison in good repair.[61] At Clerkenwell New Prison in 1670 a keeper was appointed on condition that he disbursed £300 during the ensuing three years to erect new buildings there.[62] In 1610 Maidstone County Gaol was repaired at the expense of the County, but it was the gaoler who directed the work and handled the money. At the same place in 1662 the incumbent was awarded £10 by the Justices for rebuilding part of the prison to prevent escapes.[63] After the Fire of London in 1666, Sir Jeffrey Whichcott, warden of the Fleet, removed the entire prison population to his lands in Vauxhall, then rebuilt the prison on its original site at his own expense.[64] The obligation to make and repair the prison and the control over the nature of the place that went with it was already less frequently placed on the gaoler in the eighteenth century than in the seventeenth. The architect now took responsibility for the building entirely out of the gaoler's sphere of influence.

In Hillyer's Newport Bridewell Howard found something very commendable: there was no way through from the women's side of the bridewell to the men's side and the governor's house sat astride the wall dividing the two sexes, overlooking both. Unfortunately, at the time of his visit in 1782 men and women were consorting in the same yard, but Howard was nevertheless impressed.[65] The idea of using design to enforce a definite morality on keepers and prisoners alike, which first occurred in small but regular institutions such as Newport, must surely have been closely associated with the presentation of finished, considered, regulated architectural plans, in which the prison was demarcated into zones consistent with morality as well as symmetry; plans in which the social world of the prison began to be depicted in a series of simple divisions. Into the abstract clarity of these preconceived designs, relationships between the prisoners and the gaoler were plotted which neither could escape as they were buried in the geometry of the building. Both were eventually to become mere occupants of an organ, the internal operations of which were largely resolved by architects in collaboration with Justices.

In one sense, the history of prison design from this point onwards is the history of the removal of power from those who worked and lived within to those who ruled the prison from outside, and the unnoticed role of architecture in this usurpation.

2 From correction to reformation; from dungeon to cell

The state of old prisons was subject matter for the reforms but the reform movement was not sustained solely on Howard's comprehensive picture of existing conditions. Penal reform was a cause not a reaction; it issued not just from observation, but from an implicit contrast between the way of the world as it stood and another possibility — another way of making and using prisons — that gave to the murky facts of common practice a far sharper silhouette. A fundamental tenet of penal reform was that under certain circumstances the character of an offender would inevitably shift from vice towards virtue. In order to understand the way in which the prison building was involved in the transfiguring of evil consciences, this belief will need to be looked at more closely. Two comparisons may help to convey its dimensions and at the same time illustrate its extension into architecture. The first is a comparison of correction as practised in the early houses of correction with reformation as it was to be practised in the reformed prisons; the second is a comparison of the incarcerating dungeon with the reforming cell.

Correction

When John Howard made his momentous tours in the 1770s and 1780s he found that the country's bridewells and houses of correction were no better than other prisons. They were profitless and tumbledown, they were supported on the county rates, and prisoners were allowed to while away their time in 'sloth, profaness and debauchery' that Howard sometimes found to be 'extremely shocking'.[1] He was perplexed, for he recognized these places to be relics of a much earlier campaign to make better men and women out of the idle, the profligate and the licentious by imprisoning them.

47

In one form or another houses of correction were to be found all over Europe by the middle of the seventeenth century, a response to the alarming spread of indigence that had bedevilled so many governments for so long. It was, though, a new kind of punishment; herding men and women into houses, workshops, empty convents, monasteries and abandoned palaces, disciplining them and forcing them to work. The house of correction was a penalty directed at laziness and disobedience, it was an expedient to rid the towns and countryside of beggars and vagrants, but its peculiarity derived from its taking the form of an almshouse that was both refuge and punishment at one and the same time. It was meant to be a didactic instrument that punished, instructed and improved, filling the' divide between charity and chastisement, a curious position pinpointed by Thomas Dekker's observation on the treatment of Bridewell prisoners: 'As iron on the Anvil are they laid, not to take blows alone, but to be made and fashioned to some more charitable use.'[2] It was not just that Bridewell bore a resemblance to other charitable hostels, but also that those sent there would be made into something better, though they would try to avoid it.

Bridewell was the earliest establishment of this kind. Others were more renowned in their time and would be better remembered, in particular the Dutch rasphouses and spinhouses that so impressed Howard and others of his generation,[3] but at Bridewell in London the first attempt was made to turn a disorderly rabble back into dutiful servants by introducing them into a larger, better regulated and more exacting version of the productive household, and holding them there.

In England a war against idleness was already in progress. As late as 1504 the relatively mild penalties for vagabonds had been made yet milder,[4] but in 1531, 1536 and 1548[5] a series of Acts were passed which made persistent vagabondage into a capital felony and increased the penalty for a second offence to perpetual slavery. The 1548 Act not only proscribed wandering about as practised by beggars, strumpets, gypsies and jugglers, but also included those not seeking work or leaving their work as subject to the same punishments. Bridewell came into being with these laws in force.

Bridewell Palace had been built in 1522 by Henry VIII for the purpose of entertaining Charles V of Spain.[6] It had since been deserted by the Court and 30 years after its erection was already ruinous and decaying. Nicholas Ridley, the Archbishop of London, and the London Aldermen both petitioned Henry Cecyl, Edward VI's secretary, to turn the empty palace over to the City so that 'Christ should be no more abroad in the streets', as Ridley put it.[7] Nothing could better illustrate the ambivalent position of the new institution than the language of these two petitions; Ridley writing of the hungry, naked and cold as if they were the Body of Christ, the Aldermen, in an equally fanciful text, writing in the name of the vagrants and extolling themselves as rescuers of them from 'the puddle of idleness which is the mother and leader of us into beggary and all mischief'.[8]

The petitions were granted in 1555. Sir Richard Dobbs and a committee of 24 Aldermen then set about establishing a variegated scheme of industry under the one roof. 'In a well ordered city, as in a well ordered household laziness is not to be tolerated', declared Juan Luis Vives while making proposals for the relief of the Bruges poor in the 1520s.[9] Vives, however, did not suggest supplying the poor with more than metaphorical habitation; the London Aldermen did. In fact, three sites spread around the City's edge were made ready to receive different categories of inmate. The impotent were to be put in Grey Friar's House, the casualties in St Thomas' Hospital. Bridewell was to take 'the rioter that consumeth all', 'The vagabond that will abide in no place', and 'The idle person, as dissolute women and others'.[10]

The palace, once fit for kings, was to receive beggars and prostitutes. The irony was obvious,[11] yet the site was not altogether inappropriate. Bridewell Palace had originally been the receptacle for an enlarged, hierarchical household, and that structure was now to be reinvoked. In the sixteenth century the household was both a theatre of production and a political microcosm. Indeed it could be said to be the fundamental political unit of society at that time; the one to which all others, however vaunted, referred.[12] The homeless poor were the masterless poor; having no abiding place they escaped from under the umbrella of authority. Bridewell would rectify this by supplying shelter and enforcing submission within it. The Bridewell Governors were vested with patriarchal power in all matters of policy, and were personally to supervise discipline, committal and release. The palace was to become a gigantic productive hive. A list of 26 arts, trades and labours was drawn up, including the fabrication of tennis balls, feather beds, bonnets and caps, shoes, the drawing of iron and the making of lace. In this way it was to be turned into that 'fresh field of exercise, which is the guider and begetter of all wealth, virtue and honesty'.[13]

Long before Bridewell there had been a London prison for vagrant and immoral persons: a small rotunda called the Tun at Cornhill, right in the very centre of the City. The Tun made punishment into a spectacle, surmounted as it was with an open cage, stocks and pillory for the display and mortification of offenders.[14] Bridewell, on the other hand, located outside the old City wall, was a relatively private institution despite the enormous traffic of prisoners that passed through it (2,043 in the year following 25 March 1598, for example).[15] Deprived of its function as a popular circus, the punishment for idleness and dissipation was now given a distinctly mercantile aim: to redeem the thriftless through the transforming power of work.

Between 1555 and 1557 the palace was refurbished and modified to accommodate its new clientele. There was already a strong exterior curtain wall with few windows, but on the interior a pair of spacious courtyards surrounded with an impressive string of halls and chambers belied the external appearance (Fig. 20). In 1662, not long before the Great Fire gutted the old palace, the Quaker Thomas Ellwood, sent there for non-conformity, was so struck by these splendid apartments that he committed his impressions to paper. The Great Dining Hall seemed to him 'one of the finest rooms I ever remember to have seen'. Sixty foot long and proportionately wide, it still retained a stately ambience, and its regal ornaments, though dilapidated, were intact.[16] There is no way of telling exactly how these magnificent quarters were occupied. Nevertheless, entries in the Bridewell court records suggest that the household structure was indeed paramount, although not quite as specified by the Aldermen.

The Governors established Masters of Arts in the palace buildings, each with their own workshops, their own lodgings, their own prisoners and their own business. In 1560 John Rose, on payment of £20 to the City, was permitted to build a lodging for himself and his wife in the prison and was given leave to inhabit the Presence Chamber, a small room adjacent to it, as well as the chambers above and below it, and was also to be given a part of the gallery and part of the garden for the rest of his natural life. In 1576 Mr Peck, the packthread maker, was allotted 'The Long Gallery on the ground with the chimney at the south end of it and a room for two chambers out of the garden in which to carry on his trade.[17] Once such terms were agreed the Masters of Arts were left relatively free of inteference and soon took upon themselves much of the authority vested in the Governors and more besides. In 1602 a committee investigating abuses declared the undertakers, as they were then called, to have the running of the place:

The undertakers have taken into their own use the best rooms in the house such as were most fitting for setting prisoners and the poor at work, which heretofore had been used for that purpose . . . to take and even to take rent for divers rooms and employ not a third part of the rooms to set prisoners at work.

This complaint and others like it[18] indicate not so much the dissolving of patriarchal structure as its literal reinstatement. The Governors were fathers by analogy, but to judge from the records, their overextended authority was easily usurped by the various Masters of the trade-based

20. Bridewell Palace, a nineteenth-century elaboration from Ralph Agas' map of London, 1560.

houses within the institution, and these houses were no more or less than the name implies. The Masters of Trade chose their own prisoners, administered discipline themselves and even released inmates on their own account. Within a few decades the grand scheme of production established in the carcass of a grand house had decayed into a composite of ordinary domestic workshops, and the unified habitation of the palace had been subdivided and parcelled out, as the expanded image of patriarchal authority was reduced to its modest origin.

Nevertheless, in 1576, local justices were permitted to found houses of correction modelled on Bridewell within their jurisdiction, a power that was reiterated and extended by Acts of 1597 and 1609,[19] the latter of which obliged them to establish at least one house in every county and borough, supported entirely from the labour of its prisoners. These retained their peculiar designation for the idle and thriftless until the start of the eighteenth century, when at first larcenists and then a whole variety of offenders could be sent there at the discretion of the magistrates.[20] The local houses of correction were undertaken on a more commonplace scale, the 1583 Ordinance for Maidstone House of Correction, for instance, stipulating that:

the house at the foot of Gabriels Hylle in Maydstone . . . or some other fitt house in that towne, shalbe taken to terme for yeares; at some convenient rent: and . . . the roomes therof . . . shall be of common charge made strong and severall for men and boyes by theimselves, and for women and wenches by theimselves, as well for diet as for working and lodging. And that the rest of the roomes thereof shalbe private to and for the wardein of the said house and his familie.[21]

The prescription is for something very like a prosperous merchant's household but with prisoners in place of apprentices and servants, warder in place of master. The reference to 'some other fitt house' indicates the expectation that an institution of this size and shape would fit neatly into ordinary domestic buildings.

The houses of correction were designed to punish and at the same time reclaim their inmates. But, unlike the penal institutions of the late eighteenth and nineteenth century, they were not meant to reclaim lost souls. Their aim was the simpler one of demonstrating a principle. Obedience led to industry which led to wealth. These steps ascending toward civilization were opposed by the downward course of insubordination, idleness and poverty. Obedience was the key and if obedience did not require the spiritual complicity of prisoners, it did require that they understood the results of passivity or defiance. At Bridewell any sign of either was visited with flogging, chaining and near starvation,[22] but the didactic nature of the penalties for indolence is perhaps nowhere more evident than in the contrivance known as the water cellar which has been described by Thorsten Sellin.

The water cellar was the penalty for refusing to work, malingering or slovenliness in the Amsterdam Rasphuis. To illustrate the effects of its use, a contemporary tract, parodying Catholic devotional prose, told how the spurious St Pono interceded to redeem a prisoner claiming to be infirm. The prisoner was placed in the water cellar, an underground closet containing a pump and a conduit. Water poured through the conduit into the closet and began to rise. Nothing else happened until, eventually, the water reached the unfortunate man's ears, and at this point the miracle finally took place; fearing for his life he pumped with all his might and continued to do so as the water continued to flow, until it was clear to everyone that his infirmity had departed.[23]

As well as being a facetious satire at the expense of Catholics and idlers, the St Pono story, and of course the water cellar itself, was a quite serious presentation of the necessary and unremitting nature of work for the lower orders of mankind. Idleness was the result of a misconception. If a person was lazy he was so because he had not perceived the indissoluble bond that connected labour with respite. Thus the water cellar could be said to prove a moral idea with the economy and precision of a proof in geometry. A lesson was taught in it that turned a general principle into a demonstrable reality, so obvious that even the most obdurate could not fail to see it. All forms of corrective discipline aspired to this concrete clarity. At Amsterdam and Danzig the cellar was still in use in the first decades of the eighteenth century according to Sellin,[24] and while there is no evidence of its use in England, it turns up on an early-eighteenth-century playing card amongst a medley of different treatments for poverty and idleness (Fig. 21).

As time passed the houses of correction decayed and submerged into the general scheme of imprisonment. Even so, there were occasional attempts to extend, once more, the radius of authority over a larger community of labouring prisoners. One of the last was a scheme published by Henry Fielding, novelist and magistrate, in collaboration with Thomas Gibson, an architect, in 1753 (Fig. 22). Their proposal was for a huge institution combining prison, house of correction and workhouse, for the County of Middlesex. Ribbons of workrooms studded with watchmen's lodges were spread over a vast area enclosing courts for 3,000 pauper males, 2,000 pauper females and 1,000 convicts. Their labour was to be hired out to contractors who would put them to work in sutleries within the confines of the house. Fielding likened it to 'the idea of a body of men united under one government in a large city',[25] and claimed that if the magistrates invested the poor rate, some £70,000 per year, in this immense metropolis of labourers instead of doling it out as gratuities, they might reclaim a large portion of their outlay.

Apart from its sheer size, the most extraordinary feature of the scheme was the generality of its function. Inmates were to be committed on suspicion, or for not having a special pass, as well as for

21. English playing card, early eighteenth century.

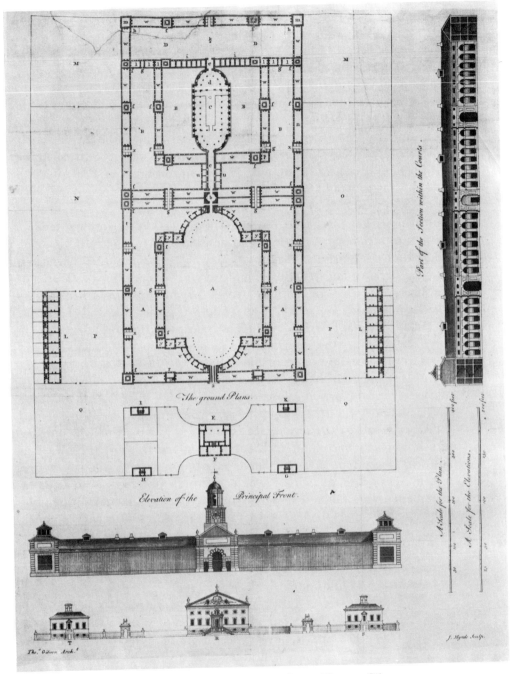

Part of the Section within the Courts.

The ground Plans.

Elevation of the Principal Front.

A Scale for the Plan.
A Scale for the Elevations.

Tho.ˢ Gibson Arch.ᵗ

J. Mynde Sculp.

22. Project for a County House for Middlesex, Thomas Gibson,
from Henry Fielding, *A Proposal for Making Effectual Provision for
the Poor*, 1753.

poverty, idleness, misdemeanour or crime. The industrious poor were expected to commit themselves voluntarily as a gesture of goodwill.[26] Fielding thought the comparative inutility of the existing workforce to be the result of two defects: demographic scattering and moral turpitude. His 'County House' would concentrate the power of the poor as an engine might concentrate natural forces, and within it idiocentric acts would be made coherent. Much of this was reminiscent of Bridewell. There was, however, one important difference. The Fielding/Gibson project would rely less on creating reflex obedience by chastisement, more on aligning institutional structure with the specification and distribution of space. The early houses of correction had made a place into a punishment but the place itself had no special properties. Like other early prisons they were, more often than not, colonizations of existing sites and structures, and were never conceived as works of architecture in any conventional sense; they were simply fixed abodes. The architecture of the Fielding/Gibson project was by contrast described in detail. At Bridewell chastisement has been inescapable: in the County House the space allotted to labour, supervision and recuperation would have been inescapable.

But it so happens that as the scope of prison architecture was increasing the scope of prison labour was diminishing. The Fielding/Gibson scheme had no real heirs within the mainstream of penal reform. During the second half of the eighteenth century, at just the time when industrialization was becoming apparent outside the prisons, the idea that industry should be the sole medium of moral improvement within prisons was eclipsed. Labour would maintain its place as an essential ingredient of morality and would retain its place in prison discipline also, but was enveloped in a doctrine that professed a deeper understanding of the human condition.

Reformation and solitude

Before the reforms of the late eighteenth century there were sporadic attempts to infuse imprisonment with more definitely Christian, even more spiritual, aims. There is nothing that distinguishes these projects from corrective imprisonment in any precise way, except for a perceptible bias towards the personal redemption of prisoners; a bias that led to a new concern with what was referred to as 'reformation of character'. While the houses of correction had focussed attention on the tangible reality of productiveness, turning the uselsss into the useful, the reforming prisons would concentrate on the moral transformation of their inmates, turning evil into good.

All that was necessary to distinguish the one kind of prison from the other was a marginal shift of emphasis in the meaning of a process; labour, still important, was valued more as a measure of piety and submissiveness than as a demonstration of prudence. Seemingly, this is an inconsequential semantic detail, yet from it developed a discernible rift between reformative and corrective discipline. The early houses of correction did not neglect the workings of the human mind; correction, after all, was a kind of moral education in its way, but reformative discipline was designed to reach deeper levels, printing its pattern more indelibly. Correction was addressed to the intellect, reformation to the soul.

By the end of the seventeenth century the notion of penal reformation had achieved rudimentary definition. At first the new discipline was restricted to particularly pathetic classes of wrongdoers — monks, young boys and fallen women; eventually it spread to cover the whole body of criminal offenders.

It was the Benedictine monk, Jean Mabillon, better remembered for his seminal contributions to modern historiography, who announced the principles of redemptive imprisonment. His *Reflexions sur les Prisons des Ordres Religieux* emphasized the profound spiritual effects that might flow from the better use of imprisonment as a penalty for religious offenders. Secular justice should terrify but ecclesiastical justice should save souls.[27] Various precedents were cited, in particular the penitential rules drawn up by the seventh-century hermit St John Climacus, but more had yet to be done. So Mabillon proposed that every French province should build an independent monastic prison on the lines of a Carthusian cloister, in which a special penitential rule of strict solitude would be observed: 'There would be a number of cells, similar to those of Chartreux, with a work room to train them [the imprisoned monks] in some useful labour. One could also add to each cell a little garden which could be opened at certain hours for them to work in and take the air.'[28] The Carthusian cell (Fig. 23) was an abode for the soul in communion with God, not with man. Inmates came

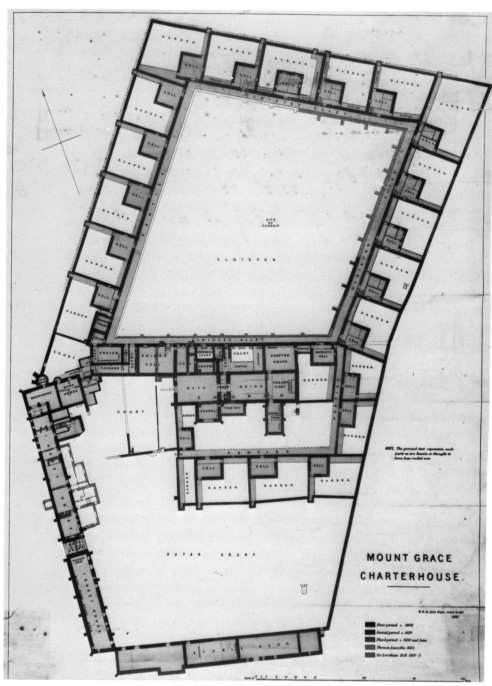

23. Mount Grace Charterhouse, Yorkshire.

together only for matins, lauds and vespers.[29] It was this kind of seclusion in austerity, relieved by occasional communal rituals, that Mabillon envisaged for the monastic prisons.

In the *Reflexions* the Catholic authorities were presented with a picture of the penitential prison that showed it to be an ecclesiastical tool, stemming from and belonging to the monastic tradition, built to stimulate remorse in the hearts of offenders rather than to exact vengeance. It is interesting therefore that the first concrete realization of a penitential prison was brought into being by Pope Clement XI, although there is no evidence to suggest a direct connection.

As part of a campaign to strengthen his moral government over the people of Rome following a sequence of natural disasters that disrupted the city in 1702/3, Clement XI founded a house of correction for boys in the Hospital of San Michel.[30] San Michel, like the Bicêtre in Paris, was an enormous complex of buildings, some 300 metres across, containing every species of human failing from senility to felony.[31] Much of it, including the house of correction, was constructed under the direction of Carlo Fontana.

In the *Motu Proprio* of 14 November 1703,[32] Clement let it be known that the wicked children of Rome who had customarily been crowded together in a fearful prison known as the Polle Drara, from whence most emerged worse than they entered, were now to have the opportunity of being reformed in the house of correction. It was a service for which their guardians were expected to pay in hard cash, and even then only promising material was to be admitted. The prospective inmates, all under 20 years of age, were first sifted by the Tribunal of the Cardinal Vicar. Recommendations were made by the Governor of Rome, the Senator, Judges and the Auditor to the Chamber. Final judgement still lay with the Papal authorities. Only the most spiritually innocent would graduate to find a place within its walls. The rest would be consigned to the common gaol.

The place was designated a house of correction and its purpose was phrased accordingly: 'That they who, when idle, were injurious, when instructed might be useful to the state.'[33] Also the building had been carefully planned by Fontana as a manufactory for woollen cloth. In the basement were vats for washing and dying, with a wide ramp leading to ground level so pack animals could haul material up and down. The ground floor was furnished with looms, above was a monumental vaulted hall lined on each side with three stories of galleried cells, and on the roof an open loggia for drying dyed wool, with a winch from the dying vats in the basement.[34] But despite Fontana's attention to the processes of production, the centrepiece of the scheme was always recognized to be the vaulted hall with its 60 galleried cells, the part least integral to the business of cloth making. Fontana himself chose a perspective of it for a commemorative medal struck in 1704 (Fig. 24).[35] Indeed, illustrations of the building published later would invariably truncate the upper and lower parts of the section, giving the false impression that hall and cells comprised the entire structure (Figs. 25, 26).

Certainly it was here that the innovation lay. At the east end was an altar, at the west end a whipping post and a sign demanding silence. Between were lines of benches to which certain children were chained and set to work spinning wool. Others were kept in their cells all the time. Each cell had its own privy in the thickness of the outer wall, each had a barred window facing into the central area from which the altar could always be seen, so that Mass could be celebrated without necessarily letting the children out. It was as if a cloister had been crammed into the interior of a church, the aisles filled with ranges of cells, and the whole then sandwiched in a factory; a concentrated and ingenious organization combining the requirements of correction and penitence by arranging production round a monastic core.

The Rome House of Correction found a prominent place in John Howard's *The State of the Prisons* as one of the 'more rational plans for softening the mind' that he commended to his readers.[36] In it he found his favourite prison inscription which read: 'it is of little advantage to restrain the bad by punishment, unless you render them good by discipline'.[37] All the same, its importance in penal history was not in the discipline as such, but in the new mainstays upon which that discipline rested: silence, solitary confinement, exposure to religious ritual, and, behind them all, architecture. In 1839 a distinguished French prison reformer could still say that it was 'the most perfect model that could be chosen for a penitentiary',[38] by which time its mark had been made and penitential imprisonment had spread much farther from its monastic origins.

While Carlo Fontana was making plans of the Rome House of Correction for Clement XI, proposals of a similar kind were being formu-

24. Rome House of Correction, sketch for a commemorative medal,
Carlo Fontana, 1704.

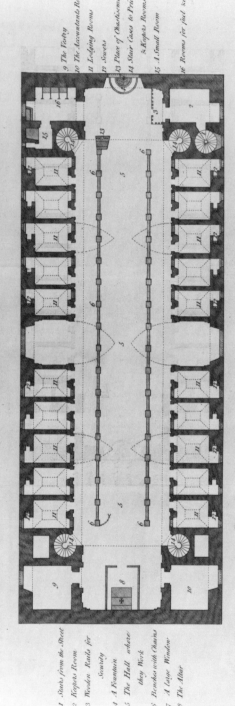

25. Rome House of Correction, Carlo Fontana, completed 1704, plan and section as illustrated in Howard, *The State of the Prisons*, 1777.

lated in protestant London. In 1701 a committee of the Society for the Promotion of Christian Knowledge (S.P.C.K.) was brought together at the behest of Bishop Crompton to look into the prisons. Thomas Bray, a founder member of the S.P.C.K., was made chairman. Bray's views were formalized in two manuscripts: the first *A General Plan of a Penitential Hospital for the Imploying and Reforming of Lewd Women*[39] describing a project he had tried to establish in 1698: the second *An Essay Towards ye Reformation of Newgate and Other Prisons in and about London*,[40] in which the horizon of penitential imprisonment was dramatically widened.

No further attempt was made to implement his suggestions at the time and the two manuscripts were soon forgotten. Still, they define the points at which the notion of penitential confinement gained entry into English penal thought, and at which its mantle was first extended over all prisoners, even the most ferocious.

Bray regarded Newgate as an incitement to felony, the evil and dissolute attracted to it by the unparalleled range of disgusting pleasures offered within. For novices it was a school of vice with 'old criminals

26. Rome House of Correction, Carlo Fontana, elevation showing the full extent of the building.

corrupting newcomers'.[41] He thought much the same of Bridewell, where the majority of London whores were sent, and this is what prompted him to plan a different kind of institution where this retrograde tendency would be reversed. The Penitential Hospital for Lewd Women was not to be anything like a prison, for its function was precisely to counteract the effects of those terrible institutions. It was to stand between Bridewell and liberty as a decontaminant for women who had already served out their sentence before the law.[42] Like the Rome House of Correction it was to have been a place of privilege. The next step was much bolder — to suggest that the existing prisons should also be reorganized on the same lines:

> The reformation of prisons may much contribute to the reformation of the public, for prisons are one great part of our correction of criminals, and if they are well managed may prove effectual to their amendment: whereas for want of discipline it now generally happens that prisoners are made much worse by them, and if an innocent person be committed by misfortune or mistake, he is commonly corrupted and turns profligate.[43]

Here Bray used the word reformation with its two classic penological meanings: applied to prisons it meant a new order, new rules, new buildings; applied to prisoners it meant a transformation of moral state effected by imprisonment. These were meanings which the word retained until the nineteenth century.

In this early vision of reform the prison was to be turned from a debauchers' paradise into a fountainhead of virtue whose effects would spread through London's courts and alleys via the agency of reformed offenders returning to old haunts. Under pious, strict rules all the traditional evils of gaols would be suppressed by a hierarchy of virtuous keepers. Prisoners were to be told of 'the good designed to their souls by these orders'; they would be exhorted 'to joyn their endeavours to promote good work';[44] they would be issued with sundry devotional books. At the same time men were to be kept absolutely separate from women prisoners, and speaking between them would be a punishable offence. All prisoners were to have single cells in which to sleep, to prevent fornication, while the older and wiser criminals, the corrupting sort, were to be 'kept in separate apartments, singly, by themselves and by no means suffered to converse with others'.[45] If the prison was to be a seed bed for the cultivation of virtue, the better strains had to be protected from the rank, so an attempt had to be made to divide like from unlike, men from women and the corrupted from the innocent because of the pernicious intercourse they would otherwise enjoy. Righteous words would brook no competition.

Given the explicitly religious character of penitential imprisonment, the question arises as to why it so easily crossed the divide between Catholic and protestant. Mabillon had given the practice an exclusively Catholic history, yet Bray was a proselytizing protestant and later in the eighteenth century the swelling ranks of penal reformers were, as Michael Ignatieff points out, packed with radical non-conformists.[46]

One significant source of convergence between these two opposed strands of Christianity was, though, to be found in the changing protestant conception of hell. Hell was the paradigm of penalties to which prisons were always being compared. They were hell on earth, the gateway to hell, the epitome of hell, the suburbs of hell, they were hell itself.[47] Geffray Mynshull made his process through King's Bench into an epic journey through hell (1618);[48] the author of *Hell in Epitome* did the same at Marshalsea (1718);[49] Edmund Gayton in 40 small pages describing London prisons, managed to restate the likeness on five separate occasions (1655).[50] The comparison had an implicit moral value and was not merely rhetorical, something brought out by *The Charitable Visit to the Prisons*, anonymously published in 1709 as advice and counsel to all kinds of prisoners. The author reminded his readers that 'some have found the fear of Hell their first step to Heaven'. The danger of pollution was considerable in prisons, but this did not matter so long as they served the greater purpose of simulating the terrors and pains of life after death for the wicked. In Hell 'How tormenting the apprehensions of an endless duration in misery, yet to come'.[51] These torments could be intimated in prison which stood as a foretaste, a pale shadow, an edifying copy of hell. It is often difficult in this tract to establish where the eschatological original ends and where its prison replica begins, so closely were the two knit together.

In the later eighteenth century, on the wave of penal reform, comparisons with hell were as common as ever, but hellish prisons were no longer being defended as a useful mnemonic depicting the wages of sin in the next world. Robert Denne, for example, complained to the London Aldermen in 1771 that:

Seldom have I passed thro' the gate of that most diabolical fabric, Newgate, that the description given by our illustrious poet of the Infernal Regions hath not occurred to my mind. And if you only recollect some parts of *Paradise Lost*, you will perceive that many of the lines in which Milton has related the employments and amusements of the evil spirits, are very applicable to the other place. At present I shall only observe that the close recess of the Pandemonium, where the chiefs of them sat in council to work the destruction of mankind, answers but too well to the principal ward in the prison.[52]

This was the martial country of the dispossessed, wilfully at war with society, and the more people were sent there the sadder it would be for the world at large. It illuminated nothing; it was merely an aggravation. Nevertheless, one quality it shared with the hellish habitations of *The Charitable Visit* was that they were both unredemptive. They made people worse, not better.

In early protestant eschatology there was no purgatory, only a heaven for the chosen and an unredemptive Hell in which the wicked were thrust for eternity, but D.P. Walker has shown how, during the seventeenth century, protestant hell was developed into a place from which sinners might eventually be redeemed.[53] Towards the end of the eighteenth century a redemptive hell was commonly accepted in enlightened protestant circles. This being the case a prison compared to the older unredemptive hell had to be condemned for its perversity. More merciful intentions were ascribed to the 'administrator of the universe' who now preferred the repentance of sinners to their everlasting torment.[54] Consequently the old prisons, still seen as hellish, unregulated and chaotic, lost the only moral utility they ever had, since the hell to which they corresponded was judged to be nothing but a vindictive figment.

Any prisons that would attempt reformation of character on the lines of the new reformatory hell would partake of a different order, more akin to purgatory than the traditional kingdom of the devil, for redemptive hell shared many characteristics with that much maligned Catholic invention. It would be necessary to introduce a structure in which it was possible to calculate sin, as in the Book of Fate where the vices and virtues of each soul were audited by angels. Bray's reformed Newgate would have been like this — not a punishment at all but a stringent test. Punishment was to be meted out separately, on the evidence of a comprehensive register of breaches, faults and omissions.[55] In terms of general practice the introduction of extensive rules and orders directed at prisoners' behaviour during the late eighteenth and early nineteenth century marks the transition, but by this time the authorities were grappling with the concomitant difficulty, of monitoring the performance of every prisoner all the time; a difficulty that would be resolved largely in terms of architecture.

As the purpose of hell changed so too did the nature of the punishment suffered there. The carefully planned geography of physical tortures so meticulously described by the advocates of eternal damnation now seemed decidedly offensive.[56] Impalings, burnings, flayings and dismemberings could only serve to exacerbate the passions and increase the culprits' hatred of God. The problem was to describe a punishment that did not alienate in this way. The solution was to put mental anguish in the place of physical tortures.[57] It was the perfect method because, as Rousseau amongst many others noticed, innocence could never be punished: 'I cannot recollect, after my death, what I was during life; without recollecting also my perceptions and consequently my actions: and I doubt but this remembrance will one day constitute the happiness of the just and the torments of the wicked.'[58] Recollection was a self-adjusting recompense for both good and evil. If hell, or for that matter heaven, were nothing but memories, then the way to reproduce hell's effects in prison was to give the criminal mind nothing but its own sordid contents to dwell on. A way had to be found of shutting out all diversions and disturbance. This was one route, a protestant route, toward solitary confinement, another practice that would have to rely heavily on architecture for its realization, as was already evident from the Rome House of Correction.

Redemption and progress moved in the same direction. Redemption affected the individual soul, progress existed in the context of nations and societies. The emergence of the prison into the political light in the 1770s and 1780s was placed in the perspective of progress by distinguishing between what Howard termed the gothic and rational modes of punishment. The trouble with medieval punishments, according to the Rev. John Brewster, who published prayers for prisoners in solitary confinement, was that they were devised to afflict the body and never reached the mind, and so were useless and cruel at the same time, but now a new penalty had been discovered to 'drive into the recesses of the heart'.[59] Jonas Hanway put it in a classical framework and boasted of 'outdoing the ancients',[60] but what linked these and all the other references to the same transition was the idea of an evolution towards a more merciful system. Sir William Eden, co-author of the Penitentiary Act, saw the progress of punishment as a gradual but as yet incomplete passage to this end. 'Reason and mercy', he wrote, 'gradually prevailed; but an ample field is still open to the exertion of their influence.'[61] In an unusually concise and pithy aphorism Howard added a note of international competition: 'We have too much adopted the gothic mode of correction, viz., by rigorous severity, which often hardens the heart; while many foreigners pursue the more rational plan for softening the mind in order to its amendment.'[62] These many foreigners included the Hanse towns and the Dutch with their houses of correction, the Italians with their child reformatories in Rome, Milan and Genoa, and, most advanced of all, Ghent in Austrian Flanders with its enormous Maison de Force, built by the architect Montfeson under the direction of Vicomte J.P. Vilain XIII, and begun in 1772. Planned as a regular octagon 190 metres across with segmental courtyards round an administrative centre (Fig. 27), the building was left incomplete. Even so English visitors were struck by the combination of architectural order and inflexible disciplinary regulation.[63] For all the acclaim it received in the decades of reform, the Maison de Force was perhaps closer to the older notion of correction. It was, though, an illustration of the potency of institutional punishment and an odious comparison with the disorder of English prisons.

Beyond the European arena it appeared that other great civilizations had, quite independently, adopted more advanced penalties to inflict on their peoples. Robert Denne, for instance, cited the Chinese and Japanese prisons as being airy, neat and all with separate cells, comparing very favourably with the best regulated European gaols.[64] Here then, was a dialectic of progress: the Dutch, the Flemish and the admirable, semi-legendary Orientals had to be outshone. This somewhat crude nationalistic dynamic, nourished on the great achievements of foreigners, together with the notion of a penal teleology propelling the authorities further and further from ignorant cruelty towards a perfect system of rational punishment, justified penitential imprisonment by giving it a proper time in which to unfold; a position in the course of things that made its appearance seem both inevitable and urgent. The penitential prison would raise both the law and offenders out of the coils of violence. The law had been trapped there by history; offenders were trapped there by passion.

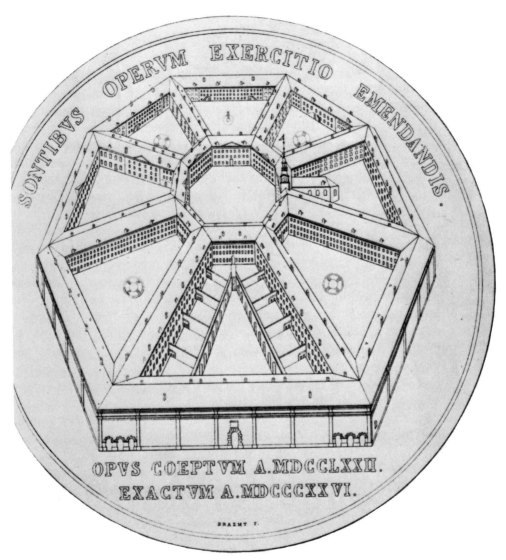

27. Maison de Force, Ghent, begun 1772, the scheme as originally planned. Only five of the eight courts were completed in the eighteenth century.

A characteristic pattern of corruption was to be observed inside as outside the prisons — a progressive spiral into evil from the smallest indiscretions. Left to themselves, prisoners would 'accelerate their own destruction',[65] immersing themselves ever deeper in their own violence and folly. But what force was it that pushed human nature into this rapid abandonment? Apart from Bentham, all the reformers were in agreement: it was passion. Passions were feelings that moved the mind as powerfully as bodily pain or ecstasy, active irrational energies that caused inexplicable desires and hatreds. Passion, always violent and egotistical,[66] had to be contrasted, not with reason, which was a different thing altogether, but with sentiment. Sentiment was at the opposite end of the scale of feelings. It was delicate, open to reason, moderate and passive where passion was gross, sensual, greedy and untamed. The image of the criminal as a wild beast, which had enjoyed wide circulation in the seventeenth century, could now be paralleled with another characterization in which he had merely succumbed to an excess of passion, becoming a victim to deranged emotions.[67] One inflaming agency was entertainment. There was, said Henry Fielding, 'a broad and well-beaten passage from places of public diversion to prison'.[68] Gaming houses, theatres, taverns and other nocturnal resorts not only consumed the meagre earnings of the poor, they magnified their appetites and indulged their senses, creating the intoxication and excitement out of which issued crime.

Passions were also roused by violent forms of punishment. Whipping in particular was singled out as an example of this exacerbation through the application of 'impolitic' penalties.[69] What was needed was an amercement that would 'curb and soften the passions into a religious, humane and obedient temper';[70] a punishment that would be gentle in that it inflicted no great physical pain, a penalty that would appeal to sentiment. Again, the remedy was found in solitude, which was known to exert a strong influence over the mind. Although associated with contemplation and religious awakening, it touched the conscience in a way perfectly tailored to the needs of penal reformation.

In the secular world, havens of solitude were first created for kings, dukes and princes.[71] In the eighteenth century the privilege of being alone still belonged to the upper strata of society, but nevertheless was beginning to alter, decisively, the shape of landscapes and buildings. The English garden with its bowers, ruins, hidden grottoes and contrived views to distant scenery, where 'all alone, and compliments apart, / I ask these sober questions of my heart';[72] and the English country house with its separate apartments, libraries, studies and closets,[73] were devoting more and more space to seclusion. Although there was a great difference between the elective, occasional solitude sought by men of culture, which in any case was easily modified into the scenery of intimate friendship, and the unremitting cellular isolation that was to be imposed on prisoners, the two conditions derived from the same idea that any form of society was suspect both morally and aesthetically.

Paul Hazard tells how the qualities of the wholly natural man were discovered in Beaurieu's story, *L'Elève de la Nature*. At birth a child was put in a cage and fed through a hatch so that he would be entirely cut off from all human contact. Introduced to others of his kind at the age of twenty, he proved himself the personification of propriety, benevolence and reason.[74] This familiar little parable showed how the intrinsic goodness of man was obscured by intercourse; remove the intercourse and perhaps the essence would reappear. This would not be easy, because the majority of mankind would go to great lengths to surround themselves with diversion and excitement rather than be left alone.

It was the philanthropist Jonas Hanway who, in the crucial period after the outbreak of the American War, proved the most effective exponent of solitary imprisonment. Together with Robert Dingley he had set up a magdalen house in 1758 where prostitutes were put to work in small chambers without company, were kept on a spare diet (to calm the passions) and given religious instruction (Fig. 28).[75] By 1786 2,415 women had passed through its doors. Of these, about 900 were discharged as incorrigible, or at their own request because they found the regime too harsh.[76] Drawing on this experience Hanway published two essays, *Solitude and Imprisonment* (1776) and *Distributive Justice and Mercy* (1781), on the plausibility of extending this regime to the prisons. Its effects were after all universal: 'There is scarce any wickedness that solitude will not work on it.'[77] The reason for this was that the 'forced reflection' it entailed was an immersion in truth. The burdens of sin, guilt and fear were increased to their correct weight on the soul. It was an inescapable confrontation with an inner force normally screened by everyday trivia.[78] In solitude truth preyed on the mind,

28. Frontispiece from Jonas Hanway, *Thoughts on the Plan for a Magdalen House*, 1759.

ridding men of any delusions, and so it would be a blessing to all those who comprehended its meaning and submitted themselves to it. Only 'monsters in human shape' could fail to respond to its imperatives.[79]

The contrast between solitary confinement and the gregariousness of existing prisons was, of course, lost on no one. It was therefore as a fitting tribute to Hanway that the Rev. William Dodds, awaiting execution for forgery, composed an encomium on solitude while suffering in the cacophony of Newgate, picturing 'The *Revel Rout* dispersed: each to his cell / Admitted silent'.[80]

Solitude found its way into the statute book as the initial stage of felony sentences prescribed in the Penitentiary Act of 1779 ('solitary imprisonment accompanied by well-regulated labour and religious instruction'),[81] and was brought into local gaols and houses of correction by Acts of 1781 and 1784. The construction of numerous prisons, entirely or partially for solitary confinement, followed (see ch. 4).

A dialogue soon developed within the reform movement over the dangers of unleashing the full power of solitude on minds habituated to diversion. Jonas Hanway, Robert Denne, William Blizard, Josiah Dornford, William Turner, George Onesiphorus Paul, the 3rd Duke of Richmond and Thomas Beevor were all convinced of its benefits and worked for it by publishing, campaigning or building. Thomas Beevor told of the unexpected benefits arising from its use at Wymondham House of Correction, where prisoners, 'their minds tortured with guilt, and unrelieved by the avocations of society, seem to feel no ease but in discharging the load from off them'.[82] Confessions of many crimes quite unknown to the authorities had been wrested from criminals touched in this way. Old stories were revived and embellished, like that of the seventeenth-century radical, James Naylor, who thought he was Christ, joyful in his delusion until put in solitary confinement where he was quickly reduced to the status of a mortal in his own mind, now decidedly sober.[83] The truth would out.

But there was another side to it. The hollow soul collapsed into its own vacuum when not sustained by external diversion.[84] There was therefore a great danger in solitude as well as a great possibility. Its overwhelming force could destroy those without inner resources, who could reflect on nothing but the emptiness within. So it was that the Comte de Lauzun, kept in a dark dungeon for nine years at Pignerol, nearly died of grief when his keeper trod on a spider, his only companion.[85] Howard was cautious. He believed that 'solitude and silence are favourable to reflection and may possibly lead them [the prisoners] . . . to repentance', but had decided as early as 1777 that separation both day and night was impractical and severe.[86] He remained unconvinced by later visits to Sherborne Bridewell, Reading House of Correction and several other prisons where inmates were kept in isolation 23 hours of the day.[87] Bentham adopted solitary confinement for his first Panopticon scheme in 1787, but by 1791 had changed his mind after being advised of its dangers (possibly by Howard, since Bentham said he sought his advice), explaining that it made the mind a 'gloomy void', leaving the prisoner 'destitute of all support but for his own internal resources . . . producing the most lively impression of his own weakness'.[88]

During this period of dialogue no one recommended unbridled use of solitary confinement. The question was how far it had to be moderated and softened. Its practical definition was never quite clear, and what A.K. Wedderburn (Lord Loughborough), for instance, described as solitude sounded little different from Howard's confinement in cells at night time only.[89] The one certainty was that, employed judiciously, the effects would be beneficial.

Any hesitancy was not for lack of conviction. The reformers had devised an ambiguous sort of punishment that combined the most terrifying characteristics with the quality of humanity. It could be depicted as worse than death or as a kind of gentle charity. The formidable Archdeacon Paley, no friend to reform, understood this: 'Of the *reforming punishments* which have not yet been tried, none promises so much as that of solitary imprisonment, or the confinement of prisoners in separate compartments. This improvement augments the terrors of the punishment . . . '[90] As Hanway also recognized, the new form of imprisonment was 'compounded of both justice and mercy', for it carried with it 'the ensigns of terror and the banners of peace and good will towards men'.[91]

The eruptions of passion that paved the way to vice and crime took place in gaming houses, taverns, brothels and theatres. The process of criminal reformation therefore required an institution that would stand as a negation of all that these places stood for. They fostered downfall: the prison would foster regeneration. It would be a turning point on the trajectory into wickedness. This ambitious objective was to be pursued through a combination of rules and architecture,[92] but during the early years of reform the crucial role of architecture in establishing solitude was only dimly perceived.

Expectations regarding architecture were high, but were at first experienced in nebulous generalizations and enigmatic allusions. Addressing an architect, Thomas Bowdler wrote of the national penitentiaries: 'Our undertaking is so different from anything that has ever been built in this country that a person may be very fit for building a church or palace and very unfit for being architect to the penitentiary houses.'[93] To redress existing evils, maintained Howard, 'the first item to be taken into account is the *prison itself*'.[94] Hanway was only a little more specific about his proposed gaol for Middlesex, recognizing at least that 'The great art in the contrivance of this building will be to prevent all kinds of communication between one prisoner and another.'[95] Existing prisons might be ancient and stupid in their construction, but the question of what to put in their place had no real answer until William Blackburn and Jeremy Bentham forged the links between discipline and building. It is interesting that the reformers perceived the links to be both practical and necessary. There was even a glimpse of a far grander aim for architecture in the work of maintaining society as a whole. Denne hinted at this when he called on architects to invent a new sort of building that would 'allure some of the giddy generation, whose closets appear dungeons to them, to indulge in a few minutes' recollection'.[96]

The dungeon

The author of *Hanging not Punishment Enough* in 1701 and Bernard de Mandeville in 1725 proposed a period of complete isolation between sentence and execution for all those condemned to hang.[97] The reason Mandeville gave for this modification of procedure was that the procession to Tyburn had been turned into a travesty. Prisoners in the tumbril were no longer a dolorous and fearful spectacle but impious and brave. Their drunken and impenitent exit was distorting the dramatic meaning of public execution.

Mandeville was concerned that the crowd would construe their behaviour as demonstration of the honour and courage of felons.[98] Just three days of utter isolation in a 12 foot square dark cell would change all that. Bypassing all reference to inner experience, Mandeville only wished to convey the corporal effects of isolation, and treated it as if it were a species of torture. The condemned man would emerge a terrifying sight. The 'paleness of his countenance and the shaking of every limb', together with the cries of anguish, the tears, the wringing of hands and the distortion of features, would convince the rabble of the 'pangs, amazing harass and unspeakable agony of his excruciated soul!'.[99] This skilful piece of manipulation would restore to public execution a propitious dramatic structure.

In 1728, three years after the publication of Mandeville's proposal, 15 condemned cells, with tiny windows high in the vaults were erected on the east side of the old Newgate.[100] These were preserved adjacent to Dance's rebuilding (and can be seen in Dance the Elder's plan (Fig. 44) marked E).

Mandeville's proposal presents an aspect of earlier practice of which nothing has yet been said but which was central to the architectural idea of the prison prior to reform. If the object of solitary confinement as conceived by the reformers was to subdue passion and calm the emotions, the object of the much older practice of incarceration was, by contrast, to accentuate them. It was the dramatic character of incarceration that gave it value, and its dramatic character overflowed easily into art. So it was that the architecture of the dungeon, as the scene of incarceration, was translated into an expressive theatrical setting. As such it laid no claim to realism and had little to do with the realities of incarceration. But the characteristically overblown representations from the world of the stage were eventually translated back into architecture and were to have a lasting influence on the imagery of the prison during the eighteenth and nineteenth centuries.

Mabillon attributed the invention of the dungeon to Abbot Mathieu Prieur, who dug a subterranean sepulchre into which he threw a monk whom he considered incorrigible.[101] Whether this was true or not, it had been common practice since medieval times to consign malefactors, political enemies and heretics to chambers cut into the depth of tower walls, in the footings of baileys, to undercrofts and cellars. Some dungeons were, like Prieur's, purposefully excavated, others, like Portman Castle (Fig. 29),[102] were largely the result of superior constructions; dark, accidental cavities beneath the grade

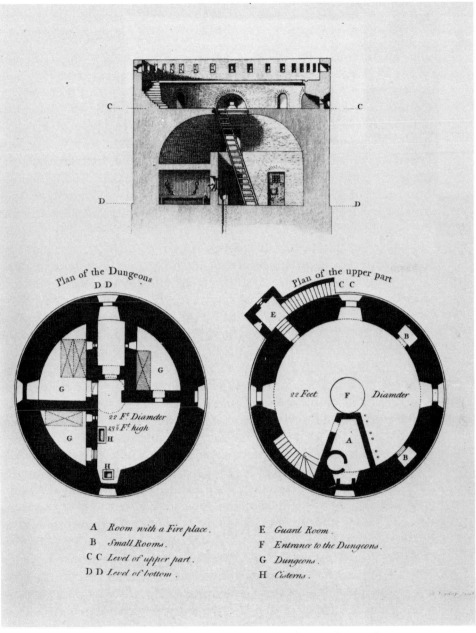

A   *Room with a Fire place.*
B   *Small Rooms.*
C C *Level of upper part.*
D D *Level of bottom.*

E   *Guard Room.*
F   *Entrance to the Dungeons.*
G   *Dungeons.*
H   *Cisterns.*

29. Portman Castle, a French naval fortification used as a prison, from Howard, *Lazarettos*, 1791.

of habitation; fitting places to dispose of those whom it was best to forget.

When the prison first appears as a distinct architectural formation it does so in emulation of these places. At Venice, between 1531 and 1552, 19 dungeons called the Wells, within the Doge's Palace, were constructed as if they belonged underground, though in fact they were on ground floor and mezzanine level. An almost identical arrangement of blind cells placed back-to-back within a larger envelope of masonry was to be found on the ground floor of Antonio Rusconi's Venice New Prison occupied in 1574 (Figs. 30, 31).[103] The first architectural treatise to offer plans of prisons, Joseph Furttenbach's *Architectura Universalis* of 1635, also showed lines of dungeons encased in building. In Furttenbach's designs this arrangement was the principal feature of the prison plan (Fig. 32).[104]

In these examples the dungeon was neither accident nor anomaly, but an endlessly reproducible item. In this respect they may be compared to the reformed prisons of the eighteenth and nineteenth centuries with their ranges of identical solitary cells, yet they quite clearly belong to another emotional world, still that of the unredeeming prison, though placing the prisoner not in the region of the damned, as did the general run of crowded gaols, but in the region of the dead, where, 'ye contemplate how to live i' th' grave before ye come to die'.[105] This may not have made for nobler punishments, but it did make possible nobler representations of punishment.

Towards the end of the seventeenth century there began a theatrical tradition of prison scene making for drama and opera, associated now with the name of the Bibbiena family (whose ten conventional sets included the *carceri*), in which the dungeon was depicted so as to produce a profoundly histrionic effect. Daniel Marot's Prison d'Amadis (Fig. 33) is a fine example of the type:[106] a vast receding cavern of decayed vaults, bridges and colossal piers decorated with instruments of torture and the tools of confinement. Across similar tromp l'oeil perspectives[107] the calumniation of heroes and heroines would be acted out in countless melodramatic scenes. The drift from practice towards representation culminated in the publication of Piranesi's *Carcere* etchings in 1745. Piranesi took the operatic set, detached it from its theatrical origins and generalized it into spatial configurations that could only exist in pictures. The *Carcere* had not the remotest connection with prison building; their incalculable influence resides not here, but in their effects on sensibility.

In these forms the dungeon was entirely within the field of representation. It thrived in painting and literature as well as on the stage (Fig. 34). But in the later eighteenth century attempts were made to transport a scenery so rich with emotion back into reality. It was then possible, for instance, to conceive the following as one of the punishments in an ideal legal code: 'Nearby, will be the walled cemetery which

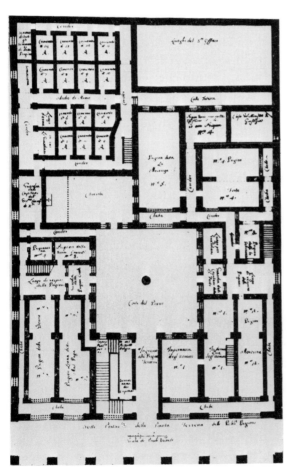

30. Venice New Prison, A. Rusconi, occupied 1574, ground plan. Umberto Franzoi, *Prisons of the Venetian Republic*, Venice, 1966.

will hold buildings of very strong stonework, a type of cavern that is rather spacious and heavily barred, to shut in forever and then entomb Citizens who deserve Civil death, that is, to be forever excluded from society.'[108] So wrote the French utopian Morelly in 1755. Also from France came a number of architectural projects attempting to create prisons from the images of incarceration in the arts. Those produced by Boullée, Ledoux, Houssin and Bellet (Fig. 35) in the 1780s and 1790s[109] are well known: oppressive, massive, and monumental, with balefully lit *cachots* surrounded by monolithic masonry. Only the capaciousness of the stage set was lost. They were declarations that architecture was, above all, an art of evocation. The incalculable weight of stone, the encasing exteriors, the immurring courts filled with shadow, the melancholy dungeons pierced with a single ray of light,[110] the entire prison was becoming a cultural reminiscence. The image of the thing belonged to its past, and that is perhaps why these projects were stillborn, compromised from the outset by the existence elsewhere of a developing

31. Venice New Prison, dungeon.

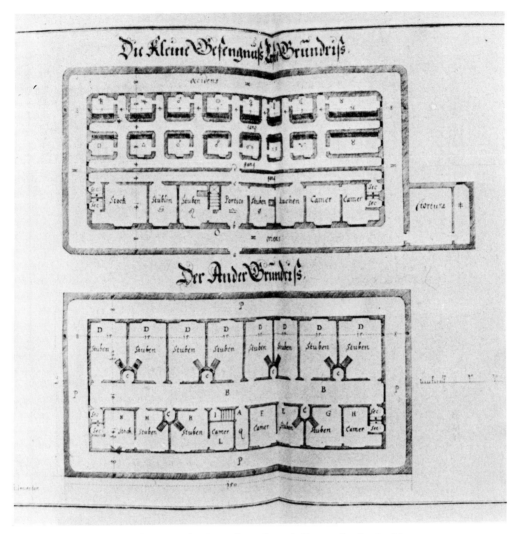

32. Design for a small prison, from Joseph Furttenbach, *Architectura Universalis*, 1635.

33. Daniel Marot, Prison d'Amadis, scene for an opera.

architecture of reform that was as yet without recognizable images but which belonged to the present.

Only one prison of this incarcerating kind was realized: the Cabanons de Surété in the Bicêtre. In 1788 the Cachots Souterreins in the prison section of the Bicêtre were demolished, and in their place a block of 18 dungeons raised (Fig. 36).[111] Nine were subterranean pits, each with a 25 cm grille at the top of a two metre shaft to admit air, light and food. Prisoners were chained to the wall. Above were nine larger dungeons,

34. Joseph Wright of Derby, The Captive, a scene from Sterne's *Sentimental Journey.*

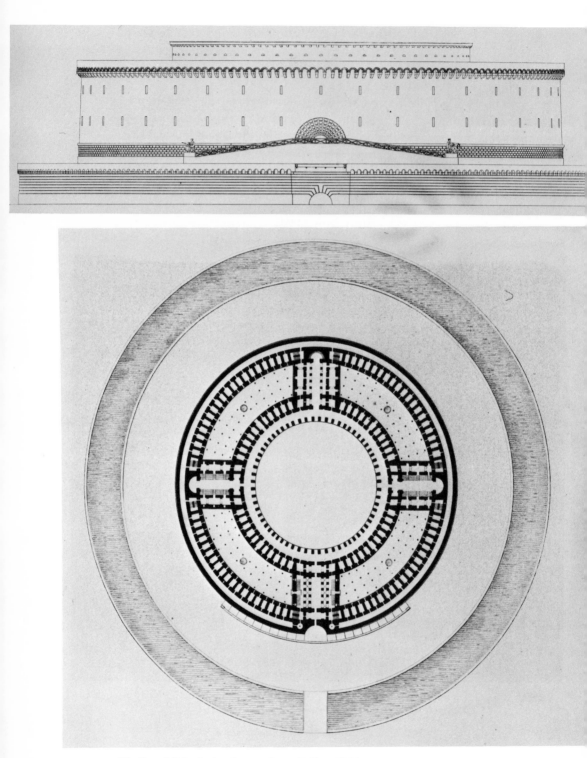

35. Grand Prix design for a prison, Bellet, 1792.

containing a lavatory and a stone bed, lit and ventilated through a pair of arches aligned to give the prisoner a tantalizing glimpse of a tiny piece of the sky. A beautifully rendered cross section of the *cachots* shows a prisoner languishing in the half light of the upper dungeon, reclining decorously like a sculpture, dressed in a Roman cloak and looking up to heaven through receding gothic vaults (Fig. 37). It was an evocation of an entirely sentimental kind — a classical posture in a medieval setting — which nevertheless shows that the dungeon now existed in order to oppress in a way that was consistent with heroic and sublime suffering. Thus it romanticized agony and garnished brutality with an aesthetic, and as such it belonged to the past, to art, but not to posterity.

In late-eighteenth-century England the dungeon was not consciously recreated in prison architecture as it was in France, except in the castellated tower of condemned cells in William Hillyer's Moulsham County Gaol for Essex, of 1777,[112] and in the spectacular design for a county gaol published by John Carter in 1778 (Figs. 38, 39, 40). Carter's plan was a medley of reformed and traditional elements, including separate wards and workrooms, a taproom and a debtors' begging cage. These things he buried in the solid carcass of a fortress as unequivocal as the French designs. Dungeons, however, in this curious hybrid, were mysteriously absent, except for a ring of nine dark cells at the foot of the east tower.[113] In the sixteenth-century Venetian prisons the image

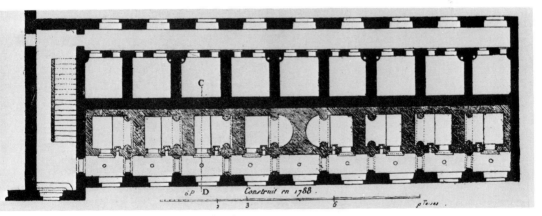

36. Cabanons de Sûreté, Bicêtre, Paris, begun in 1788, ground plan.

Coupe sur la Ligne — C. D.

37. Cabanons de Sûreté, Bicêtre, section.

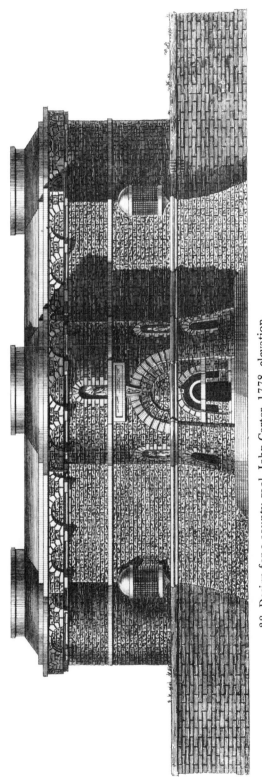

38. Design for a county gaol, John Carter, 1778, elevation.

of the grave had been tied to an experience as vivid as torture. In Carter's design this was no longer the case. The dungeon resembled the grave, Carter's prison resembled the dungeon. The allusion, now two layers deep, was that much more sophisticated, and that much further from its original object.

John Carter's project exemplifies a theme that recurs throughout the late eighteenth and nineteenth centuries: reform acknowledged in the programmatic organization of space, incarceration represented in the appearance of the building. While in Carter's pattern book design the reference to incarceration bit deep into the plan, in practice such imagery was restricted to the entrance portal.

In Britain the dungeon was not admitted as an ingredient of contemporary prison architecture. It might be evoked as the symbol of imprisonment but real dungeons were nonetheless relics to be rediscovered in old gaols and exposed in a lurid and unsentimental light. On the continent they may have been lonely and dolorous places, in England they were populous, foetid and obscene. The most publicized bad prison in the 1780s was the Bishop's Prison at Ely where men and

Plate CLXXX.

39. Design for a county gaol, John Carter, section.

women were chained to the walls or stapled to the floor, according to the magistrate James Collyer who petitioned George III to close it. There were others just as awful, like the room in Stafford County Gaol where Howard found 52 male felons 'chained down, hardly 14 inches being allowed to each'.[114] The moisture from their breath ran down the walls. Seven prisoners had died here of gaol fever in 1787 and nine in the infected debtors' apartment above. This was a dungeon. So too was the pit in the yard at Warwick Gaol that was used as a dormitory until 1797. Nineteen years after it had been abandoned, an appalled visitor estimated that up to 45 prisoners could have been kept in it, chained together through ankle rings like a string of beads (Fig. 41). Thomas Bowdler considered the Warwick pit the worst prison in the country. When he inspected it in 1789, he found 41 prisoners, of whom only 35

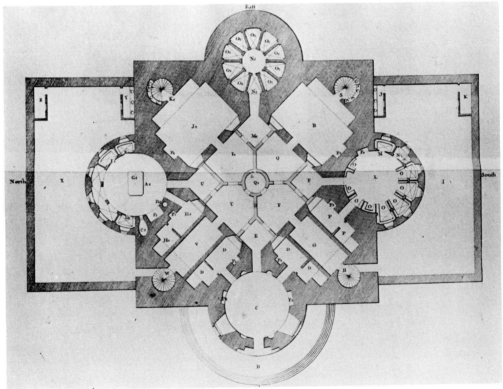

40. Design for a county gaol, John Carter, ground plan.

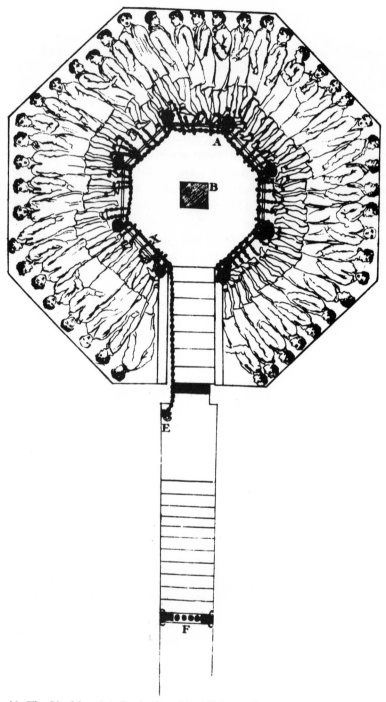

41. The Pit, Watwick Gaol, closed in 1797, an illustration published in 1818. A chain (X) was threaded through ankle irons, through fixed rings (A) and then anchored to the wall in the passage (E).

could find space to lie. They slept in a ring round an open cess pit (marked B in the figure) in the centre of an octagonal cellar, 19 feet below ground with only a small grating let through the top for ventilation. In the winter months human steams would billow out of this like smoke from a chimney.[115]

There were other subterranean pits at Bristol, Nantwich and Worcester. Although probably excavated only a few decades previously (the Nantwich Town Gaol Round House was dug in 1782),[116] they were made to appear the cruel remnants of a perverse medievalism. Although there were not many like them, they became a vortex towards which all unreformed prisons would inevitably gravitate; a type to which they all approximated to a lesser or greater degree.

The dungeon thus redefined — distasteful and without sublimity — did not provide a platform for heroics, neither did it provide an opportunity for the soul to disengage itself from the flesh in the way described so often by prison authors since Boethius.[117] Instead there was the compelling vision of a living hell.

Did the unreformed prisons duplicate the conditions of hell as suggested by the reformers, or did they duplicate the conditions of everyday life? For the reformers it was not so much a question of the facts as of the positioning of facts. On the one hand the prison was seen as cure for general malaise: 'Were our prisons newly modelled', said Josiah Dornford, Mayor of London, 'it would be one considerable step towards a reform of the lower orders of the people.'[118] On the other hand there could be no political future in a war against ordinariness. At this point the prisons had to appear on the nether side of normality for reform to be contemplated at all, but a far larger segment of social life could have been characterized in a similar way, and would be so, when the time was ripe, in the 1840s, the decade when housing became a political issue.[119]

The reformers were applauded for their benevolence. Howard in particular was treated to lavish praise. He was said to be a 'God-like man', a saint whose virtue could not be measured against the yard-stick of average human goodness.[120] Among his contemporaries only Wilberforce was of comparable stature.[121] Poems were written, plays performed, medals struck and monuments proposed in his honour.[122] While this is no place to probe Howard's character (which, as a fitting act of venveance, has been dissected already),[123] in so far as his personality was present in his public action, he displayed a paradoxical combination of severity and gentleness, rigid autocracy and dispassionate altruism — an ambiguity of disposition that could be extended to the entire movement for penal reform.

Nonetheless, he was hailed as the great deliverer of neglected prisoners, and was portrayed as such by the painter Francis Wheately (Fig. 42). An old man, a debtor no doubt, lies ill on a rotting straw pallet, covered with a piece of sackcloth and surrounded by his dependents and other prisoners. The great reformer stands pointing to the offensive pallet, an abashed gaoler by his side. Howard's servants stand by with a basket full of bread and a decent mattress to replace the straw bedding. A light is thrown on this scene by a small grating, but the sepulchural vaults of

42. Francis Wheatley, John Howard Offering Relief to Prisoners, 1787.

the prison dungeon recede immediately into the darkness beyond. This dextrous canvas is the perfect illustration of a chosen moment, bringing together the finest and most tender features of the reformers' mission. Only neglect and bad buildings stand in their way. Omitted was all sense of ambiguity. Absent also was any hint of the nastiness in human nature with which the reformers felt themselves confronted.

Still, if the ambiguities of penal reform were lost in contemporary adulation and for a while lost to posterity, they were evident to the reformers themselves. Prisoners were going to be delivered from their dungeons and reeking wards, but they were going to be delivered into a measured, regulated, silent world, dominated by an architecture of inescapable relationships.

3   Gaol fever

In the 20 years between 1775 and 1795 a wholesale rebuilding of the country's gaols and bridewells was accomplished. These were not the cottages and hostels of earlier years, but expensive and unique types of building — reformed prisons. At least 45 of them were erected during this period in England alone.[1] There were two proximate causes of this rebuilding: the American War of Independence and an unexpected out-break of gaol fever.

Ever since the law had first regularized the deportation of convicted felons in 1717[2] the majority of transportees had been sent to North America and the West Indies. So when hostilities between the Crown and the American colonies turned into outright war in 1775, the scope of penal transportation was suddenly and drastically reduced. It was this entirely unconnected political event that produced the crisis necess-ary to trigger off the legislative and executive mechanisms in the cause of reform. Some alternative arrangements had to be made to fill the enormous gap in the system of secondary punishments that had been created by the war. But the war did not affect the form of prisons any more than a hand affects the stone it throws. It was a different matter with gaol fever, the other precipitant of reform, which did alter the prisons, leaving an indelible print on their architecture.

There is a lot in a name; gaol fever belonged in gaols, the army fever belonged in the army and the hospital fever belonged in hospitals. Francis Bacon had rated the smell of a gaol to be the most pernicious infection besides the plague. No writer on early prisons neglected to mention the ubiquity of fevers, sores and infections in them.[3] It was fear of disease that made Baxter's sojourn in Clerkenwell House of Correction so much less pleasant than it might have been (see p. 33).

For a long time the authorities had been aware that the fever might escape from the gaols to bring down those who had never ventured inside their walls, but there was an acknowledged pattern to this kind

of accident. It would always occur after an assize. In the mid eighteenth
century many medical men and reformers busied themselves in tracing
how many gaolers, keepers, judges, lawyers and jurors had been tragically
killed in this way. The surgeon Thomas Day reminded his readers of the
'Black Assizes' of Taunton in 1730 during which over 100 died.[4] G.O.
Paul told of 300 deaths within 48 hours at the Oxford Assizes of 1577[5]
and Howard, too, had a collection of historical examples to add to those
disclosed in the gaols of his own day. These were nasty reminders of the
fever's power to break the boundaries of its proper location, culling
victims from all walks of life, and in particular from the legal profession.
Opening the prison for an assize was like opening Pandora's Box.

There was one example that would have been familiar to everybody.
In April 1750 attendants at the Old Bailey sessions remembered being
struck by a 'noisome smell' in the court.[6] A week later a number were
taken with a highly malignant fever. Most died. The death toll included
the Lord Mayor of London, two judges, an alderman, a lawyer, an
under-sheriff and several of the jury, not to mention 40 others.

Whether it was this one event that stimulated a wider interest in
prisons or not, it is certainly true that after 1750 the reform movement
became more purposeful, and there is no doubt that the Old Bailey
deaths were the major cause of the Aldermen's prudent decision to
rebuild Newgate Prison,[7] for it now appeared that there were two
reasons for doing so: to reform criminals and to stamp out the fever.

It was not just that magistrates felt that they too might one day fall
victim to the disease fostered in their own gaols. Medical practitioners,
with a new sensitivity to causal sequence, were beginning to cast doubt
on the accepted nomenclature of fevers. A breakthrough seems to have
been made by Dr John Pringle in the year of the Old Bailey deaths. In
Observations on the Nature & Cure of Hospital & Jayl Fevers Pringle
demonstrated that not only gaol fever and hospital fever but army fever
as well were all one and the same disease; a disease caused not by a
type of institution, nor by some peculiar elective affinity between sin
and illness, but by a linked chain of events under particular conditions.
'This fever is proper to every place that is the receptacle of crowded
men, ill aired and kept dirty . . . wherever there is a collection of putrid
animal steams, from dead or even diseased bodies.'[8] The significance of
this clearly stated aetiology was to suggest that prisons could be made
healthy if the conditions for the propagation of fever were removed. It

also suggested that all sorts of curious local fevers starting with 'gentle horrors and feverish heats' could well be the result of this same boundless affliction being spread by released prisoners.[9] So while this made the disease appear more pervasive and immanent, it also contained the possibility of its control.

There were other good reasons for attempting to suppress the fever at source. Howard, Pringle, Janssen, Dr Lind and G.O. Paul would all point to the depredations it caused in the army when, in periods of national emergency, the gaols were used as recruiting houses.[10] This, like the assize epidemics, emphasized the spread of fever from the gaols. Inside them fever had been wiping out many hundreds and possibly even thousands every year.[11] The same writers who had pointed out the public hazards of the fever were just as quick to show the injury it did to prisoners, some of whom were committed only for want of sureties, to give evidence for the crown, or for trifling debts. Howard contended that in the country as a whole more prisoners died of gaol fever by chance than were sent to the gibbet by process of law. Day and Paul bore witness to the truth of this indictment. Of 114 felons 7 had been hanged and 14 had died of fever at Maidstone in 1782. In the same year at Gloucester three times as many died of fever as were executed.[12]

Apart from the sentiment this might arouse in the hearts of the benevolent there was an issue at stake. The problem was that this made the penalties of the law into a lottery. It was one of the great aims of eighteenth-century penal legislation to introduce proportion between the degree of crime and the degree of punishment.[13] The random deaths through fever were making a mockery of this principle. So two equally powerful motives existed for controlling the fever in prisons: to prevent a general epidemic and to establish the necessary concordance between offence and penalty.

The three fevers that Pringle identified as one and the same (along with a number of others that went under the title of putrid and pestilential fevers) were none other than epidemic typhus — a disease that flourished with great intensity in eighteenth-century England.[14]

Aerial infection

Epidemic typhus is transmitted by lice, but in the eighteenth century the vector spreading gaol fever was thought to be a far more subtle vehicle than a crawling parasite. Prevailing opinion was that the disease was engendered by a change of quality or of constitution in the air we breathe. The atmosphere of the old, dark, close and putrid prisons was supposed to act as a reservoir of infection. The air, pent up in unventilated chambers, was thought to develop its own vapour into an irresistibly contagious gas. The first phase of reformed prison architecture was therefore dominated by a concern to design prisons in such a way that they could not possibly harbour putrid air.

The air had been made an independent subject of scientific enquiry by Stephen Hales, whose *Vegetable Statiks* (1727) included numerous experiments devised to illustrate the properties of this most encompassing and penetrating of all substances. Hales' findings and methods cleared the way for the identification of the major gasses over the ensuing half-century, and, since he was also responsible for the construction of ventilators in a number of public buildings, it is tempting to seek the origin of the technology of ventilation in the foundation of this new area of study, an advance in practice stemming from an advance in knowledge. But this was not the case. Pretty well every treatise on architecture from Alberti onwards had advised against siting buildings near or orienting them towards sources of noxious vapour — marshes, swamps and middens in particular — which would corrupt air and promote fevers, a view substantiated by a long tradition of medical opinion. Thomas Sydenham, for instance, explained the typhus epidemic of 1685/6 as due to an exhalation from the bowels of the earth which infected the atmosphere as a whole and was then assimilated into the human body. Similarly, Robert Boyle traced the epidemic to 'subterraneous miasmas'.[15] Forty years later Hales believed he had discovered another, even more potent source spoiling the atmosphere. According to him, air was a cleansing medium and the purpose of breathing was to evacuate waste from the body. He was able to show that, contrary to expectation, a measured volume of air was *reduced* when exhaled and concluded from this that, as it had to contain more matter after being breathed out, the air had collapsed into a denser, less elastic substance which he called 'fixed air', composed to respirable air plus acidic and sulphurous fumes. He went on to demonstrate its increasingly poisonous effect by re-breathing his own exhaled air for 8½ minutes.[16]

Hales' great contribution to the advancement of chemical science was the apparatus of his experiments; his contribution to the advancement of ventilation was the grafting of a new error onto some old ones, filling the air with yet more dangers. Not only could infected air generate from mineral action under the earth, from rotting corpses or decaying vegetation, it could arise from the healthy operation of living human bodies too, from breathing. Soon a variety of more or less respirable, more or less noxious airs were being held to account for a variety of illnesses. In many cases authors would mix the old aetiologies with the new. What they held to be beyond dispute, however, was the pre-eminence of air in the geography and economy of ill health in general and of fevers in particular.[17]

In 1733 Dr John Arbuthnot, a Fellow of the Royal College of Physicians and, like Hales, a Royal Society member, published his enthusiastic *Essay Concerning the Effects of Air on Human Bodies* expounding the insights provided by Hales' work. Grotesquely methodical, Arbuthnot listed the complex additives and impurities in the air we inhale. It was permeated with quantities of dews and waters, calcined rock from volcanoes, salts, vapours, tiny seeds and abrasions from vegetables, particles of gold, sulphur and quicksilver plus a whole catalogue of other atoms and effusions. Above and beyond all these was the respirable matter breathed out by men and animals. According to his calculations, if the respirable matter and the effluvia from the skin of exactly 2,904 men was collected over a period of precisely 34 days it would cover an acre of ground one inch deep. It seemed astonishing that civilization had not perished in a mire of its own effluvia long ago, and it would no doubt have done so were it not for the mixing and cleansing action of winds and the purifying action of thunder, lightning and eruptions.

Over the globe as a whole there was a dynamic balance of pollution and purification, but at the same time there were local fluctuations and concentrations. Many illnesses were produced by exposure to such imbalanced mixtures. One class of ailments would be due to too great a dryness in the air, another to air which was over-moist. Pestilential fevers, including gaol fever, were caused by the air absorbing decomposing organic matter.[18] The remedy was as obvious as it was simple; mix the air to keep it moving and you prevent contamination.

Later there were to be many interpretations of the way in which air served to purify and pollute, and of the way it spread putrid fevers.

Most would believe that the air acted as a vector carrying some diffused impurity as the source of contagion — but then it was difficult to tell what was real air and what was impurity, since the atmosphere was known to be a complex concoction of different elements. The source itself was identified variously as a 'hidden diathesis' that changed the texture of the blood on inhalation (Arbuthnot), air vitiated by respiration (Pringle), dispersed animal filth in general (Mead), or an 'envenomed nidus' impregnating the air (Lind).[19] Some said they honestly did not know what it was that caused contagion, like Thomas Day, who only knew that perspiration and pure atmosphere 'if long confined in the same room or place without mixing with the fresh air, will become infectious'.[20] Subtleties of interpretation like these could not detract from the fundamental agreement on the need for ventilation, but there were still pockets of resistance to the theory of aerial infection even in the 1770s. Dr William Fordyce, for one, thought putrid fever was caused by liquids putrescing within the body, fizzy blood, morbid foams and poisoned bile. Regular blood-letting and a daily ration of beer was, he said, the best preventive.[21] Another enterprising doctor thought he had discovered a 'medicine of singular efficacy' that would cure gaol fever, which he advertised to the London Aldermen so that they might try it out in their gaols.[22] Even Pringle was experimenting with cures from camomile flowers and barks to turn febrile tissue healthy,[23] but these were diversions. The mainstream of opinion was for preventive ventilation rather than curative treatments. Progress had led science to air but had not yet brought the atmosphere under sufficient control. A minor technology was now in the making in which air was to be put to use in the service of health.

Respiration

It was Stephen Hales himself who pursued the possibilities of making gaols more salubrious by ventilation. Hales, a Doctor of Divinity and a Fellow of the Royal Society, had worked briefly with Bray, Oglethorpe and Lord Perceval on a philanthropic scheme to settle debtors discharged from the London prisons in the colonies,[24] which may have alerted him to the prevalence of fever in existing gaols. Fourteen years later, in 1741, he presented a paper to the Royal Society concerning some patent ventilators he had designed for ships but which he also commended for use in public buildings. According to Hales, buildings and ships were too frequently conceived as inert vessels, even though they had to sustain life within. He found that it was useful to compare them to animals. Animals did not harbour stagnant air inside themselves and nor should any human habitation; they should breathe. Thus:

Were an animal to be formed the size of a large ship, we are well assured by what we see in other animals, that there would be an ample provision made to furnish that animal with a constant supply of fresh air, by means of large lungs, which are formed to inspire and breath out air in the same manner as these ventilators do . . . Can it therefore be an unreasonable proposal to furnish ships, gaols, hospitals etc., in the same manner with the wholesome breath of life in exchange for the noxious air of confined places?[25]

In 1749 Hales, an old man of over 70, was installing ventilators for the artificial respiration of the Savoy Prison. He had already put a small wind machine in Winchester County Gaol and would later do so in Northampton Town Gaol, and the county gaols of Shrewsbury, Maidstone, Bedford and Aylesbury.[26] At the same time he was cultivating the Duc de Noialles with a view to ventilating the French prisons and *hôtels dieux*. By 1752 he had done the same for Newgate in London. Directly after the fever outbreak of 1750, Sir Theodore Janssen had ordered the clearing of Newgate's interior and had supervised the removal of three entire cartloads of 'the most abominable filth' to an uninhabited spot where it was buried ten feet below ground, a measure understood to be no more than a temporary check.[27]

R.B. Pugh tells us that in 1509 an examination was made of the 'corrupt air' of Newgate, and by 1535 the prison had an air moving machine.[28] Hales knew of a ventilator that had been operating for many years in Winchester Gaol, while another had recently been fitted at Durham County Gaol.[29] Nothing is known of these, but they were most likely single bellows or fans worked by hand once every now and then to vomit out the rotten stench that built up inside individual chambers. Rather than rely on the fickleness of keepers to work his machine, Hales attempted to use the power of the wind to pull the foul air from the bowels of the building. Like breathing it was meant to be a continuous, not an intermittent process.

The Newgate ventilators (Fig. 43), which had taken five years to perfect and complete in conformity with 'nature's own method of working',

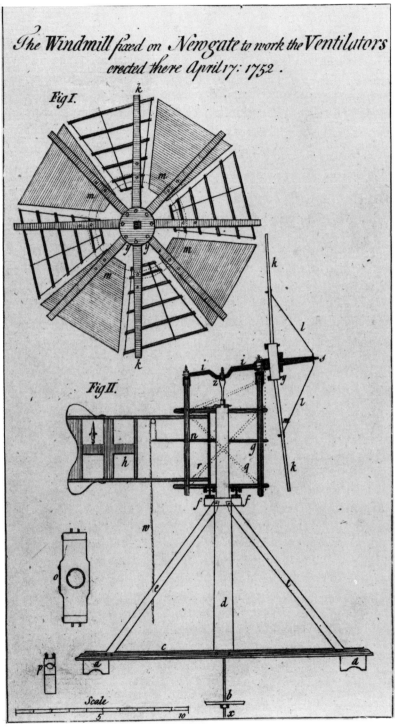

43. Stephen Hales' windmill to drive the bellows that drew out the foul air from the interior of Newgate. It can be seen in operation above the prison in Fig. 14.

functioned like a gigantic and extremely inefficient lung. There was a main duct which passed from the gaol roof down through a central light well to penetrate into 24 rooms through so many branching ducts. This was the respiratory network. At roof level was the mouth from which foul air was exhaled and the pump which pulled the air out. A windsail on top of the building was connected to a low-pressure bellows which Hales claimed could move the air at up to 27 miler per hour through the ductwork. This pump was modelled on the action of the muscles in the midriff which push and pull the air in and out of our bodies.[30]

Fever was not entirely abolished from Newgate by the ventilators, but both Pringle and Hales made strenuous efforts to prove to the Aldermen and the public that many lives had been saved by their instal-lation, which was not made any the easier considering that as soon as it started to work all the prisoners fell ill. Pringle attributed this initial bout of sickness to the drawing out of putrid atmospheres confined in the vaults of the building, undisturbed for many years until sucked out by the turbulence in the rooms above. The prisoners seemed, anyway, to recover after a while. If any doubt remained Pringle was inclined to vindicate the system by taking people up to the roof to watch a small torrent of befouled steams pumping from the mouth of the stack.[31] Occasionally an important visitor might still die of the fever, as did Dr Duntze's German companion who had come specially to see the venti-lators in 1754,[32] but notwithstanding this, it was generally accepted that there had been a marked improvement in the health of the pris-oners. During the first four months of operation only seven had died.[33]

Although this result might now appear inconclusive, the contention that ventilation would eliminate gaol fever was afterwards accepted as proven. For over fifty years salubrity and airiness were to be major determinants in the shaping and construction of prison buildings, not to mention hospitals, a host of other institutional forms, town plans and, eventually, in the nineteenth century, housing.

An inspired example of the use of an organic analogy as the basis for technical innovation, Hales' ventilators were just that bit too ambitious to succeed in practice. Forced ventilation, even by this new and improved method, was cumbersome, complicated and expensive. The amount spent at Newgate was £276.6s., including compensation to the relatives of the artisans and apprentices who had died of the fever while constructing the machine.[34] When finished it could only generate the power to evacuate one room at a time. Each of the 24 branches was controlled by a lid, and 23 of the lids had to be closed, otherwise the effect was nothing more than a slight, aimless stirring of the air within the building. Because of this it became necessary to employ a full-time operator to see to the bewildering variety of valves and lids, to furl and unfurl the windmill sails, to ventilate the 24 rooms in proper sequence, to work the manual pumps in the peripheral rooms that could not be connected to the main stack, and to maintain the machinery. There was also an insurmountable difficulty in using wind as a motive force to work the system. On windy days, when the prison would in any case get some air, it worked well enough. On still days, when a change of air was all the more urgently required, there was no power to be had at all. Although the Newgate pumps could be worked manually, the operator was said to be 'insufferably idle' and the ventilators rarely worked for more than a few hours a day.[35]

The rebuilding of Newgate

It was understood at the time that there were too many drawbacks to this method. Pringle regretfully accepted that little else could be done with an ancient pile like Newgate. But he felt that new prisons should be built in such a way that they did not require this enormous breathing apparatus.[36]

In the first edition of *The State of the Prisons* Howard recommended that manual ventilators be installed in all prison infirmaries, but later declared them to be unnecessary in a well-designed institution, as was all the paraphernalia of air-purifying showers, exploding gunpowders, brimstone fires, steamings and dousings with lime and vinegar that had recently been devised to combat the fever in its traditional environment.[37] Dr William Smith agreed. During the spring and summer of 1776 Smith visited the gaols in and around London. This was more than an exploration; he went to heal the sick. Twice a week between March and September he visited each of the 'dreary and loathsome mansions' in turn and claimed to have cured upward of 380 prisoners of putrid complaints. He said he was able to relieve the acutely sick, but, because no physician could preserve health in vitiated air, he could not rid the prisons of the fever. The gaols needed rebuilding.[38]

Hales had demonstrated the theory of aerial infection, but was unable to find a satisfactory solution to the problem he had raised, and as a result the emphasis soon moved from the provision of forced ventilation to the provision of natural ventilation. Three years after Hales had fixed up his ventilators the Aldermen decided to rebuild Newgate. A committee was set up and three architects submitted plans. The designs by Isaac Ware have been lost but those by George Dance the elder (1755) and William Jones (1757) have survived,[39] both with similar layout and accommodation.

Pringle had come to the conclusion in 1750 that the unhealthiness of gaols was as much the result of their not being provided with courtyards as anything else: 'The fault here seems partly to lie in the contrivance of the jayls, which never can be so healthful whilst they are too small for the number of prisoners or too insecure to be without dungeons, and without any convenience of a court for the freedom of air.' Theodore Janssen, as sheriff in 1750, had also advocated rebuilding the prison with an extensive courtyard, on the model of York Castle County Gaol (Fig. 17).[40] It is not surprising then to find that the designs were organized around as large a trio of courtyards for felons, debtors and women that could possibly be got on such a restricted site. Both were stark, solid and unfenestrated towards the street and more or less open towards the interior, although the two architects treated their facades very differently. Both had large reservoirs in the courtyards. Both had individual cells in the felons' wards but not in the debtors' ward. The plan forms were almost identical. We may judge from all these similarities that the Committee for Rebuilding stipulated a very precise brief, and that this brief was no thoughtless compromise but a careful exploration of the two new functions of the prison: to promote moral health through cellularization and division of males from females, felons from debtors, and to promote physical health by the provision of running water, drainage and open courtyard planning. These plans are the evidence of the Aldermen's intentions at this early stage in the rebuilding and they show quite clearly a conscious attempt to revise traditional arrangements in favour of something cleaner and more respectable.

The architects found themselves caught in a dilemma; the demands of security and seclusion were not easily compatible with the demands of health and open planning. On such a small plot the outer walls of the prison had to stand adjacent to the street. If these walls were opened up for the purposes of ventilation, the gaol would no longer be cut off from the surrounding community and the felons in their cells, which lined the outer surface of the building, could spend their time chatting with whomever cared to pass the time of day, rather than in silence. They could also escape with greater facility. So, Dance the elder left no exterior openings at all, except for a single small door into each court (Fig. 44). He then turned the otherwise blank facade into a regular sequence of blind niches.

Of the two sets of plans Jones' were the more detailed and complete (Fig. 45). His facade, a rather feeble imitation of a castle curtain wall, with a few frivolous crenellations on top — and the first conscious exploitation of medieval architecture as an emblem of imprisonment in this country — was, like Dance the elder's, blank, except for the occasional mock archery slot. The interior was classical, with four spacious arcaded galleries round the courts, yet some of the cells were dreary little chambers with no windows. Nor was this the only irresolute element in Jones' design. There were several carry-overs from the old regime, such as the debtors' begging grate, the taproom and the common hall. How these were understood to fit in with cellularization is anyone's guess, but the committee could not have envisaged a very severe system. (It is known that the cells were only for sleeping.) The same hesitancy is evident in the imprecise demarcation of the territories belonging to male and female felons. To get to the chapel, which was placed in the upper part of the Newgate Street arch, the women would have to pass right across the male precinct. Washing facilities and the taproom were also shared.[41]

A hierarchy of social divisions, based on wealth and status, had evolved in the old Newgate. The less complicated but more distinct divisions in the projects for rebuilding were made on moral grounds, not on grounds of purchasing power, and an attempt was made to restrict each group more or less within its own quarter (to this end there was a watch room between the male and female felons' courts). A step had been taken to assert moral authority through architecture; it was a faltering step, but the direction was unmistakable.

Returning to the issue of airiness and health, neither Jones nor Dance the elder could have had more than limited success with an impenetrable wall wrapped round the outside of their buildings. Jones, in particular,

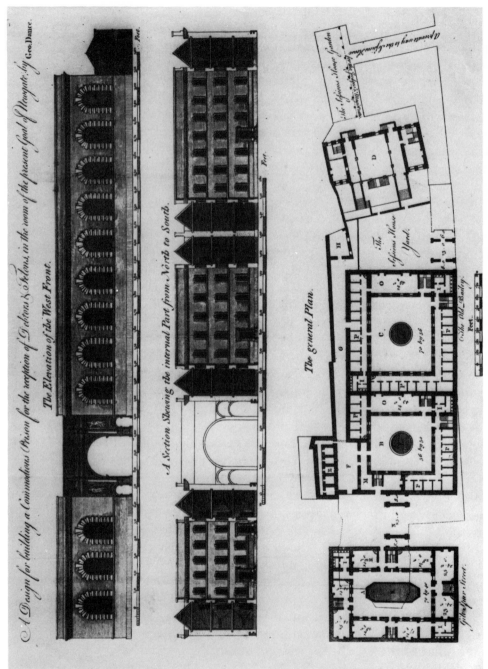

A Design for building a Commodious Prison for the reception of Debtors & Felons, in the room of the present Goal of Newgate, by Geo. Dance.

The Elevation of the West Front.

A Section Shewing the internal Part from North to South.

The general Plan.

106

44. Project for the rebuilding of Newgate, George Dance the elder, 1755.

did his best to make up for this deficiency. He furnished both the male and female felons' quadrangles with a corner tower containing an enormous number of privies (one for every two prisoners). Here great attention was paid to ventilation as a precaution against the spread of fever from the steams of human detritus (Fig. 46). At the core of the tower was an open shaft ventilating the half-rings of privies attached to it at each level. Under the privies the trays containing the detritus were further ventilated by two tubes bedded in the wall and rising to the

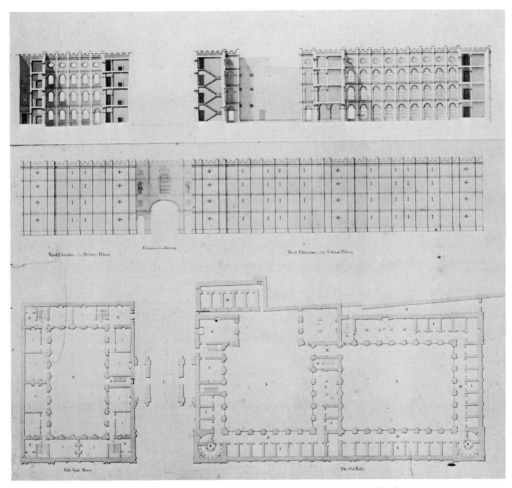

45. Project for the rebuilding of Newgate, William Jones, 1757.

roof, which Jones graphically termed 'nostrells'. Next to each closet was a basin supplied with running water pumped from the courtyard reservoirs.[42]

It was not until 1767, ten years after these plans were produced, that the Aldermen obtained Parliamentary consent to spend £50,000 on rebuilding from money raised on a coal tax of 6*d*. per cauldron.[43] Before consent had been obtained they had flirted briefly with the idea of moving Newgate from its historical location to some more open spot. Had they persisted, the new gaol might have been subjected to less criticism, as many of its much publicized defects were due to its being so constricted and hemmed in, but the committee gave up the idea early on. Dance the elder was appointed surveyor to the prison but soon resigned for reasons of health. In February 1768, George Dance the younger, who had been Assistant Surveyor, replaced his father and immediately proceeded to redesign the prison, not from arrogance, but because the Old Sessions House was now to be demolished leaving a plot of land on the south side that he considered large enough for the whole gaol. A completed design was ready in April, only two months after he had taken office.[44]

Dance the younger's Newgate is the only prison to have become a

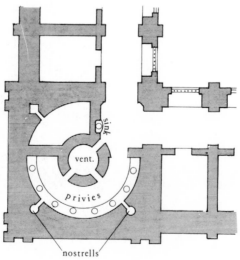

46. Project for the rebuilding of Newgate, William Jones, the privies.

constituent element of the general history of British architecture. It has achieved this position because of the massing and styling of its facade — an impressive essay in neo-classical composition regarded by Summerson as magnificent because of the Piranesian drama of its rustication, and the vivid play of receding and projecting elements.[45] And of course the exterior was magnificent, even sublime — about that all contemporary commentators were agreed (Fig. 47). After its completion they would also agree that it was a bad prison from any other point of view. In particular the interior was close, airless and insalubrious.

In his first sketches Dance the younger introduced circles of venti-lated privies almost identical to those in William Jones' plan, and retained the complete cellularization of the felons' wards.[46] The designs of April 1768 show a diminishing number of privies and a sub-stantially reduced number of cells. The final contract design of 1769 had just five cells for refractory male felons. The courtyards had shrunk from the capacious dimensions of earlier designs and the outer wall was still unventilated. The younger Dance consolidated the institution into an almost symmetrical plan with a perfectly symmetrical, articulated but unperforated facade, and made a more complete division between men and women, but the only hint that the prison resulted from a fever scare were the ten semi-circular ventilation wells behind the still numerous privy closets (Fig. 48).

As time passed Newgate was becoming a less and less adequate instrument or reform. Decisions made on the grounds of economy and security were pushing it back into an unregenerate form. Even so, by 1778 an extra £25,000 was needed to complete the building.[47] New-gate was a botched but instructive prelude to the reform movement. It was an object lesson. For the reformers it figured as an unhappy example of the folly of skimping, of concentrating on security at the expense of salubrity, and of concentrating on the exterior at the expense of the interior. Howard, who had offered the Aldermen the benefit of his wisdom only after the gaol was building, was not at all pleased with the end result, implying that by neglecting to take his advice they had erected an impregnable but unhealthy citadel which was sure to spawn new outbreaks of fever,[48] which it did, but not in the old epidemic way. During October 1793 malignant fever broke out in the State Prisoners' ward. Pitch barrels were burnt daily, vinegar sprinkled and the place kept very clean. In the same month Lord Gordon, whose mob

47. A French engraving of Dance the younger's Newgate in an imaginary landscape, 1790.

had razed the new prison building in 1780, died there, a lone casualty. Dr J.C. Lettsome, and the Newgate house surgeon, Mr Gillespey, determined the causes of the outbreak to be the special anxiety suffered by State prisoners that predisposed them to illness, the dirty bedding and, of course, the paucity of ventilation within the prison as a whole.[49]

There were other new prison buildings of the 1770s and 1780s that mixed the 'gothic' and 'rational' modes of correction, and which like Newgate sat uncomfortably on the line dividing the reformed and the unreformed. The architects would enforce partial cellular confinement, would separate the sexes and would tentatively set out to convert their prisons from engines of putrefaction to places of prophylaxis. Yet many old institutions such as the taproom, parlours and masters' rooms would still find a place in their plans.

These uncertain half-measures are found, for example, in the Essex County Gaol designs of William Hillyer. In 1767 a committes of Justices recommended that the gaol at Moulsham be rebuilt. There are plans for two alternative sites. The 1770 plan for the new site at White Horse Lane borrows a good deal from Dance the younger's Newgate. Exactly the same apsidal staircase and privy details were used and the gaol is similarly strung around a pair of introverted rectangular courts with no

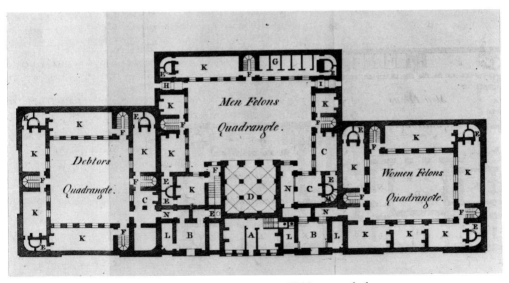

48. Newgate, George Dance the younger, 1769, ground plan.

outward facing ventilation.[50] (Needlessly so in this case, as there was another boundary wall beyond.)

After a great deal of argument it was decided to rebuild the Essex gaol on the old site. Hillyer's Moulsham design of 1773 (completed 1777)[51] was provided with a severely classical but not unequivocally prison-like frontage. Internally it was a lot less cramped than the White Horse Lane plan, being arranged round one large rectangular court (Figs. 18, 19). There were only eight night cells for felons, and a tap-room was provided (which the Justices later decided to remove on the grounds that it 'impeded the free circulation of air').[52] An attempt to provide enclosed foul drainage proved more a nuisance than a benefit. Rings of privies were connected to an ingenious disposal system of cast iron pipes which persisted in giving out a most offensive smell into the wards of the prison. It was thought that this stench might generate fever and there were problems with vermin too. At Bristol City Bride-well an enclosed drainage network had become infested with such bold rats that a cat had to be kept in each room to protect the sleeping prisoners from attack.[53] Still, it was from these fumbling efforts in the 1770s that there came a better understanding of the difficulties and expense of building prisons that would function in the interests of reform. It was becoming clear that it was going to be a costly exercise.

During this period of gestation architects, surveyors, magistrates and aldermen alike may have been perplexed and unsure of what to make of their new prisons, but there was no shortage of helpful hints from philanthropists and the medical profession on the crucial question of how to promote airiness. Jonas Hanway told them to simply put large windows in their gaols and to replace absorbent wood with impermeable stone flooring. If the cold floor were to cause chills then the prisoners should be issued with cork-soled slippers.[54] Denne approvingly recalled that Stephen Hales had tried to balance his extract systems at Newgate and the Savoy by knocking as many ventilator holes as he dared in the prison walls to get good air in.[55] Denne himself felt it would be wise to impose complete cellular isolation on prisoners and thus prevent cross infection. Capel Lofft advised that prisons be constructed of plain brick rather than stone or plaster, as brick was porous enough to allow any confined air to percolate out.[56] Dr John Jebb designed a dry moat boundary which was as secure as a wall 30 foot high, but which left the interior of the prison open to the effects of the gentlest breeze.[57]

William Smith thought the answer might be to employ prison 'scaven-
gers' whose job would be to clean, sweep, wash and empty slops.
Prisoners should be frequently bathed, walls regularly limed, and doors
should always include a large area of open grating to ensure a continuous
flow of air into every room.[58] Bentham preferred the opinions of Dr
Maret who had been experimenting with ventilation in a Lyons hospital. Dr Maret considered it essential to change the air in a room once
every day. By hanging fresh meat at various elevations in the hospital
wards and waiting for it to putrefy, he had discovered that, contrary to
conventional beliefs, foul air did not rise but fell to the floor. Extracts
should therefore be placed at low level. All recesses and corners were to
be avoided as corrupt air would harbour in any crevice, however small.
He favoured oval hospital wards with smooth half-round mouldings
between ceilings, walls and floors.[59] John Coakley Lettsome thought
that wool and linen protected little pockets of vitiated air in the mat of
their fibres. So he proposed that a uniform be exchanged for each
prisoner's clothes on entry, that bedding be frequently changed, and
also designed a folding iron bed-frame which allowed air to circulate
around the mattress while in use.[60]

But it was John Howard more than any of these gentlemen who was
to be the architects' mentor, and he had much to say on the subject of
salubrity. First there was the question of where to put your prison. It
should not be cramped amongst other buildings, but should be in open
country — perhaps on the rise of a hill to get the full force of the wind,
and it should be close to a running stream.[61] All this might seem very
bucolic but there was more to this decision than the quest for pure air
and fresh water. Having been relegated to the edge of the town in earlier
times, the prison was now to be thrust out of it altogether. This was no
mere gesture either. A more isolated location would have been unthink-
able before the reforms; alms-collecting, the sale of work, and the
supply of day to day needs, to say nothing of the interminable comings
and goings of friends and relatives, were all reliant on the prison being
part of the city or town.[62] To take the prison out of this context was
to acknowledge that it would no longer relate to the external world in
so familiar a way. It was being abstracted from everyday life and made
very special. Of course, the explicit reasons for this retreat were entirely
prophylactic. Had not Robert Palmer's Hertford Gaol, built on an
exposed site some way beyond the town between 1774 and 1776,

quelled the fever where it had once been endemic, even though the new prison was on a bad plan?[63]

Then there was the prison building itself: Howard's model plan for a county gaol (Fig. 49) was an assortment of half a dozen irregularly spaced pavilions each for a different class of prisoner and each raised wholly off the ground on arcades 'that it may be more airy, and leave

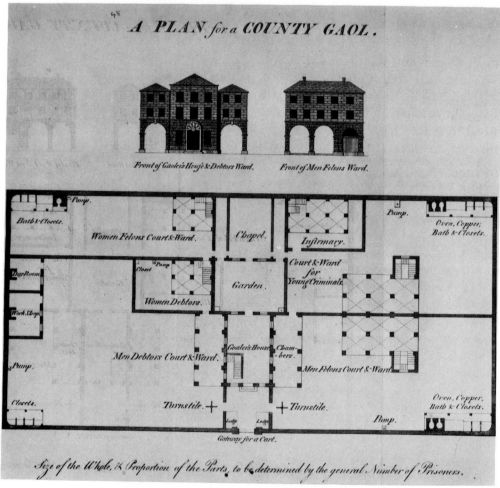

49. Design for a county gaol published by Howard in *The State of the Prisons*, 1777.

under it a dry walk in wet weather'.[64] Only the staircases, the chapel and the keeper's house reached the ground. There were pumps, baths, closets and ovens distributed around the perimeter of the gaol as further aids to hygiene. These would find their way into new prisons, but it was the arcades that were to become the liet-motif of the first generation of reformed gaols and bridewells. Howard's prison is suspended in the air because if it were to touch the ground it might corrupt itself with dampness and stagnant, vitiated vapour. The purity of the reformed gaol seemed to be threatened by every form of contact.

Two kinds of contagion

It had been noticed that there was a quite close similarity between the way that fever spread itself and the way that vice spread itself. When Henry Fielding maintained that 'Bad habits are as infectious by example, as the plague itself by contact',[65] he was reminding his readers of an old maxim and repeating a literary commonplace. But it was already becoming increasingly difficult to distinguish the irony of the comparison from the mechanics of an established relationship between moral psychology and medical pathology. The analogy could be drawn more closely. It was a matter of great contemporary significance that, in Howard's words, 'The general prevalence and spread of wickedness in prison, and abroad by the discharged prisoners, will now be as easily accounted for, as the propagation of disease.'[66] Both physical and moral contagion were spread through invisible substances that passed from body to body in some subtle effervescence, too rarified for the human intelligence to fix upon in transit and yet so profoundly ugly in their effects that no one could doubt the fact of transmission. Vice after all was never reasonable — it had to be some kind of mental mal-function.[67] It was surely a brand of madness in which the human passions were commandeered against the individual and society. 'Vice and folly' together were always working to 'carry on a war against the interest of mankind'.[68] This was why Lord Loughborough considered it so much better for prisoners to be controlled by pre-ordained discipline than to let them pursue their own fancies. For him the worst oppression of unreformed gaols was the 'oppression of virtue', dooming prisoners to suffer under the free play of their own passions.[69] It was therefore as much an act of philanthropy to try and cure prisoners of their vice as it was to try and cure them of fever — even if the cure was unpleasant.

The symptom of this malady as it was perceived in the eighteenth century had nothing directly to do with criminal culpability. Vice was most commonly revealed in a proclivity for sensual pleasures which if let to develop would quickly spiral into the sump of depravity. Hogarth depicted the complete course of this disease from beginning to end in *Marriage à la Mode*, *The Idle Apprentice*, *The Harlot's Progress* and *The Rake's Progress*. More than anything else he fascinated his contemporaries with detailed pictures of its revolting terminal manifestations, as in the hideous *Gin Lane* and *The Times of the Day — Night*. Perhaps these horrid vignettes of low life were no more than phantoms of the educated imagination, yet they always seemed easy enough to corroborate by reference to particular crimes. The people had absorbed the venom of immorality; they were at once its victims and its manifestation. Vice may appear of 'frightful mien' to the virtuous, but to those more familiar with her face she had become the object of tender affection.[70] Familiarity bred attachment. Vice, like the most tenacious gaol distempers, was now entrenched. More disquieting still, it seemed to be inextricably bonded into the fabric of everyday life.

All this was compounded in the old prisons, where justice was 'converted to the most deadly *evil*, and instead of curing, adds virulence to the disease'.[71] How then was the prison to be converted to its proper therapeutic aim — how could it mend morals? The lesson was all too plain. If the prison building could be used to prevent the propagation of fever, it could be used in some similar way to prevent the even more insidious propagation of vice.

The theory of aerial infection was erroneous. There can be no doubt, though, that the improvements and rebuildings of the 1780s and 1790s, together with the emphasis on bathing, washing and fumigation, were extirpating the fever from prisons. By 1789 the Proclamation Society could claim that 'gaol fever . . . is now almost eradicated',[72] and when fever appeared in the new and reformed Chester County Gaol in 1800/1, Dr Peploe Ward, investigating the occurrence, considered it no mean achievement on the part of the gaoler to run such a filthy and pestilential gaol within such a well-ventilated structure.[73] The new building was not only absolved, it was also used as evidence against the gaoler, who was immediately dismissed. The reformers had won an unequivocal victory against fever in the prisons. It is no exaggeration to say that they expected a success just as spectacular in the battle being waged against vice in the same place. As the two were so alike this did not seem too sanguine a hope.

4 Penitentiaries and reformed prisons

During the 1780s William Blackburn emerged as an authoritative figure, dominating prison architecture till long after his premature death in 1790. Next to nothing is known of him, except that he was born in 1750, that his father was a Southwark tradesman, his mother a Spaniard, that he was portly, a presbyterian, and that despite common schooling he gained admittance to the Royal Academy, where, in 1773, he received a minor prize for architectural drawing. It was this obscure figure who first turned prison design into a kind of technology, translating the doctrine of reform into the practicalities of construction. This chapter, which deals with the rebuilding of the prisons during the last quarter of the eighteenth century, is essentially an account of his work. There are, though, issues more significant than the demonstration of his personal preeminence. What all of Blackburn's prison designs and those of his contemporaries show is a critical change in architecture as it was applied to a new class of buildings. This is not just to say that formal academic principles were often laid aside in the interests of function, a point so conspicuous it hardly needs to be said. While it is clear that the majority of new prisons had little to do with the conventions of architecture as an art, it must be emphasized that they had a great deal to do with its procedures and practices: consistent, scaled plans, working drawings, thorough annotation of uses — in the eighteenth century these were the practicalities of architecture, not the practicalities of building — together with an over-riding concern with the distribution of parts relative to one another, with completeness, and with the employment of geometry as the generator of the plan, if not as the generator of visible form. This then was not the demise of academic architecture but its selective extension into foreign territory.

118

The Penitentiary Act

To judge from the statistics produced by Janssen and Howard, for every execution in the years between 1750 and 1770 there were about ten sentences to transportation.[1] The American War of Independence brought penal transportation to a virtual halt, so a revision of the system of secondary penalties could hardly be avoided now this convenient and relatively merciful method of despatch was blocked. Three alternatives were introduced. In 1776 an Act was passed[2] permitting those sentenced to transportation to be employed on local river works. Two old sailing vessels, the *Justicia* and the *Censor*, were set up as dormitory hulks for convicts who laboured during the day on raising silt and gravel from navigable estuaries. Other possibilities were opened up by the 1784 Transportation Act,[3] which allowed convicts to be sent anywhere in the world. A few hundred unfortunates were delivered to Gambia, on the West African coast, where they mostly perished, and in May 1787 the first of them set sail for Botany Bay in New South Wales. There was also the penitentiary. The word was a new one in the penal lexicon. It had been coined by the authors of a piece of legislation which had taken five years to reach the statute book. Sir William Blackstone, first Professor of English Law at Oxford, and Sir William Eden, an ambitious young lawyer, started work on it in 1774, encouraged by the emergence of John Howard, whose recent evidence to the House of Commons had been received as the speech of a national hero.[4]

The Penitentiary Act or Hard Labour Bill of 1779[5] was an amphibious law, combining elements of correction and reformation. As the Penitentiary Act it was the harbinger of penal reform. The obsolete term penitentiary referred to a monastic cell, set aside for sinful monks — a place of penitence and remorse. As the Hard Labour Bill it had a great deal of the corrective morality of work written into it. All offenders, it decreed, 'are to be kept to labour of the hardest and most servile kind'. A long, but familiar list of occupations followed: hemp beating, log rasping, stone sawing, capstan turning, rag chopping, and so on.[6] Blackstone and Eden were inspired by Howard's descriptions of the Dutch houses of correction, but their bill was not just a slavish imitation of Tuchthuis regulations sanctified with a pious title. As at the Rome house of correction, techniques for inducing remorse took their place within the reassuring format of corrective discipline. It would be foolish to pretend that this one Act transformed the value of prison labour. It did nothing of the sort. Labour remained much the same as in the early bridewells, only it was no longer paramount. The hard labour of the Blackstone and Eden Act was one tactic in a larger strategy of penal reformation.[7] Again Howard's views serve to pinpoint the change in attitude. He denounced the profit motive not just in the old gaols but in the new as well, 'for surely, it is impossible to place any degree of *profit* in competition with the prospect of meliorating the minds of our fellow creatures'.[8] Other reformers felt the same way. Work was still glorified as an essential ingredient in prison discipline, but the motives for doing it had been redefined.

The 1779 Act made it possible to substitute penitentiary imprisonment for transportation. Minimum sentences of six months for women and one year for men were set. The maximum was seven years. Only the most 'atrocious and daring' criminals were henceforth to be committed to the hulks, where the notoriously high mortality rate had already become a source of severe embarrassment to the government; in the first 20 months of operation 150 out of 600 convicts sent there died.[9]

A commission of three supervisors was to be appointed for the purpose of erecting two buildings, 'substantial edifices to be called penitentiary houses', one for 600 male convicts and one for 300 females, financed and run by Parliament. Here began the centralization of the penal system. In contrast, an earlier draft of the Act, published in 1776, had proposed that penitentiaries should be built at the expense of and under the control of local authorities, as were gaols and houses of correction. Furthermore, the magistrates were urged to provide similar establishments for 'femmes couvertes', infants and lunatics.[10] This early draft set out to revolutionize secondary punishment in a single move. It was confidently predicted that with a penitentiary in every jurisdiction, capital statutes could be reduced, while penitentiary sentences could be graduated to fit every degree of felony. Atrocious crimes would diminish and all would be well.[11] The Bill is said to have failed because the punishment it outlined was incompatible with the British ideas of liberty.[12] Yet opposition to the revised Act of 1779 was much less vigorous, quite possibly because the burden of support had by then been removed from the local authorities to the Treasury, although the form of discipline remained the same. So the revised Act was a more modest proposal even though its finance and administration were unprecedented; the two National Penitentiaries were little more than a cautious experiment in comparison with the grand design of 1776. The number of penitentiary sentences that could be imposed at each assize were to be strictly limited, and the quotas would be nowhere near adequate to substitute for transportation.[13]

Thus 'mangled and distorted from its first comely form',[14] the Act was made law. Blackstone persuaded Howard to become one of the supervisors. A committee was then formed with the non-conformist Dr John Fothergill who was a personal friend of Howard, and George Whately, Treasurer to the Foundling Hospital. These three were duly appointed as the Penitentiary Commission. They never progressed beyond an acrimonious debate over choice of sites, which now, of course, was a matter of crucial significance. On the one hand Howard and Fothergill, with the support of Blackstone, were determined to recommend a site at Islington. On the other, Whately, with the support of the Lord Chancellor, favoured a site at Limehouse, considered too damp by Howard. Neither side would capitulate, and when Fothergill died in 1780 Howard took the opportunity to resign. The committee was dissolved. It was hardly an auspicious beginning.[15]

On 2 March 1781 a second, more businesslike trio of supervisors replaced the first. Four months later Sir Charles Bunbury, Thomas Bowdler and Sir Gilbert Elliott had chosen an 82 acre site at Wandsworth Fields for the Male Penitentiary and a smaller one on Battersea Rise for the females. Negotiations for purchase were undertaken, and an architectural competition was advertised. Sixty-three entries were considered and on 23 March 1782 the results were published. The first prize of £100 for the best Male Penitentiary was awarded to an unknown architect from Southwark, William Blackburn, and £60 went to Thomas Hardwick for the best Female Penitentiary.[16]

Little can be traced of the 63 designs entered for the competition. Plans by Soane and Thomas Baldwin survive, the general form of Blackburn's entry is known, but, apart from two other drawings of uncertain designation, perhaps penitentiaries, that is all.

John Soane, who had high hopes of getting a prize, produced two very fine essays in composition, effortlessly combining the detailed demands of the brief into coherent and symmetrical geometries (Figs. 50, 51, 52).[17] The crystalline triangular configurations of his plans

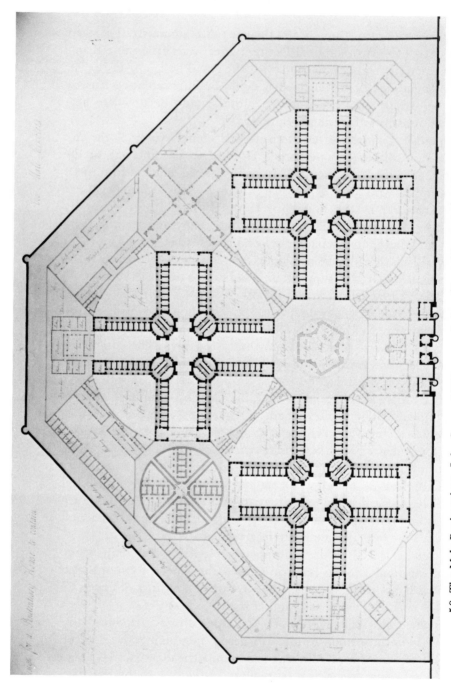

50. The Male Penitentiary, John Soane, 1782, ground plan. Three identical cruciform elements, one for each class of convicts, were grouped round a chapel. In the intervening spaces were workrooms, the governor's house (behind the entrance), infirmaries (right), and balancing the latter, a quatrefoil of 'dark and airy dungeons' for refractory prisoners (left).

51. The Male Penitentiary, John Soane, aerial view in a fanciful setting.

123

52. The Female Penitentiary, John Soane, 1782, ground plan.

followed from the tripartite classification of prisoners proposed in the Act. Between commital and release every convict had to progress through three classes, each with a distinct regime. To the first belonged a period of cellular confinement with the most irksome labour performed in solitude. The second allowed better conditions and work in small groups, while the third permitted communal work of a less arduous type.[18] In this way the fact of reformation was to be tested and rewarded simultaneously. Convicts would have to resist the temptation of company and intercourse as they rose towards liberty — with the threat of demotion if they did not. Each class required its own domain with distinct facilities. In both his plans Soane grouped the three sections of cellular accommodation around a chapel, which, though a small element in the composition, was the focal point of the entire complex. Beyond the circle of cells and airing yards (also required by the Act) were the work rooms, where, in the Male Penitentiaries, the sequence of classes was most clearly visible, from the small solitary compartments for the first class to the large workshops for the third class.

Soane's designs moulded the specific and relatively complex spatial requirements of the 1779 Act to his own stylistic ends, a capability recognizable as the hallmark of the professional. They were airy, with arcades and well-spaced buildings. They were cellularized and secure. They embodied the provisions of the Act but did not develop the architecture of imprisonment beyond it, although they compare well with Baldwin's entry which hardly reflected the demands of the Act at all, being layed out like a sequence of miniature town squares (Fig. 53).[19] The plan for a penitentiary house or house of correction that found its way into Howard's *Account of the Principal Lazarettos* (1st edition 1789) was probably conceived as a proposal for the Male Penitentiary. Like Baldwin's it was a multiple courtyard scheme (Fig. 54). It contained cells for the requisite 600 inmates and as no local authority would have seriously contemplated building such a gigantic institution in the 1780s or 1790s, it is reasonable to suppose that it originated as a national project. A section of yet another large unidentified courtyard prison by William Newton among the R.I.B.A. drawings may also have been a penitentiary exhibit (Fig. 55).[20]

None of these proposals, characterized by their vast symmetry and orderliness, did more than cope, skilfully or hamfistedly, with the specifications of the Penitentiary Act. Blackburn's Male Penitentiary design seems to have gone further, opening a new avenue of development. Information on his plan is scanty. A later design for the Borough Gaol at Liverpool, built between 1785 and 1789, was said to resemble it,[21] and a survey published in 1849 (Fig. 56)[22] shows details of the internal arrangements at Liverpool, still easily identifiable as part of the original building programme and almost indistinguishable from a design by James Wardrop made in 1791 for Calton Gaol, Edinburgh (Fig. 57).[23] But only so much can be read into this. Liverpool gaol was for 270 prisoners, enormous by eighteenth-century standards (a local wit speculated that it would contain half the population of the city).[24] It was, all the same, less than half the capacity of the Male Penitentiary.

Without more details of the Penitentiary, the full significance of its layout cannot be ascertained. There is no doubt, however, that the Liverpool design was deliberately contrived so that all the exterior parts

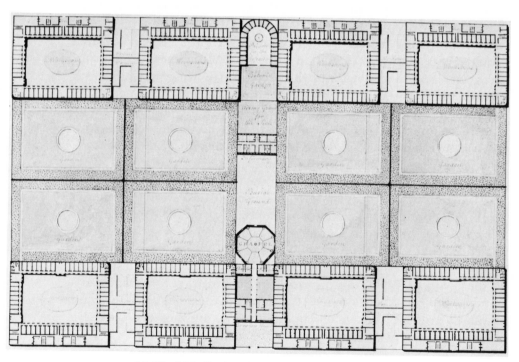

53. The Male Penitentiary, Richard Baldwin, 1782, ground plan.

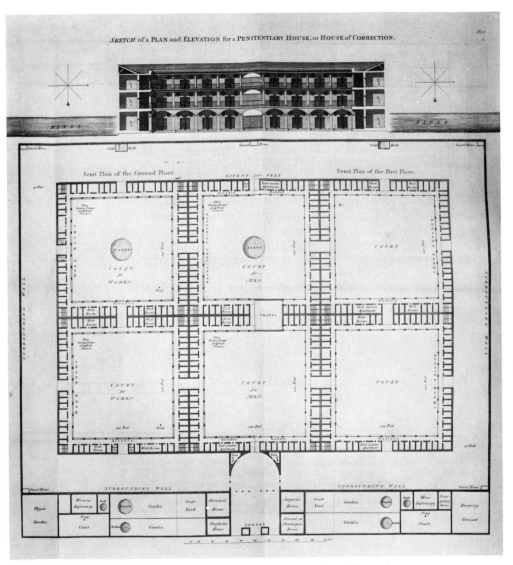

54. Penitentiary House or House of Correction, from Howard,
Lazarettos, 1789.

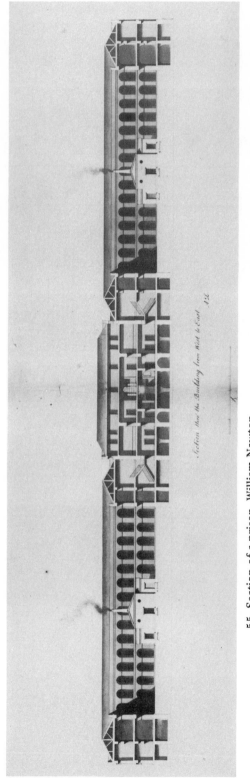

Section thro' the Building from West to East. 454

55. Section of a prison, William Newton.

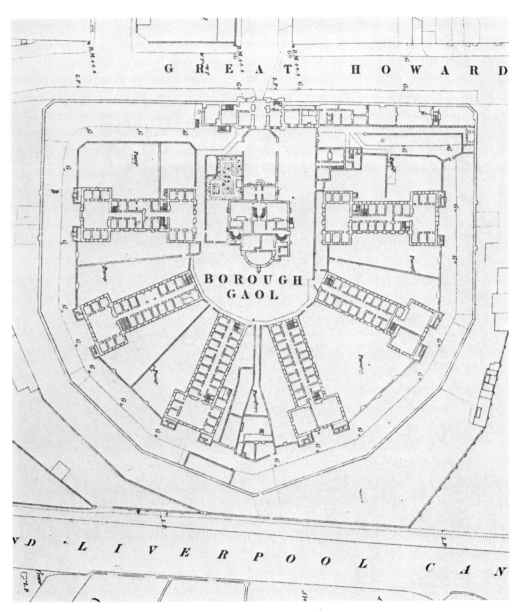

56. Liverpool Borough Gaol, William Blackburn, 1785–9, from the
Ordnance Survey of 1849.

of the prison were visible from the gaoler's and turnkey's apartments in the central hub.[25] The prison building was fragmented into six unconnected blocks exposed to the air. These blocks were held in place by imaginary radii emanating from the gaoler's parlour, bringing the entire range of buildings under his eye. Wicket fences took the place of walls along the inner and outer boundaries of the airing yards so as not to inhibit the vista stretching right out to the edge of the prison. Radial and circular plan geometries were the neo-classical stock-in-trade, but it

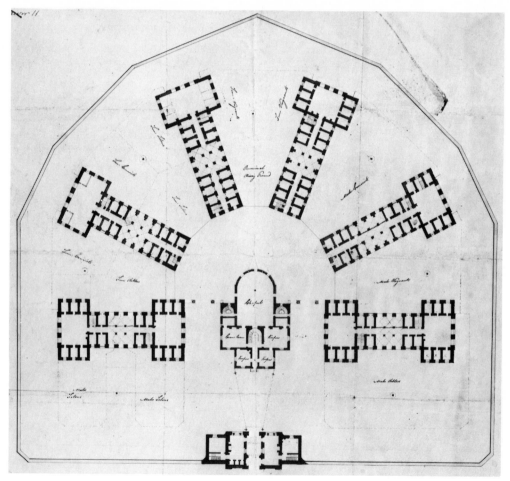

57. Project for Calton Gaol, James Wardrop, 1791, ground plan.

is rare indeed to find isolated radii left stranded in space. It was this, with the new functions accompanying it, that distinguished Blackburn's plans from the superficially similar Maison de Force (Fig. 27).

The same ruthless radial geometry was later to be employed in order to exploit the 'surveillance' or 'inspection' principle that loomed so large in prison design. Blackburn's two plans did give the first hint of the value of this arrangement, but he got no great credit for it afterwards. In 1826 that bastion of surveillance, the Society for the Improvement of Prison Discipline, looked back on Liverpool as a naive bungling, so badly handled that it led other architects to abandon the radial plan altogether, until it was rediscovered in the early years of the nineteenth century.[26]

After some modifications suggested by the Commissioners, the two winning designs were approved by the Lord Chancellor and went out to contract in August. Things seemed to be going splendidly when, in September, a vague statement from the Treasury made it known that 'new measures were about to be taken with felons which made the hastening of the penitentiary houses less necessary', and money to purchase the sites was withheld on a slender legalistic pretext.[27] Depressed but undaunted the Commissioners arranged for drastic economies to be made, thinking they would convince the government of the scheme's viability, but at the same time lamenting the effects of the cuts. Blackburn turned his estimate of £149,982 into a mere £30,165, and a similar miracle of parsimony was performed by Hardwick.[28] But all this conjuring was in vain. When Pitt's administration took office in 1784 the Transportation Act was hustled through Parliament and the penitentiaries were shelved.[29]

Reformed prisons

It was the local magistrates and not the central government who actually initiated reform by building new prisons. During the 1780s the country's prison population was rapidly inflating as more offenders had to be sentenced to a spell in gaol or bridewell in lieu of transportation. Howard witnessed an increase of 84% between 1776 and 1787/8 (Fig. 217). According to Bentham, the prison reformers in Parliament had seen the American War not as a disaster but as an opportunity. In the

Grand Juries it was the same. Every time a prison was presented at quarter sessions as insufficient (a necessary preliminary to rebuilding) the reasons were bound to include overcrowding. The fundamental issue was still the reform of the prison system, but it was the immediate necessity for expansion that prompted new building. Even so, old prisons were rarely suffered to remain in existence after new ones were completed, however pressing the need for space.

The escalating urgency of reform and its effect on prison construction can best be illustrated by the changing policies of the Dorset Grand Jury. In 1783 they decided that the old gaol, built in 1633, should go. Plans submitted by an architect, William Tyler, were approved (Fig. 58), and his gaol was soon built on the same site, using the material from the demolished structure.[30] About £4,000 was spent. Then, in 1787, Howard came. He thought the new prison most unsatisfactory in conception and too small in size. He indicated that a more ambitious proposal designed by one of the magistrates would have been far more appropriate. The magistrate in question was William Morton Pitt, who, encouraged by this unexpected source of support, reopened the issue of rebuilding at the next quarter sessions. In April the magistrates approached William Blackburn, now a celebrity, asking him to comment on Tyler's prison. He sadly informed them that it was utterly bad, as it did not allow 'solitude and separation from whence the hope of reformation springs'.[31] The cells were unventilated and damp and the yards were too small. This indictment was considered at the November sessions, where it was agreed that Blackburn himself should be invited to prepare a better set of plans. Blackburn's proposals were adopted in July 1788. The second rebuilding, only five years after the first, on a new and exposed site north of the town of Dorchester, cost over £16,000 (Figs. 59, 60). The Tyler gaol within the town was closed.[32]

Usually there was but one rebuilding. The first prison to be erected as a direct result of Howard's probing enquiries was the gaol at Horsham. The 3rd Duke of Richmond, as Lord Lieutenant of the County, seems to have taken the Grand Jury by storm. He had his own architect, William Ride, draw up plans for a larger, healthier gaol on the lines suggested by the great philanthropist, with 40 cells in two storeys raised on arcades, a separate infirmary, a commodious gaoler's house and a chapel, which the quarter sessions meekly accepted when it was placed before them on 2 October 1775[33] (although the prospect of a second

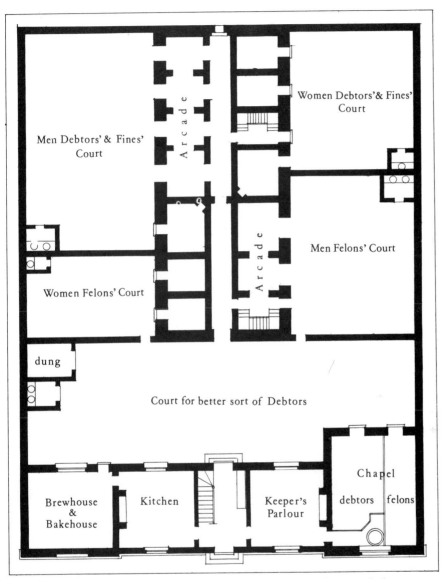

Women Debtors'& Fines' Court

Men Debtors' & Fines' Court

Arcade

Men Felons' Court

Women Felons' Court

Arcade

dung

Court for better sort of Debtors

Chapel

debtors   felons

Brewhouse & Bakehouse

Kitchen

Keeper's Parlour

58. Dorchester County Gaol, William Tyler, 1783, ground plan.

expensive reformed prison at Petworth produced a petition of protest from local ratepayers in 1786.[34]

In Cornwall, two years later, another magistrate, the gentleman farmer John Call, instigated moves to build a combined county gaol and house of correction at Bodmin, designed the new prison himself, and supervised its erection (Fig. 61).[35] Horsham and Bodmin were both completed in 1779. Between this date and 1785 there was a pause

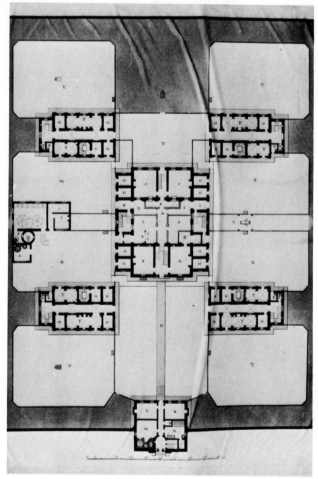

59. Dorchester County Gaol, William Blackburn, 1785–9, ground plan.

while the magistracy waited for the National Penitentiaries. The revival
of local activity was due to the government's failure to deliver these, to
the enormous upsurge in prison population and to an Act sponsored by
the Tory Member Cecil Wray, which reintroduced the somewhat diluted
substance of the original Penitentiary Act.[36] Wray's *Acts to Explain
and Amend the Laws Relating to Gaols and Houses of Correction* (1784)
were largely permissive. They did not force the Grand Juries to build,
but obliged them, when they did build, to provide prisons that were
divided into 'distinct apartments' for up to ten types of prisoner from
convicted male felons to female debtors, to provide chapels and much
else. They legalized the mortgaging of rates as well, which at last made
it possible to raise large sums of money on credit, in order to finance
costly projects.[37]

Consequently, in 1785, local prison building began in earnest. The
Norfolk magistrate Sir Thomas Beevor built his industrious little bride-
well at Wymondham. The architect James Wyatt started the House of
Correction at Petworth (Fig. 62) for West Sussex. William Blackburn

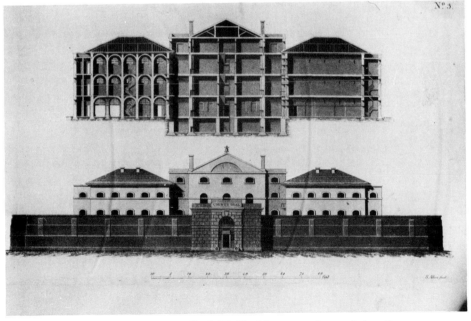

60. Dorchester County Gaol, W. Blackburn, section and elevation.

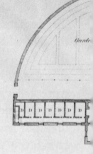

To John Howard *Esq.* This *PLAN. ELEVATIONS*

BODMIN *in the County of* C

Plan of Second Floor

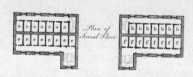

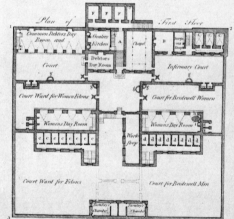

Plan of   *First Floor*

Common Debtors Day Room, and

Gaolers Kitchen

Chapel

Court

Debtors Day Room

Infirmary Court

Court Ward for Women Felons

Court for Bridewell Women

Womens Day Room

Womens Day Room

Work shop

Court Ward for Felons

Court for Bridewell Men

Turnkeys Chamber

Turnkeys Chamber

References

A *Head Gaolers House*
BBBB *Separate Rooms for Infirmary*
CCC *Condemn'd Cells*
DDD *Common Debtors night Rooms for two each*
EEE *Chambers in Gaolers House for Master Debtors*
FFF *Vaults for Coals*
aaa *Night Cells for Women Felons*
bbb *Night Cells for Bridewell Women*
ccc *Night Cells for Men Felons one in each on the first Floor over the Arches*
ddd *Night Cells for Bridewell Men one in each on the first Floor over the Arches*

This Gaol is built on the side of a steep Hill facing the South on a spot rather too confined in Extent but as no more con...
contrived that the Steepness of the Ground which at first appeared a great obstacle seems to be of advantage in many...
purest fresh Water is brought in above the Gaolers House, and divided through every Ward to supply the Baths and other use...
any communication of Speech or otherwise, between the different kinds of Criminals, and to keep each Six distinct by th...
so that no escape can be concerted or effected by mining. One Hundred Men and Women may be lodged in the seve...

Scale of

Designd by & Executed under the Directio...

London, Printed for I. &...

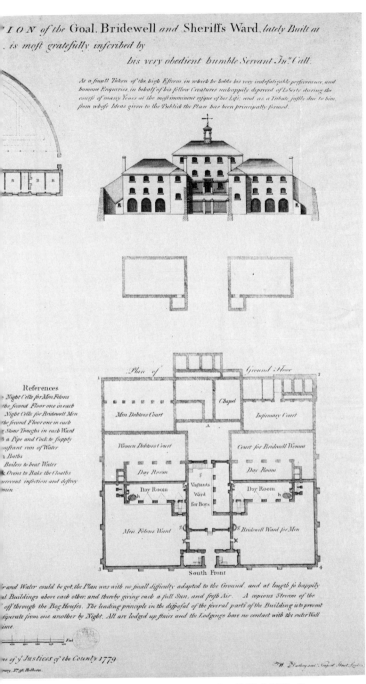

61. Bodmin Prison, John Call, 1777—9.

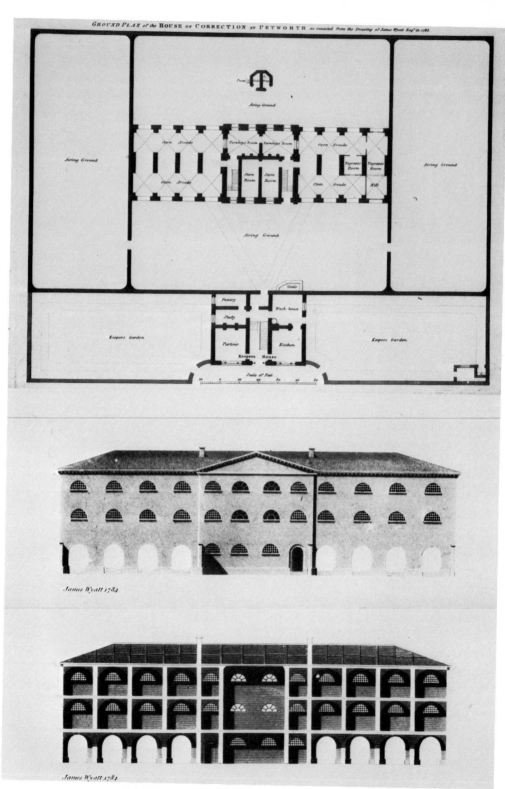

62. Petworth House of Correction, James Wyatt, 1785.

started the Borough Gaol at Liverpool and produced designs for the county gaol and four bridewells for Gloucestershire. The next three years saw the inception of another 12 major prison projects. Everywhere John Howard's dispensations were being used to justify great changes in the penal system. Bodmin, Oxford, Winchester, Lancaster, Salford, Dorchester, Chester and Middlesex — it was always Howard's name linked with the genesis of the scheme. At Shrewsbury County Gaol the central niche above the entrance contained, not the traditional effigy of blind justice, but a bust of the great patron of reform (Fig. 63). At Liverpool the road to the gaol was named after him, at Lancaster the prison workshop.[38]

There were also places where the reformist effort did not succeed. Bedfordshire, curiously enough, as it was the county in which the muck had first been stirred, performed its own parochial version of the penitentiary fiasco by rejecting an open site offered to them by Howard in 1786 for which Blackburn had prepared plans, choosing instead a site in the High Street that the owner refused to sell. Here they let the matter rest — some gratefully, no doubt.[39] Still, most of the time the evident crisis of numbers, coupled with the enthusiasm of individual magistrates, was enough to carry the reforms.

Having got so far the magistrates would normally seek precedents and advice. The plans and the rules of Horsham, Bodmin, Petworth and Wymondham were all being circulated as desirable models, but the bold experiment in prison building conducted by the County of Gloucester was by far the most highly praised and the most widely known. So much so that 30 years later, in 1815, an enquiry into the organization of gaols would still commence with a pilgrimage to the Gloucester County Gaol.[40] Even King George III deigned to take a look, an unusual thing this, although he seemed unable to make much of it, rousing himself only to say that the edifice showed 'judgement' and 'masterly workmanship'.[41]

The exemplary County of Gloucestershire built not one, but five prisons all at once. The magistrates were led to embark on this thoroughgoing programme of reorganization by one man — George Onesiphorus Paul. Paul, son of a wealthy cloth manufacturer, had never met Howard, though familiar with his work, when, at the Lent assize of 1783, he first suggested that 'nothing less than a general and entire correction of the principle of prisons' was called for.[42] At the August

63. Shrewsbury County Gaol, William Blackburn and John Haycock, 1786–93, entry lodge.

assize Paul delivered the first of two lengthy, tendentious addresses to the assembled magistrates at the end of which they resolved to build new bridewells. Two months later he was back again, insisting that this would not be enough: it was no use just reforming a part of the system. The County ought rather to build 'on a plan that may effect a total change of that system which has hitherto been suffered to exist — new prisons — new regulations — and new attentions to their operation — nothing less can establish a police — prevent pestilence — and produce an amendment in morals'.[43] He went on to measure the recently remodelled Castle Gaol's power to corrupt morals by the number of women who had been made pregnant during imprisonment. It turned out that five or six had lately been so.[44] Again, swayed by his aggressive espousal of reformist ideas, they let Paul have his way and resolved to rebuild the Castle Gaol from scratch. By the end of the year Blackburn had been brought in as 'the most proper person to be appointed surveyor'. He was directed to prepare plans for a county gaol to house 185 prisoners in eight classes plus five bridewells in various parts of the county, one of which was incorporated into the county gaol at Gloucester.[45]

The county gaol was designated a penitentiary house, as it was to accommodate convicted felons who would otherwise have been transported. Paul had made use of a permissive clause in the 1779 Act as he made use of a local fever outbreak and the licentious goings on in the Castle — as a bludgeon to convince others of the validity of his scheme. Penitentiary and all, the Gloucester reform was far more than a substitute for transportation; it was an attempt to mobilize the County effort against all forms of vice and disorder. The effort was to be financed as if it were a business venture, with annuities sold at commercial rates of interest. For unlike the reforming magistrates of Dorset and Cornwall, Paul saw no place in his machinery of law and justice for magnanimous gestures of charity. The prisons were for the advantage of a particular group, property.owners. The burden of their creation and maintenance should therefore rest equally on all within that group.[46] As the new prisons opened the Castle Gaol and the Old Bridewell at Lawford's Gate closed. By 1792 the barrage of new institutions was complete. Already there were stories going about that in the less populous district of West Sussex, the Duke of Richmond's two reformed prisons were having a most extraordinary effect. Criminals and idlers were taking flight from the county in droves to avoid the terrible fate of being reformed, and in future would regard the place 'as Europeans would the Gold Coast or a Hindoo the Arctic regions'.[47] When, in 1791, Petworth was found to be three-quarters empty, it was taken as conclusive proof of the Exodus. The same phenomenon was observed in Gloucestershire. The ultimate demonstration of the effectiveness of reform became an empty new prison, and during the 1790s the Gloucester bridewells were rarely more than half full.[48]

Reforming magistrates did not confine themselves to making general resolutions. Where records exist of committee proceedings they show, as often as not, that much time was spent discussing both the architectural form and the internal organization of prison buildings.[49] The combination of all their requirements into a concrete proposal was now the job of an architect or surveyor. These words were still sometimes used loosely to describe any builder with pretensions, but all the same there was a considerable difference between the local artisans employed in earlier days, whose plans were perfunctory sketches at best, and the prison builders of the 1780s and 1790s, many of whom had received academic training. It was these architects, and in particular William Blackburn, who, collaborating with the magistrates, began to develop prison design into a kind of moral geography.

Security, salubrity and reformation

These were the three cardinal requirements of a reformed prison. The formula, derived from Howard, had obtained the status of a cliché by the 1780s.[50] In Blackburn's buildings each element of the formula acquired its own techniques of construction and its own characteristic planning. The rest of this chapter takes the form of an enquiry into them. Once having examined the means employed by prison architects to these ends, it should be possible to define the connection between the doctrines of reform and eighteenth-century prison design more exactly.

Security

Put simply, security required enclosure; salubrity required exposure and

fragmentation; reformation required compartmentalization. In a reformed prison all these needs had to be reconciled.

Although compartmentalization and enclosure were easily compatible, difficulties arose, as they had at Newgate,[51] when the inimical
logic of exposure was superimposed upon the other two. The arcane
tradition of incarceration would therefore give way to a more sophisticated type of confinement. Boundary walls moved outwards on
enlarged sites and were fixed at between 15 and 20 feet high. They
were isolated from the rest of the prison by an encircling patrol path,
from which the turnkey could inspect the prison airing yards through
paling fences.[52] If on a restricted plot, the perimeter wall might be
punctured with ventilation grilles as at Kirton Bridewell,[53] although
this was not regarded as good practice because it encouraged the surreptitious passing of messages and articles in and out. However, George
Dance the younger, whose unenviable task it was to fit several London
prisons into very small sites after completing Newgate, devised a ventilation slot for prison walls directly adjacent to the street which rendered
this more difficult (Fig. 64).[54] Perimeter walls were always battered
and buttressed on the exterior side so that no foothold would present

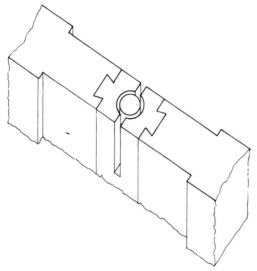

64. Ventilation slot, Southwark Compter, George Dance the younger,
1785.

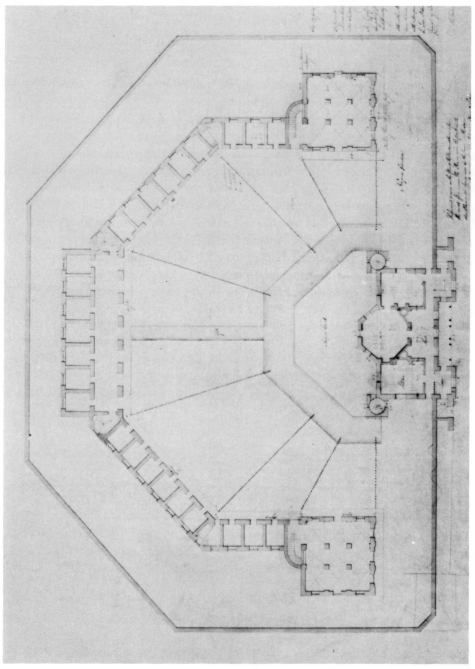

65. Northleach Bridewell, William Blackburn, 1785, ground plan. The octagonal room was the keeper's parlour.

66. Northleach Bridewell, W. Blackburn, entrance facade.

itself on the inner surface. Other methods of scaling the wall were countered by leaving the top few courses of brickwork in loose mortar, so they would collapse as the escaping prisoner put his weight on them.[55] Bentham recalled Blackburn explaining his own practice thus:

> If a man gets to the other side of the wall it must be by either getting through or under or over it. To prevent his getting through, I make it of stones too massy to be displaced, as bricks may be by picking. To prevent his getting under, I make a drain. As he undermines, no sooner is he got within the arch, than out flows the water and spoils his mine.[56]

This then was the reformed prison boundary wall; a medley of simple, but not necessarily obvious foils brought together to frustrate every variety of escape attempt.

Security did not consist of containment alone. What the reformers called the policing of prisons — the maintenance of discipline and order within — was just as important. It was to improve policing that Blackburn took advantage of radial geometry in his designs for the Northleach Bridewell in Gloucestershire (designed 1785; Figs. 65, 66, 67), Ipswich County Gaol in Suffolk (commenced 1786; Fig. 68), and Salford New Bayley (commenced 1787; Fig. 69), as well as Liverpool Borough Gaol (Fig. 56). Northleach was later used as the basis for Thomas Harrison's very similar design for the County Gaol at Chester Castle (designed 1786).[57] Salford New Bayley was copied detail for detail by John Baxter in his proposal for Calton Gaol and Bridewell (designed 1791; Fig. 70)[58] and the same plan type (octagonal hub with four equal wings attached) was taken up by John Nash at Hereford County Gaol (commenced 1792; Fig. 71).[59]

Within this new genre three varieties of plan can be distinguished, all with similar characteristics and all originated by Blackburn: a hub with detached radial wings (Liverpool); a hub with attached radial wings (Ipswich, Salford, Hereford); a hub facing onto a polygonal range of buildings (Northleach, Chester). Harrison's gaol for felons at Lancaster Castle (designed 1787) was a hybrid of polygonal and radial types (Fig. 72).[60] These designs fostered what was, in a very literal sense, the centralization of authority. At the focal point was always the 'governor's parlour', the 'rendezvous for keepers' or the turnkey's lodge with windows facing out onto every facet of the prison.[61] The institution was brought under observation from one key position, but it was, at this stage, a policing measure and that was all. Observation was directed into the spaces between buildings to make sure that no one got out. When Bentham developed the principle of central observation and allowed it to penetrate the interior, a dramatic change of purpose occurred (see ch. 5). Meanwhile Blackburn and his followers were content to use it as a means to prevent rebellion or escapes. No more need be said of security, which was, anyway, the least controversial of the three requirements except in so far as it interfered with the others.

Salubrity

The preoccupation with salubrity, as explained in chapter 3, resulted from the widespread belief that typhus fever was generated and disseminated by the atmosphere. In the Gloucester prisons a number of new techniques for encouraging 'perflation', the continual movement and changing of air, were introduced. Blackburn made use of two

67. Northleach Bridewell, W. Blackburn, view across the airing yards.

complementary principles to draw air into his prisons. The first was a principle of planning; the fragmentation or extrusion of the building as a whole. The second was a principle of detailing; the puncturing of the fabric — external walls, internal walls, floors and ceilings — until air could leak through to every corner. The same details were used in all five designs for Gloucester. They were much admired and much copied. (Thomas Harrison, for example, was specifically directed by the Lancashire magistrates 'to view the county gaol there and to examine carefully all the interior arrangements, locks, separations, furniture, etc.'.)[62] Fortunately the original working drawings of appertures, fixtures and fittings which were invisible on most plans but which were such an important feature of the new reformed prisons, have survived (Fig. 73). From them a great deal can be learnt about Blackburn's technique of ventilation.

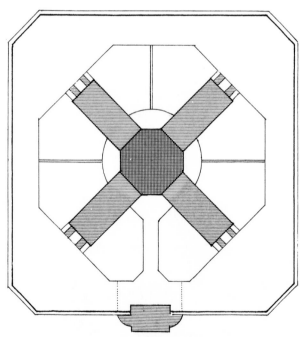

68. Ipswich County Gaol, William Blackburn, started 1786, block plan. Redrawn from S.I.P.D., *Remarks on the Form and Construction of Prisons*, 1826.

69. Salford New Bayley, William Blackburn, started 1787, entrance facade.

149

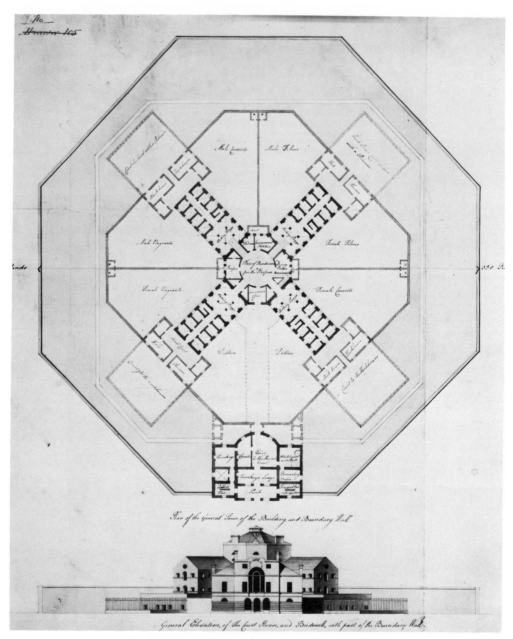

70. Project for Calton Gaol and Bridewell, John Baxter, 1791, ground plan and front elevation. A close copy of Salford (compare facades). Governor's and keeper's offices overlooked the airing yards, while the central 'Rendezvous for Keepers' led directly into the four arcaded 'working piazzas'.

A look at the plan of the Gloucester County Gaol (Fig. 74) shows the cell blocks to have been lifted completely clear of the ground on pier supports as in Howard's Ideal County Gaol of 1777 (Fig. 49). Many other prisons were elevated on arcades: James Wyatt's Petworth (Fig. 62), Blackburn's Littledean Bridewell (Fig. 75), Blackburn and Haycock's Shrewsbury County Gaol (Fig. 76), Harrison's Chester Castle (Fig. 83) and Leroux and Middleton's Cold Bath Fields (Figs. 77, 78) may serve as examples. At Cold Bath Fields the magistrates must have felt that arcading was indispensable, as the terrain of the site, a marsh previously used as a lay-stall, was ill adapted to sustain this form of construction. Reverse arches had to be sunk into the mud to spread the loading more evenly, hence the opinion expressed by a correspondent of the *Gentleman's Magazine* that there were more bricks below ground than above it.[63]

71. Hereford County Gaol, John Nash, 1792–6. The cell block in the left foreground was a later addition. The central observatory and attached wings were original.

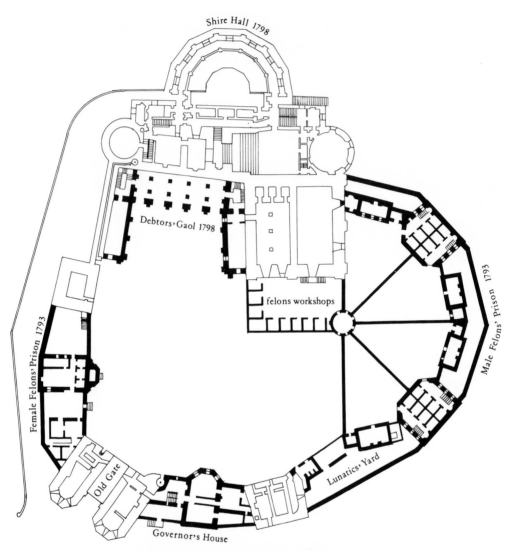

72. Lancaster Castle Gaol, Thomas Harrison. In the small circular observatory at the centre of the male felons' prison (1787–93) the occupation of keeping watch was for the first time disengaged from other activities.

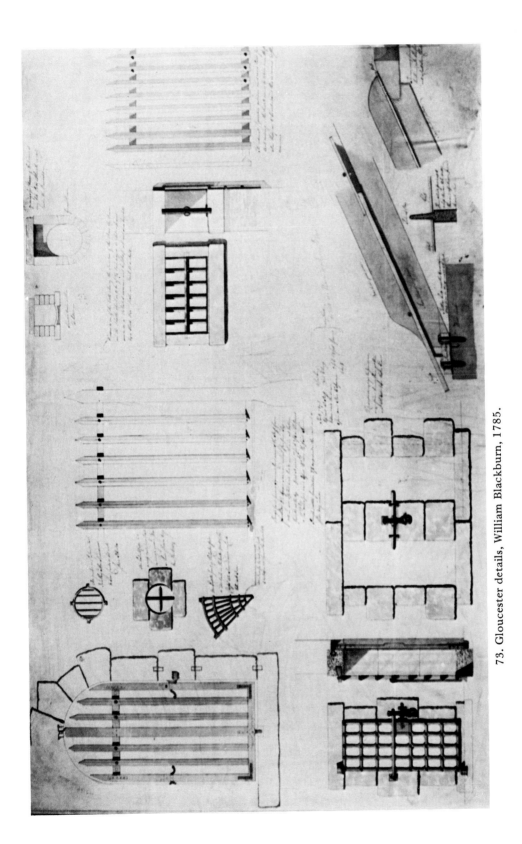

73. Gloucester details, William Blackburn, 1785.

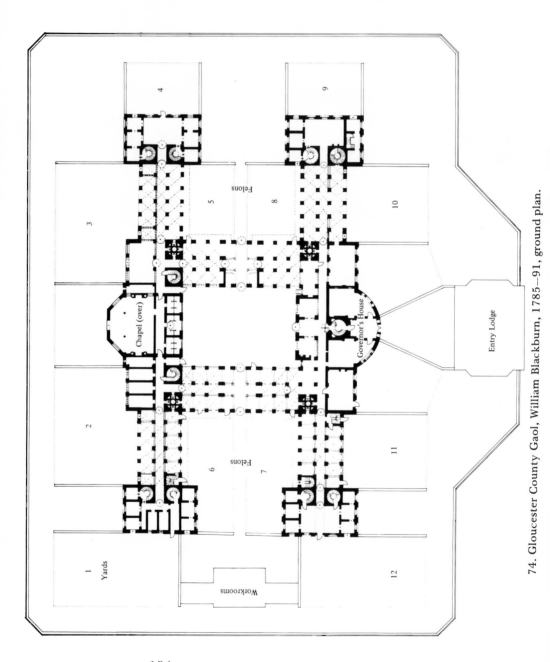

74. Gloucester County Gaol, William Blackburn, 1785—91, ground plan.

154

75. Littledean Bridewell, William Blackburn, 1785, elevations.

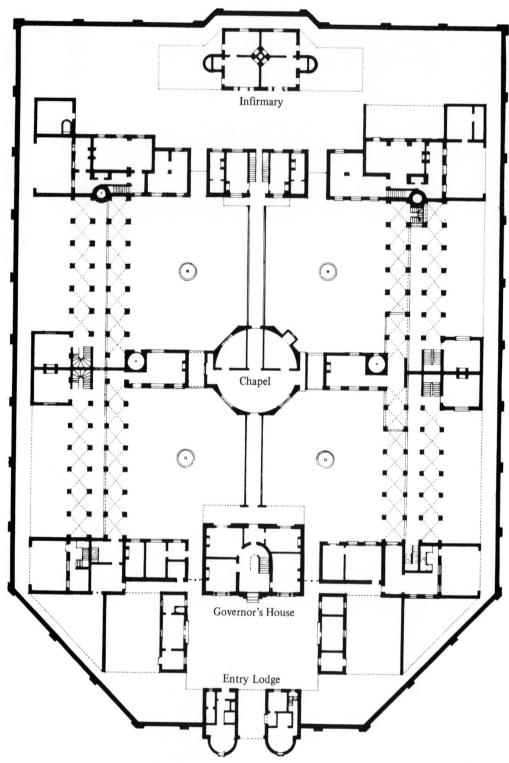

Infirmary

Chapel

Governor's House

Entry Lodge

76. Shrewsbury County Gaol, William Blackburn and John Haycock, 1786–93, ground plan.

It should be said that this practice was in no way derived from the rational architecture of columns and lintels unencumbered with walls that had been proposed by theorists like the Abbé Laugier, though some of the more elegant plans might suggest such a derivation. The prison architects used arches to span between supports, not beams as did the rationalists; they used heavy piers, or even slabs of wall, not graceful columns, to carry their loads; they did not employ the classical orders, primitive or otherwise, and they were happy to build any amount of unarticulated load bearing wall in the upper storeys of their buildings. So it is clear that arcading in reformed prisons was a response to the demand for ventilation and was more directly related to contemporary medical theory than contemporary architectural theory.

Sometimes panels of walling would be built up to the arch springing, but this did not necessarily compromise the function of arcading, because large grated openings were always left under the vaults (Figs. 78, 79). The semi-enclosed areas left under the elevated prison, incongruously labelled 'piazzas' by Blackburn,[64] opened onto the airing yards and were generally used as work places for the prisoners, but their primary function was as a bridge under which air could flow. The cells, corridors, and other rooms above the arcades were then perforated with a variety of openings. Circular iron gratings were let into passage floors, wicket turnstiles took the place of solid wood doors in the main circulation areas (Fig. 73), cell windows were barred but not glazed, and each cell was cross-ventilated with iron grilles opening out into aerated passageways (Fig. 78), or with arched openings above the door lintel (Fig. 79). These openings were windowed at Gloucester, so, to ensure the infiltration of fresh air when closed, a small unglazed hole was left in the lintel itself. Where double leaf cell doors were installed (e.g. Horsham and the Gloucester prisons; Fig. 80) one leaf would be solid oak and the other an open iron lattice. Even bedsteads were turned into iron frames or riddled iron plates (Fig. 81). At Cold Bath Fields, Lawford's Gate and Littledean the chapel served as a ventilation well, drawing air from the bottom to the top of the building (Figs. 78, 82). James Neild, visiting Lawford's Gate in 1802, was fascinated by the incidental use that Blackburn had made of this chapel area. Gratings opened off the well into the infirmaries on the upper floor, in such a way that the bed-ridden sick could look down on divine service from their beds, as from the galleries of certain medieval hospitals.[65]

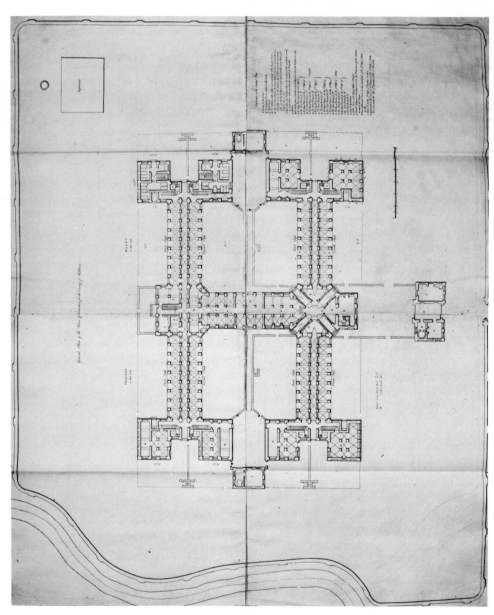

77. Cold Bath Fields House of Correction, Jacob Leroux and Charles Middleton, 1788–94, ground plan.

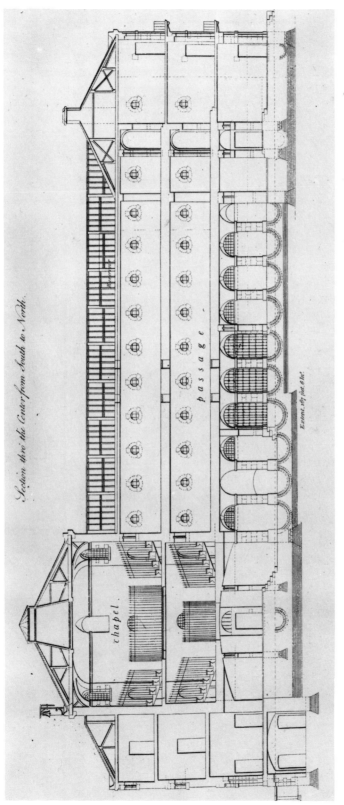

Section thro' the Center from South to North.

chapel

passage

78. Cold Bath Fields, Leroux and Middleton, section of the chapel and policing passage between rows of outward facing cells. Ventilation apertures are visible in the passage floor.

79. Gloucester County Gaol, William Blackburn, a view across the felons' courts published in 1795.

80. Northleach Bridewell, William Blackburn, cell doors.

The best reformed prisons were a mass of small holes; large colanders jacked up on stilts, ventilated by the percolation of air into a uniformly porous container. There was no organized pattern of air flow, which meant that it was extremely difficult to control the rate of ventilation, but this might have been considered a good characteristic, as cold prisoners would, if they could, block up vents and inadvertently cause fever to ferment. Prisoners were later reported to have ruined the good

81. Northleach Bridewell, William Blackburn, interior of cell.

ventilation at Bury St Edmunds Gaol in this way, 'considering that there is a comfort in the exclusion of air, and in dirt'.[66] The same issue arose in an unexpected way at Cold Bath Fields when a Commission, including G.O. Paul, and W.M. Pitt, looked into the state of the prison in 1800. Only in individual small rooms, such as the cells, could the rate of air change be regulated. Cold Bath Fields, as the Commissioners found out, could get very cold indeed during winter nights. Still, they did not find real fault with the fabric as such, though they admitted it to be less than perfect. The real fault was in the degree of latitude allowed to prisoners. The architect had provided wooden shutters to control the ventilation of each cell, which could be adjusted from inside by the occupants, 'but such improper use had been made of this power, that in not less than 70 of the cells the prisoners have torn down the shutters', thus exposing themselves and their successors to the night air.[67] This seemed strange to the Commissioners — a widespread sabotage that affected only the prisoners who committed it — but they offered no explanation. All they did was to draw a conclusion. Quite obviously the privilege of adjustment should not be left in criminal hands. Applied to ventilation this question of the privilege of adjustment was of marginal significance in the eighteenth century because the controls employed were not particularly complex, but the question would recur in exactly the same form in the model prisons of the 1840s.[68] The answer, too, would be the same.

After Gloucester the suspended colander principle was widely applied as the solution to the problem of expelling stagnant, vitiated air. It dominated the design of prison fabric and resolved the difficulty of getting fresh air to the heart of intricately compartmentalized buildings. The Howard/Blackburn prisons did not, therefore, breathe by inhalation like Hales' Newgate, but allowed air to infiltrate over a wide surface.

Getting air to flow in the spaces between buildings was judged to be at least as necessary as getting it to flow inside them. So, either the plan was pulled into a thin ribbon (Fig. 65; Horsham, Northleach) or it was fragmented into a series of independent pavilions (Figs. 56, 61; Liverpool, Dorchester, Preston, Oxford and Bodmin). At Dorchester and Preston, Blackburn sewed the separated pavilions back together again with a string of iron bridges and galleries, superimposing an integrated network of walkways on to the fractured parts of the prison. Policing and salubrity were both enhanced by planning detached buildings

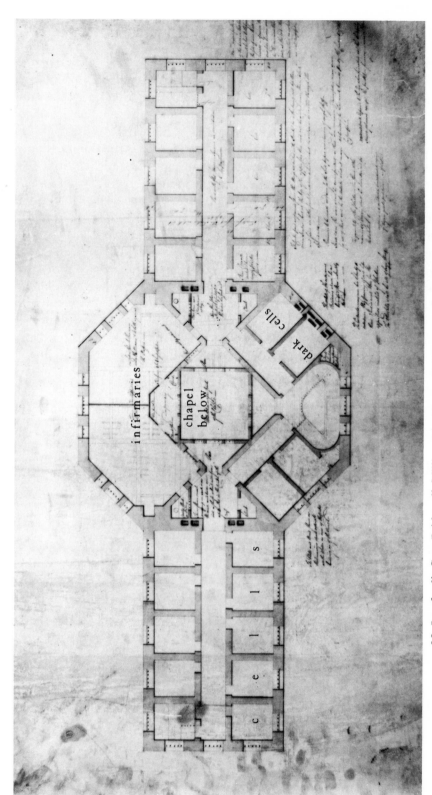

82. Lawford's Gate Bridewell, William Blackburn, 1785, upper floor plan.

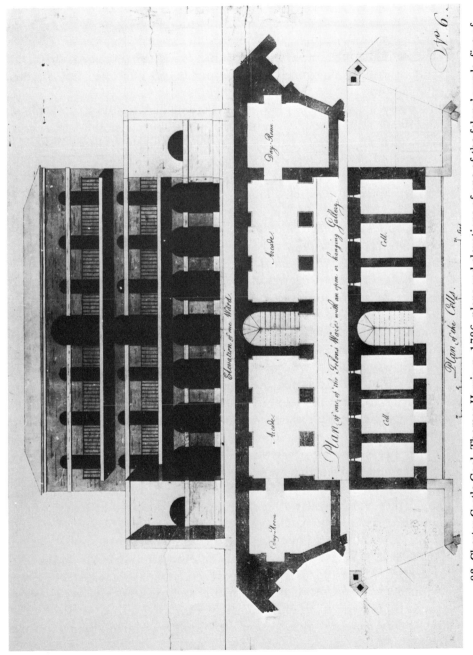

83. Chester Castle Gaol, Thomas Harrison, 1786, plans and elevations of one of the felons' wards, five of which were joined together in a half octagon.

165

(Fig. 59).[69] More was exposed and more could be seen. But whilst salubrity required centrifugal and dispersed planning, policing required centripetal and condensed planning. Blackburn's flying iron galleries cleverly balanced these two opposing forces by breaking apart the building and at the same time maintaining an unbroken net of communications.

Usually a more conservative and limited disintegration took place. Architects still produced courtyard plans, but enclosed courtyards, after such an example had been made of Dance's Newgate, were no longer considered correct. In an early design for Chester Castle Gaol, Harrison therefore split the half octagon of the felons' wing into five distinct arcaded pavilions joined only at ground level (Fig. 83).[70] Similarly, Blackburn at Gloucester, Stafford, and Shrewsbury County Gaols, and Leroux and Middleton at Cold Bath Fields, removed whole slices of the surrounding structure to expose the interior. In this way the courtyards were contained but not enclosed (Fig. 79).

Ventilation was of central importance in the battle against filth and disease, but water supply and drainage played their part too. A plan of the 'great drains' at Cold Bath Fields, for example, shows a network of accurately graded surface and soil drains furnished with rodding plates, interception chambers, sedimentation pits and — because the main conduit was nearly 4 feet in diameter — escape-proofing (Fig. 84). This type of princely sanitation, not neglecting properly ventilated privies, was, from Blackburn's time, a normal provision in all prisons (Fig. 85).[71] To supplement these methods of promoting health there were also new categories of accommodation to be found: fumigating rooms, copper baths, and most essential of all, the separate prison infirmaries for men and women that were required by the Popham Bill (1774).[72] A rare case in which magistrates were held to account for non-compliance with the laws regulating prisons occurred at Essex, where Lord Loughborough, as Secretary to the Home Department, fined the County £500 because they had failed to provide such accommodation for the sick.[73] Where practicable, infirmaries were isolated from the rest of the prison to avoid all risk of contagion, either at some distance from the main buildings or on top of them in an attic storey, where patients would be assured a copious stream of purifying air, as at Gloucester where they were put above the gaoler's house and had airing yards on his roof.

The prisons of the 1780s and 1790s dispelled gaol fever. They were prophylactic but draughty and cold; an urgent response to the fear of aerial infection. Soon, holes were being filled in. First to go were the arcades. The government, when they took over Cold Bath Fields from the Middlesex Magistrates, enclosed and cellularized the entire ground floor.[74] Prisons built in the nineteenth century often abandoned arcading altogether. Even so, elements devised by Blackburn were retained in prison building practice long afterwards. Floor ventilator gratings, apertures for cross-ventilating cells, iron access galleries, partial arcading, discontinuous enclosure, and open fence boundaries can all be found in much later specifications,[75] while the fragmented radial plan

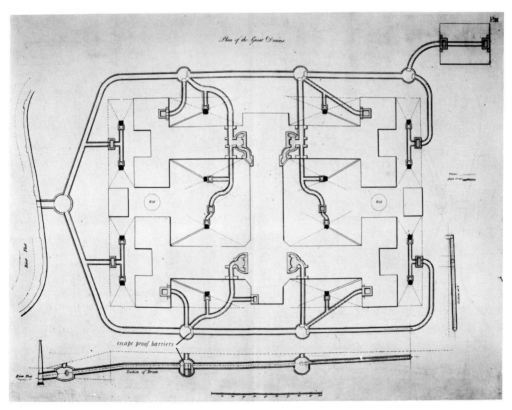

84. Cold Bath Fields, Leroux and Middleton, 1788–94, the great drains.

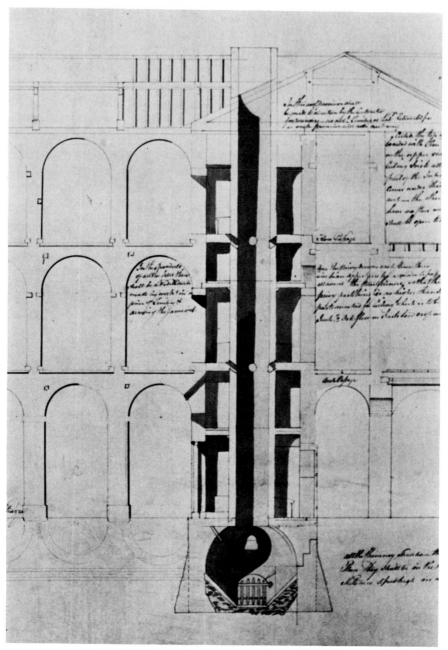

85. Gloucester County Gaol, William Blackburn, 1785, privy stack.
Escape-proofing on the main drain can be seen below.

was being used ever more frequently. The technique of inducing salubrity through architecture was no longer pursued so relentlessly because it had served its purpose; the prisons were healthy at last.

Perhaps as a result of this success, salubrity was later regarded as the shibboleth of the Howardian Movement. By 1824 John Headlam could look back on the prisons of Howard's time and see in them a rest-cure for criminals, that pandered to physical needs and therefore neglected the discomforting business of reformation.[76] Such interpretations of the immediate past were common in the 1820s, but in fact the Howardians were as determined as anyone else to make their prisons 'places of real terror, to those the law would terrify'.[77]

Reformation

Reformation did not dispense with or neglect punishment — it was just that punishment was now supposed to be for the criminal's own good rather than for the benefit of others. The programme of reformatory discipline outlined by the philanthropists, which put great faith in the redeeming effects of separation and seclusion, could only be implemented in a building designed for the purpose. Because reformation relied so much on demarcation and division, to isolate prisoner from prisoner, architecture was acknowledged to be the crucial factor setting the process in motion. The reformers, from the very beginning, recognized that the problem was one of communication. John Call described the properties of his Bodmin Gaol to Howard in the following terms: 'The leading principle in the disposal of the several parts of the building is to prevent any communication of speech or otherwise, between the different kinds of criminals; and to keep each sex, distinct by day, and every individual separate from one another by night.'[78]

The technical complexity of the problems that these criteria raised were shunned in an initial attempt to divide, separate and subdivide, maybe in the hope that the fact of division would itself suffice to break down the criminal conspiracy against reason. George Onesiphorus Paul actually listed the third function of the prison as separation rather than reformation, so closely did he identify the instrument with its purpose.[79]

Separation was a generalized form of solitude and it had identical attributes. 'Separation both day and night is the principle of all improvement: to a certain degree it is an object of prime necessity, to constitute a legal prison; and there is no possible degree of separation that will not bring with it additional perfection: — it favours every species of reform.' Like Rousseau's afterlife it would only be a punishment to the wicked because 'it favours retreat to those, whom a conscious innocence inclines to privacy under their misfortunes', and yet 'if carried to solitude, is the most sovereign corrector of a hardened heart'. Then there was also the matter of dividing to rule: 'It is by cabal and participation of design, by confidence in numbers, that desperate deeds are undertaken.' Separated the prisoners were under the power of their keeper.[80] Any division between one kind of prisoner and another was desirable and the more divisions the better.

In reformed prisons there were three levels of division: (1) cellular night separation for all prisoners; (2) the isolation of various groups such as males and females, felons and misdemeanants, into distinct classes; (3) the seclusion of individual prisoners both by day and by night. All of these arrangements can be easily traced in contemporary prison plans. Most prominent of all were the night cells. The typical Blackburn night cell was vaulted, whitewashed, contained no timber and measured anything from 8ft 9in. by 8ft 2in. at Gloucester to a meagre 7ft 2in. by 5ft 9in. at Salford (Figs. 80, 81).[81] The only fixture was the bed. Blackburn claimed that his night cell vents were 'so managed as to exclude conversation, while they admit air',[82] by which he meant that they were located high up in the vault and did not face any corresponding apertures on the opposite side of the dividing passage, making intercourse awkward, but hardly impossible. The problem of soundproofing had not yet arisen. When it did, it would provide the technology for a more profound quarantine.

Architecture is ideally suited to the task of keeping people apart; walls do nothing quite so well as this. The pattern of walls in a plan and the distribution of apartments in a section are abstracts of a social reality defined by interdicted or extended communication between one place and another. So long as the distribution of occupants, their circumstances and their authority over one another can be fixed, either by the force of architecture alone, or bolstered up by rules and regulations, the building can be regarded as a frozen image of intercourse. This correlation betwen social and physical shape was well understood by William Blackburn, who began to make very good use of it in his 19 prison plans, in which the buildings were conceived as a nesting sequence of containers, the perimeter walls enclosing the ward boundaries, in turn enclosing the cells.

Standing between the outside world and the inside of the prison, attached to the boundary wall, was the entry lodge, a unit that occurs first in just those institutions where the rules defined an exacting, almost ritual, procedure of admittance: the Gloucester County Gaol and Bridewells (Fig. 86).[83] The prisoners, once through the gate, were received by a surgeon. They were stripped, examined, bathed, their clothes taken from them, fumigated and stored, their heads were shaved and they were issued with a uniform. All this took place in a cluster of well-equipped chambers around the gate. The process of reformation commenced with this secular initiation in which all superficial signs of the criminal self were removed. Here again, the whole process was understood and justified as a necessary precaution against infection (and, true enough, it was measures such as these that must have been responsible for the abatement of typhus fever), yet its impact was to mark the enormous gap that separated prison from everyday life and to define the excruciating moment of passage between the physical pleasures of debauchery and the mental pains of reformation. As the only point at which the prison met the ordinary world the entry lodge filtered all transactions between the two. Kitchens were often located here to avoid the necessity of delivering goods into the heart of the gaol. At Shrewsbury the last vestige of the begging grate was incorporated into the new lodge (Fig. 63). Two apertures were left in the doorway to receive charitable donations. But the practice was a charade. No longer collected or distributed by the prisoners, the money was handled by the administration and given to 'debtors in a state of industry' and 'prisoners in a state of reformation'.[84] The Shrewsbury charity, far from being a deliverance from need, was a system of rewards for diligence and obedience.

Once within, prisoners were severed from ordinary society, all contact with which was now mediated by the authorities. In this same period visiting and letter writing were more strictly curtailed and occasionally disallowed altogether. It is worth quoting the note to Blackburn's Dorchester designs published in 1795, which, in describing how prisoners are to receive visitors, illustrates the close alignment between procedure and plan (see also Fig. 87) that made this mediation effective:

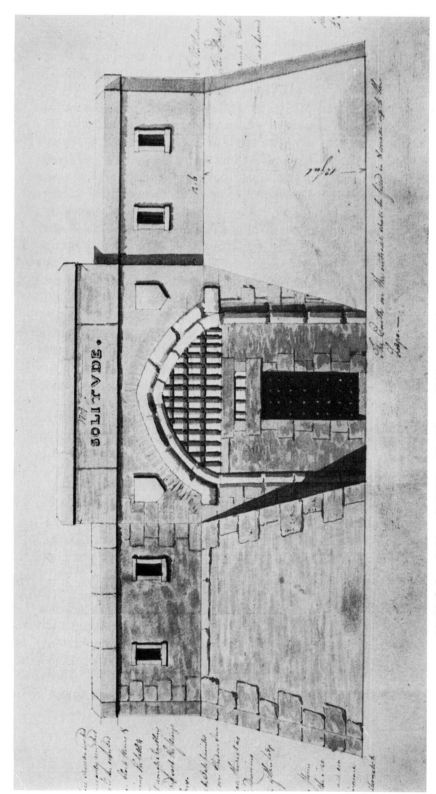

86. Littledean Bridewell, William Blackburn, 1785, entry lodge.

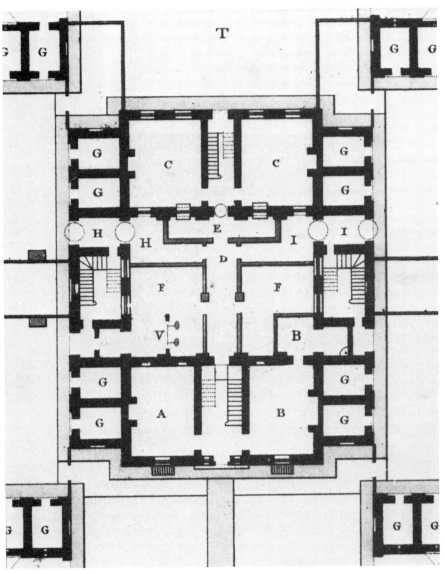

87. Dorchester County Gaol, William Blackburn, centre pavilion, ground plan.

When visitors come to see the debtors, they are permitted immediately to go to their visiting room [E on plan], the inner door of which is constantly kept locked, the outer one open; there are two windows opening from it, one into each debtors day room; these windows are barred, but a table goes through each of them, one half being in the debtors room, the other half in the visiting room. Debtors are not therefore excluded from the society of their relations or friends, yet the visitors are not allowed in general to come into the rooms, by which means many irregularities are prevented. In particular cases, the keeper, where he finds it proper, unlocks the inner door and suffers the debtor to take his friend with him into his cell or court. Fines and felons have not the same indulgence, their friends cannot see them but in the presence of the keeper; the three gates to their visiting rooms [H, I] all being locked. The keeper, on application, lets the friend into the space between the first and second gates and stands himself in the space between the second and third, the prisoner remaining in the court. He can thus effectually prevent the introduction of weapons, liquor or other items the use of which is forbidden in the prison, as well as be a check on any improper conversations.[85]

Such were the ways administrative regulation combined with architecture. It was an architecture comprised of apertures, barriers, interceptions and distances, not of space, volume and surface.

The class wards functioned as prisons within the prison. The isolation of groups of prisoners, each with its own type of stigma and its own degree of malignance, into independent zones required the replication of facilities as well as subdivision. Each enclosed ward would generally have its own staircases, privies, wash-house, workrooms and its own airing yard. Often they served only a few inmates. The Littledean Bridewell, for example, could accommodate only six prisoners in each of its wards. The simplest way to divide one ward from another was to demarcate territories and fit each into a distinct plot (this was the usual arrangement in radial, pavilion or small prisons). To preserve the integrity of this division, walls were built down the middle of the corridors at the Winchester County Gaol (1788) and also in the Bridewell (1787) (Fig. 88). Blackburn was more ingenious. In his plans, particularly the larger courtyard plans, the ward territories interleave and weave over and under each other but rarely do their paths cross. At first a single wall was regarded as an adequate separator, but a network of policing passages soon pushed their way in between, both inside and outside the building (Figs. 77, 78), islanding the wards to make intercommunication between classes more difficult. Chapels, too, begin to be compartmentalized with timber partitions (Fig. 89).[86]

Finally, there is the question of solitary confinement. How widely was it practised and in what form? Evidence from local plans, regulations and contemporary descriptions shows that most reformed prisons did attempt to impose solitude to a lesser or greater extent. As early as 1771 the Middlesex Justices ordered cells to be erected in Clerkenwell House of Correction 'for the confinement of disobedient and disorderly apprentices, separate from each other and from other prisoners' as a means to reclaim and preserve their morals.[87] At Gloucester County Gaol a three-stage imprisonment, as defined in the Penitentiary Act, was in operation, the first third of any sentence being served in absolute solitude.[88] At Petworth the rules laid down that: 'The keeper and turnkey take especial care that the prisoners are kept separate night and

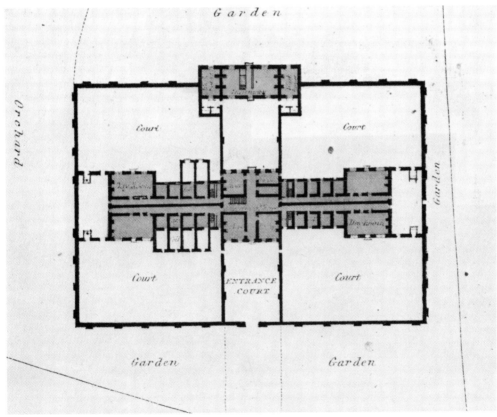

88. Winchester County Bridewell, 1787, ground plan.

day, and that they perform such work as may be allotted to them in their respective cells; and that they, upon no pretence whatever, permit them to have any communication with one another.'[89] Howard noted a similar practice at Wymondham Bridewell.[90] The absence of workrooms at Horsham (1775), the Essex County House of Correction (1802–5),[91] the Herefordshire County House of Correction (1790)[92] and the new cell block at Fisherton Anger (1791) (Fig. 90),[93] is a good indication that all prisoners were 'kept separate night and day' in these prisons, but in many layouts there were distinct apartments for work and sleep even where solitary confinement was practised. The penitentiary workrooms at Gloucester County Gaol, the individual work cubicles under the piazzas in the Gloucester bridewells, and the extraordinary hive of weaving shops on the misdemeanants' side at Preston (Fig. 91), as well as the 102 single workrooms at Liverpool Borough Gaol,[94] were all used in this way. Night cells were supplemented with a graduated hierarchy of workrooms, some for 'single persons to work in solitude', others for 'two, three or more persons'.[95]

There was yet another variant in which a section of prison accom-

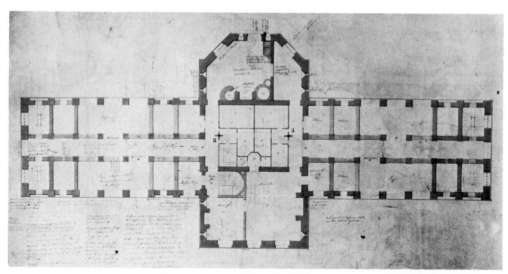

89. Littledean Bridewell, William Blackburn, 1785, ground plan. Entrance to the compartmented chapel was controlled by two turnstiles.

modation would consist of solitary cells for both night and day, each with its very own airing yard, so that exercise, as well as work and sleep, was brought into the realm of solitary activities.[96] At Lincoln Castle Gaol four of these were added some time between 1788 and 1800, but the six at Winchester Bridewell seem to have been part of the original 1787 design (Fig. 88).[97] At Kirton Bridewell in Lincolnshire (1790–9) eight 'solitary cell yards' were incorporated.[98] Harrison's early plan for a string of 12 cell-and-yard units at Chester Castle was eventually abandoned, as also was the most uncompromising proposal of all by George Dance the younger for the Southwark Compter.

In 1780 the Gordon rioters razed the old Compter. By 1785 Dance had produced two plans for its reconstruction. The first of these, rejected by the Aldermen, was an intricate demonstration of the architecture of separation (Figs. 92, 93). The site was impossibly small — a plot measuring hardly more than 65 X 104 feet. Judged by the demanding standards of the time, any plan on such a site was bound to be full of faults. As it turned out, the debtors' prison was far too airless and enclosed, the felons' section opened directly to the exterior and the

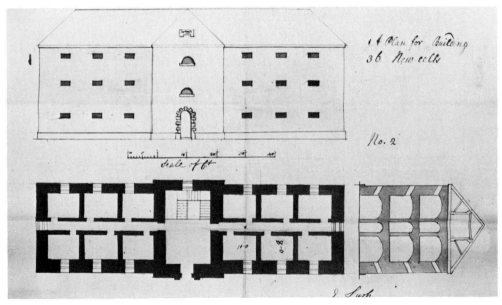

90. Fisherton Anger County Gaol, cell block, E. Lush, 1791.

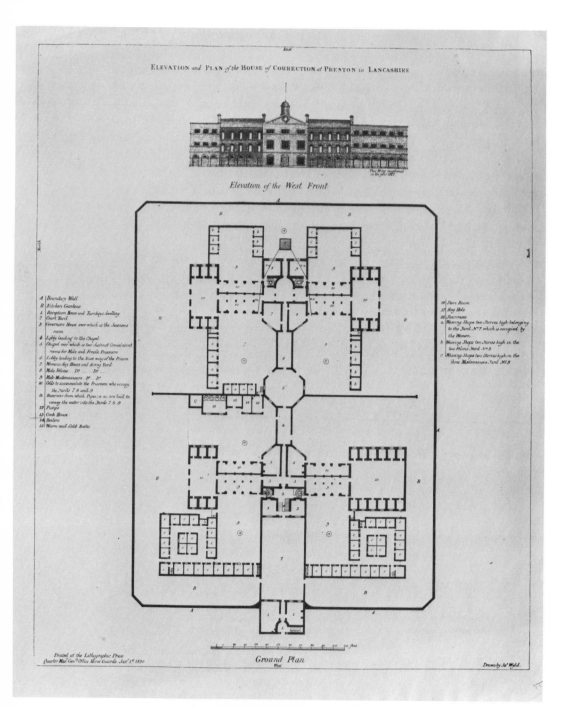

91. Preston House of Correction, William Blackburn, 1784, ground plan. The accumulation of 124 solitary weaving shops in two storeys can be seen behind the entrance. The date of building is uncertain.

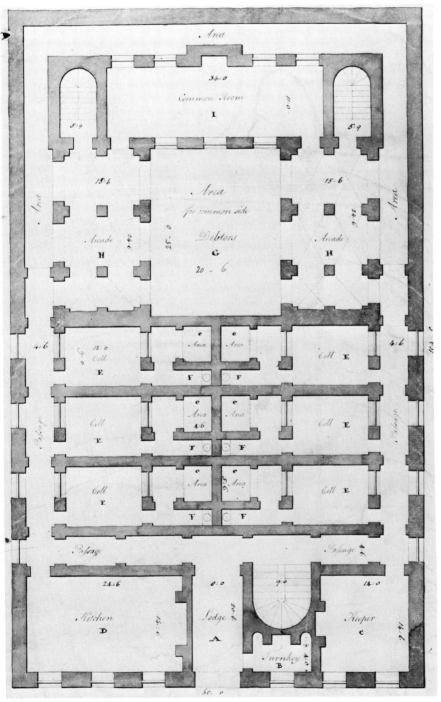

92. The Southwark Compter, George Dance the younger, between
1780 and 1785, ground plan. The individual privies to the felons'
cells are marked F.

gaol was not in view from the keeper's house. On the other hand, Dance shrewdly made part of the roof into a debtors' airing yard and excelled himself with the layout for 12 well-ventilated solitary cells in which a prisoner could spend his entire sentence, except for a weekly visit to chapel.[99] To each cell was added a privy and a yard, so that the requirements of both law and nature could be met within it. The art of it was to arrange all this into a sort of Chinese puzzle without sacrificing ventilation or seclusion. Dance did this by stacking smaller cells on top of larger ones, making space for open yards on the first floor as well as

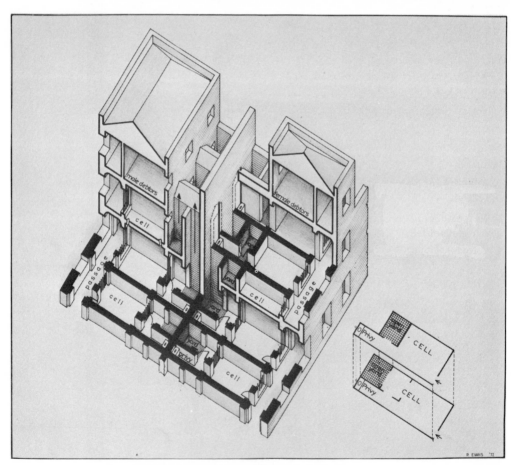

93. Analytic drawing of Dance's design for the Southwark Compter.

at ground level. Each unit became an L-shaped shaft for the passage of air and each yard a vertical walled funnel,[100] screening prisoners from the sight of any of their fellows above, below or about them (Fig. 93).

Undoubtedly, Dance's cell/yard/privy suites, with their complex three-dimensional organization, marked the furthest extension of the technology of isolation in the eighteenth century. There is no way of telling why the Aldermen did not pursue the plan, but most probably it was just too expensive.[101]

Compared with the regular and pleasingly formal layouts for the penitentiary competition (Figs. 50–55), the new local prisons seem rather tawdry and lacking in architectural grace. Many appear at first sight incoherent and piecemeal. This lack of visible formality was not the result of halfwitted design but on the contrary resulted from the pursuit of an original insight. These plans could be described as the terminal distribution of buildings caught between opposing forces. In the local prisons of the eighteenth century an attempt had been made to reconcile the antagonistic demands of security, salubrity and reformation. Security required the prison to be enclosed (for the prevention of escape) on a fragmented but condensed plan (for policing); salubrity required it to be exposed and open, on a dispersed plan (for universal ventilation); reformation required that the whole be composed of isolated compartments and cells (for the prevention of communication). The resulting conflict between centripetal and centrifugal forces on the one hand and between exposure and enclosure on the other gave rise to a form of building which did not correspond to the canons of either classical or picturesque composition. What appears to be a lack of order was in fact the imposition of a different species of order; what looks like the decline of architectural skill was in fact the development of techniques that led beyond appearance, or rather, techniques which were not in the least concerned with appearances. Nothing could demonstrate the invisible order of the new prisons better than a comparison between the clear hierarchical plan of Liverpool Borough Gaol and Herdman's water colour sketches of the resulting formless building (Figs. 56, 94, 95, 96). Geometry, unity, proportionality and symmetry in this, the most experimental phase of prison construction, had been sublimated to the requirements of reform. They were still there, locked into the abstract figure of the plan, but they were no longer visible to

94. W. Herdman, water colour of Liverpool Borough Gaol in the nineteenth century.

95. Herdman water colour of Liverpool Borough Gaol.

96. Herdman water colour of Liverpool Borough Gaol.

the occupants. In most plans the underlying geometrical figure can be made out — the ghost of classicism. Sometimes this geometry was integral to the operation of the building, as with radial configurations, but usually it represents no more than a point of departure; an original shape to be fractured, cut, dismembered and subdivided to conform with the requirements of security, salubrity and reformation.

'The ingenious Mr. Blackburn'[102] was the indisputable originator of this type of architecture. Practically every new technique reviewed in this chapter was evolved and refined by him during eight active years.[103] Certainly, Howard recognized Blackburn's talent for translating principles into reality, sizing him up nicely with the comment that he was 'the only man capable of delineating my idea of what a prison ought to be'.[104] When he died Blackburn was at the height of his brief preeminence. In October of 1790 he set off for Glasgow, having been requested to design a prison for that city. On the way, at Preston, he suffered a fatal stroke. He was only 40 years old. The same year John Howard contracted yellow fever at Cherson, while on an extensive prison tour in Russia, and died. But it was not these deaths that put an end to the first phase of reformed prison construction, as is sometimes maintained, though few projects were embarked upon after this date. The fall-off in building was, more prosaically, due to the beginning of the Napoleonic Wars, and to the more active local authorities having completed their business. New prisons had been built and that, for the time being, was the end of the matter.

Although some prisons exemplified the new techniques more adequately than others, none were entirely untouched. John Soane's felons' prison, boxed inside the old twelfth-century keep at Norwich, was hardly airy and salubrious, but was cellularized, arcaded and nothing if not secure (Fig. 140).[105] George Gwilt overlaid a radial configuration of yards on a conventional rectangular court plan at Horsemonger Lane (1791–8) with little correlation between the two. Nevertheless, he provided every reformed requisite from a centrally placed governor's house to a fumigation chamber. Possibly the least praiseworthy new prison from the point of view of reform was the Leicester County Gaol by the Derby architect George Moneypenny (1789–93) (Fig. 97),[106] yet this same building would have appeared progressive and ingenious fifteen years before, with its four yards, its single cells, partitioned chapel, baths, pumps and privies — an indi-

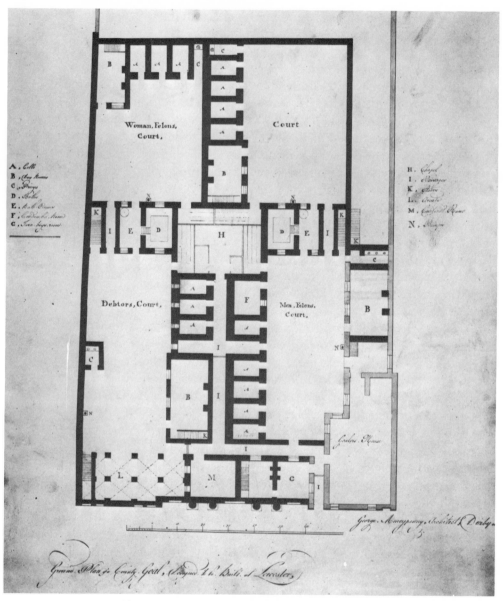

97. Leicester County Gaol, George Moneypenny, 1789, ground plan.

cation of the revolution in expectations that had taken place during the 1780s. Leicester County Gaol, like Newgate, was praised for its fine facade. It was still, in 1815, the most splendid edifice in a town well supplied with public buildings when John Nichols complimented the architect for 'his knowledge of grand design bordering on the terrific' (Fig. 98),[107] and Moneypenny was proud enough of his building — and indeed of himself — to inscribe his name and profession boldly on the centre lintel. Dispensing with the stringent, exacting criteria of reform, he chose to concentrate on the appearance of the elevation. The composition of a prison plan and the composition of a prison facade were already seen as distinct operations with quite different rules. They might be co-ordinated, as they had been by Harrison at Chester County Gaol, which possessed an admirable facade (though of the court house, not the prison), had a regular plan and was also acclaimed as a fine piece of reformed design, but no deeper correspondence between them was recognized. For Moneypenny it was altogether more convenient to disengage them completely: the reforms, for what they were worth, were buried in the plan; the elements of neo-classical architecture were exhibited in the facade. In this instance the dissociation was a passive affair, disdainfully giving up part of architecture to the alien requirements of the prison so as to reserve what was left for art, but soon this very dissociation would itself be put to use, and the facade employed to propagate impressions of imprisonment quite distinct from what in fact went on behind it.

Active as these years had been only about half the local Grand Juries had considered rebuilding any of their prisons, and some of these, like those at Leicester, Norfolk and Bedford, were indifferent to the doctrines of reform. The sceptical apathy of unconvinced justices was continually challenged by the reformers, but in the closing years of the century reform itself came under attack for the first time. The issue was solitary confinement, and it was raised by a small group of radicals. Ironically enough, it was a form of penal discipline that had been lately adopted in liberated America and in Revolutionary France. The Walnut Street solitary block at Philadelphia was constructed in 1790, and the French Criminal Law Reform of 1791 prescribed solitary confinement on bread and water as an alternative to capital punishment.[108] But in this country it was applied to a wider range of offenders than elsewhere. Here, owing to the deep belief in its reforming power (for how else can

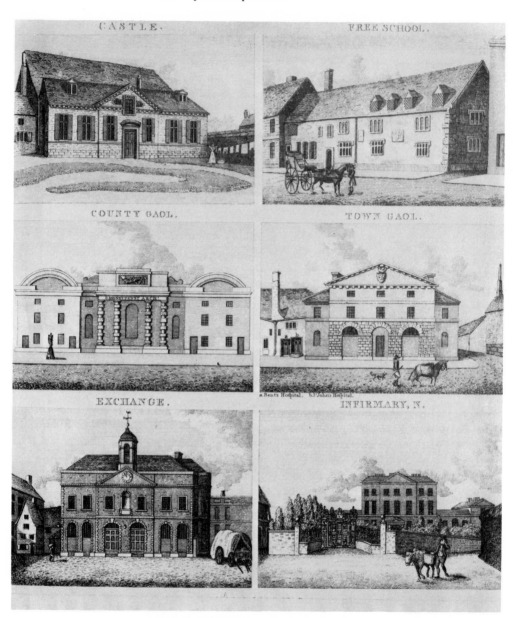

98. Leicester's public buildings, an illustration from John Nichols,
The History and Antiquities of the County of Leicester, 1815.

it be explained?), solitary confinement was more frequently employed against petty offenders than against felons. At Essex and Hertford the gaols allowed work in common when the adjacent bridewells were uniformly solitary. As Lord Loughborough pointed out, petty offenders were much better material for reformation than felons and hardened convicts. The first priority would therefore be to impose solitude on the meekest, not the boldest.[109]

In 1792 an emotional tract, *Gloucester Bastille!!!: Pathetic Particulars of a Poor Boy*, accused the Justices in that most praiseworthy County of sentencing a 16 year old boy to seven years solitary confinement for stealing a few clothes — 'surely worse than the punishment for murder'. It portrayed the irreparable decay of the mind under solitude. It claimed that the personality was 'depressed into a state of inanity', that eyes 'roll in wild horror upon a vast emptiness' and the tongue 'forgets the articulation of words', and pleaded with the County to call a halt to this atrocious 'mental punishment'.[110] The new discipline was also used on literate political offenders, and from these men came first hand descriptions of reformatory solitude. In 1799 Kidd Wake, a bookbinder sentenced to five years in Gloucester Gaol for uttering 'No George — No war',[111] somehow managed to publish a poster of himself in his cell (Fig. 99) with this plea:

Five years confinement, even in common gaols, must surely be a very severe suffering; but if Judges or juries would only reflect on the horrors of solitary imprisonment, under penitentiary discipline! If they would allow their minds to dwell a little on what it is to be locked up, winter after winter, for 16 hours out of 24, in a small brick cell — without company — without fire — without light — without employment — and scarcely to see a face but those of criminals and turnkeys . . . Above all, to be subject to a thousand insults and vexations impossible to be described, and therefore scarcely to be remedied; but by which continual torment may be and often is inflicted. If they would but consider what an irreparable misfortune it is to have a considerable portion of life so wearisomely wasted; they would surely be more tender of dooming any man, for a long time to such wretchedness. It is a calamity beyond description, more easy to be conceived than explained.[112]

In London Francis Burdett, the radical Westminster M.P., championed the cause of Colonel Edmund Despard, confined for sedition in Cold Bath Fields. It was a popular campaign.[113] Despard was finally released and Burdett managed to engineer a Parliamentary enquiry into the state of the prison, but he was careful not to raise the issues of solitary con-

KIDD WAKE,

IN A SOLITARY CELL,

AND CLOATHED IN THE UNIFORM OF GLOCESTER PENITENTIARY HOUSE.

99. Kidd Wake in Gloucester Gaol, 1799. The uniform consisted of alternate panels of bright blue and yellow material.

finement or reformatory discipline in his public statements, preferring to rely on more expedient accusations of misconduct and neglect directed at the gaoler, Aris. A similar tactic was adopted by Orator Hunt in 1821 when he accused his gaoler of 'playing cards with a prisoner', 'suffering males and females to mix together', 'swearing and blaspheming' and omitting to attend Divine Service. A woman was committed to solitary for singing but this was hardly noticed. Hunt did not question the nature of reformatory discipline, he only questioned the regularity of its practice in terms not markedly different from Howard (Fig. 100).[114]

In these opportunistic attacks the radicals adopted the rhetoric of reform to score an immediate victory over their opponents. To do so

100. The cruelties of Illchester Gaol illustrated in H. Hunt, *A Peep into Illchester Prison*, 1821.

they had to make the prison appear in its traditional guise as a den of petty exploitation and vice, and the issues raised at Gloucester were all too easily submerged. Burdett nevertheless continued to press for enquiries into reformed prisons. In more reflective vein, the philosopher William Godwin restated the Beccarian principle, never really acknowledged in this country, that true reformation could not be forced on anyone by laws and should not, therefore, be confused with or identified with punishment. For Godwin the new prisons, with their 'tyrannical and severe' regime, were perhaps 'the bitterest torment that human ingenuity can inflict',[115] and were in any case doomed to fail in their mission. Coleridge also opposed reformatory punishment and helped publicize solitary confinement and the Despard affair with this frequently quoted quatrain which pointed a hackneyed metaphor towards a new target.

> As he went through Cold Bath Fields, he saw
> A solitary cell;
> And the Devil was pleased, for it gave him a hint
> For improving his prisons in Hell.[116]

Solitary confinement was quietly deleted from the list of reforming requirements. Although it never disappeared, it was used less and less regularly, ending up as a special form of discipline for refractory prisoners. This was not solely due to radical agitation. The first sign of frustration was in 1789, when Paul heard of 'ignorant tales' being put about, describing the 'scenes of horror' in his new gaol and bridewells, which he relished as the cause of the 'wondrous diminution of offences' that had been noticed as soon as the prison building commenced. At the same time he complained that the public had amplified and exaggerated solitude into something far worse than it actually was.[117] The Gloucester system, he insisted, was mild. By 1800 frustration with the public was turning into frustration with prison buildings. The Commission of Enquiry into Cold Bath Fields, of which Paul was a member, could only reflect that: 'with regard to solitary imprisonment accompanied by well-regulated labour and religious instruction as directed by the Penitentiary Act aforementioned, one doubts if it has ever been really practised on any regular and temperate system', an opinion made more striking as the increasing volume of public criticism had forced the government to set up the enquiry in the first place. According to them reason for despair was to be found neither in the oppressive

101. T.H. Shepherd, view of Cold Bath Fields Prison in 1814.

discipline, nor in the volatile response of public opinion, but in the sad fact that the technical problem of isolating prisoners against their will had never been satisfactorily solved.

The disillusioned Commissioners reported that 'for the several weeks during which our eyes have been attentively fixed on the management of this prison . . . we have observed the entire number of every yard or division passing their time in unrestrained intercourse with each other'.[118] The realization that all these carefully planned discriminations could be so easily flaunted, was a disturbing one. The prevention of communication would need to be more seriously studied, or the hope of reformation would have to be abandoned. In 1808 solitary confinement was phased out of the Gloucester system. In 1816 the Sussex Magistrates declared it was time 'to reconsider the principles of solitary confinement in all its circumstances' and proceeded to fill in the arcades at Petworth with communal workrooms.[119] The apparatus of a penal experiment was to be dismantled. It had been expensive as well as controversial and ineffective. A good reformed prison cost anything from £151 to £283 per cell-place during the 1780s and 1790s (Fig. 182). A reforming county would now spend at the very least a quarter of its revenue on the mortgaging and administration of their prisons. At Gloucestershire in 1797/8 the prisons accounted for 61% of the entire budget.[120] One might expect this to read as an epitaph. In fact, after a modest pause, the whole issue of prison reform was to be revived, though within a somewhat modified framework. In the meantime Jeremy Bentham solicited, persuaded, pleaded with and finally fought with successive governments for the privilege of building a National Penitentiary on his new plan.

5   A way of obtaining power

The building *circular* — A cage, glazed — a glass lantern about the Size
of *Ranelagh* — The prisoners in their cells, occupying the circumfer-
ence — The officers in the centre. By *blinds* and other contrivances,
the inspectors concealed . . . from the observation of the prisoners:
hence the sentiment of a sort of omnipresence — The whole circuit
reviewable with little, or if necessary without any, change of place. *One
station in the inspection part affording the most perfect view of every
cell.*[1]

Such was Jeremy Bentham's description of his new, and less expensive,
mode of employing and reforming convicts. At the time it was clear to
everyone that this scheme for a penitentiary was not within the mainstream of prison design, nor did it represent the mainstream of penal
doctrine. In fact its uniqueness, lovingly dwelt on by its inventor, was
so well established that when finally it was rejected by Parliament in
1811, twenty years after it had first been taken up, it was this very
quality which proved its undoing. The Panopticon or Inspection House
was original, of that there is no doubt, but for all the claims of its
author and for all the fears of its detractors it was very much a part of
the reform movement. With its considerable dissimilarities so frequently
highlighted, it is easy to lose sight of this essential continuity. The
Panopticon was thus a development of, as much as a departure from,
Howardian practice.

Bentham had become interested in penitentiaries after the publication
of the first draft of Blackstone and Eden's Act in 1776. He approved of
its 'many capital improvements'[2] but proceeded in his immodest way
to write down corrections and additions that he thought ought to be
incorporated. This grew into a pamphlet printed in 1778 and entitled
A View of the Hard Labour Bill. The *View* was not a criticism of the
Act so much as an extensive catalogue of technical solutions to the
problems posed by it, prefiguring the precise verbal pictures of gadgets

195

and contrivances which made up such a large part of *Panopticon*. It was not about legislation, as one might be led to expect, but about the means of implementing the desired ends of legislation; a handbook of design with each objective laid before the reader and each solution following. An example of his reductive, analytical and undeviating method of tackling practical problems will demonstrate how unortho-dox were the results of its use. Section 40 of the draft declared the purpose of prisoner apparel firstly to be 'the humiliation of the wearer', and secondly the prevention of escape. A coarse uniform with badges was prescribed by Blackstone and Eden, but Bentham pointed out that a uniform could be discarded, so surely an indelible marking would be better. Shaving off a convict's eyebrows might be one answer (for shaved heads can be covered), but most effective of all would be a pain-less semi-permanent dying of the skin:

Instances of chymical means of producing marks are washes applied to the forehead, or to one or both cheeks, or, in short to the whole face, so as to discolour it. Chymestry furnishes many washes of this sort. Of several of these I have often undesignedly made trial upon myself. Various metallic solutions produce this effect in a state so diluted as prevents any objection on the score of expense. The stain lasts without any fresh application as long as the stratum of skin which it pervades; that is, to the best of my recollection about a week. No other washes have ever yet been found to discharge it.[3]

In the *View* Bentham was already pursuing a line of thought that would preoccupy him for the better part of his life; how could human behav-iour, and through behaviour the human condition as a whole, be con-trolled and made certain by design? For twenty years he devoted himself to the advancement of a single project, spending most of his money on it, in which every aspect of this question was to be answered, and his whole philosophy made manifest. The project was the 'Penitentiary Panopticon'.[4]

The idea came to him in Russia while visiting his younger brother, Samuel, a naval engineer who was them employed by Prince Potemkin to reorganize the industries on his Critchef Estate.[5] There Samuel was building a sizeable manufactory around a core of directors' rooms from which the whole establishment could be easily overlooked. This caught his elder brother's fancy and while he waited for Catherine the Great to pay him court,[6] Jeremy Bentham enlarged on the idea and gave it a name — Panopticon: the all-seeing eye. In 1787 a bundle of contrived 'letters' on the subject was sent to London, but they were not immediately published. When, in 1791, they finally reached the presses, a long postscript had been added, describing in exhaustive detail a plan of construction and management for a Panopticon Penitentiary House. The previous year an architect, Willey Reveley, had been employed to draw up plans,[7] and Samuel Bentham, having returned from Russia, was called in as engineer.

The governments of England, Ireland and France were all approached with the offer of the new invention, and the services of Jeremy Bentham as governor of it. A Panopticon in Dublin was being promoted by Sir John Parnell,[8] Chancellor of the Exchequer for Ireland, and a proposal made to the newly established Paris National Assembly, through Brissot, was warmly and gratefully received. Bentham suggested that the Revolutionary Government hand the management of the enormous Bicêtre Hôpital Genéral with its 3,850 patients and prisoners over to him. He would then build a great variety of timber Panopticons for the great variety of inmates, by way of an experiment.[9] But it was only in March 1792, when the death of Jeremy's father, Jeremiah Bentham, had made available enough capital to finance the venture directly, that overtures were made to Pitt (1st Lord of the Treasury) and Dundas (Secretary of State) to reconsider the matter of an English Penitentiary.[10] They were shown models, given lists of undertakings and the workings of the scheme were explained to them. In 1794 a second Penitentiary Act, this time composed by Jeremy Bentham himself, was passed easily through Parliament. It was, of course, perfectly fitted to its author's needs. The Bentham brothers, philosopher and engineer, were to have the running of the National Penitentiary, under a contract that specified financial obligations with exactitude, but left the planning and administration of the penitentiary largely up to them. As a preliminary payment £2,000 was disbursed by the Treasury,[11] and the brothers began the practical business of acquiring a site.

The most noticeable difference between the Blackstone and Eden penitentiaries and the Benthams' was that the latter was to be run under contract; the government would have no direct involvement in its management. Others saw this as regressive. One of the major aims of reform was to curtail the gaolers' autonomy in prisons. Why should the principle be abandoned at the behest of one gentleman? Yet Bentham insisted on it in his case, not because of any deep conviction of its general applicability (he heartily commended management by 'the united wisdom of the nation' as opposed to profiteering by contractors in the *View*)[12] and not because of a craving for the income so confidently expected from it, but because it would be a demonstration of the validity of his entire philosophical system. There is no other way to explain his fanatical devotion to this one idea and his profound disappointment at its final rejection. Wilberforce lamented, perhaps not without reason, that the failure of the Panopticon under conventional government had driven Bentham into Radicalism.[13] One of the philosopher's last works was a vindictive history of his pet scheme in which George III was portrayed as the arch-villain in a plot to prevent him realizing his dreams.[14]

In many other respects the Panopticon Penitentiary resembled its predecessors. The prisoners were to be properly fed, washed, clothed, aired and housed, they were to be kept isolated, first in solitary cells, later in compartments for three or more. They were to be put under a vigorous discipline and made to work. But there were differences too. Besides contract management, three features set it apart from anything that had gone before. The first and the most extraordinary was that the Panopticon brought the prison into the realm of utopia. Its construction and regulation were to determine the workings of a strange kind of model community, subject to the dictates of reason alone. Second was the raising of one organizing principle above all others in the design of the building — the Inspection Principle. Third was a new explanation of its function, replacing the pious language of Christian redemption with a comprehensive materialistic psychology. This psychology described the mechanisms of civilized society as dependant on the manipulation of only two driving forces: pleasure and pain; a manipulation which could be effected by controlling the form and content of our surroundings.

The Panopticon was more a contraption than a building. Its queer machinery was set to 'grinding rogues honest' with a degree of inexorability that even William Blackburn had not approached. Also, its scope was wider. Blackburn had begun to use his architecture as an instrumental part in the process of reform. Bentham now used it to generate and stabilize a complete social system. Here technology was not merely an aid to morality — it was a necessary precondition of the very morality it created.

Bentham's Utilitarian doctrine made ethics into nothing more or less than a system of checks and spurs that propelled human action one way or another. His Felecific Calculus was nothing more or less than a set of rules for determining human responses, and the Panopticon an arena for its enforcement. The technology of construction, the art of rule making, the business of production and the science of morality were all to be synchronized under the direction of a man who felt them to be subject to the same overriding rule.

The Panopticon was, in a very real sense, a physical extension of Jeremy Bentham, built to magnify his potency. He openly acknowledged this, describing it as 'a way of obtaining power, power of mind over mind, in a quantity hitherto without example'.[15] Monarchy, he thought, was 'the only tolerable form of government for such an empire', and he the philosopher king,[16] or, in Burke's rather less flattering metaphor, 'the spider in his web'.[17] When criticized for allowing himself so much power he responded with the assertion that this was exactly the *virtue* of the scheme.[18] Although in the 1790s the office of gaoler was still not 'very elevated', Bentham saw in it an opportunity for the practice of omniscience and omnipotence, for as gaoler he would be the Deity in a microcosm of his own making (Fig. 102).[19]

The form of the Panopticon building defined the power structure within it. In the 1787 scheme (illustrated in the misbegotten drawing, frequently reproduced as if it gave a representative picture; Fig. 103),[20] the governor was billeted with his family in a well-fenestrated cylindrical kiosk inside a much larger rotunda. The kiosk looked out across an intermediate space onto a circle of 192 cells four storeys high. All the light for the kiosk filtered into the middle of the rotunda through large windows in these encircling banks of cells. Hence the prisoners, themselves brightly illuminated, would be unable to see into the darkness of the kiosk, much as people out in the street cannot see into a house window. The privilege of those within this protected core — the governor, his family, assistants and visitors — was to observe the prisoners without themselves being seen to spy on them. To ensure this directional property blinds or curtains were to be hung over the kiosk windows, and the doors of the rooms inside were positioned so that they would not show up silhouettes when open. Family and friends were, by their presence, to contribute to the work of surveillance: 'It will supply in their instance the place of that great and constant enter-

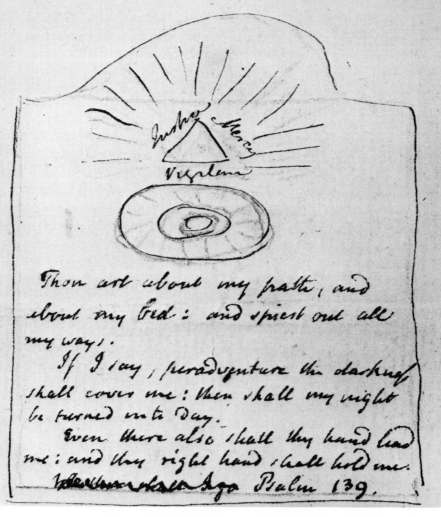

102. The 139th Psalm quoted by Jeremy Bentham in what appears
to have been a sketch layout for the frontispiece of *Panopticon*.

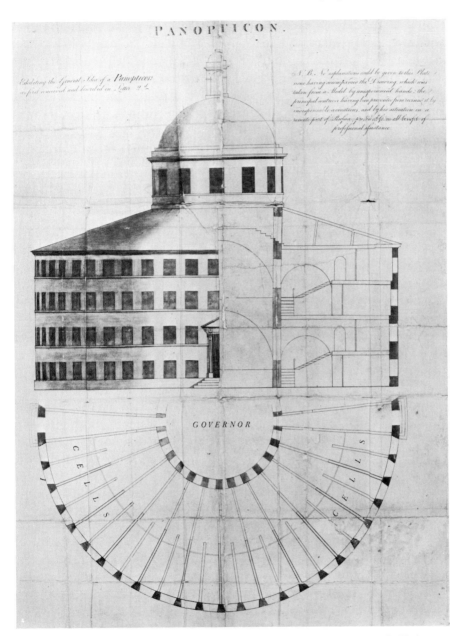

103. The Critchef Panopticon, 1787, section, elevation and half-plan.

tainment to the sedentary and vacant in towns, the looking out of windows. The scene, though confined, would be various and not altogether an unamusing one.'[21] This was all very well during daylight hours, but not during the night. So, in order to 'extend to night the security of day', Bentham proposed to fit a ring of innumerable small lamps around the outside of the Panopticon rotunda. Reflectors were to direct light back into the cells where a dim replica of daylight would suffice to maintain the prisoners in view of the master, still hidden in his shrouded lodge.[22]

In the mature scheme, as drawn up by Willey Reveley in 1791 (Figs. 104, 105, 106), the governor's house and the administrative offices were removed from the centre into an enlarged portico, appended to the rotunda, leaving only a single chamber in the middle. This was still to be 'the heart, which gives life and motion to this artificial body'.[23] The arrangement was now somewhat more complex, because the subordinate turnkeys had been expelled from the centre. They now inhabited a ring of inspection passageways ('annular galleries') between the centre and the cells. This innovation was Reveley's contribution to the plan.[24] Blackened on the inside, with screened openings facing towards the cells, the inspection passageways were also designed to render those within 'invisible from the outside'. Peripatetic turnkeys, thoughtfully provided with a portable writing desk and stool for the recording of irregularities and infractions, were to spend their day roving round and round watching the prisoners. Watching both prisoners and turnkeys was the governor, ensconced in his central chamber, which was 'pierced every inch or two with eyelet holes about the size of an ordinary silver spangle' and covered with coarse muslin. Thus the prisoners, sequestered from one another in their cells, would be under surveillance from a patrolling corps of invisible turnkeys, but the transactions between turnkeys and the prisoners would be under surveillance from the governor's muslin draped citadel. There were now three levels of authority in the hierarchy. Even the staff were to be subject to the logic of the 'commanding principle of inspection'. It was a principle that concentrated knowledge and, through knowledge, power in the hands of the governor to the exclusion of all others; 'Here issue all orders: here centre all reports.' There was even the possibility of extending this pyramid of authority to a fourth tier. Bentham made a sketch of a gigantic multiple Panopticon some time after 1824[25] in

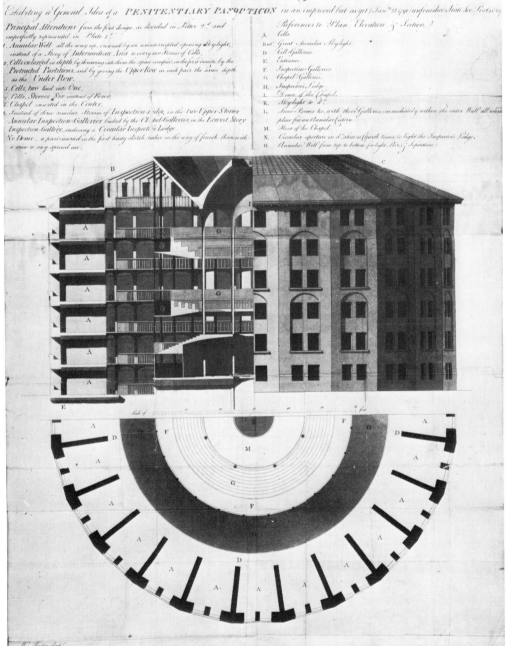

104. The 'Penitentiary Panopticon', Jeremy Bentham, Samuel Bentham and Willey Reveley, 1791, section, elevation and half-plan, corresponding closely but not exactly with the description in the *Postscript*.

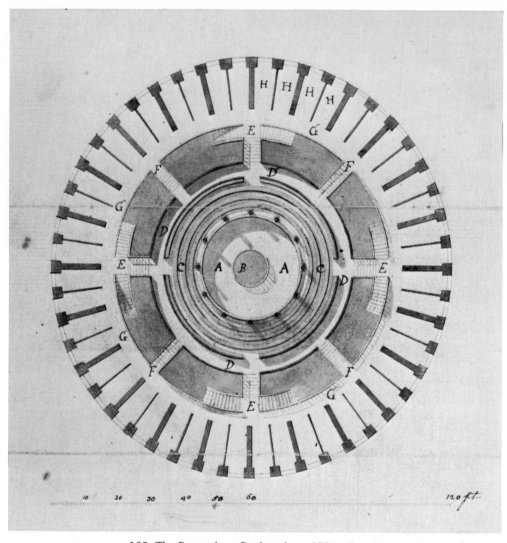

105. The Panopticon Penitentiary, 1791, plan. Drawing by Reveley.

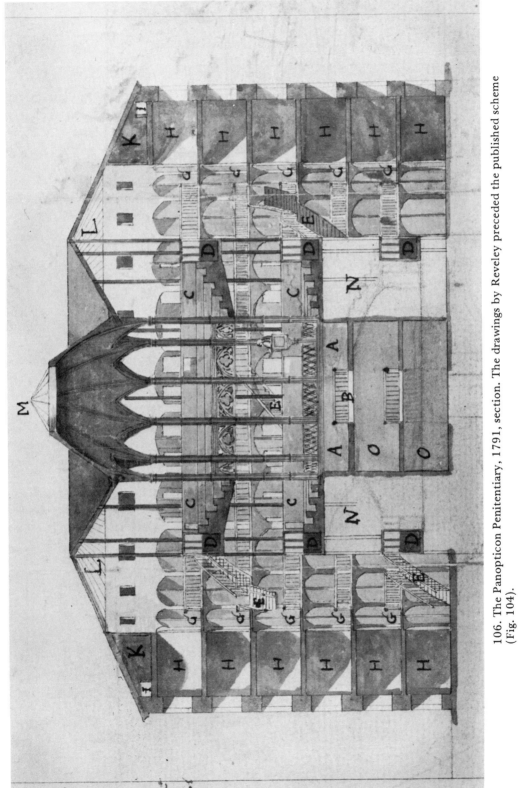

106. The Panopticon Penitentiary, 1791, section. The drawings by Reveley preceded the published scheme (Fig. 104).

which the governors of each segmental Panopticon were subject to scrutiny by a governor of governors (Fig. 107).

Bentham liked to draw attention to the similarity between the 'apparent omnipresence' of the invisible governor of the Panopticon and the ineffable qualities ascribed to God in the 139th Psalm.[26] The

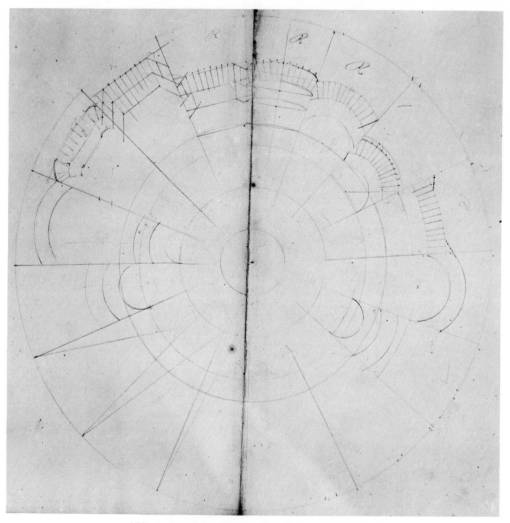

107. A sketch by Jeremy Bentham watermarked 1824, for 16 segmental Panopticons emanating from a common centre.

half facetious, half serious biblical analogy could be pushed further with the prisoners as mankind after the Fall and the turnkeys as angels. In an attempt to reinforce this structuring of human relationships through architecture, Bentham devised a lantern which extended the principle of 'seeing without being seen' about as far as it could go. A waisted cylinder, just large enough to seat one person inside, was to be placed near the geometrical centre of the building, reached by an enclosed spiral stair. The inspector would sit on a stool adjusted so that his head was within the waisted section of the lantern, where there were to be a multitude of small lenses (Fig. 108): 'The lantern might be of the thinness of paper: in short it might in that part (that of the apertures) be of paper, and then a pin-hole would be sufficient to give him a view.'[27] From this flimsy capsule an encompassing view of the entire

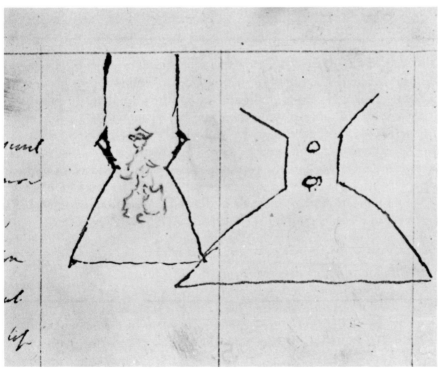

108. Marginal outlines of the inspection lantern from the Bentham Papers.

building was to be had. With the lantern the systematic application of a single principle encroached on the liberty of the governor to such an extent that he too became its prisoner as much as were the convicts under his charge, its concentric centripetal geometry fixing him in an exact position just so that he might fulfil the duties of his office.

'In a Panopticon prison one general problem applies to all . . . without exception or relaxation', said Bentham. The problem was to reveal to the governor every last detail of the life of his employees and prisoners, and to put in his hands the means to control them. This was the source of what the French architect, L.P. Baltard, later regarded as 'le génie de la mécanique' perfected by the English, whose prison buildings 'fonctionnassent comme une machine soumise a l'action d'un seul moteur'.[28] In this instance the *seul moteur* was working to increase the powers of the supervising eye. The building was disposed so that the sight lines from the governor's lodge and the inspection galleries penetrated every inch of space within the rotunda, with no corner hidden, but it was not only the power of sight that was increased. A system of tin 'conversation tubes' was to be installed, to work as an accoustical analogue of the system of visual surveillance. Bentham first envisaged an array of separate tubes from every cell, terminating in his central chamber.[29] The governor could pull wires inside the tubes to ring a bell at the other end, and so draw the attention of individual prisoners for instruction or reprimand. At the same time the 'slightest whisper' of every prisoner was transmitted to the lodge. Then of course, the slightest whisper of the governor was also transmitted to all the prisoners, which is perhaps why the conversation tubes were only to be found as a means of communication between turnkeys and governor in the 1791 scheme.[30]

This pinpoints an interesting feature of the Panopticon: the speaking tubes to the cells were discarded because they worked the same way in both directions — they were isotropic. Such a system was out of character in a building the function of which was to foster an unimpeded flow of 'useful' information towards the centre while simultaneously acting as an almost totally refractory medium to 'dangerous communication' in any other direction.[31] The Panopticon remained an essentially visual system not only because the watching eye was the most abstracted and disengaged of the organs of perception, a fitting medium for a philosopher of Bentham's temper, but also because it was, before the advent of electronics, much easier to construct an environment that was visually anisotropic. The attempt to design a similar system for the listening ear had to be abandoned because there was simply no way it could be accomplished.

Concealment, oversight and overhearing made possible the 'omniscience' and 'apparent omniscience' of the governor. These though, had to be balanced with 'omnipotence'; an equal measure of executive power to curb and command the inmates he knew so much about. In the end Bentham relied on the turnkeys in their inspection passageways to carry out his instructions, as they were within easy reach of the cells, and specified a ring of loud-hailers around his chamber with which to issue orders to the prisoners. There is, though, a brief description of a more ambitious if impractical plan to devise a complex of wire operated controls to open and close each of the cell doors from the central chamber.[32]

The directionality, making of the prisoners a 'multitude though not a crowd' from the point of view of the governor, but 'solitary and sequestered individuals' from their own point of view,[33] was the most important characteristic of the Panopticon's hierarchical configuration. There are buildings whose plan looks very much like that of the Panopticon. Usually the affinity is formal, not operational. Bentham always compared his penitentiary to the Ranelagh Pleasure Dome in Vauxhall Gardens (William Jones, started 1742). Except for its conscious irony, it does not seem an appropriate comparison. Ranelagh looked similar but it did not work in the same fashion. Most circular buildings were, like chapels and theatres, distributed in such a way that one central event could be observed by many people.[34] However, there had been two earlier types of building in which this principle was inverted, turning the stage into an observatory. Giulio Camillo's mysterious Memory Theatre, as described by Frances Yates, performed a quite different function to the Panopticon in a similar way (Fig. 109). A semi-circle of seven rising ranks of images were disported round a stage. Standing on this stage someone instructed in the meaning of the icons would find displayed before him 'all that the mind could conceive and all that was hidden in the soul'.[35] Like Panopticon it was a divulger of secrets. There was also a tradition going back to Lucullus of aviaries in which the observer, instead of being placed outside the cages, was placed in the centre looking outwards. Louis Le Vau adapted the idea in his

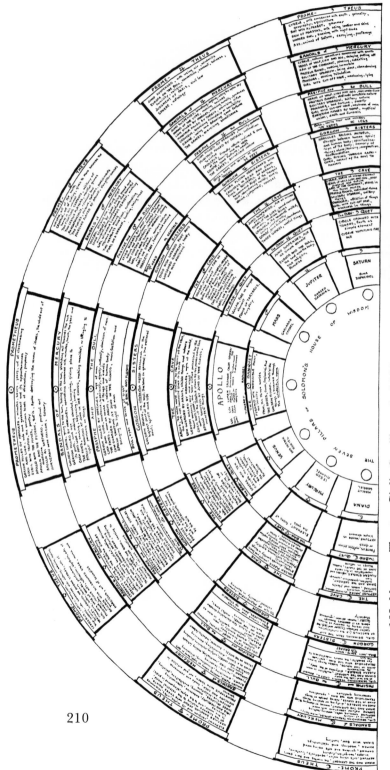

109. Memory Theatre, Giulio Camillo, early 1530s, reconstructed plan by Dame Frances Yates.

210

Versailles Menagerie for Louis XIV (Fig. 110), and others followed.[36] In all these buildings the privileged eye determined the shape of the world.

Although it was Blackburn who first made use of the inspection principle in prisons, Bentham let it be known that this 'simple idea in architecture'[37] belonged to himself and his brother, and even implied that Blackburn stole it to use in the Dublin Penitentiary.[38] Nevertheless, the Panopticon brought surveillance to a new perfection. Yet by introducing more and more inspection, more and more pervasive control, by orienting every aspect of design and construction to this one advantage and condensing the prison into a single volume, he changed the nature of the principle itself. Where at Northleach, Ipswich and Liverpool it was merely a means of peripheral policing (see pp. 144–7), in the Panopticon it became the very source of morality.

To explain the connection between surveillance and morality, a few words will have to be said about Bentham's Utilitarianism, which put a rationalistic interpretation upon the conventional reformist notions of imprisonment. In this he was heir to the French Sensationalists, particularly Claude Helvetius, with whose work he was certainly familiar. The epistemological root of Sensationalism and Utilitarianism alike was to be found in John Locke's theory that the mind of man was a *tabula rasa* at birth. According to Locke, ideas were put in the mind like words into a lexicon. Impressions were thus stored in the memory to be organized into patterns by the association of similar ideas. The result was coherent thought. Only two innate qualities of mind were required to explain the human condition: a desire for happiness and an aversion to misery. These were 'the constant springs and motives of all our actions'.[39] Locke went as far as to define good and evil in terms of pleasure and pain, yet felt it necessary to exclude moral thought from his otherwise mechanical model of human psychology. But Bentham and indeed many of the *philosophes* (d'Alembert, Condillac, d'Holbach, Condorcet and Helvetius) adopted Locke's epistemology as the foundation of morality as well as all other varieties of knowledge.

This connection of epistemology and morality made a great deal of difference. It meant that one could assert that 'in man all is sensation'.[40] It meant that the mind was capable of 'acquiring' moral ideas through the same channels as it might acquire ideas of colour and space – the senses. Sight, sound, smell, touch and taste; these were the ingredients

110. Versailles Menagerie, Louis Le Vau, started 1662.

of morality as surely as they were the foundations of the understanding. It meant that morality was a branch of psychology which itself was considered as an aspect of physiology. Free will and innate moral ideas could be dispensed with or could be reduced to incidental decorations. Because of this, Offray de la Mettrie, deciding that crimes were the result of involuntary spasms, called for the resignation of all judges so that physicians might take their place as the only profession competent to distinguish guilt from innocence.[41] Civilization was raised up on the elusive mechanisms within the mind, and nothing in the world could be of greater importance than the contents of this strange organ: 'Time eats away fetters of iron and steel, but has no effect upon habitual associations of ideas, except to strengthen them; and thus the immutable base of the strongest empires rests upon the soft fibres of the brain.'[42] Everything from artistic taste to the conception of Tristram Shandy could be put down to the association of ideas. What rendered it all reducible to an order was the simple tension between pleasure and pain. What made it a justification for the wholesale reconstruction of society was the concomitant belief that environmental conditions manufactured human responses.

The new psychology was applied to education, where Helvetius discovered that 'the true preceptors of a child are the *objects that surround him*' (my italics); these were now the 'instructors to whom he owes almost all his ideas'.[43] A graze on the elbow might lead to a more profound illumination of conscience than any amount of edifying literature. The sight and smell of a pot of flowers in an empty room might transform the sensibilities of a young man without a word being spoken.[44] Moral character was built up through a sequence of such events. In 'an infinity of minute articles, now regarded as insignificant' were to be found the seeds of virtue and vice. It was an American Professor of Chemistry, Benjamin Rush, who first attempted to catalogue these influences in his *Enquiry into the Influence of Physical Causes upon the Moral Faculty* (1786).[45] In this extraordinary work the determinants of moral behaviour were listed as follows: climate, diet, drinks, extreme hunger, diseases of the mind, idleness, excessive sleep, the effects of bodily pain, cleanliness, solitude, silence, music, eloquence of the pulpit, odours, airs and medicines. Each had its own effects. Dephlogisticated air, for instance, when taken into the lungs, 'produces cheerfulness, gentleness and serenity of mind'.[46] As for music, 'we are able to differentiate the virtues and vices of different nations, by their tunes, as certainly as by their laws'.[47] The influence of odours was demonstrated by the peculiar wickedness of those who lived in the sulphurous zone around Etna and Vesuvius. Most of Rush's physical causes, however, were not found in nature but were created artificially by man himself.

A question presented itself: was there not just a possibility that, having put this contingent universe of psychological influences under observation, its workings could be analysed, understood and then regulated? Could a society be brought under the thumb of reason solely through the reorganization of its institutions? If good and evil were not bred in the mind but in the 'infinity of articles' that surround us, then by ordering these articles in a certain way a certain quantity of good or evil would result. This was the tantalizing prospect: '*a situation in which it would be almost impossible for a man to be depraved, or wicked*, or at least *where there would be as little evil as possible*'.[48] These were the words of that obscure but influential French utopian Morelly, whose aim was to define and then bring into being such a situation. He chose the law as the medium of its creation, as did Helvetius, d'Holbach, Brissot and Beccaria.[49] Bentham too considered himself as first and foremost a composer of legal codes. Yet, the nation state was too large a thing altogether for there to be any certainty in it. 'To guide the motions of the human puppet', wrote Helvetius, 'it is necessary to know the wires by which he is moved.'[50] He might have added that it is also necessary to have the wires in one's grasp. The Panopticon, like the system of education thought out by Helvetius, like Rush's reformed Philadelphian prisons (see p. 318 below), like Fourier's Phalansteries, like Robert Owen's industrial community at New Lanark, and like Ledoux's Royal Salt Works[51] was an isolated and restricted society where the strings could be sorted out and their movements choreographed.

What distinguished the Panopticon from these utopian or institutional experiments was the lengths to which its designer was prepared to go in order to render its workings predictable through the agency of architecture. The vision of a community methodically governed into 'motions of course' gave Bentham deep satisfaction, so much so that he could eulogize his penitentiary thus:

Here may be observed the first opening of that sense of clockwork regularity, which it would be so easy to establish in so compact a microcosm. Certainty, promptitude and uniformity are the qualities which may here be displayed in the extreme. Action scarcely follows thought, quicker than execution might here be made to follow upon command.[52]

As has been pointed out, this kind of submissive social order was just as attractive to the general run of prison reformers. The Howardian prisons were, in the same way, conceived as a set of physical influences determining the morality of the inmates. Again, it was only the extremity — the 'pitch of perfection' — of Bentham's solution that distinguished it (Fig. 111).

Bentham's Utilitarian philosophy as laid out in *The Principles of Morals and Legislation* (published 1789) was an amalgam of the pleasure/pain principle, the association of ideas, materialism, and moral determinism. It differed little from French Sensationalism, except perhaps in its petty thoroughness. Put briefly, he maintained that the interest of an individual was his own happiness. His happiness was the pursuit of pleasure and the avoidance of pain. His life might therefore be expressed in the form of a double entry account of pleasures minus pains. An aggregate computation could be made for society as a whole and a figure given to a nation's felicity.[53] The business of government was to create a system of rewards (pleasures) and punishments (pains) that would promote the greatest happiness of the greatest number. The precise proportion of the pains and pleasures that went to make up human life could only be discovered by 'investigations as severe as mathematical ones, and beyond all comparison more intricate and extensive'.[54] It was the function of the Felicific Calculus to fix these precise proportions, but the calculus was applied to the Panopticon in a rather strange way. The fate of the convict was to suffer a certain amount of pain. It was only sensible that this pain should be to someone else's advantage;[55] consequently the arithmetic of pain and pleasure in a prison had to be expressed differently. In the special case of the Panopticon it thus became the greatest happiness of the contractor compatible with the least unhappiness of the convicts, which, as it turned out, was a classic formula for the exploitation of labour.

Bentham was such an avid partisan of his Penitentiary that his statements on it, which were after all very extensive, were not always consistent. By selective quotation a good argument could be made for his believing in moral reformation of the Howardian sort, yet on the whole it appears that he rejected it. He was after something else from his convicts, as is made clear in the statement that he knew 'of no test of reformation so plain or so sure as the improved value of their work'.[56] Profit was once again the measure.

The Panopticon was to be a factory with a monopoly of cheap labour

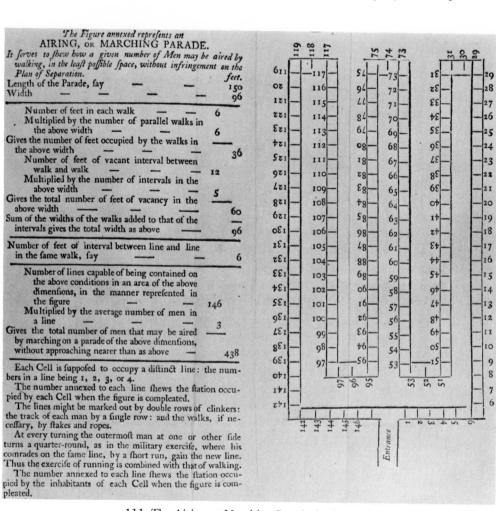

111. The Airing or Marching Parade for Panopticon prisoners, Jeremy Bentham, 1791.

protected by the state. 'What other manufacturers are there who reap their profits at the risk of other people, and who have the purse of their nation to support them, in case of any blameless failure?'[57] Where else could hands be prevented from combining for higher wages or getting drunk? Moreover, convict labourers *needed less* as they did not have to support their families. As in the mercantilist houses of correction, Bentham's prisoners were to be classified according to their ability to work, not according to the degree of their offence. The good hands, the capable hands, the promising hands, and the drones would be put to hard labour for maybe fifteen hours each day on a spare diet. Artificial light would allow as long a work day in winter as in summer. At first a diversity of trades were to be pursued in the penitentiary, but this idea gave way to that discovered by Adam Smith as the essence of rational production; a single large scale manufacturing process was to be broken down into a sequence of discrete operations — the division of labour. It too was overtaken in 1794, by which time Samuel Bentham had perfected his patent wood working machine. This was a mechanical planing device, originally run by a steam engine, redesigned so that it could be worked by the exertions of the convicts in their cells, in such a way that 'merely moving the machine answered all the purposes of completing manufacture'.[58] Labour could now be 'extracted from a class of persons on whose part neither dexterity, nor goodwill were to be reckoned upon'.[59]

As with contract management, the emphasis on material production was thought to be a grave fault in the Panopticon, which in some ways was closer to the Dutch Tuchthuis than were Blackstone and Eden's penitentiaries. However, this was a question of motive rather than a question of administrative practice. The day to day regime in the Panopticon would have been remarkably close to that within a good Howardian prison. In a manner of speaking, Bentham seems to have taken the soul out of the structure of Christian penitence and made thoroughly good use of the carcass. His rationalist penology borrowed its forms largely from the pietistic tradition.

Production was Bentham's pleasure and the convicts' pain, but his concern went much further than this, and indeed one would expect no less from someone who, in the estimation of the Procès Verbal, 'breathed the most ardent love of humanity',[60] and who, in his own estimation, was very probably 'the most benevolent man that ever lived'.[61] Bentham felt no vindictiveness towards malefactors; the very idea was ruled out by his philosophy. Convicts were distinguished from the common run of people 'more by suffering than by guilt'.[62] The root of their immorality was to be found in the quality of their minds, which were 'weak and disordered'. Perpetual surveillance made it possible to forestall their folly: 'Delinquents are a peculiar race of beings, who require unremitted inspection. Their weakness consists in yielding to the seductions of the passing moment.'[63] The benevolence of inspection was in its capacity to prevent transgressions ever taking place. Careless infractions were to be controlled by eliminating all temptation and by making discovery certain. Prescience would take the place of ineffectual punishments. What could be kinder? The minds of delinquents might be peculiarly weak, and their habitual associations less strong, but in all else they were fairly typical. It was thus as a sample of humanity – a humanity that Bentham saw as more or less universally 'weak and disordered' – that they took their place within the Panopticon Penitentiary.

The principle was not restricted to penitentiaries. Anything that required government could be accomplished better in a Panopticon. Proposals for bridewells, houses of industry, poorhouses, lazarettos, magdalen houses, factories, madhouses, hospitals, schools (Fig. 112), institutions for the deaf, dumb and blind, nurseries and orphanages were worked out by Bentham at one time or another.[64] After the smooth passage of his Penitentiary Act he seems to have been overtaken with a boundless enthusiasm for Panopticons, and his manuscripts for that period are littered with odd fragments extending the principle ever more widely. In one of these can be found plans for a Panopticon chicken coop called the Ptenotrophium.[65] In another the penitentiary was to be the nucleus of a colony which would include the Sotimion, for unsupported mothers, the Paedotrophium, a nursery for their infants, and, since the site was some distance from the metropolis, a hill tavern for the entertainment of visitors curious to inspect these establishments. The tavern was a most outlandish conception, being everything that the Panopticon was not; a luxurious orchestration of titillating contrivances including 'rooms perfumed by invisible electrical [?] fountains of rose water', magic lantern exhibitions, 'columns of hollow glass filled with coloured fluids' and more traditional tromp l'oeil. Humphrey Repton was to landscape the site.[66] In projects like the Paedotrophium the autarkic utopianism of the Panopticons was

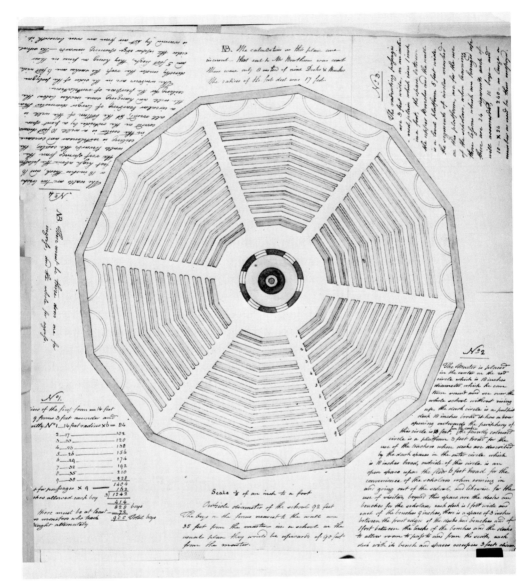

112. The Chrestomathic Schoolhouse, Jeremy Bentham, 1816, plan.

most amply revealed. Describing himself as a 'child fancier', Bentham confessed that his aim was to breed up a 'score of pretty children' so as to 'make good subjects of them'.[67] All the evidence brings us back to the same point. The Panopticon was an artificial universe, an enclave of reason and order within a larger society still hopelessly irregular and ectopic. Perhaps it was not a universal remedy, but it was certainly a universal rectifier. As such, Bentham's is the only prison ever to have been conceived as a possible model for the good society.[68]

Upon one thing all historians are agreed: the Panopticon was a singularly unconventional piece of engineering. Every page of description contains some architectural innovation, or some technical refinement. Because Jeremy Bentham was prone to push things just that bit beyond the point of feasibility, all this has too often been dismissed as impractical or even childish. The prevailing view was summed up by Gilbert Geis' statement that 'the philosophy of the proposed prison . . . was admirable, but the precise method of carrying it out often shows more vivid imagination than practical knowledge'.[69] A similar criticism was being made by Robert Edington as early as 1803. This dividing of the Panopticon into two parts, a philosophical idea about punishing, which was good, and an instrument for the realization of that idea, which was not so good, deserves close scrutiny. Those who accept it find the faults of the Panopticon in its technical insufficiency — nothing more. This seems a very odd notion, especially so when the technological eccentricities of it are put into perspective.

Together with the admittedly improbable items, such as the governor's lantern and the wire operated doors, came a number of well-considered and fascinating advances in construction and servicing. Two of these, the use of iron and glass and the design of an integrated heating and ventilating system, are of some interest because of the incidental light they throw on the development of modern building technology.

'They will all get out', observed the Lord Lieutenant of Ireland when shown the Panopticon Penitentiary plan.[70] Reveley had been instructed to put in as much window as possible, so that by opening up the rotunda wall, the interior would be illuminated.[71] This he had done, as far as it was possible in a load-bearing brick structure (Fig. 105). Bentham was intrigued by the properties of glass. He indulged himself by inventing curious glass ornaments and decorations for the Panopticon Hill Tavern. Lucid transparency was very much to his taste, as is evident from his recollection of a French fairy-tale in which the heroine had been imprisoned in a palace of solid glass: 'of this archetype the Panopticon was as near a similitude as the limited power of human art could admit'.[72] The problem was one of structure. The dissipation of the outer wall could only go so far with masonry construction. In the Reveley scheme (Jan. 1791) the outer ring of vaulted cells was retained for durability and incombustibility, but within this circle a new structural material was tried out: iron. Once the idea of the family lodge was dispensed with it became possible to open up the whole interior. 'Space took the place of matter from the bottom of the building to the top.'[73] Since the conception relied on a clear field of vision through 360 degrees, this was a very useful improvement. Between them the Bentham brothers and Reveley devised a double ring of iron columns upon which rested the roof, the inspection galleries and two tiers of chapel seating, which Jeremy had felt obliged to include in his scheme for the sake of convention (Figs. 104, 106). 'Airiness, lightsomeness, economy and increased security' were the benefits achieved through the use of this slender open palisade inside the rotunda. Iron, unlike most building materials, was 'impregnable to putrid contagion' as well. A hollow tube section was chosen. Not only was it strong; it could serve a double purpose. Cast iron water pipes might be used as columns and chimneys:

Upon enquiry at a great foundry where it is cast for such purposes [i.e. rain pipe], I learnt that in that manufactory it could be cast hollow for a length of 12 feet, but no more. Upon consulting with my professional advisor, I was informed that that length could be made to suffice and it occurred to him that . . . some might be made to answer the purpose of water-pipes for conveying the water from the roof; and to me that others might be made to serve for chimneys — articles for which it might otherwise be not altogether easy, in a building of so peculiar construction to find a convenient place.[74]

By integrating the services into the columns further space savings were made. To use iron for free standing structural supports in a building this size was adventurous, to say the least. There can be no doubt that the Benthams were going to see it through, for there were soon to be complaints that 'several thousand pounds' had been spent on cast iron work for the frame of the building which was left to rust on site for want of government approval.[75]

However, the most extensive use of iron and glass was not in the penitentiary but in a Panopticon House of Industry designed by Samuel

Bentham in collaboration with the architect Samuel Bunce in 1797.[76]
Pitt's ill-received Poor Bill had set Jeremy Bentham off on a campaign
to institutionalize the nation's paupers as well as its convicts. His influence on Chadwick and the 1834 Poor Law is well known. There were,
he surmised, about half a million paupers up and down the country. In
two decades the number would probably double, but in the meantime
250 large Panopticons to house 2,000 inmates spread evenly over
England and Wales on a 10 2/3 mile square grid, and administered by a
single National Charity Company, would solve the immediate difficulties.[77] The 250 houses of industry were all to be the same, each a
regular twelve sided polygon framed in iron and sheathed in glass in
order to effect a 'universal transparency' within for the sake of inspection (Fig. 113). Mirrors were to be fixed up around the centre to direct
extra light into the governor's apartments and to give him unusual views
of the paupers at work. The external skin of small glass panes was held
in a network of iron leadings, mullions, transoms, columns and lintels,
with not one inch of walling. The effect, though hardly beautiful in its
simplicity, was nevertheless uncompromising. Nothing quite like it
would be seen again until the middle of the next century.[78]

The combination of iron, or steel, and glass to create unified, brightly
illuminated interior spaces is familiar in modern architecture. What is
less familiar is the early appearance of the same combination as part of
a scheme to impose an unremitting rule on the patterns of human
action. The function of inspection was greatly enhanced by the use of
these materials. With masonry, nothing like the same panorama could
have been achieved. Considerations of economy and aesthetics played
their part, but this eminently modern construction was justified primarily in terms of a philosophy of government, based on an idea about
the way the human mind worked. In other words, it was an essay in the
engineering of behaviour through the manipulation of architectural form.

Architecture, now an item impinging on the Felicific Calculus, was
tacitly redefined. It became not just the container, but the organizer of
human functions: an active agency in the formation of experience and
morality. If Blackburn's work stood at the very edge of a practice
stretching back to the Renaissance, of dovetailing formal composition
with the convenient distribution of space, Bentham's was outside it. In
the Panopticon the principle of utility was to have been translated
directly into architecture without the intervention of academic rules of

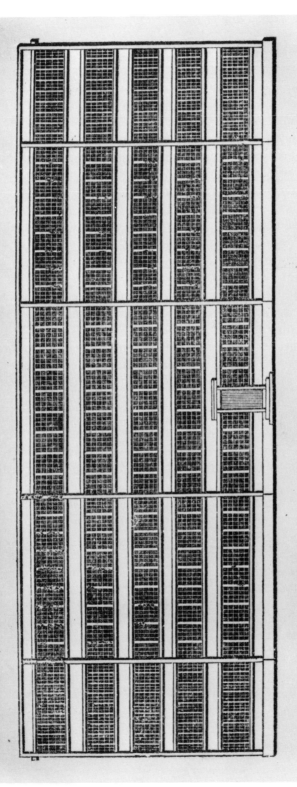

113. Panopticon House of Industry, Samuel Bentham and Samuel Bunce, 1797.

composition. While it is ironic that the act of designing was finally divorced from visualization in a project so fundamentally concerned with the eye, the significant thing was the change in focus: the eye of the beholder and of the designer no longer rested on the building (as it did for example in Ledoux's famous contemporary engraving of the theatre at Besançon reflected on a retina) but on the human figures within it.

Art did have its place, though. Bentham was not exactly an iconoclast. He did not believe that any harm would come from the use of images as such, but he regarded beauty as comparable to any other source of pleasure, claiming that for the philosopher the game of push-pin was of equal value to the best poetry and music, so long as the resulting quantum of joy was the same.[79] No place was left for art in his chrestomathic scheme of education. There was no system in it. It was too dependent on the individual vagaries and foibles of the imagination. But art need not only be used for the production of pleasure, for there was another side to it. Imagery could evoke painful impressions on the mind as well as pleasurable ones, and painful impressions could be manufactured more surely. When considering a mass-produced bas-relief to be fixed above the entry of all local authority penitentiaries, Bentham paid minute attention to the meaning of what was to be depicted. A similar relief at Metz House of Correction showed stags, boars and lions yoked to a cart driven by the governor. As these animals could never be domesticated, it implied that after imprisonment criminals remained untamed, and gave the impression that the authorities were attempting the impossible.[80] He would have foxes and wolves instead to make the prospect seem a little more promising. To heighten the impression of fear and guilt in the Panopticon, he took heed of the practices of the Spanish Inquisition, his aim being to turn the chapel into an 'auto de fe' with the prisoners in hideous or dolorous masks.[81] Art too was an instrument of government, but only in its fearful forms. It was with this unexplored nether-region of iconography and expression that Bentham concerned himself. The aesthetics of pleasure were of no interest at all to him except as a personal diversion.

The early Panopticon scheme was shown to John Howard, who criticized its lack of ventilation.[82] By condensing the prison back into a single enclosed volume, salubrity had been sacrificed to surveillance. Recognizing the truth in this, Bentham set to discover a method of ventilating the interior without modifying the form of the building. He never really solved the problem, but on his way to doing so he more or less inadvertently stumbled on something of more lasting importance. The 1779 Act required that workrooms be heated. In the Panopticon no part of the interior could be warmed independently of the rest, as all spaces interpenetrated. The whole building had therefore to be warmed or nothing at all. Seeing that if the whole had to be ventilated and the whole had to be warmed, Bentham also saw that the two pro-cesses could be combined — air could be the medium of heating. In pursuit of this insight he developed something very similar to the thermo-ventilation plant so extensively used in early Victorian insti-tutions. With iron, glass and the inspection principle Bentham let no one go in doubt of his originality; but not so with heating and venti-lation, which as much as anything was his (or more likely Samuel's) invention.

The principle of ventilation adopted by Blackburn with its uncon-trollable percolations of air was replaced by an organized, controlled system of air movement driven by convection. Fresh air was to be drawn through an 'aeriduct' into a Franklin stove under the centre of the rotunda. Once heated it would be distributed through a radial array of tubes out towards the cells (Fig. 114). It had been pointed out to Bentham that the warm air would tend to rise in the intermediary space without passing through the cells, so he designed a chain of vertical, inter-linked ventilator tubes to foster air movement in this zone as well.[83] The tubes were to stand in the centre of each cell to reduce the risk of their being used covertly for conversation between prisoners. In 1794 Bentham thought that he had solved the two problems of dis-tributing warm air through the building and evacuating noxious effluvia with the ventilator tubes. By 1797 he had absorbed the significance of Maret's erroneous experiments (see p. 113), and supplemented the tubes with extracts at floor level in each room to dispose of 'the heavy part of the foul air' as well.[84] This was the arrangement adopted by Jebb at Pentonville. In its development, as with the other Panopticon systems, the Bentham brothers put technology in the service of a moral order, so that the building became a fulcrum for the exertion of authority. Every function centralized was an increase, not of efficiency or economy, but of power. The prisoner's every need was to be satisfied by an ever more complicated machinery for no other reason than to divest him of all influence over those needs. So the earliest attempt to supply a compre-

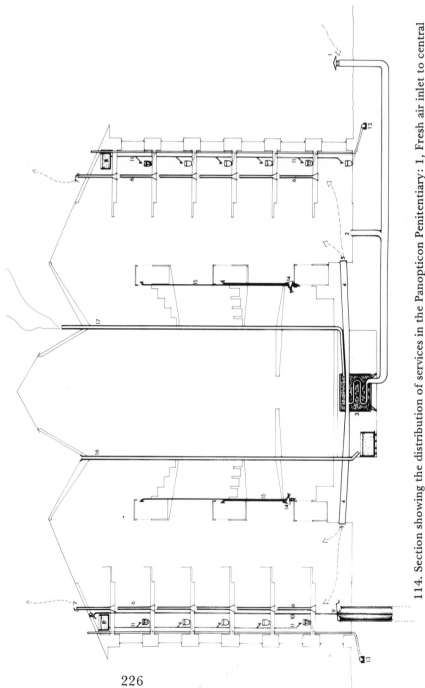

114. Section showing the distribution of services in the Panopticon Penitentiary: 1, Fresh air inlet to central stove; 2, Recirculated air inlet; 3, Modified Franklin stove; 4, Radial hot air ducts; 5, Hot air outlets; 6, Ventilation tubes to draw air through cells; 7, Valve outlet; 8, Annular fresh water cistern; 9, Well and pump; 10, Water supply to cistern; 11, Individual water supply stacks serving each cell; 12, Privies and soil stacks in each cell; 13, Closed sewer; 14, Loud hailer for general commands; 15, Tin speaking tubes from governor to turnkeys' galleries; 16, Structural iron rainwater pipe leading to storage tank for fire-fighting in sub-basement; 17, Structural iron flues from stove.

226

hensive technology of services arose from a desire to dominate, not a desire to serve.

The first obstacle in the way of a Panopticon Penitentiary was Lord Spencer, whose estates included the Battersea site. He was unhappy with Bentham's proposals, or indeed anyone else's, to build a prison there,[85] even after he had been assured that a Panopticon would be 'an ornament to the neighbourhood', drawing inquisitive persons of good quality from many miles around, as did Hanway's Magdalen House and Bedlam.[86] In 1797 a sympathetic Parliamentary Finance Committee, consisting of two close friends and a relative of Bentham's, reviewed the matter and advised him to seek a new site, since it was clear that Lord Spencer was not inclined to sell. Fruitless negotiations at Tothill Fields, south-east London and Woolwich followed, and Bentham grumbled about sites which vanished at his approach. By June 1798 he claimed to have spent £9,000 over and above the £2,000 already received.[87] Finally he used his own capital to purchase a marshy site at Millbank from the Earl of Salisbury. Still he could get no commitment from the evasive Treasury bureaucracy nor from the King himself. The Panopticon was out of favour. His first response was to offer a variety of compromise deals: why could he not take over one of the Thames hulks in the meantime? Should he not build a Temporary Panopticon of wood as an interim measure?[88] Still no decision was forthcoming. By 1800 he really had the bit between his teeth. Incensed by the Treasury's diffidence he threatened to get embarrassing motions called in the House, and, with open disregard for his friend Nepean, who was his source of information, accused officials of having confided that they hated the very sight of him.[89] Overtures were made, offering compensation, which served only to confirm Bentham's fears and increase his irascibility. The business dragged on until 1811 when, on the recommendations of the Holford Committee, whose members were suspicious of the impious maverick philosopher, the contract management of prisons was declared illegal. In 1813 the Treasury released £23,000 compensation to Bentham, who was now thoroughly embittered by his experiences.

It should be made quite clear that the Holford Committee did not object to the inspection principle, neither did they object to Jeremy Bentham as governor (or they said they did not, which is not quite the same thing). What they objected to was the fact of the penitentiary being outside government control in the hands of a private individual.[90] The Panopticon Penitentiary floundered because it was to have been managed by contract, but the inspection principle upon which its design was based became the unifying feature of early-nineteenth-century prison architecture.

What is perhaps surprising, considering the wide influence of the inspection principle, was the infrequent copying of the Panopticon form. Only three rotunda prisons were constructed in Britain. First was Robert Adam's Edinburgh Bridewell. Bentham had approached Adam in May 1791, after a disagreement with Willey Reveley, with every intention of inviting Adam to take Reveley's place.[91] At that time Adam's designs for the Edinburgh Bridewell were multiple courtyard plans in an academic neo-classical idiom,[92] but having seen the Panopticon he drastically revised his scheme, creating a semi-circular inspection house of four storeys (Fig. 117). The abundantly castellated building, nearing completion in 1795, borrowed the plan, but not the mechanical systems from Bentham's prototype.[93] The same could be said of Gandy's small Female Felons' Wing at Lancaster Castle Gaol (Fig. 118), built much later, between 1818 and 1821. Here centripetal geometry and internalized inspection were considered so successful that the Male Wing was remodelled on similar lines. In this last building, inspection, which had been interpreted in the Female Wing and at Edinburgh solely as a principle of architectural planning — a pattern of distribution for walls — was extended to a crude acoustic surveillance as well. The officer in his station was:

enabled not only to inspect the rooms which are on the same floor with his own apartment, but also to overlook the prisoners in the rooms below, through conveying apertures in the ceilings, which terminate in small openings next to the point of view. This ingenious contrivance has, besides, the advantage of conveying sounds from the lower rooms to the officer's apartment above.[94]

The word Panopticon was soon stretched to cover radiating wing or polygonal terrace plans arranged round a central observatory and became identified particularly with the radiating form. This confusion was encouraged by Samuel Bentham's wife, Maria Sophia, who, as late as 1853, was attempting to impress on the public that her husband and not Jeremy had invented it.[95] Samuel had indeed used various plan forms in his several 'Panopticon' projects after Critchef. Some, like the Woolwich Cadet School (1797, not built), were polygonal terraces strung round an inspection pavilion; others, like the Naval Dockyard for Sheerness (1812, not built; Fig. 119) and the Ochta School of Arts and Crafts, were radiating wings on a central hub.[96]

The direct influence of the Panopticon would be felt intermittently into the twentieth century (Figs. 120, 121), but in Samuel's projects, as in the greater number of early-nineteenth-century prisons, inspection was accommodated to a less demanding technology. What it lost in the way of omniscience, omnipotence and omnipresence it gained in every-

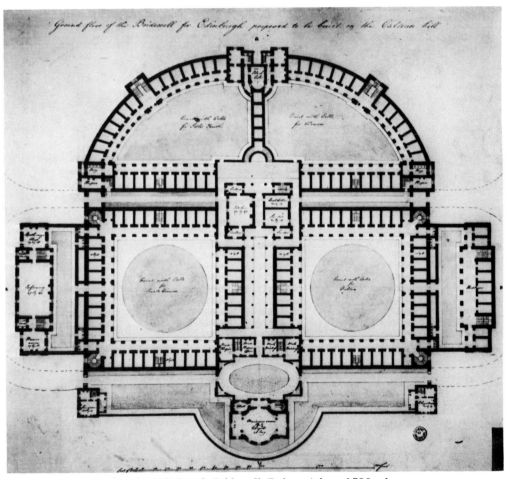

115. Project for Edinburgh Bridewell, Robert Adam, 1790, plan.

day practicability. What it lost in totality it gained in typicality. Not until Joshua Jebb's Pentonville was the attempt to construct an entirely predictable, synthetic reforming environment repeated. Only then were architecture and engineering amalgamated, as they had been in the Panopticon, in a final attempt to prove the moral effects of sensation on the mind.

116. Edinburgh Bridewell, Robert Adam, 1790, elevation and section.

117. Edinburgh Bridewell, Robert Adam, plan as executed, 1791–5.

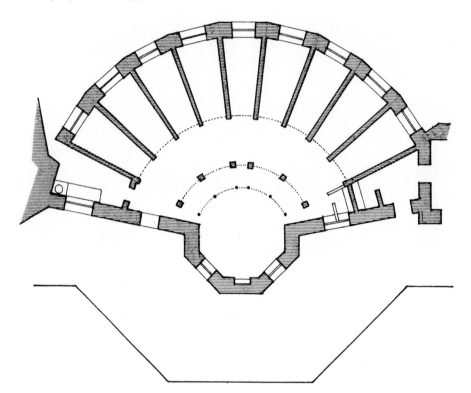

118. Lancaster Castle Gaol, Female Wing, J.M. Gandy, 1818–21,
plan.

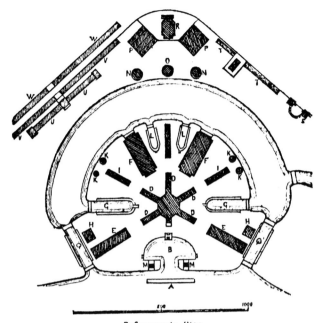

References to Plan.

A. Floating Breakwater.
B. Boat Cove.
C. Offices.
D. Storehouses and Workshops.
E. Sallery and Riggery, and Present use
    Storehouses.
F. Covered Docks.
G. Docks.
H. Receiving Rooms.
I. Timber Seasoning Houses.
K. Deal Seasoning Houses.
L. Docks.

M. (between L, L,) Boat house.
M. (near B) Master Attendant, and
    Foreman afloat.
N. Mast Store Towers.
O. Masting Tower.
P. Working Mast Towers.
Q. Entrance Locks or Docks.
R. Chapel.
S. Entrance Gate.
T. Officers' Houses.
U. Seminary of Naval Arts.
V, W. Artificers' Houses.

119. Unexecuted plan for the development of Sheerness Dockyards,
Samuel Bentham, 1812.

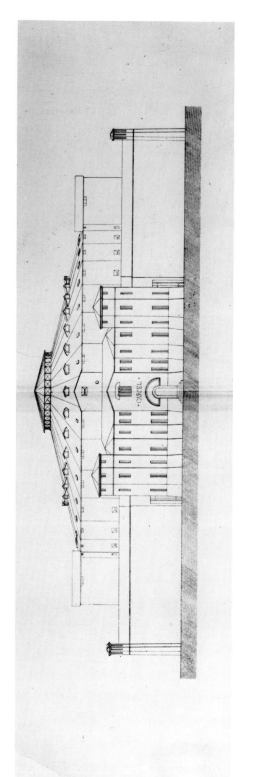

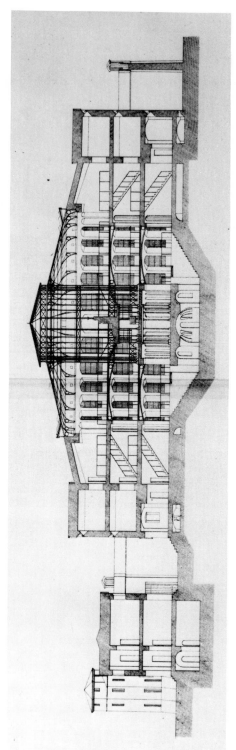

120. Project for a Departmental Prison, Abel Blouet, 1841.

DOORLESS PRISON-CELLS : CUBA'S GREAT EXPERIMENT IN PENOLOGY.

121. Panopticon rotunda, Isle of Pines, Cuba, 1932, from *Illustrated London News.*

6   Classification, inspection and labour

The climate of improvement

Between 1800 and 1832 the English local prison system was consistently enlarged. Almost every year would see the inception of at least one substantial new prison or the complete rebuilding of an old one.[1] Altogether there were to be more than 50 such undertakings, producing familiar yet distinct landmarks beyond the edge of towns and cities. In the same period the average prison population doubled from roughly 7,000 to 14,000 (Fig. 217).[2] The total number of prison institutions dwindled as the tiny, decaying cottage bridewells and empty gaol houses were closed, but the size of new prisons increased. In the early years of the century the ten largest contained 2,299 inmates; by Michaelmas 1833 they contained 3,997 (Fig. 122).[3] This consolidation of the national system, concentrating more prisoners into fewer prisons, was important because it affected both administration and architecture, and would eventually contribute to a second crisis in prison design, but the statistical picture also shows how radically the prison system had been altered by the 1830s. The Howardian Reforms had been far more effective than is generally realized, but when James Neild, following in the wake of Howard, travelled to every gaol and bridewell in the country between 1800 and 1806 he found that the reformed prisons were still no more than a solid rump on an attenuated body. All the old practices, liberal and exploitative, could still be witnessed in the rest. Many of the buildings were the same, or worse than they had been 30 years before.

In 1833, however, the picture was very different. By this time what were referred to as 'old' prisons were none other than those built in the 1780s, anything more ancient having been demolished, turned over to less exacting uses or sold off. Explicit institutional regulation had entirely replaced traditional and commercial practices in common gaols

236

and houses of correction. Although survivals were still to be found in some debtors' gaols, nearly every vestige of prison history prior to 1779 had been erased.

These were the years in which the first transformation of the prison system was completed. It was the unfurling of a pattern derived in large part from familiar precepts. The reformed prisons matured, grew more uniform, became more organized and reached a point beyond which they could not advance, but Howard was still the guiding light, immorality was still conceived as epidemical, the imposition of central authority was still understood to be essential and the reformation of character was still the aim. The early-nineteenth-century prisons were thus organs of a persistent ideology; their design was less a tentative search for the points of contact between architecture, conduct and morality, more a methodical application of 'general principles of construction' in search of increased certainty and effectiveness. William Blackburn had devised a repertoire of techniques; Jeremy Bentham had singled out a crucial unifying precept of design. The nineteenth-century architects moderated what Blackburn and Bentham had left them, discarded the unnecessary and the visionary to synthesize their inheritance into a typical form; a first genotype of the prison — which, as it happens, was superceded almost as soon as it was perfected.

At the beginning of this consolidation, in 1808, the architect Richard Ingleman described the state of the 'science of prison building' as it appeared to him. It was, he said, in the doldrums. William Blackburn, the most gifted interpreter of Howard's ideas, was still without peer, but even his buildings were grossly deficient. Their oak paling fences were already rotting and useless, they afforded little or no inspection, different classes on different floors freely communicated with one another through ventilation gratings, they contained too many sleeping cells, too few workrooms, and prisoners could sometimes see over the boundary walls from the upper stories. Despite all this, Ingleman had to agree that Blackburn's prisons were better than anyone else's, because few other architects had a sufficient grasp of principles. After the deaths of Howard and Blackburn 'the art of prison building became at first stationary, and then retrograde'.[4] This is how it appeared, but although little seemed to be going on, George Byfield's Bury St Edmunds Gaol of 1802–3 (Fig. 123) and Ingleman's own designs for Southwell House of Correction in 1807 and Devizes house of Cor-

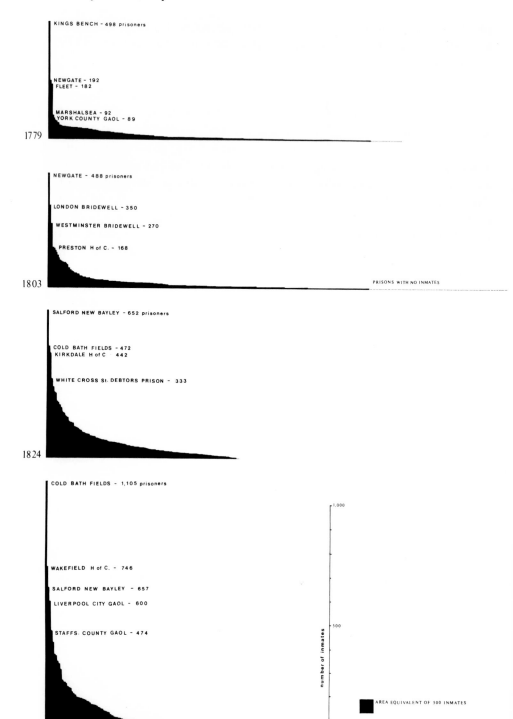

KINGS BENCH - 498 prisoners

NEWGATE - 192
FLEET - 182

MARSHALSEA - 92
YORK COUNTY GAOL - 89

1779

NEWGATE - 488 prisoners

LONDON BRIDEWELL - 350

WESTMINSTER BRIDEWELL - 270

PRESTON H of C. - 168

1803   PRISONS WITH NO INMATES

SALFORD NEW BAYLEY - 652 prisoners

COLD BATH FIELDS - 472
KIRKDALE H of C   442

WHITE CROSS St. DEBTORS PRISON - 333

1824

COLD BATH FIELDS - 1,105 prisoners

WAKEFIELD H of C. - 746

SALFORD NEW BAYLEY - 657

LIVERPOOL CITY GAOL - 600

STAFFS. COUNTY GAOL - 474

1843

number of inmates

1,000

500

AREA EQUIVALENT OF 500 INMATES

50   100
number of institutions

rection in 1808 (Fig. 124) had already begun to push the prison into two similar but distinct forms, the radial and the polygonal.

Whether prison architecture would thrive from this point onward was seen to depend on two things: the devising of new techniques and the understanding of principles. In the event architects were unable to establish undisputed claim to either, for while there were perhaps fewer amateurs intruding into the field of design than in the 1780s, there was a countervailing concentration of independent expertise on the subject of prisons, challenging that from within the architectural profession. This new body of knowledge, concerning discipline, management and construction, centred on the Society for the Improvement of Prison Discipline and for the Reformation of Young Offenders (S.I.P.D.), set up in 1816 by three anti-slavers, Lushington, Harbord and Buxton. In fact the S.I.P.D. was not a new organization but the confluence of two existing bodies, the Society for the Diffusion of Knowledge Upon the Punishment of Death and the Improvement of Prison Discipline (founded in 1801) involving Basil Montagu, Samuel Hoare and the Gurneys, and the Society for Investigating the Cause of the Increase of Juvenile Delinquency, which in 1815 had made a survey of youth in the nation's gaols.[5] Out of their campaigns against hanging and for the protection of the young arose the amalgamated society which was to remove emphasis from prisoners and legislation and place it on prisons and administration.

The S.I.P.D. dominated the theory and practice of prison management and design from 1818 until well into the 1830s. At its core were philanthropists like Samuel Hoare, the brother-in-law of Elizabeth Fry, William Crawford, who was also to play an important part in reintro-

122. *Opposite*. The number of inmates in prisons (England and Wales) 1779–1843. The four profiles were built up by arranging the prisons according to the size of their population. The height records the number of inmates in each prison. The area of each profile is equivalent to the total prison population, the overall length to the total number of institutions. The noticeable leftward shift during the nineteenth century adds weight to the contention that not just a few reformed prisons but the entire system had been consolidated before the erection of Pentonville.

Sources: for 1779, Howard, *State of the Prisons*, 4th edn; for 1803 (averaged for the years between 1800 and 1806), Neild, *General State of the Prisons*; for 1824 and 1843, *P.P.*, Gaol Returns, Schedule B (1825 and 1844).

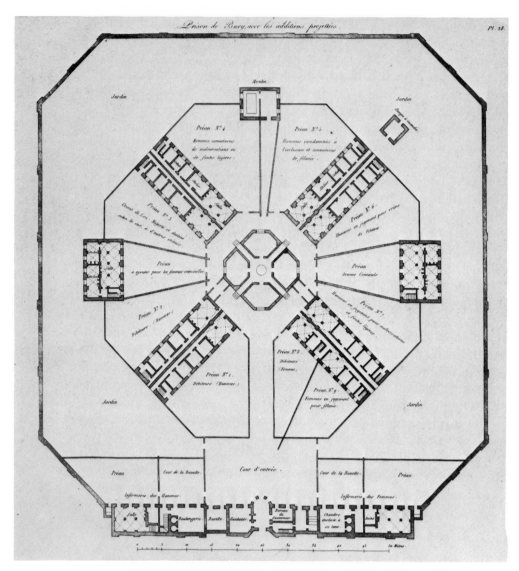

123. Bury St Edmunds County Gaol, George Byfield and John Orridge, 1802–3, ground plan. Originally a simple four wing plan; the other pavilions were added later.

ducing solitude during the thirties and forties, and Thomas Fowell Buxton, who helped to establish the society. But the S.I.P.D. was able to engage the active support of more illustrious and well-connected figures. In 1826 the list of vice-presidents alone comprised a duke, a marquis, 11 earls, 4 bishops, 11 lords, 15 Members of Parliament and one untitled gentleman, none other than William Wilberforce. Society members were customarily included on government commissions and

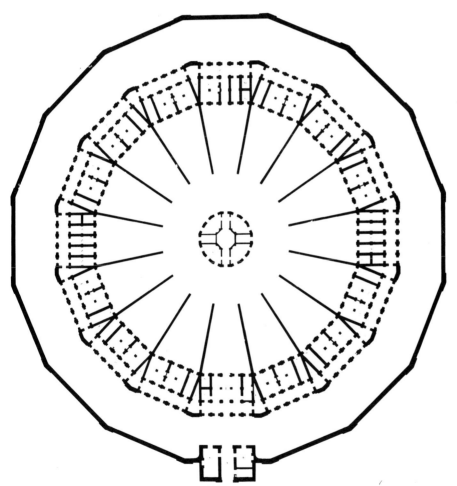

124. Devizes House of Correction, Richard Ingleman, 1808—17, ground plan.

enquiries into prisons. Extending influence in yet another direction, the S.I.P.D. published detailed handbooks on the regulation and construction of prisons.

Two works, *Rules Proposed for the Government of Gaols, Houses of Correction and Penitentiaries* (1820) and *Remarks on the Form and Construction of Prisons* (1826), form a landmark in prison history, not just because of their direct influence on subsequent events, and not only as evidence of the S.I.P.D.'s martialling of knowledge, but because they illustrate the mentality of early-nineteenth-century improvement more clearly than any other documents. The language was slightly different from that of earlier years, its tenor more moderate, its claims less sweeping, its bias subtly skewed away from general questions of morality towards practical issues. Unlike the reformist literature of the 1770s and 1780s, the S.I.P.D. publications did not deal with free will, criminal culpability, the rule of law, the relationship between vice and passion, the nature of character reformation or the history of corruption and depravity. All such things had either been forgotten or resolved into commonplaces. Rhetorical digressions and theorizing were displaced by thorough, businesslike, but still intense discussions of the precise means to effect the required changes. The society devoted a tremendous amount of time and attention to architecture: a measure of its importance within the scheme of improvement. They surveyed existing prisons, investigated their performance, drew up their own plans and vetted other people's. Attention focussed on details, on very important but small adjustments. There was no question as to the utility of inspection; there was no question as to the necessity of centripetal prison planning. All doubt was resolved to a choice between three types of prison. First, should polygonal or windmill plans be adopted; then should the wings of a windmill plan be joined or separated from the central observatory? These were the issues of the day, for it was a matter of the utmost importance that in prison construction 'correct notions should prevail'.[6]

Buxton, whose father, as Sheriff of Essex, had contracted gaol fever while visiting a prison, was the most prominent society member in the early years. He was appalled by physical suffering and was to take over from Wilberforce the leadership of the anti-slaver's lobby, and he was a philanthropic gentleman of a recognizable type. So were Samuel Hoare, also active in the S.I.P.D., James Neild, who had trudged round the country in emulation of Howard to compile his alphabetical dictionary of prisons published in 1812,[7] and J.T. Becher, pioneer of institutional poor relief and a supervisor of Millbank Penitentiary, who was also responsible for the rebuilding of Southwell House of Correction, a small but influential building.[8]

They were soon joined by new men. The growing preoccupation with practical details helps explain how certain gaolers rose to prominence as experts on prison construction and management. John Orridge, 'active, intelligent and humane',[9] collaborated with the architect George Byfield to produce the gaol at Bury St Edmunds in 1803 which he afterwards ran (Fig. 123), then worked with Buxton and the architect William Wilkins on the prison plan for the Emperor of Russia in 1819 and finally with John Dobson on the winning design for Carlisle County Gaol in 1822. He was the best known gaoler, but Thomas le Breton, the keeper at another of Byfield's gaols at Canterbury, matched education and respectability with a thoughtful shrewdness. Like Orridge he put his ideas into a book. Daniel Harris, an Oxford builder, and keeper of the County Gaol there, worked with Jeffrey Wyattville designing and then building Abingdon Bridewell with prison labour between 1805 and 1811.[10]

Orridge, le Breton and Harris were hardly typical of their calling, yet the idea of a gaoler joining the ranks of reform and advising on the lay-out of prisons would have been inconceivable in the eighteenth century. Great changes had taken place. Reformers now welcomed the appearance of a new class of prison keepers characterized by their 'humanity' and quite different from the 'merciless race of men . . . conversant in scenes of misery' who had preceded them.[11] At a time when 'moral supervision' had 'to a certain extent replaced mere physical restraint' in prisons,[12] the keeper had also to assume the responsibility of moral guardianship. However, the ill-fated reign of Daniel Nihil as both governor and chaplain at Millbank in the 1830s would prove how unwise it was to combine the moral authority of the chaplaincy with the moral duty of governorship. Life at Millbank under Nihil was popularly rumoured to be an interminable litany where a contrite and devout expression could conceal the most desperate crimes.[13] In general, the relationship between keepers or governors and their prisoners was carefully circumscribed by rules promulgated by the magistrates, who sometimes, as at Devizes, ordered that the governor himself should 'not hold unnecessary conversations with the prisoners, but should give the necessary commands and relieve their wants in as few words as possible', and always required him to obtain a letter of permission from the Chairman of the Quarter Sessions before leaving the prison at night time.[14] A new breed of 'sober and steady' employees 'of respectable character',[15] at once deferential and authoritarian, were being recruited into the prisons; as often as not they were ex-military men whose humanity extended as far as their adherence to the rules, but whose reflex reaction to command made them exemplars to the prisoners — the same breed in a higher state — as well as good emissaries of authority.[16] And that is why mere good character was no longer considered enough, whether in keepers, deputies or assistants. Of the recruits at Millbank it was said that 'We have found a wide difference between military men taken with good testimonials from their late commanding officer, and manufacturers out of work, or decayed tradesmen bringing characters from former employers or their neighbours.'[17] This was not because the soldiers were better men, but because they had been trained to act in a certain way. The observation was made by George Holford, M.P., about whom a few words should be said before describing Millbank, for which he was responsible.

Holford was beyond the pale of the S.I.P.D. He championed polygonal plans; they championed radials. He deprecated the liberal use of the treadwheel; they proclaimed it. The exchanges between Holford and the more numerous, less vulnerable S.I.P.D. members, the press and various other individuals developed into a number of set-piece controversies over key issues of design and discipline, and Holford, although not a man of great intellectual distinction, nevertheless performed a special role in exposing these latent differences. It was not a part he played willingly. In 1810 he had been chosen as the chairman of the committee which went on to recommend that the government abandon Bentham's Panopticon and build an even larger penitentiary for 1,200 convicts to serve London and Middlesex alone. This proposal was accepted by Parliament, and the large marshy, riverside site below Westminster, at Millbank, was purchased. As a Supervisor of Works with J.T. Becher and Charles Long, Holford laboured from 1812 to 1822 to see the Millbank Penitentiary completed (Figs. 125, 126), and for many years remained its most ardent defender.

Holford, Becher and Long had selected a design by William Williams

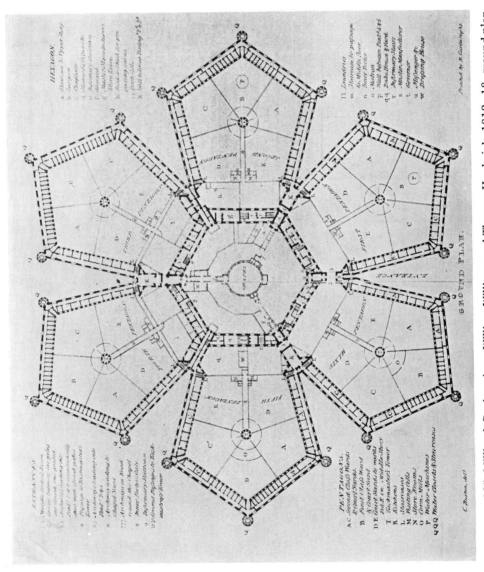

125. Millbank Penitentiary, William Williams and Thomas Hardwick, 1812–18, ground plan.

245

Drawn by Tho. H. Shepherd.

PENITENTIARY, MILLBANK, WESTMINSTER.

Engraved by J. Tingle.

126. Millbank Penitentiary, Williams and Hardwick, view of entrance from riverside.

from among 43 competition entries, which was nevertheless considered far from perfect, so Thomas Hardwick, a veteran of the 1782 penitentiaries competition was appointed to revise the plan and superintend its erection. Millbank was to be the largest prison in Europe; the building alone covered seven acres. At its centre was a circular chapel and around this was a hexagonal range of buildings containing offices of the central administration: governor, chaplain, surgeon and master manufacturer. Extending out from the hexagon were six nearly identical pentagons, four for men, two for women, each one a semi-autonomous prison with its own staff of ten overseen by a taskmaster who acted as resident deputy to the governor. What looked on the plan like small circular booths in the middle of the pentagons were in fact three storey surveillance towers within which were the taskmaster's bedroom, his parlour where he took meals with an assistant, and, on ground floor, a warders' mess where information was received and orders given.[18] The architecture of the pentagons resembled Richard Ingleman's house of correction at Devizes, designed four years earlier, but the scale of the operation, the multiplication of prisons within the prison and the consequent separation of central and subsidiary authority set Millbank apart, as did the unprecedented subdivision of its population into 30 independent wards, although housing only two grades of prisoner.

The discipline was modelled on the rules at Gloucester Penitentiary, still highly regarded, and Becher's Southwell House of Correction, both in turn derived from the specifications of the Penitentiary Act of 1779. Prisoners were admitted to a regime of solitude, but could graduate to a second class where they were permitted to work in small groups. To explain its intended effects, Holford published two poems, *The Convict's Complaint* and *The Convict's Thanks*, supposedly penned by a reformed character who had been transferred to Millbank after languishing in the Thames hulks. The *Thanks* opens with a peal of praise for 'those who planned the silent cells' and goes on to illustrate the close alignments between the definition of activity, the subdivision of time, and the subdivision of space, by a simple list of consecutive events:

> Here every action is by rule defin'd;
> To each its proper time and place assign'd;
> Oft sounds the prison bell, and as it rings,
> Its brazen voice a known commandment brings;
> By rule our several duties we fulfil,

> Now throw the shuttle, and now turn the mill,
> Now march in pairs, and beaten circle trace
> Around the gravell'd course with measured pace.
> Now take our meal, and now, with listening ear,
> Attentive stand the word of God to hear.
> And now in school we learn to read and write,
> Or letters to our friends, with leave indite.
> Now homage to our heavenly Father pay,
> And prayer, which usher'd in, concludes the day.[19]

The poem was published after seven baneful years of attempting to enforce the discipline it describes so happily, an indication of Holford's unwavering faith.

Despite claims that it was based on principles laid down by Howard, Millbank failed to employ the technology of ventilation and was situated on a marsh. Despite claims that it was a Panopticon, it applied the inspection principle in such a way that it overwhelmed the plan without extending central surveillance. Its snowflake symmetry gave the appearance of finality and resolution, but Millbank represents a passing moment in the development of prison architecture. An attempt had at least been made to come to terms with the critical problem of its gigantic size; a problem which would recur soon enough elsewhere, first at Maidstone, then at Derby and Tothill Fields (Figs. 164–167). Still, the project was remembered as a failure.

Difficulties were first encountered when the enormous girth of its boundary wall began to rise from the site late in 1812. The ground was soft to an unknown depth. Eminent engineers and architects were consulted: Rennie, Lewis, Cockrell and Browne. 'Puddled walls' of lime-bonded gravel on timber piles were decided upon for the foundations, but by the time the outer wall had reached a height of six feet it had already begun to tilt and crack. The area was then drained, which only made things worse by causing displacement and subsidence over the entire site. The contractor had to demolish and start again. After 18 months, £26,000 had been spent and there was nothing to show for it. But work continued despite Hardwick's resignation, and in February 1816 the first convicts were received. Seven months later the governor recorded the following incident in his journal:

September 21st 1816 — Arose at six o'clock in the morning in consequence of being informed that the passage gates of Pentagon 1, next the angle towers, were all fast and incapable of being unlocked by the turnkeys. Went there and found it was so, and that it was occasioned by all the three angle towers having sunk a little lower, which had cracked the arches and wall in several places.[20]

Ominous noises and windows shattering spontaneously at odd times of day and night convinced some of the staff that the building was about to collapse on top of them. John Rennie the engineer and Robert Smirke the architect, appointed to investigate, had to recommend the demolition of the three crumbling towers and the substantial under-pinning of the rest of the structure, which consumed a further £70,000 and brought the final cost to £458,000. The edifice was finally made stable, but public opinion was moving against what proved to be not only the largest prison in the country but also by far the most expensive per prisoner (Fig. 182). Confidence in the penitentiary slipped further when it became known that the first consignment of convicts had rioted in an attempt to increase their food allowance in the spring of 1817. This did not, however, prevent the place being labelled as 'Mr. Holford's fattening house', nor did it prevent odious comparisons between the lot of the comfortable convict and the hard-pressed and hungry free labourer who steadfastly supported wife and children in hard times. Bowing to public pressure Holford reduced the diet and calamity struck once more, this time in the shape of a mysterious sickness, first noticed in the autumn of 1822, which steadily spread until over half the convict population were victim to diarrhoea, debility, feebleness and faintings. Fifteen months later, after 30 had died, and after the whole convict population had been evacuated from the prison, Holford was convinced that the disease had been sea-scurvy.

It is hardly surprising that there should have been a certain dis-enchantment with the penitentiary, considering this sequence of disasters involving the over-spending of public money, defective con-struction, sickness and rebellion all before it was even complete. Holford stood firm, publishing three successive *Vindications* of the building and its regime between 1822 and 1825. Even so, changes were eventually agreed upon. Holford had insisted that the sickness of 1822—4 was due to a slight imbalance in the prison diet.[21] A Parliamentary Commission enquiring into the incident disagreed. They preferred to see the sickness as the result of poor ventilation and unhealthy atmosphere. The peni-tentiary, with its enclosed courtyards, without arcades, and sited on damp ground, was to be opened up and aired. Humphrey Davy knocked holes through the cell walls and installed stoves, Michael Faraday fumigated the whole prison with chlorine, and the Commissioners, who were struck by the prisoners' excessively low spirits, recommended the introduction of 'rational amusements' and 'innocent recreations . . . conducive to health' into penitentiary discipline.[22]

This request for the introduction of 'cheerfulness' was unique.[23] Others might call for the relaxation of certain specific rigours, either of solitude, of the treadwheel or of flogging, for fear of warping the mind or harming the person, or they might call for better conditions in the interests of physical health but that was all, otherwise the correct balance between tenderness and severity, proclaimed by eighteenth-century philanthropists as the basis of penitentiary imprisonment, but so difficult to achieve, would be upset. For this reason, as the prisons were improved they became bleaker; as the level of servicing and accommodation became more commodious they became more dismal, since each additional comfort of the body required a compensating subtraction of mental sustenance, a calculation not fully appreciated by the public during the lean years after the French Wars when prison building was at a peak, yet made abundantly clear by the evidence given to successive Commissions enquiring into prison discipline. The more stringent regulation of visiting was a gauge of this tightening up. The eighteenth-century practice of lodging families with debtors had been curtailed by the reformers and the visiting of all classes of prisoner had been restricted to particular times and to a particular place within the prison designated for that purpose alone, often a kiosk or room occupying the no-man's-land between central observatory and radial wings with a cage between visitor and prisoner in which sat a supervising turnkey. Now the prison authorities were discussing whether there was any virtue at all in either visits or letters, for, as Sibly the governor of Brixton put it, such things 'interfere with prison discipline'. In 1835 ten witnesses at such an enquiry held that no visiting or letters should be permitted at all once a man or woman was sentenced. Only three suggested that a quota of letters, at least, might be allowed 'under very strict control'.[24]

As this process continued, as the sophistication of prison building increased, and as the last threads between the world of the prison and everyday reality were cut, architects came to recognize that the outward appearance of the new institutions might be used to counteract their growing reputation, fostered in the press, of being sponging houses full of well-fed, well-housed, idle felons. Ingleman believed that the prison was very similar to a palace, for both buildings were meant, in their way, to dominate the lives of men.[25] Yet because they defined, so to speak, the two ends of a spectrum, they were not to look the same. To the magnificence of the palace belonged decoration; to the austerity of the prison belonged simplicity. Strength and utility devoid of embellishment should prevail throughout.[26] 'The absence of embellishment', affirmed the S.I.P.D., 'is in perfect unison with the nature of the establishment. The elevation should therefore be plain, bold and characteristic, but divested of expensive and unnecessary decorations.'[27] There were those who still put the conventions of academic design above the conventions of prison building, in particular the notorious George Moneypenny who, after building Leicester County Gaol, had modelled the Exeter House of Correction facade (1809) on Burlington House in Piccadilly, and applied to the front of Winchester County Gaol (1805) a doric cornice from the Theatre of Marcellus in Rome and an entrance derived from Vignola's Farnese Gardens Gate. In most prisons, however, decoration, where it appeared at all, was restricted to the entrance portals, the ponderous massing, vast overscaling and starkness of which all conspired to give a bleak, oppressive aspect, 'as gloomy and melancholy as possible'.[28]

To achieve this effect a wide range of stylistic devices were employed: emphatic Italian machicolation (Fig. 127), heavy rustication, doric simplicity (Fig. 128), battered profiles suggesting monolithic solidity (Fig. 129), rotund, squat towers in imitation of medieval baileys (Fig. 130). There was a studied Saxon entrance from Richard Ingleman (Fig. 131), a facade of primitive Levantine massing though classical Greek in detail by Francis Goodwin (Fig. 132), and of course continued borrowings from Newgate (Figs. 133, 134). The best of these were exercises in abstract propaganda, rather as William Blackburn's entry lodges had been; attempts, familiar enough at the time, to give architecture a voice that would transmit a universal language of emotion derived from the immutable bond between the substance of building and the sensations of the beholder. An early design for the lodge at Northleach, for example, heightened the effect of a weak facade by removing the entrances to the sides and diverting an adjacent stream so that it would appear to be swallowed by a gaping low arch in place of the centre portal (Fig. 135). All the same, this universal language had to be sup-

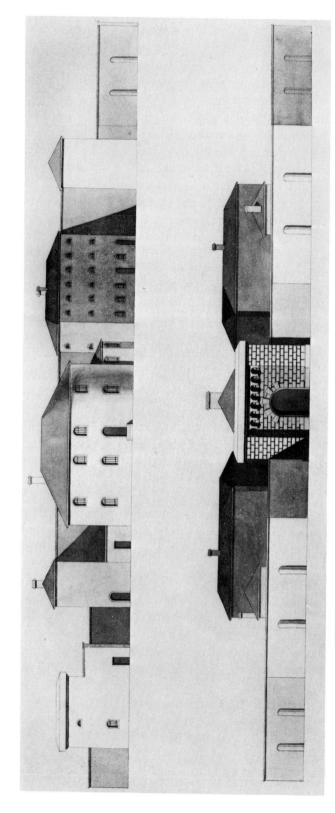

127. Unexecuted project for Springfield County Gaol, Chelmsford, Thomas Hopper, 1820, front and side elevations.

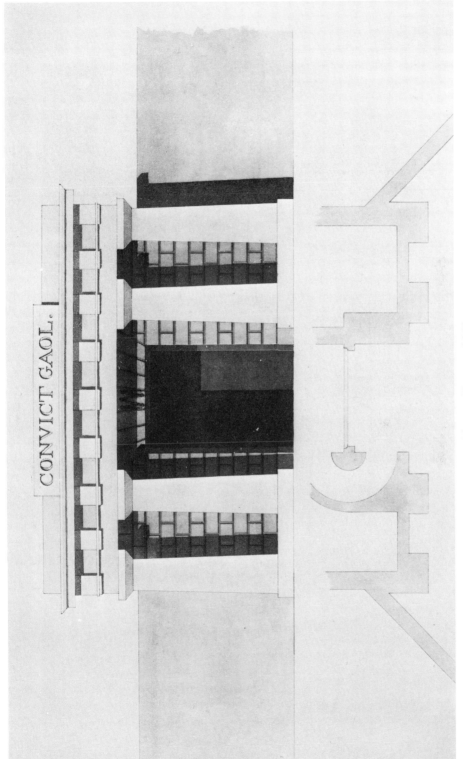

128. Design for a prison entrance, Thomas Hopper, 1820.

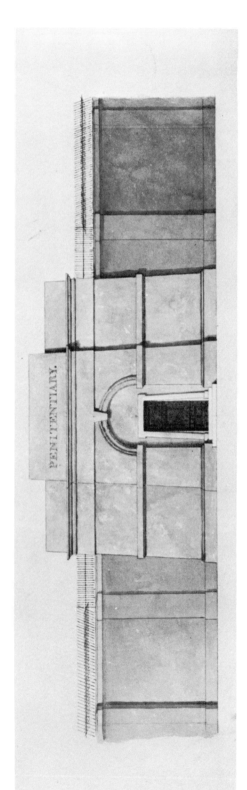

129. Design for the entrance to Bedford Penitentiary, John Wing, 1819

130. Unexecuted project for York Castle County Gaol, Robert Wallace, 1824.

plemented with symbols of a defunct cruelty in the shape of fetters and castellation if only to underline the point. Fetters had recently been outlawed except for use on refractory prisoners; at Millbank an empty cell festooned with these useless chains was set aside as a museum of vanished practices (Fig. 136). Castle dungeons were already archaeological curiosities. The persistence of castle and fetter as the principal emblems of imprisonment bore no relation to the realities of contemporary discipline, nor were they meant to. They were employed as a consciously deceptive deterrent, keeping old fears alive by reflecting a popular, melodramatic picture of the prison back towards the public. This silent, empty rhetoric of the prison facade was the more persuasive

A SAXON ENTRANCE.

131. Saxon entrance to Devizes House of Correction, Richard Ingleman, 1808 or after.

since the disappearance of prison life into a secret precinct behind the walls.

Perhaps the expressive power of architecture is always at its height when uncompromised by any distracting human presence. At any rate, having put prison life behind a series of architectural shields for the purpose of reform, the same agency was used to falsely declare the nature of what had been hidden away to make it appear more terrifying.[29] To say that the facade failed to express the nature of the building would be to miss the point entirely, as it belonged to a different world and was part of a distinct stratagem. Its lame fictions were in any case subsidiary to the architecture of the prison interior, a point which should be emphasized, as architectural historians still tend to look hardest at the facade and, what is more, fall victim to the hoax by making it represent the prison within.

As with the reformed prisons of the 1780s, the internal arrangement of the early-nineteenth-century prisons was based on three principles, but they were not quite the same ones. John Orridge declared the three 'grand ends' to be security, the preservation of health, and the amelioration of morals; in other words, security, salubrity and reformation, the

132. Derby County Gaol, Francis Goodwin, 1823–7, entrance facade.

133. Newgate, George Dance the younger, 1769—84, portal.

PARUM EST COERCERE
IMPROBOS POENA
NISI PROBOS EFFICIAS
DISCIPLINA.

134. Dover Town Gaol, Richard Elsam, 1818—21, entrance facade.

three cardinal requirements of Howardian prisons. Superficially nothing had changed. But then Orridge went on to tell the reader how 'with regard to morals, — it is well known that a combined system of classification, inspection and employment, ensures and improves the moral character of prisoners'.[30] As to security, it was bound up with inspection, while healthiness was sought by ventilation as before: 'by the detached situation of the different buildings, by the opposed ends of the airing grounds being connected with open iron palisades and by the provision made to obtain a current of air through every cell and passage of the prison'.[31] What this meant as far as Orridge was concerned was that health and security could be promoted by the observance of accepted building practices, but he was certain that morality, as yet, could not. Emphasis therefore shifted from security and the preservation of health to the acknowledged but not yet perfected methods of enforcing morality: classification, inspection and employment. Orridge's

135. Northleach Bridewell, William Blackburn, 1785, entrance facade.

understanding of the matter was borne out by events; classification, inspection and labour had supplanted security, salubrity and reformation as the fundamentals of a good prison.

Classification

The classification of prisoners into groups and the isolation of those

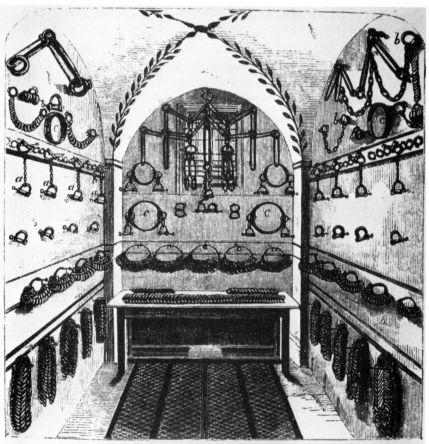

THE CHAIN-ROOM AT MILLBANK.
a, Handcuffs; *b*, Shackles for the legs, fastened round the ankle, and secured to *c*, an Iron Ring or the waist.

136. The chain room at Millbank as witnessed by Mayhew and Binney in 1856.

groups from one another by means of architectural separation was commonly practised in the eighteenth century. The methods employed were not particularly effective, as the Cold Bath Fields Commissioners had pointed out (p. 194). Although early-nineteenth-century architects were that much more careful, they did not make any great advances in the technology of separation, one of the more original contributions being made by the prison officer Thomas le Breton, who published an ingenious section for radial prison wings in which windows were replaced by roof lights in the upper cells to prevent the prisoners looking down into the adjacent airing yards. He also copied Blackburn's technique of providing an access corridor for one side of the cell-block and an external gallery or path for the other side, so that a two storey wing could be divided into four exclusive wards with independent circulation (Fig. 137).[32] No such building was ever erected. Instead the great majority of radials followed the plan at Bury St Edmunds, splitting each wing lengthways with a spine wall down the centre of a corridor, as had first been done at Winchester Bridewell (Fig. 88).

If the technology did not advance, the number of classes did. To take Bury as a typical example, in 1803 it had eight classes disposed in quadrilateral symmetry around the centre. By 1819 Orridge had felt it necessary to compromise the plan by inserting three new courts and two new blocks, making eleven separate classes plus two infirmary wards in a prison for 104 persons. This was not enough; 14 classes were required. The ideal prison plan produced by Orridge, in collaboration with T.F. Buxton and the architect William Wilkins, for the Emperor of Russia in the same year (Fig. 138), leaves no doubt as to the direction of events: a gradually increasing number of prisoner types were being identified as time went on. The ensuing proliferation of classes was evident everywhere. Throughout the country, in the smallest as in the largest prisons, walls were being raised to keep up with it. Cold Bath Fields had 11 classes in 1801, 13 classes in 1818, 18 in 1824, and 24 in 1843 (Fig. 139). At the beginning of the century there were only four prisons containing ten or more wards; in 1843 there were 50 of them.

The multiplication of categories does not really seem to have taken hold until the end of the French Wars,[33] during which sections of prisons were sometimes left empty for years, after being divided into separate wards in the enthusiasm of the 1780s. Neild recorded that several of the 14 yards at Exeter County Gaol had been dug into

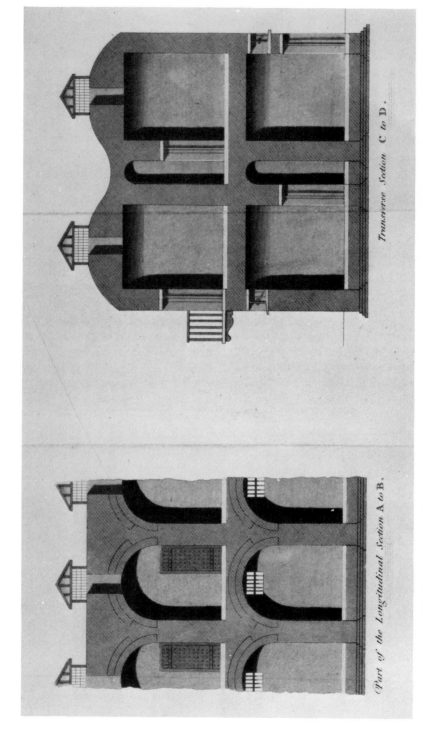

Part of the Longitudinal Section A to B.

Transverse Section C to D.

137. Section of a radial wing from Thomas le Breton, *Thoughts on the Defective State of Prisons*, 1822.

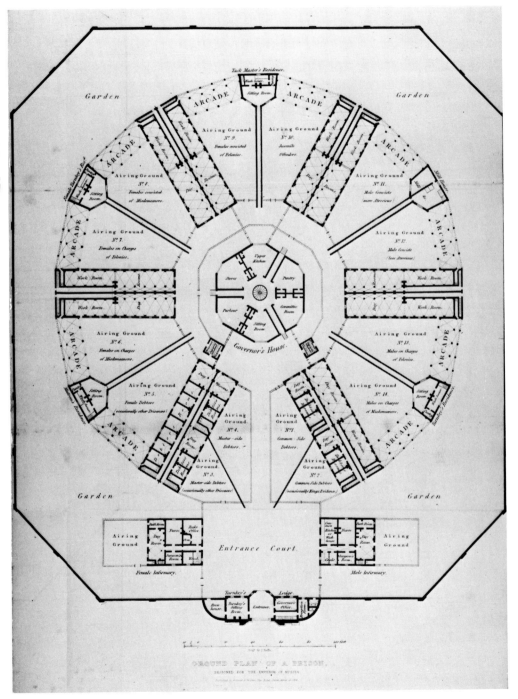

138. Prison designed for the Emperor of Russia, William Wilkins,
John Orridge and Thomas Fowell Buxton, 1819, ground plan.

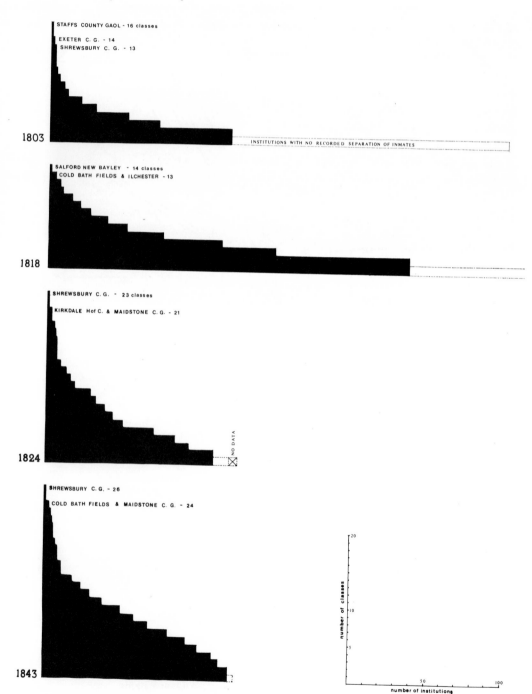

gardens, 'there being at the time . . . no prisoners of the class for which they were originally intended'.[34] That was in 1802. In contrast the S.I.P.D. topped all previous calculations by distinguishing a minimum of 20 categories worthy of sequestration in 1820: 6 for houses of correction and 14 for gaols.[35] Two years later Thomas le Breton, pronouncing classification to be 'the very basis of prison reform', came up with a figure of 21.[36] The year after that the Derby Magistrates were preparing to build a new gaol and house of correction with 23 classifications mapped into it,[37] and Parliament passed an Act requiring 12 divisions for gaol prisoners and 8 for bridewell prisoners.[38]

This extraordinary escalation stemmed from the rejection of solitary confinement after the Despard affair (p. 189). Solitude had been abandoned as much because it was difficult to impose as because of its unkindness. Belief in the excellence of the principle of seclusion had not really been shaken by the complaints of a few prisoners against its severity. Classification was a modest revival of the same basic principle, pursued more relentlessly. Indeed it was pursued so relentlessly that it came full circle to the point of departure when reformative solitude was reintroduced in the 1830s. Meanwhile the meticulous parsing of the criminal population was reflected in the increasingly complex geometry of prison plans.

The reason for making classifications, as for enforcing solitude, was to stop prisoners from corrupting one another. In the words of Thomas Hopper, surveyor to the County of Essex and architect of several

139. *Opposite.* Classification in the prisons of England and Wales, 1803–43. Constructed in the same way as Fig. 122, only with the prisons graded according to the number of classifications enforced. A similar pattern emerges. At the head of the list in 1803 came Stafford County Gaol and House of Correction with 16 classifications. In 1843 it was Shrewsbury County Gaol and House of Correction with 26 classifications. More importantly there was a wholesale increase of classifications throughout the system. Even in 1803, 179 prisons, well over half the total, had no classifications at all while nearly 100 more contained fewer than six divisions. In 1843 only 26 contained fewer than six divisions. On the other hand institutions with ten or more classes increased from four in 1803 to 50 in 1843. In 1803 the average number of classes per prison was 2.08. Forty years later the average was seven classes.

Sources: for 1803, Neild, *General State of the Prisons*; for 1818, *P.P.*, 1819, vol. XI, 'An Account of the Gaols etc.'; for 1824 and 1843, *P.P.*, Gaol Returns, Schedule B (1825 and 1844).

prisons, 'The division of the prison ought to be so ordered as to prevent the possibility of communication between the different classes of prisoner, and so that prisoners passing to or from one class may not be seen by those of any other.'[39] The quality of innocence was still fragile, unable to flourish surrounded by corruption and iniquity, and because of the peculiar susceptibility of innocence most prisons were, then as now, 'nurseries of crime', in so far as they were not properly classified. Vice was the dominant, more vigorous force, so innocence had to be protected. Evil spread like disease and classification was a means of assuaging the epidemic. If, for example, an untainted youth mixed with criminals, what would be the consequence? The question was asked by Samuel Hoare, as spokesman for the S.I.P.D. The answer was that 'experience, the nature of man, teaches us that the infection would spread'.[40] T.F. Buxton had the perfect example to illustrate the truth of Hoare's judgement. A youth, taken for the illegal vending of religious tracts in Bishopsgate, was committed to Bridewell for a month. Buxton, bursting with indignation, viciously parodied the magistrate who was so foolish as to put an uncorrupted lad into an *unclassified* prison where he would spend his days 'amongst the worst thieves with which this metropolis is infested', and his nights 'with those who are infected with a desperate and contagious disorder — taking lessons from the one in blasphemy and dissoluteness, and from the other imbibing the seeds of a disease which you shall carry home to your family'. The conviction that a terrible moral disease was contracted by tender souls in 'promiscuous association' led the authorities to proclaim that such mixing was an awful hardship — 'a cruelty too dreadful to be endured',[41] but behind the calculation of losses to civil society was an apprehension of the appalling ugliness of low company. The cruelty of mixing was an issue of aesthetics as well as morality.

The architect Richard Ingleman was more concerned with the practical consequences of the analogy between vice and disease. He proposed a mathematical model which would predict the rate at which moral contagion would spread under given conditions: 'When prisoners are carefully separated by the rules and regulations, as well as by the mechanical construction of the house, the contagion of vice and idleness may be said to increase by units, but when they are collected together, it increases in proportion to the square of the number confined.'[42] In this neat formulation of prevailing opinion it was demonstrated that, although contagion could not be prevented, 'careful separation' would reduce its virulence. As the number of divisions in a prison increased arithmetically, so their protective value increased exponentially. The practical purpose of classification was thus to quarantine the vile with the vile, the vicious with the vicious, incorrigibles with incorrigibles, novices with novices and so on. Each prisoner would be assigned a position on a graded scale, which incidentally gave to classification a special judicial meaning.

The Norfolk Magistrates adopted classification, not just because it counteracted the spread of wickedness, but because it also re-established a connection, admittedly tenuous, between types of crime and types of punishment. In John Soane's Norwich Castle Gaol only men, women and debtors had been separated. There was no distinction between the different degrees of crime. It was decided in 1819 that if such a distinction was not made by the authorities then the prisoners would fail to register the enormity of their own guilt. All individual sense of sin was lost in an egalitarian community of unclassified prisoners: 'A gaol which thus defies any discrimination of character and punishment, must confound in the minds of the prisoners the various degrees of crime, and its tendency cannot be less mischievous than it is illegal and unjust.'[43] A new plan for Norwich Gaol, originally designed by William Wilkins, was sent to the S.I.P.D., redesigned on their advice and built by Francis Stone (1824–8) to contain 12 independent divisions in which a 'sense of shame' would be nurtured by differences in treatment and discipline (Fig. 140). All the same, these differences were slight. Classification raised, once again, the prospect of a thoroughly differentiated scheme of punishment, as had been advocated by the great continental reformer Cesare Beccaria, who proposed different kinds of penalties for different kinds of crime. But the great range of penal practices he had described were now narrowed into the relatively homogeneous discipline of the prison which, in compensation, developed its own internal geography to mark in another way distinctions which had been nearly lost to view. They were not to be read off the same scale, though; classification was an attempt to index the character of culprits, while diverse penalties were to have indexed their crimes.

How then were the classifications made? At first a simple division between men and women, felons and debtors had seemed enough (as at Newgate). Howard thought that young beginners and old offenders, the

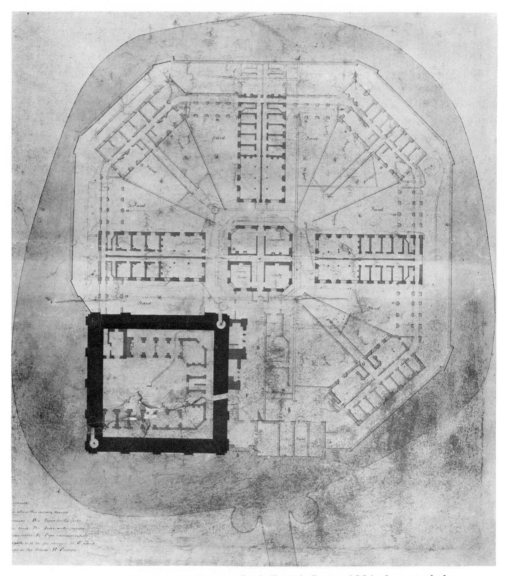

140. Norwich County Gaol, Francis Stone, 1824—8, ground plan.
The horseshoe of building contained within the twelfth-century
keep was John Soane's felons' prison, 1792—3.

sick and the healthy ought to be kept apart as well.[44] When bridewells were amalgamated with gaols, the number of divisions increased yet again to include misdemeanants. The Cecil Wray Bill of 1784 added a distinction between those charged and those convicted.[45] It was customary to keep the condemned apart from other prisoners, and it was common sense to keep those supplying King's evidence away from their old accomplices. On a different principle altogether, the 1779 Penitentiary Act had introduced three classifications through which any convict would have to progress before being released. As if this were not enough the S.I.P.D. introduced a division by occupation for bridewell prisoners; servants, apprentices, poachers and vagrants were each to have their own accommodation.[46] Other types soon emerged: those imprisoned for want of fines, those committed for bastardy, the less atrocious and the more atrocious, juveniles, those summarily convicted, and those committed for 'unnatural crimes'. Sections for the reception of new prisoners and for the refractory were needed too. The miscellaneous piles of classes that grew out of all these could not be comprehensive — the possible permutations were nearly inexhaustible — and so few prisons adopted exactly the same classifications. Nevertheless, in each case the chosen schema was meant to define an inclusive typology at once moral, administrative and legal, as the list of 29 classifications for 460 prisoners housed in 38 wards within four distinct institutions at Maidstone County Gaol in 1826 indicates:[47]

GAOL

2	Male prisoners under Sentence of Death
1	Male Misdemeanants convicted but not sentenced to hard labour
1	Ditto, who maintain themselves
2	Males for trial for felonies not Capital
2	Males for trial for Capital felonies
1	Male recommittals
2	Males for trial for misdemeanours
1	Males for unnatural crimes
1	Male deserters
1	Males giving evidence for the Crown
1	Male Juveniles for trial
1	Master debtors (being allowed rooms of superior accommodation)
2	Debtors

PENITENTIARY

2	Male convicts during the first third of their sentence

2   Male convicts during the second third of their sentence
2   Male convicts during the remainder of their sentence

THE HOUSE OF CORRECTION
1   Male Offenders against the game laws
1   Male servants in husbandry, or for want of sureties in bastardy cases
1   Males summarily convicted
1   Male juveniles
2   Male vagrants

FEMALE PRISON
1   Females under Sentence of Death
1   Female convicts in the penitentiary
1   Female convicted of misdemeanours
1   Females for trial for felony
1   Females for trial for misdemeanours
1   Female bridewell prisoners
1   Female vagrants
1   Female debtors

For all the legalistic nomenclature, classifications were not meant to be an exact reflection of established degrees of judicial guilt. A committee of the S.I.P.D. had decided in 1818 that it was not *crime* that prison punished, but what they described as 'the habits and inclinations' of prisoners:[48] a clear formulation of something implicit in much eighteenth-century penal thought. The question of judicial guilt was a matter of purely legal importance. Anyone who manifested the signs of vicious behaviour would be improved by the process of imprisonment. On the other hand it was just these lingering evidences of badness ingrained into the personality of the offender which caused such alarm; they after all were imported into the prison, the crime was not.

To sort the prisoners, reference had to be made to certain easily verifiable characteristics of age, station or crime. It was still felt that the fundamental criterion of classification should be the magnitude or type of crime for which a prisoner was committed, rather than his character or his behaviour once within the prison. This was the predominant view, but there were those, like Orridge, who thought it to be impractical. Discretion was needed. At Bury St Edmunds the magistrate left the burden of classification to him as gaoler, and he had learnt that it was 'much better to classify by conduct and character, and not by crime, because I very often find that the worst character we have is committed for the lesser offence, because he has artfully avoided being charged with the larger crime'.[49] If crimes represented character accurately, convictions did not. Experience and intuition were, he thought, better guides than any rigid taxonomy of offences, no matter how small the steps between one class and the next. All the same it was apparent that increasing numbers of divisions were not dispelling administrative confusion but adding to it. The simple act of telling vice from innocence was proving difficult. But the effort continued and the divisions became more exact as they grew in number.

Architects would go to great lengths to insure that classification was compatible with symmetry. Everyone agreed that classified prisons should be 'proportionate': that is, the accommodation in each class ward should correspond to the number of prisoners committed within that class. In polygonals, where the continuous circuits of passageway could be subdivided into convenient lengths to include anything from 2 to 50 cells in one section (Holford proposed demountable gates for this purpose),[50] adaptions could easily be made without reference to the shape of the building. In radials it was not so easy. Usually local committal statistics were used as the basis of a brief.[51] In Byfield's Worcester County Gaol (1802; Figs. 141, 142), the wing lengths were adjusted in accordance with these figures, and consequently symmetry was sacrificed. Others, however, were loath to give it up. Richard Elsam, after a long dissertation on the need to match the size of wards to statistically derived proportions, managed, by a bit of mathematical casuistry, to show that at Dover the statistics were symmetrical, so his plan for Dover Town Gaol followed suit (Fig. 143).[52] Similar magical correspondences were discovered by many architects.

An intellectually satisfying solution to this conflict between formalism and statistics was provided by Francis Goodwin in his early plan for Derby County Gaol (1823; Fig. 168). With scholastic ingenuity Goodwin had manipulated his 23 classifications so that the least offensive categories were towards the front and the most heinous at the rear. Within this series the women's prison was inserted on one side and a corresponding section for males on charge on the other. The sizes of the individual wards varied from 3 to 18 cells yet a complex overall symmetry was deftly preserved. Goodwin's plan was a sophistication; in the main, prison architects pushed and pulled their committal statistics to fit the Procrustean bed of symmetry with less finesse.

A drift back towards neo-classical composition was discerned: 'the

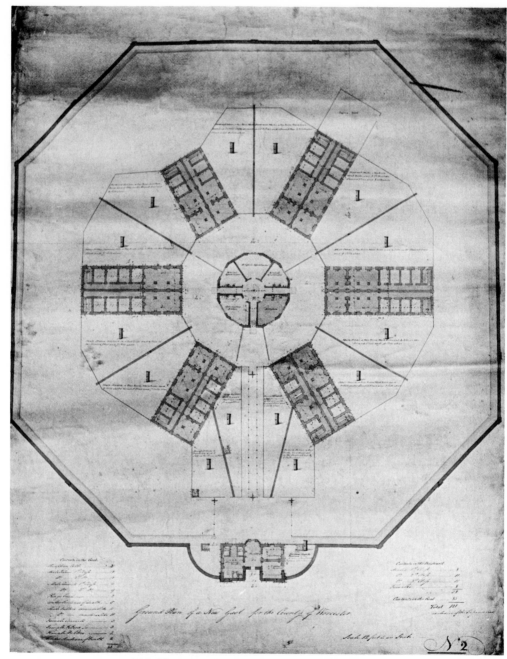

141. Worcester County Gaol, George Byfield, 1802—14, ground
floor plan. This design, dated 1802, was taken over by Francis
Sandys when he built the prison in 1809—14.

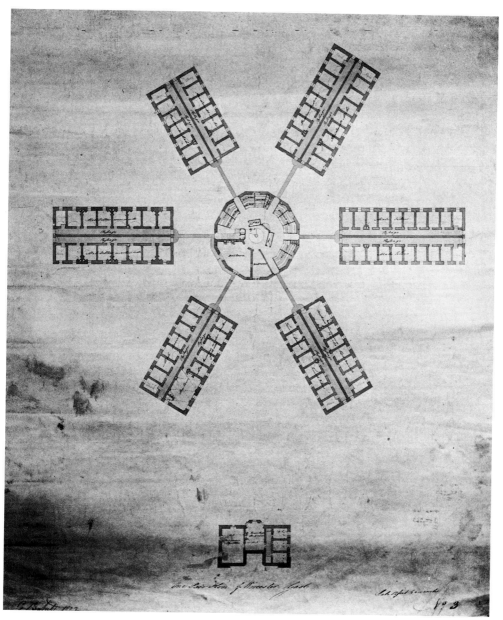

142. Worcester County Gaol, upper floor plan.

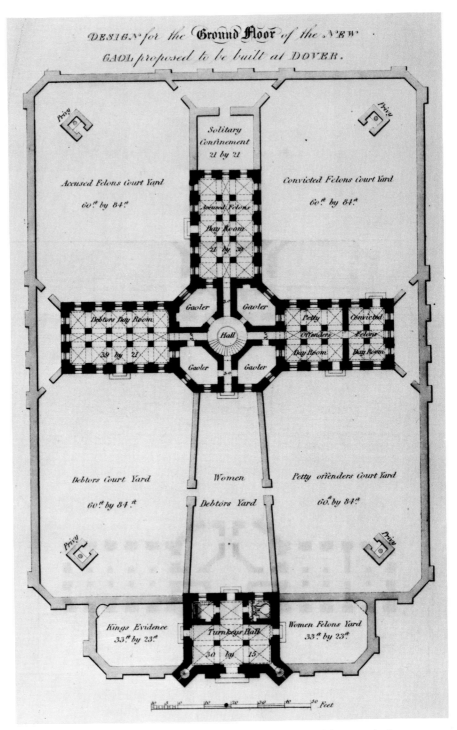

143. Dover Town Gaol, Richard Elsam, 1818–21, ground plan.

defects in the general plan of prison building', said Thomas le Breton, 'appeared chiefly to proceed from architects adhering too close to uniformity, various forms may look pretty on paper but be exceedingly defective'.[53] A comparison of the plans illustrated in this chapter with earlier reformed prisons (see ch. 4) indicates the change. The typical prison plan was now a regular, geometrical figure of crystalline complexity, maintaining a balance between composition and utility.

Was pure architecture, with its own laws undeflected by external conditions, encroaching on practicality, as le Breton supposed? Or was it that advantage had been taken of a fruitful concordance between utility and formal planning? The latter is perhaps more likely, for it was only the niggling matter of statistics which showed up an irreconcilable difference between the two. In other respects the requirements of the functioning prison translated easily enough into stylized geometries, a convertibility that doubtless helped fuel its rapid architectural development. Nor was this correspondence entirely fortuitous. The generalized, disengaged, emblematic order of neo-classical plans had entirely different origins from the instrumental order of prison buildings harnessed to the specifics of administration and discipline. But if their origins remained distinct they nevertheless ran parallel courses, both aimed towards an ideal of unrestricted regularity and gradation − the one applied directly to spatial subdivision, the other via spatial subdivision to the definition of conduct. As in the eighteenth-century prisons, differences between instrumental and emblematic geometry did arise; incompatibilities were sure to leave their trace. But it should be noted that emblem and instrument were relatively close to one another and that the newer instrumentality was sustained by a transcending but apparently useless artistry.

So here is a picture of a new species of architecture strengthened by feeding off the body of the old. Yet while this was taking place there were also signs that architects were beginning to lose claim to the prison, at a time when the emerging profession was confidently laying claim to it. Two works by architects on the subject of prisons, a 'most unpleasant, but not least requisite branch of their profession', appeared in consecutive years: the first James Elmes' *Hints for the Improvement of Prisons* (1817); the second, Richard Elsam's *Brief Treatise on Prisons* (1818) − both conventional statements of prison doctrine, both dedicated to Howard, both searching for definitive forms (Elmes chose the radial, Elsam the polygonal (Figs. 152, 143)), both written by dilettantes whose small knowledge on the subject of prison improvement could produce no more than a mixed bag of derivative nostrums, a fact in itself significant. Already the specialized task of prison building was becoming institutionalized. These monographs were the first and the last published by architects not operating under the aegis of some larger expertise, and they were deficient — mere parodies of good practice in the advancing science of prison construction. Soon afterwards the S.I.P.D. and the government would take in hand the business of formulating and codifying the principles of prison building. This became noticeable in the 1820s, when there is evidence that a number of architects engaged to design county gaols had their work checked by the S.I.P.D. and were then directed by the magistrates to alter their schemes in accordance with the society's opinion. When such vetting had been deemed necessary in earlier years, the custom had been to approach a more experienced or more eminent architect. Now architects were being told to interpret their brief into forms validated outside the profession.

Inspection

The characteristically dense patterning of early-nineteenth-century prison plans was determined by the logic of classification. The policy of moral segregation, described above, obliged architects to make their plans into complex atlases of vice, with each of numerous sectors cordoned off, screened and introverted. The equally characteristic, and even more noticeable, concentric, kaleidoscopic geometry was of course determined by the logic of inspection. Bentham in his Panopticon had magnified this one function beyond all others, and it remained from 1800 onwards the predominant organizing force in prison architecture. Despite this it was William Blackburn's radial and polygonal prisons of the 1780s (Figs. 56, 65, 68, 70) that were now taken up, not the Panopticon. What the improvers did scruple to take from Bentham was the language of inspection, though only very grudging acknowledgements were given to either, as at the time matters of provenance were overshadowed by the urgent need for such an obvious necessity as this: 'We', said the authors of a pamphlet published in 1818, 'if asked what are the three great requisites for prison management should answer "INSPECTION! INSPECTION! INSPECTION!" '[54]

The S.I.P.D., though more reserved in their judgement, were no less earnest. In 1826 they were arguing not just for inspection but for 'unobserved inspection' of the Benthamian sort.[55] George Thomas Bullar, an architect who later became the society's Secretary, had been producing model prison plans for them since 1820 — always detached wing radials. He now published a sequence of nine plans (Figs. 144, 145, 146) all affording 'constant unobserved inspection' from a central station, all pure radials with wings divided down the centre and all uniformly symmetrical.[56] Bullar's 1826 designs were a classic statement of improved radial prison planning, illustrating a succession of ideal solutions in which the classifications and the number of prisoners accommodated grew in increments from 4 to 16 classes and from 30 to 400 prisoners. The smallest plans had two or three wings attached to a central core, but as the size increased so the wings detached from it and multiplied in number, leaving it as a separate nucleus around which the rest of the prison revolved. In fact the detached wings in these, as in the majority of improved radial plans, were connected at first or second floor level with iron galleries passing from the cell corridors into a classified chapel (Figs. 142, 146) placed over the governor's apartments. On Sundays, at the ringing of a bell, the various classes of prisoners would proceed in appropriate sequence across these iron bridges into the chapel, where an exact replica of the larger moral geography of the prison was made in miniature by partitions raised across the banks of pews. The paths of different classes never had to cross, they merely approached one another along converging radii. Iron walkways, binding detached radial wings to the chapel, had first been introduced by George Byfield in his prisons at Worcester and Bury St Edmunds, then at Canterbury County Gaol and Cambridge County Gaol.[57] Their use, though new in radial prisons, was probably adapted from Blackburn, who had employed iron galleries to tie the five pavilions of Dorchester Gaol together (Fig. 59).

The question as to whether wings should be attached or detached was resolved by Bullar in terms of the scale of the undertaking. As the size of a prison and the number of classifications increased, so the wings were pushed further from the centre for the simple reason that if they were drawn closer they would block the views across the airing yards to

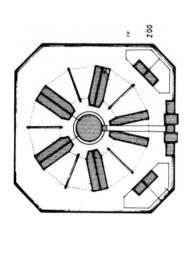

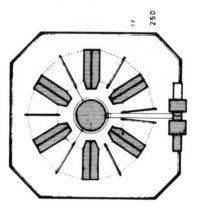

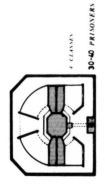

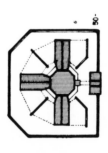

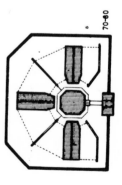

278

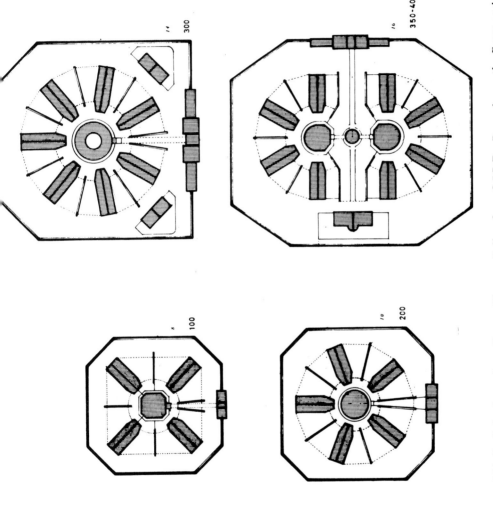

144. Radial prison plans, George Thomas Bullar, from S.I.P.D., *Remarks on the Form and Construction of Prisons*, 1826.

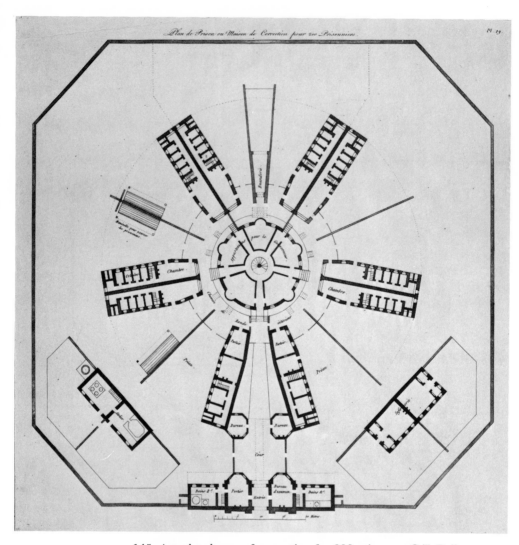

145. A gaol or house of correction for 200 prisoners, G.T. Bullar, 1826, ground plan corresponding to the sixth outline in Fig. 144.

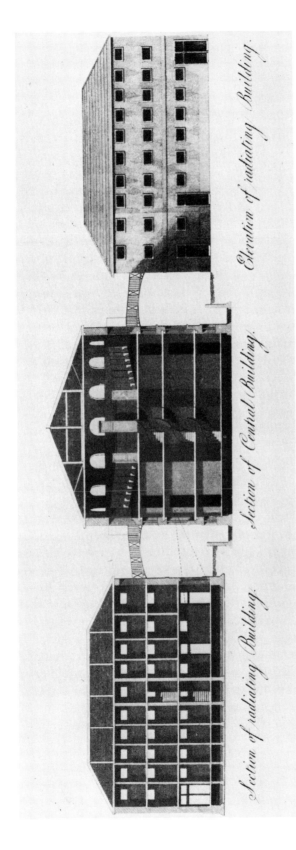

Section of radiating Building.   *Section of Central Building.*   *Elevation of radiating Building.*

146. Gaol or house of correction, Bullar, 1826, section.

the outer wall of the gaol, and the universal surveyability of the interior would be compromised. To allow the radial wings to come closer to the governor's apartments while at the same time preserving views of the yards, Bullar tapered the ends into lozenge shapes so that they corresponded more closely to the geometry of sight lines from the lodge. He also fenestrated the entire width of the wing ends so that the governor could see directly into all the workrooms, and raised the floor of the central lodge five feet above the surrounding prison to give a commanding view.

These sophistications of radial planning went with the increasing reliance on inspection as a means of ensuring morality as well as security: something well illustrated by an observation made by T.F. Buxton in describing Ilchester Gaol. Ilchester was known to be well managed but on a bad plan, as it lacked inspection, that 'requisite of every new prison'. The effects of this serious architectural omission were at once apparent to Buxton: 'The loud laughter and conversation of the prisoners during their hour of recreation, seemed to imply, that this want of observation was not unattended with evil.'[58] No words should be exchanged between prisoners even when working together. At Bury, Orridge enforced silence, 'because it produces reflection'.[59] At Southwell Becher's list of punishable infractions included 'making signals or noises',[60] but rules such as these could not possibly be brought to bear unless inspection was constant and immanent. The new prisons, while they did not make inspection absolutely pervasive, increased its scope considerably.

In this effort two contradictory principles were at work: on the one hand the governor was placed in the midst of his prisoners, on the other he was to be kept at a distance from them to preserve his inscrutability. It was this very contradiction that Bentham had never been able to resolve in his Panopticon design. Orridge chose to run Bury Gaol without, if he could possibly help it, entering the prison itself. His administration was accomplished from the central pavilion which contained his house. By oversight and delegation he maintained control. If he had to talk to a prisoner it was done through a wicket in the day-room door specially placed for that purpose. In his ideal prison the governor's residence was further protected by a double circle of iron palings.[61] Thomas le Breton's approach was different. He found that the fragmented, detached wings at Canterbury Gaol hindered inspection. The best arrangement in his view was to have wings that crossed in the centre, which would allow the keeper to *hear* what the prisoners said as well as to *see* what they did.[62] He was of the opinion, surely quite correct, that architects and reformers had occupied themselves with the niceties of obtaining visual inspection without so much as a second thought about sounds and noises. This omission seems doubly curious when it is remembered that the object of reformatory imprisonment was to prevent corruption by communication. Where whispers were a token of evil, whispers had to be heard:

The principle object hitherto studied, has been to see every prisoner, under all circumstances, during the day; this, no doubt is essential, but assuredly not so much as to hear their conversation; with the lower orders neither quarrels, conspiracy or gambling are pursued in silence; in short, no extensive mischief can occur without verbal communication.[63]

Another advantage of being able to hear was that a keeper could hear both day and night, whereas he could see only during daylight. Le Breton's observations were not translated into architecture at the time. Even his own model design for a county prison maintained a narrow divide between centre and wings (Fig. 147). Inspection remained visual above all else, although the S.I.P.D. did include in their description of prison furniture an item lifted directly from the Panopticon, which would indicate that they were quite aware of the advantages of listening to prisoners, though possibly unaware of the reasons it was abandoned by Bentham: 'The transmission of sounds, at night from the prisoners' buildings, may be facilitated by tubes of tin or copper, communicating with the sleeping cells, and terminating with a wide funnel in the bedroom of the keeper, or other officers.'[64]

In gathering information for their *Remarks* of 1826, members of the S.I.P.D. had visited 96 gaols. Only 28 afforded inspection and in most of these it was partial inspection; in the rest, so they reported, there was none at all. Yet of 48 prison buildings constructed between 1801 and 1832, only ten failed to adopt the concentric geometry of visual surveillance, a geometry that was similar to, and by now thoroughly confused with, the Panopticon principle, as has already been pointed out (p. 228).

The evidence from actual practice confirms that concentric planning was widely accepted as the norm of prison design by architects and the local magistrates throughout this period. But there were two varieties of

plan vying with one another for recognition: the radial and the polygonal (Fig. 148). Put briefly, their history was as follows: William
Blackburn had designed the first detached wing radial prison (National
Penitentiary 1782) and then the first polygonal prison (Northleach
1784). George Byfield revived the detached wing radial in 1802 (Figs.
123, 141, 142),[65] improved it and classified it. In 1808 Richard Ingleman performed the same service for the polygonal in his plan for Devizes
House of Correction (Fig. 124). Holford enthused over polygonals. The
S.I.P.D. proselytized for radials, and it appears that the society's views
predominated, for, of the 38 above-mentioned concentric prison plans

147. Design for a county prison, Thomas le Breton, 1822, ground
plan.

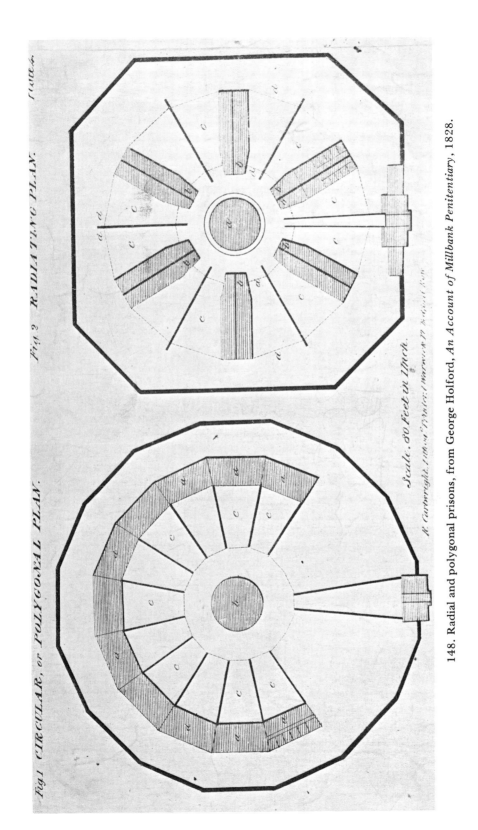

148. Radial and polygonal prisons, from George Holford, *An Account of Millbank Penitentiary*, 1828.

actually built, 30 were radials and only 8 polygonals.[66] After 1818 there were a few projects which attempted to combine both forms, for example James Bevans' penitentiary for 600 prisoners (Fig. 149), a five wing radial within a decagon, which the architect claimed had been approved by the S.I.P.D. and which he then submitted to the Surrey Magistrates as a design for Brixton County House of Correction.[67] Another example is the model prison by Orridge, Buxton and Wilkins (Fig. 138). A house of correction built at Wakefield in 1821 (Fig. 150) and an unexecuted design by Thomas Hopper for Springfield Gaol went some way in the same direction.[68] By and large, however, radials and polygonals were kept distinct.

The argument against polygonal plans was that they put too great a distance between the keeper and his prison, particularly in large institutions where a vast circus of exercise yards interposed between the central pavilion and the rest of the building (Figs. 124, 125, 151, 152). This was why le Breton admitted their beauty to the eye but found them otherwise objectionable. Not only was it impossible to oversee — let alone overhear — the prisoners unless they were out in the yards, but polygonal prison buildings also formed enclosures and were thus more difficult to ventilate.[69]

These difficulties had been encountered by Ingleman at Devizes House of Correction. It was to be his major work: a 16 sided regular polygon 330 feet across, encircled by a range of cells and workrooms facing onto a small rotunda at the focus of it all, where, said the architect 'the Governor and the taskmaster are invisible to those who are continually under their observation'.[70] Each side of the polygon, together with a thin slice of walled yard where prisoners were exercised one at a time for half an hour a day, contained one class. Each class contained a maximum of 12 prisoners — at first in solitude then in moderate but silent association on an 'uncommonly strict' system based on the Gloucester Penitentiary Rules.[71]

The prison buildings at Devizes were kept very low to prevent prisoners being able to see out over the boundary wall from the upper storeys (a fault Ingleman had noticed in many of Blackburn's prisons), and it was this that caused the plan to spread so widely. The lowness of the buildings, coupled with a regular punctuation of open arcades at first floor level, also solved the difficulty of getting air to flow into the interior courts of the prison; at the same time its compensating breadth

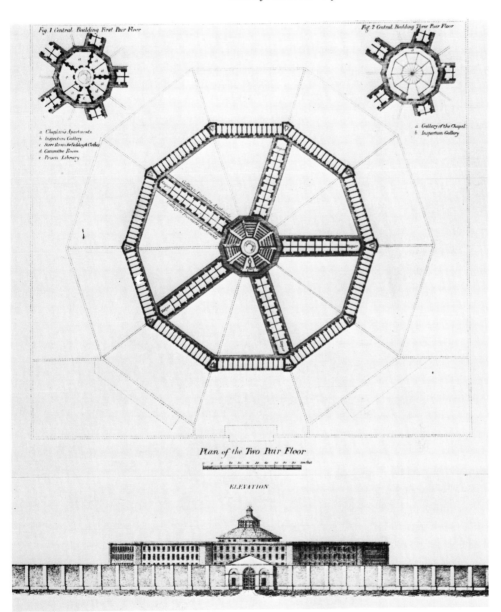

149. Penitentiary or gaol for 600 prisoners, James Bevans, 1819, upper floor plan and elevation.

put 160 feet of open space between the gaoler and his gaol. He might remain 'invisible' in his rotunda but he would have to emerge into full view of the whole prison each time he ventured from it. The executive utility of inspection was reduced by such vulnerable isolation of authority. So, when in 1817 the Wiltshire Magistrates decided to rebuild the old county gaol at Fisherton Anger, Ingleman produced a design in which he tried to overcome this crucial flaw in a plan he regarded as in all other respects unrivalled (Fig. 153). The gaol was kept low and wide (Fig. 154) but now contained a diametrical 'inspection passage' passing from the governor's apartments to the surrounding buildings. The central pavilion was still as far from the cells and workrooms but at least the staff were permitted 'unobserved egress and ingress'; at least their coming into the prison was not made a public event. Still, as Ingleman

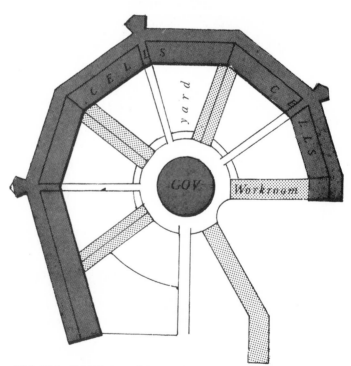

150. Wakefield House of Correction, architect unknown, 1821, plan from S.I.P.D., *Remarks on the Form and Construction of Prisons*, 1826.

151. Kirkdale House of Correction, Thomas Wright, 1819–21, view from the gaolers' gardens. The semi-circular range of building was the main prison (left background). The small tholos between the prison and the gaolers' house (far right) was the chapel.

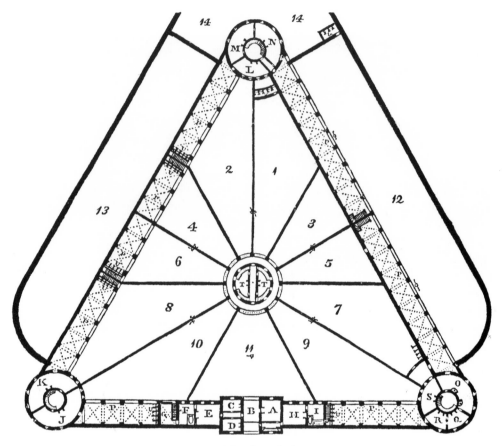

REFERENCES.

A. Governor's parlour.
B. Public entrance.
C. Governor's office.
D. Turnkeys' room.
E. General kitchen.
F. Bake-house.
G. Store room for ditto.
H. Laundry and Cold bath.
I. Hot bath. Oven for tainted clothes, &c. Room for examining felons.
J. Work room for class 10.
K. Ditto ditto——— 8.

L. Work room for 20 male felons of the best class.
M. Dining room, &c. for the debtors.
N. Common room for ditto.
O. Public kitchen. Copper for ditto.
PPP. Piazzas under the cells for each class.
Q. Living room for cook or superintendant.
R. Sleeping room for ditto
S. Work room for female debtors.
T. Turnkeys' rooms, with stairs to chapel for different classes.
UUUU. Privies, &c. to every class.

1. Extra court for felons of the best class.
2. Court and ward for 20 felons of the best class.
3. Court for criminals condemned to hard labour.
4. ——— for 12 felons of the second class.
5. Court for male debtors to work, &c.
6. Court and ward for 12 felons of the worst class.
7. ——— for female debtors only.
8. Court and ward for 20 deserters, King's evidences, &c.

9. Court and ward for 18 female felons.
10. ——————— for 18 young criminals, and for assaults, misdemeanours, &c.
11. Court for turnkeys, state prisoners, &c.
12. Court and wards for the debtors.
13. An Extra court for gardens, work and rope grounds, &c.
14. Ditto——— ——— &c.

152. Triangular prison plan, from James Elmes, *Hints for the Improvement of Prisons*, 1817.

himself was aware, the Fisherton plan was an improvement only in so far as it resorted to radial components.[72]

Although secrecy had been achieved, accessibility had not. In all polygonal prisons interminable lengths of passageway were made to serve as arteries for policing. Within them it was very easy to lose all sense of direction as there were no distinguishing features inside the prison and no visible landmarks without. Arthur Griffiths, describing the most labyrinthine of all, Millbank (Fig. 125), with its 'angles every 20 yards, winding staircases, dark passages, innumerable doors and gates', told the story of a warder who, after many years of service, was unable to find his way through the 2¾ miles of corridor without a piece of chalk. Only by making marks as he went about his business was he able to retrace his footsteps.[73]

The Wiltshire Magistrates rejected Ingleman's improved polygonal plan for Fisherton Anger, perhaps in part for the reasons given above, more certainly because of their experience in building Devizes House of Correction. Ingleman's original cost estimate of £16,000 had inflated to £40,208 by 1817. At this time the building was only two-thirds completed – it was left so, with the last five segments missing.[74] In preference to Ingleman's Fisherton plan they chose an unusually conservative design by Thomas Hopper that reverted to Howardian planning practices (Fig. 155). Devizes House of Correction and Millbank Penitentiary, set up as models of construction, had only demonstrated how very expensive polygonal prisons were (Fig. 182).

The argument against radial plans mustered by Ingleman and Holford was that they lacked security. There was nothing between a desperate prisoner and his freedom except for a low boundary wall and a few flimsy railings. All he had to do was run away from the governor's apartments – a direction he might anyway choose out of preference. Holford added that radials were easier to inspect than to administer, and that prisoners, if they had a mind, could, by overpowering one turnkey, cut the governor off from the outside world, surround him and make him a prisoner in his own prison.[75] These criticisms applied equally well to many polygonals but they also point to the source of the dispute. Holford did not trust preventive inspection: he did not believe that it was a sufficiently powerful or reliable force to control all the prisoners all the time. He therefore preferred to use the prison as a means of internment as well as a means of inspection by containing the

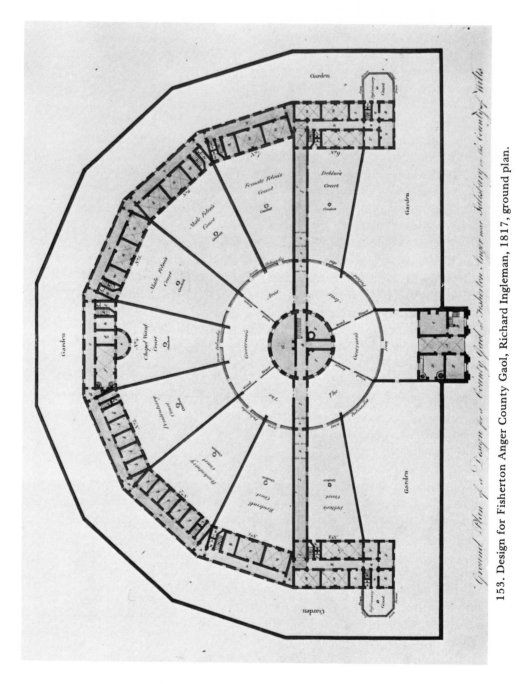

153. Design for Fisherton Anger County Gaol, Richard Ingleman, 1817, ground plan.

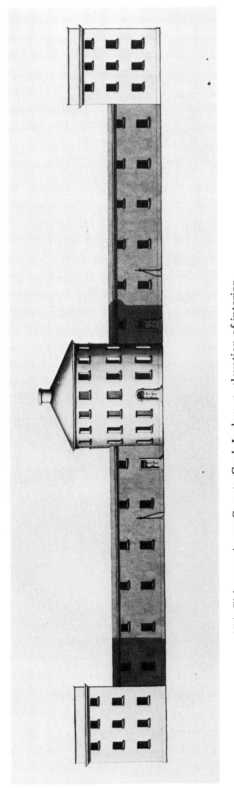

154. Fisherton Anger County Gaol, Ingleman, elevation of interior.

prisoners within an unbroken ring of solid buildings. The S.I.P.D., on the other hand, preferred to use prison buildings as a means of inspection alone, and that is why they chose the radial. So the victory of the radial over the polygonal was the victory of unlimited inspection over limited inspection. It marked the ascendence of the power of central authority over and above the containing power of secure buildings.

The radial was the more perfect organ of surveillance. The history of its development had been the history of a transition. What started off at Ghent Maison de Force as an icon of central authority (Fig. 27) — a picture of an institutional structure in a plan, with the administration and the chapel in the centre and the prisoners round about — was transformed, by a series of practical measures and architectural improvements, into an instrument for the imposition of the very authority it had set out to symbolize. The relative position of governor and prisoners remained the same while each part of the building was put in the service of this one over-riding purpose: vesting more and more knowledge and power in the person of the keeper, revealing more and more of the

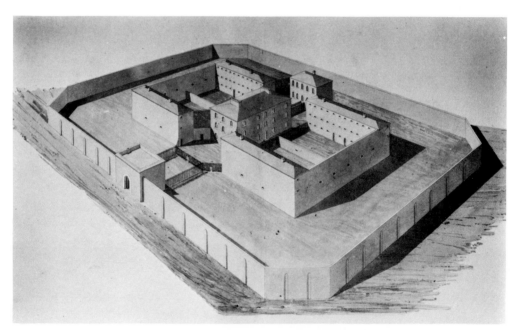

155. Fisherton Anger County Gaol, Thomas Hopper, 1820.

prison to his eye and bringing it more closely under his command until the symbol was merely contained within its own realization. The Maison de Force had depicted the concentration of authority, much as Boullée's Palais de Justice had depicted the relationship between the law and offenders: through the metaphorical language of geometry. The depiction did not affect the exertion of authority in any way, it only signified it. The improved radials were very different; they were contrived not as the expression of central authority, but as the vessels through which that authority flowed. The prison building was now a necessary and crucial element in prison discipline, without which the power of the keeper would be dwarfed, and the autocratic, rigid regulation of behaviour rendered utterly impossible. The change, though barely noticed by penal historians, and unrecorded in the general history of architecture, could hardly have been more significant.

Labour

In 1818 a new type of treadmill was invented and patented by William Cubitt, a civil engineer from Ipswich. Two years later the resourceful inventor was given an opportunity to publicize and explain its excellent properties under the auspices of the S.I.P.D.[76] Four years after that there were Cubitt treadmills installed in 54 prisons throughout the country with space for a total of 1,162 prisoners.[77]

The reason for the considerable success of the wheel, its great attractiveness to philanthropists, magistrates, keepers and governors alike, lay beyond economics, although at first it was introduced to tap a useful form of power. In the 1820s the produce from it — usually ground flour — was sold on the open market, or the mill shaft plus the labour of the prisoners was hired out to a contractor for whatever purpose he chose to use it. Cubitt himself regarded the work of prisoners as analogous to a natural energy source, and the mill as a harness to that energy:

The operations of the convicts would be precisely the same as that which is now effected by the ordinary powers of wind, water, steam or horses, and they would have no more concern with the object of the machinery, or manufacture, than any of the above-named agents; and there would be no more difficulty in establishing a mill or manufactory, near the boundary wall of a prison, through which only a single shaft, or axle, would have to pass, to communicate the power and motion.[78]

If manufacturers sited mills by streams why should they not site them by prisons?

The utilization of prison labour as a source of motive energy was not unprecedented. Samuel Bentham's planing machine, which was to have been worked by the Panopticon convicts, had been devised with the same idea in mind, and the turning of capstans or mills had been listed in the 1779 Penitentiary Act as a suitable means of extracting hard labour.[79] But perhaps the most curious example of its early use is found in Robert Seymour's account of the grinding mill perfected by John Pain. In the 1570s the Lord Mayor of London was pressing the Governors of the Poor to put one of Pain's mills in Bridewell. It was said to grind more than other machinery of the sort, but its most wonderful recommendation was that it could be worked by cripples: 'The lame, either in arms or legs, might work at it if they had but use of either, and accordingly these mills are termed handmills or footmills.'[80] Through it, invalids could be turned into industrious citizens, and the work of ten men could be accomplished by two. Treadmills had been used for centuries in Europe, but there is record of only one within the English reformed prisons before 1818. This had been installed by Orridge at Bury St Edmunds to grind barley meal for pigs.[81]

Cubitt must have known of the wheel at nearby Bury, and it is not altogether unlikely that he was led into designing a new one in an effort to improve it, since in November 1819 a prototype of his own mill — the first of its kind — was erected in that very gaol. In a traditional treadwheel the labourers stood inside. Accordingly, the diameter had to be at least 15 feet to fit a standing man within it. Cubitt, learning from the Chinese, turned this arrangement inside out and reduced the diameter of the wheel to 5 feet (Fig. 163).[82] The downward weight of the labouring prisoners was now exerted at a tangent to the wheel, where the momentum was most effective in turning the shaft, and so far less energy was wasted in useless forward motion. Cubitt could demonstrate that his wheel performed four times the work for the same distance traversed. But this was not all; the work was harder, being more like climbing than walking, and it was also measurable. An exact quantum of work could be got from every prisoner by regulating the speed of the wheel: 'If the men are not doing proper work, a bell is placed in the roof of the building, which will ring itself when the wheel goes too slow.'[83]

The value of the wheel was not its industrial potential (there is record of only one Cubitt mill outside of the penal system, installed as a hoist in the East India Company's Bengal Warehouse),[84] but rather in its capacity to reduce the act of labour to an inescapable sequence of necessary movements. Mention has already been made of the belief that the moral component of labour was in its regularity rather than in its productiveness. The widespread appreciation of the treadwheel demonstrated that this point of view was not uncommon. Soon enough some authorities would dispense with production altogether, at which point the wheel became nothing more than a device for equalizing, measuring, regulating and timing the performance of toil. Having thus lost all connection with profit it nevertheless maintained its position within the prison system, demonstrating that labour could be abstracted from complicated procedures of fabrication to exist in the concentrated form of pure exertion.

The severance of labour from profit was very disturbing to James Mill who, as a Benthamite witnessing these events, registered his misgivings in an article on prison discipline for the 1824 edition of the *Encyclopaedia Britannica*. 'Men', he said, 'seldom fall in love with their punishments.' To make labour an affliction and to deny a man recompense for it was unwise. The monotonous drudgery of the mill was quite acceptable, however, so long as a certain pleasure was obtained as the profit. For the prison to instill a *desire* to work in shiftless and lazy inmates it would need to function as a miniature model of the free-trade economy; advantage must always accrue from the performance of labour, disadvantage from its avoidance. It was folly to break the bond.[85] At this time a number of prisons — certainly Bury, Leicester, Lewes and Aylesbury[86] — paid those who worked the wheel either in extra bread rations or in money (1*d*. a day), and many more were still grinding corn. The S.I.P.D., Orridge, le Breton, and John Headlam professed agreement with James Mill, at least on the need for production, but as the years passed the mills turned less and less profitably.

Before the depth of the post-war depression had become apparent, it could reasonably be maintained that prison labour was a resource like any other to be exploited to the full. Bentham had argued thus, and his views were echoed by the pamphleteers who held that the forced labour of the prison was 'similar to the case in which the invention of a new and more perfect machinery enables a commodity to be sold much

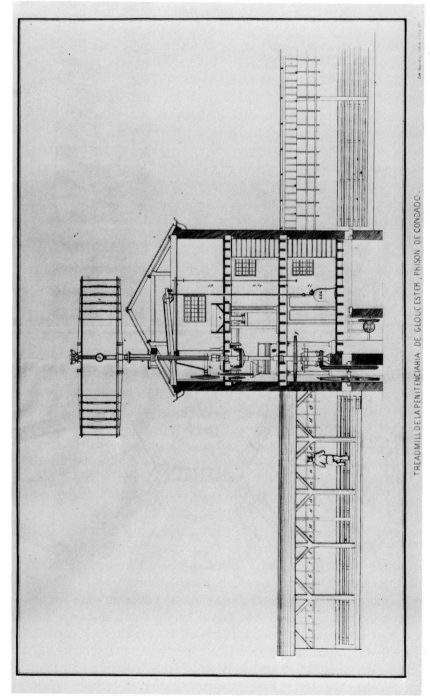

TREADMILL DE LA PENITENCIARIA DE GLOUCESTER, PRISON DE CONDADO.

156. Treadwheel and section of the mill at Gloucester County Gaol.

298

cheaper than it was sold before'. This, they held, was not an evil. Yet even in 1817 they were predicting concerted opposition to their views.[87]

All the same, it is very difficult to tell what treadwheel labour was used for in the 1820s and 1830s, because the issue simply dropped from sight. In the most comprehensive reports ever compiled on prison discipline, the House of Lords Reports of 1835,[88] we are told at what rate wheels revolved, what type of regulators were in use, how healthy the prisoners on them were and how conversation was prevented, but there is no mention of how much they yielded or of what. Only Peter Laurie, a clever and fractious Middlesex Magistrate, raised the question, and he was put down by the Chairman (the 5th Duke of Richmond) for doing so with the comment that it was not always easy to find practical occupations for prisoners.[89] Later the sheer pointlessness of the Cubitt mills became a favourite literary theme for writers on prisons. This piece from Daniel Nihil is fairly typical: 'The Poets have omitted to inform us by what self-acting machinery Sisyphus was constrained to this useless and unvaried toil. It was reserved for the modern age to complete this part of their image by the invention of the treadmill.'[90]

On the whole it was pointlessness by default, not by design. Laurie had complained that it was more expensive to set up prison industries than not to do so, and with a few exceptions this does seem to have been the case. The great advantage of the wheel was to make labour exact as well as exacting, leaving no room for deviation, malingering, or diversion, epitomizing the irreducible essence of labour as exertion dissociated from manufacture. As regulated labour replaced productive work, complicated windsail masts were raised above the treadwheel mill-houses, signifying the inutility of the prisoners' efforts (Figs. 156, 157). These sails gave a measured resistance to the rotation of the wheel. When driven at a certain rate centrifugal force would push out a governor that controlled the surface area of the rotating blade, increasing the resistance of the sail and slowing down the treadwheel until the governor subsided and the resistance decreased once again. The sails were used as a primitive form of controlling device to ensure that a certain known distance would be covered by prisoners walking the wheel for a given length of time. In the end they were found to be too imprecise and revolution counters were added, while fly-wheels and brakes substituted for sails. A further refinement was the 'ergonometer' designed by John Mance, keeper of Petworth House of Correction, in

157. Treadwheel at Brixton, William Cubitt, 1821. The friction regulator and sail can be seen above the millhouse. The bench was for prisoners taking a measured interval of rest every 20 minutes.

1832. This instrument 'notifies by an alarm bell when each day's labour is completed for seventy-eight days over which neither the officers or the prisoners have any control' (Figs. 158, 159).[91] Mance also introduced the hand-crank in preference to the treadwheel and compartmentalized each work station to prevent whispering or signalling between prisoners.

Cubitt supervised the erection of many of his treadwheels, designing the machinery, advising and inspecting the work of the local millwrights who fabricated them. There were many varieties of wheel: there were two storey wheels (Devizes), wheels with spy passages behind for 'seeing without being seen' (Springfield Gaol, Essex), single wheels and interlinked wheels and wheels partitioned for use by distinct classes. There were also wheels that, due to faulty regulators, went faster and faster until the prisoners either jumped off or were thrown off (Brixton), wheels that simply broke to pieces while in motion (Maidstone), and wheels that mangled and killed unwary prisoners dragged into the machinery (Cold Bath Fields).[92] Cubitt, undaunted, set about redesigning the radial prison around his invention (Fig. 160). The resulting plan was made the centrepiece of C.C. Western's *Thoughts on Prison Discipline*. It consisted of 14 identical four storey radial wings with iron gallery access, facing onto yards furnished with 12 large, interlinked treadwheels. The wheels made a huge ring punctuated by turnkeys' inspection rooms, and were overseen from the central lodge as well. There was no real need for exercise yards or for workrooms. Exercise and labour were now one and the same, and consequently prison accommodation need be little more than an accumulation of night cells and wheels. The Brixton House of Correction, where Cubitt built six of his wheels in 1821,[93] was a design of this type, although on a polygonal rather than a radial plan (Fig. 161). The various plans produced by Thomas Hopper for Springfield County Gaol in 1820 also feature the treadwheel, possibly influenced by C.C. Western, since he was the M.P. for Essex County, but in this instance the wheels were supplemented with extensive ateliers for other employments as well (Fig. 162).

The progress of the treadwheel was bound up with a revival of austerity. It was introduced at an auspicious time, soon after solitary confinement had been given up, and thus took its place as the most notoriously unpleasant feature of prison life. Searching for something else to 'connect the idea of discomfort with the prison'[94] the magis-

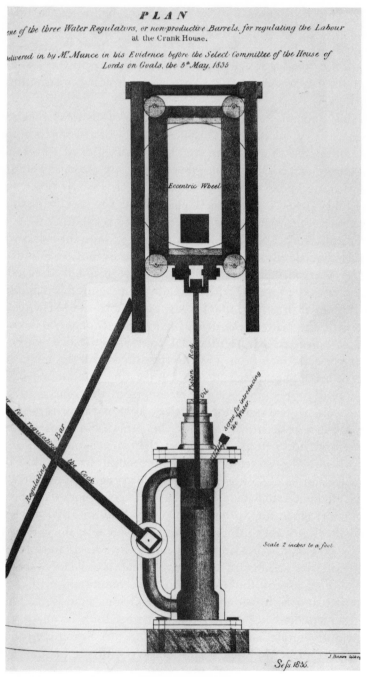

158. Unproductive water pump, John Mance, 1832.

tracy and the government found the treadwheel to be an 'excellent instrument of corrective discipline', an 'irksome penalty' which 'excites a strong dislike'. That the wheel fulfilled a comparable role to that of solitude in the prison system was pointed out by Western, who saw punishment as a delicate balancing between insufficient deterrence and the 'breaking down of the moral structure of the mind'.[95] Of the two the wheel was more certain in its operation but equally dreadful. 'The horrors of dungeon imprisonment, to the credit of the age, no longer exist: but if no cause of dread is substituted, by what indication of common sense is it that we send criminals there at all.' The words 'dread' and 'terror' were heard with much greater frequency now. Where the philanthropists had introduced solitude as primarily a method of reformation and incidentally a source of deterrence, the improvers introduced the wheel as primarily a source of deterrence — not that it was devoid of reforming qualities, but they receded into the middle distance as its capacity to instill a 'strong dislike' came to the fore.

So the treadwheel was a sure and healthy way of reintroducing terror into the prisons. When Robert Peel, Secretary of State for the Home Department, circularized the local authorities to gather information on the effects of treadmill discipline in 1823, they replied in

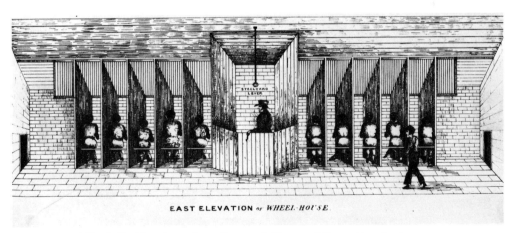

EAST ELEVATION *of* WHEEL-HOUSE.

159. Stalled hand cranks at Petworth House of Correction for turning the unproductive water pump. Labour was governed by the ergonometer. John Mance, 1832.

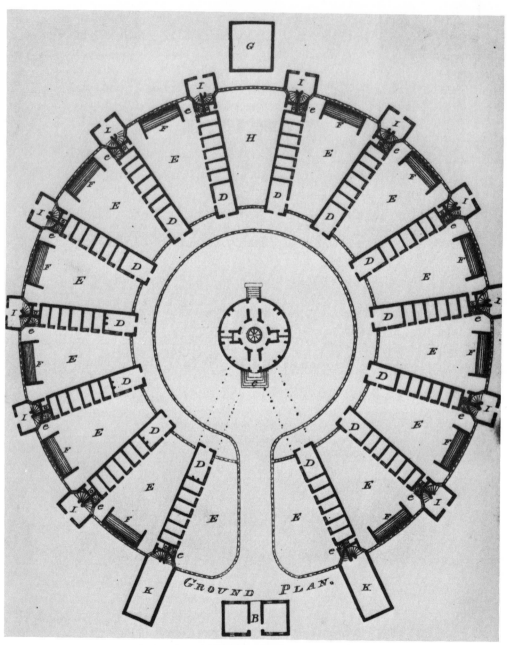

160. Design for a House of Correction for 400 prisoners, William Cubitt, 1823.

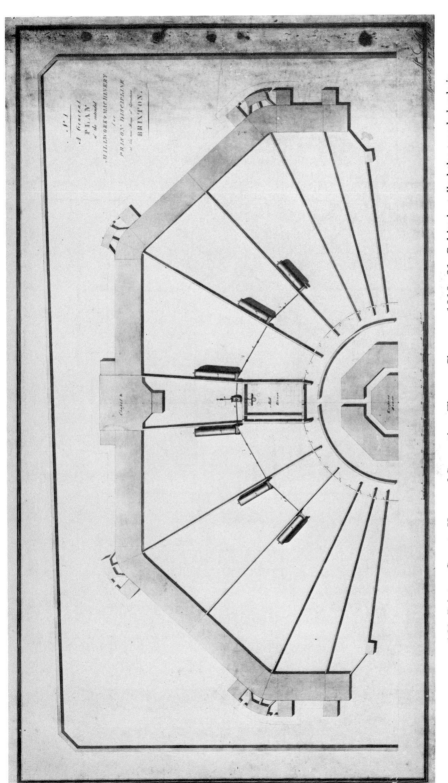

161. Brixton County House of Correction, Thomas Chawner, 1818–21. Cubitt installed the treadwheels in 1821.

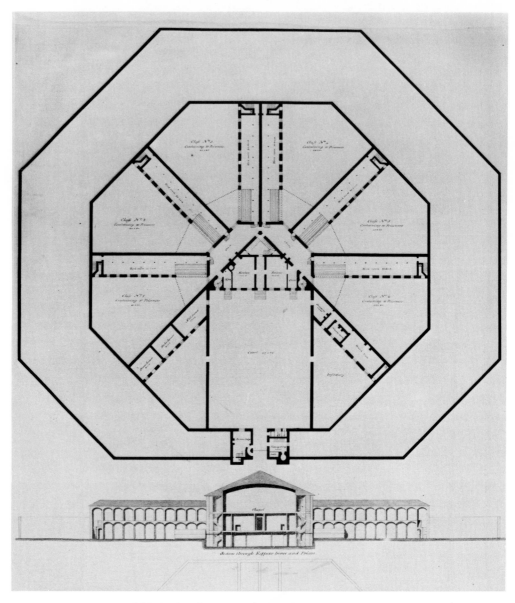

162. Design for Springfield County Gaol, Chelmsford, Thomas Hopper, 1820, ground plan and section.

chorus that 'no bodily mischief' had been perceived by their prison surgeons. Indeed, far from being injurious to health the wheel was discovered to have been positively beneficial at Lancaster, Buckingham and Gloucester. At Ipswich, where Cubitt lived, the visiting Justices were gratified to find prisoners queuing for the privilege of working on it.[96] One intrepid female had demonstrated her ability to knit while treading,[97] and the women at Northallerton declared it to be nowhere near so hard as washing clothes. It transpired that anything from eight to ten hours a day in summer and five to eight hours in winter were spent on it. The returns for 1825 were not quite so closely harmonized.[98] Giles Lyford, the surgeon at Winchester Gaol and Bridewell, recorded that pulmonary and rheumatic complaints were vastly increased by use of the wheel. At Lancaster and Maidstone inflammations of the groin were detected, and at Shepton Mallet, where it had caused eight hernias, it was described as having a 'strong disposition to produce rupture'. Voices of protest were raised. John Mason Good, M.D., an old reformer who remembered Howard, claimed that the *quality* of labour on the wheel was more injurious than its quantity, and no amount of juggling with the number of revolutions or the number of hours' labour would alter its tendency to produce varicose swellings, as the posture required of prisoners was so unnatural (Fig. 163).[99] This was confirmed by K. Briscoe, who made himself very unpopular as a visiting magistrate to Guildford House of Correction by condemning the use of the treadwheel there. Briscoe discovered from the prison records that practically all the prisoners had lost weight, one man from 11 st. 10 lb. to 9 st. 3½ lb., another from an already emaciated 7 st. 5 lb. to 6 st. 3 lb. He found a vagrant mother put on the wheel and unable to produce milk for her child, and heard also that several ruptures had recently been suffered because of it. The inquisitive magistrate then took to the wheel himself to experience at first hand its effects. He started with the slow wheel of Newport Bridewell, which made only five revolutions a minute; even this was exhausting. He went on to try other, more arduous, models and compared them to the hand-crank which he found to be much less crippling. Finally he published his views in an open letter to Sir Robert Peel in which he also disputed the wheel's deterrent effects (the prisoners at Brixton, where the wheel was in unremitting use, were flocking back for more!) and called for legislation against such an 'unnatural and profitless' invention: 'The treadmill is indeed a plan so multifariously defective, although tried and retried, propped up and praised to society, that the longer it lasts the more it must lose ground in the eyes of all moderate and reflecting men, who were at first disposed to think well of it.'[100] He was wrong. His letter was treated as the object of a most profound execration by the other Surrey Magis-

163. Section of interlinked wheels, illustrating the awkward tiptoe posture required.

trates. An answer came from one of these, H. Drummond, who managed — by what techniques we may only guess — to extract from every prisoner interviewed by Briscoe statements exactly contrary to those they had made earlier. The wheel at Guildford stayed.[101]

The function of the treadwheel was to aggravate toil, measure it and equalize its distribution amongst prisoners. If eminently successful in the first, it was discovered, by the 1830s, to be inadequate in the last. There were those who were constitutionally fitted to such labour — the sturdiest and strongest — who it was said, were usually the wickedest; and there were those who were not — the frail and the weak — whose health the wheel might most easily destroy. On the other hand, there were enormous differences in the application of it. At Bedford the labour performed each day was 'equal to an ascent of 5,000 ft. in summer and 3,600 ft. in winter, while at Knutsford House of Correction it is 14,000 ft. in summer and 9,800 ft. in winter'.[102] No doubt these irregularities and inexactitudes would have been ironed out by further technical refinements of treadwheel machinery and administration if the wheel itself had not been overtaken by the reintroduction of solitary confinement.

The limits of improvement

A crisis of confidence in the prison system was building up during the 1830s that was far more momentous than that which had occurred in the early years of the century. Ruminations on the unequal demands made by the treadwheel were but a small part of this. The crucial problems were to do with classification. As the number of classes grew, as central authority was advanced and the size of local prisons increased, so the canonical radial plan, with its one Cyclops eye in a central hub sporting tentacles of prison accommodation, became more awkward to manage. This difficulty was tackled by Bullar in the S.I.P.D. designs of 1826 (Fig. 144). As his plans increased in size so the number of radial wings around the nuclear eye of the prison grew in an entirely predictable pattern until he reached the plan for 300 prisoners in 14 classes. Here the nucleus expanded into an annular ring to keep proximity to the surrounding workrooms, but the consistent pattern of growth was preserved. In the last plan, for up to 400 prisoners in 14 classes, the pattern broke down. No more wings than seven could be supported around a single hub without too large a gap developing between the centre and the rest of the prison (a fault more typical of polygonal buildings but which was also well exhibited in Cubitt's 14 wing radial for 400 prisoners (Fig. 160)). And so mitosis occurred; the nucleus split into a mirror image of itself and authority was divided into two centres. The same point had been reached at Maidstone County Gaol (1810–17, 30 classes), designed by David Asher Alexander (Fig. 164), where four nearly identical radials modelled on Blackburn's Ipswich County Gaol each with its own point of convergence, were distributed across a tri-angular grid of interconnected inspection passages. It had also been reached at Westminster New Bridewell in Tothill Fields (1829–32, 24 classes), by Robert Abram (Fig. 165), where a plan with three five wing

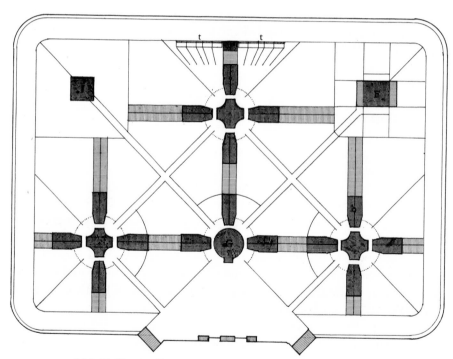

164. Maidstone County Gaol and House of Correction, David Asher Alexander, 1810–17, G, gaolers' house; I, infirmary; F, female prison; tt, treadwheels.

radials round an enormous entrance courtyard was finally agreed on. Seven earlier schemes for Tothill Fields submitted between 1819 and 1829, all with between 24 and 26 class divisions, show variations on similar themes (Fig. 166).[103] Only one attempted to unify the prison round a single centre; a hopeless task, as indicated by the substitution of a 'room for dead bodies' in place of the governor's observatory at the heart of the prison (Fig. 167). In these instances the whole radial prison

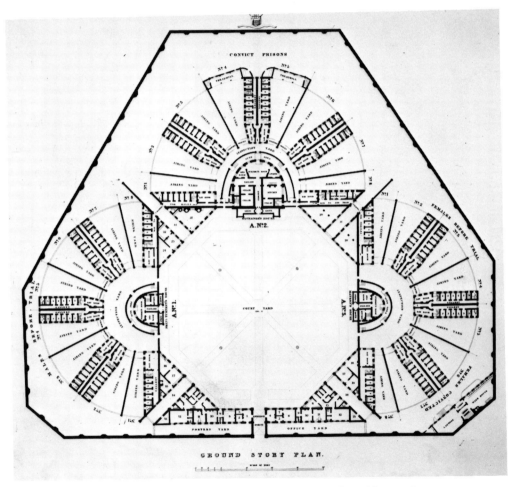

165. Westminster New Bridewell, Tothill Fields, Robert Abram, 1829–32, ground plan.

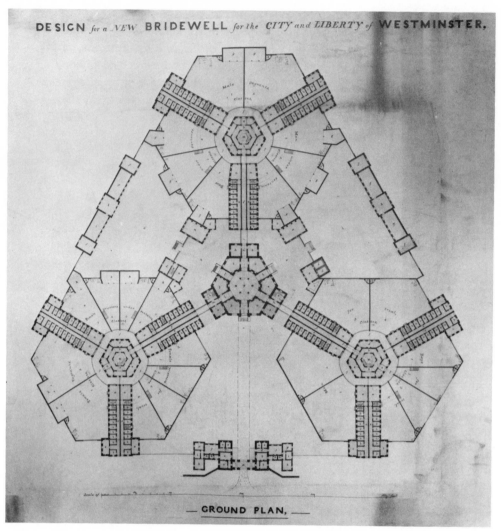

166. Project for Westminster Bridewell, architect unknown, 1819, ground plan.

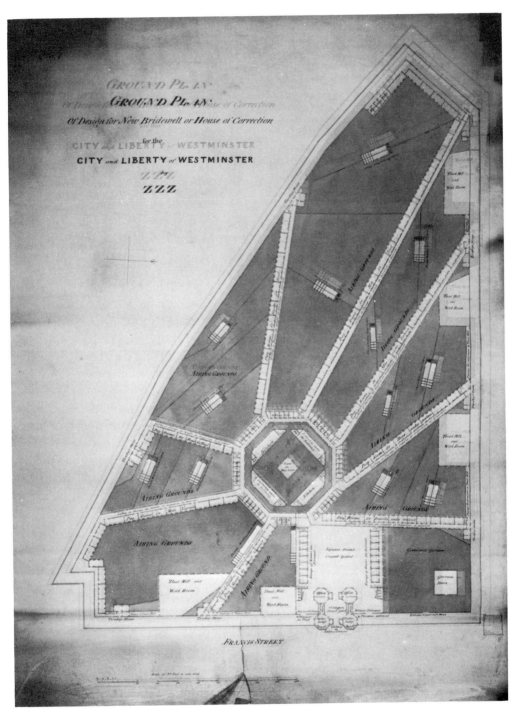

167. Project for Westminster Bridewell, architect unknown, 1819, ground plan.

had replicated itself to keep pace with the continuing subdivision of its component parts. Another solution was attempted by Francis Goodwin in his early design for Derby County Gaol and House of Correction (1823). At first sight the Derby plan appears to be a conventional radial martialled about a single centre, but closer scrutiny reveals six other points of convergence — and at the focus of each, a turnkey's chamber (Fig. 168).[104] While preserving the formal expression of central authority, Goodwin had in fact inserted these six subsidiary surveillance stations with overlapping fields of vision at key points along the edge of the prison. With the increased efficacy of inspection that this allowed went a corresponding devolution of central authority. No longer could the whole prison be dominated from one point.

Goodwin's plan was adopted by the Derby Justices and then sent, post haste, to the S.I.P.D. for comment. There is no record of the S.I.P.D.'s answer, but the revised plan, which incorporated their suggestions, went back to a more conventional layout with surveillance emanating from the very centre and nowhere else (Fig. 169).[105] In order to accomplish this reunification Goodwin had been forced to relegate seven of the class wards and yards to an outer ring, from where they were only tenuously connected to the centre.

The two plans for Derby illustrate clearly the two varieties of compromise which prison architects could make as classifications increased. In the first plan a pervasive surveillance had been maintained at the expense of centralized authority; in the second, central authority was reasserted at the expense of surveillance. The classified radial had reached a limit — a limit of scale and divisibility — beyond which its dual functions could not be sustained.

This was not the only trouble. The logic of classification was approaching an impasse, independent of the technical problem of maintaining surveillance and subdivision. Orridge had pointed to the necessary imprecision of any scheme of categories, drawing attention to the artfulness of the most atrocious and deceitful prisoners, who could always beat the classification system and turn up in a ward full of innocents, where, with their peculiar power over weaker minds, they would be able to pervert their fellow inmates with effortless facility.[106] This was the worm in the fruit; the artfulness of the wicked who were somehow able to overcome the most scrupulous classification and evade the most vigilant surveillance. During the 1830s there was a

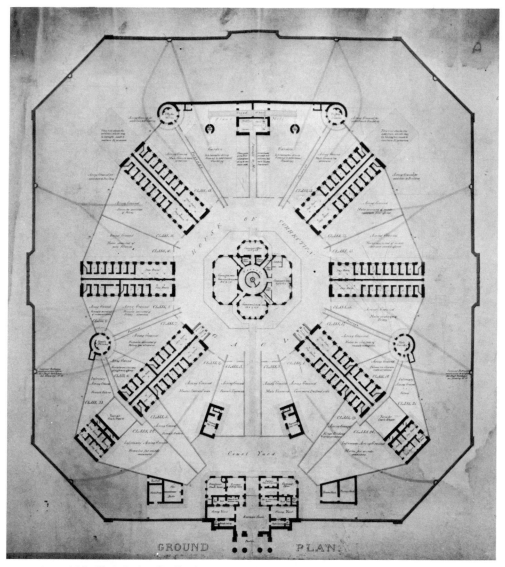

168. First design for Derby County Gaol, Francis Goodwin, 1823, ground plan.

growing scepticism over the plausibility of classification. It was a scepticism of a particularly corrosive kind. Observations regarding its shortcomings and imperfections were in abundance: 'It has indeed been imagined that the propagation of crime during imprisonment could be prevented by a judicious system of classification. Experience has however shown the fallacy of all such arrangements.' Classification had not precluded vice and disorder from the English prisons in which, it was now angrily testified, 'even an innocent man sent for trial can hardly escape contamination'.[107] In language reminiscent of the first phase of reform Cold Bath Fields was condemned as a 'sink of abomination' in which men and women prisoners could freely converse, and so on it went; always the same dismal tale. Nothing was right. Things were too lax.

Just before these disparaging words were heard, the news of some vitally important experiments into new methods of imprisonment taking

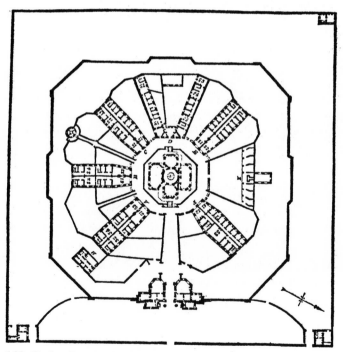

169. Derby County Gaol, Francis Goodwin, 1823—7, ground plan.

place in Philadelphia and New York began to trickle through.[108] It was hardly a coincidence that the existing prison system, a very recent product stemming from 50 years of agitation, reform and improvement, now came under a most damaging attack from the very people who had helped build and maintain it (Bullar, Sibly, Chesterton, Orridge, Mance, Crawford, Russell, Nihil, Hoare).[109] With new proposals at hand current practices could be dissected, discredited and anathematized. Silence and separation would yet be the salvation of prisoners. The task that remained was to re-establish the need for them. This was done during a period of intense self-criticism in the 1830s. By insisting that things had not yet gone far enough, and by showing that two of the three mainstays of reformation — classification and the wheel — were ineffective, the authorities themselves ushered in the final phase of prison reform.

Three attitudes to imprisonment have been discussed in the preceding chapters: the mercantile attitude as exemplified by Bridewell; the eighteenth-century doctrine of reform with its mixture of piety and reason; and the out-and-out rationalism of Bentham's Panopticon. If characteristic aims were to be assigned to each one of these they would be the enforcement of work in the Bridewell, the enforcement of seclusion in the reformed prison, and the enforcement of central authority in the Panopticon. The era of prison improvement saw the revival and reintegration of forced labour in the prison system and the development of central authority as well as the continuation of seclusion in the form of classification. In this sense improved prisons were a culmination of prison history; a fusion embodying these three commanding principles in one kind of building. In another, more urgent sense, they were simply preliminaries to the last act.

7   Architecture against communication

The English rediscovered the reforming power of solitude in America, where the earlier practice of solitary confinement had not been renounced as it had been in this country.

On 8 May 1787 the Philadelphia Society for Alleviating the Miseries of Public Prisons met for the first time. Under Benjamin Rush's guidance the society was to campaign for solitary confinement and hard labour in prisons but, although they achieved some limited success in these early years,[1] it was not until 1818 that the Pennsylvania State Legislature voted $60,000 for the construction of a penitentiary at Pittsburgh, and then, in 1821, a further $100,000 for another in Philadelphia in which a regime of unmitigated solitude would be enforced.[2] An even more severe incarceration was practised for ten brief months at Auburn Prison in New York State, where reformation was pursued in a special block of 80 claustrophobic cubicles measuring no more than 7 feet by 3½ feet. The closeted convicts were subjected to such complete seclusion that they died or went mad: 'In order to reform them they had been submitted to complete isolation; but this absolute solitude . . . is beyond the strength of man, . . . it does not reform, it kills.' So wrote de Tocqueville and de Beaumont after their extensive tour of American prisons in 1831.[3] The disappointing results at Auburn led the New York authorities to abandon unmitigated solitude in 1823. It was replaced by a regime of hard labour in 'silent association' during the day with cellular confinement at night. Any communication between convicts — even a glance — was henceforth punished by vigorous flogging in order to prevent moral contamination.

Back in Pennsylvania the Pittsburgh Penitentiary, designed by William Strickland, was completed in 1827 (Fig. 170). Although intended for unmitigated solitude 'defects in the construction of the prison rendered the execution of the system impossible'.[4] The prisoners could talk to one another with no difficulty from within their cells. Pennsylvania

318

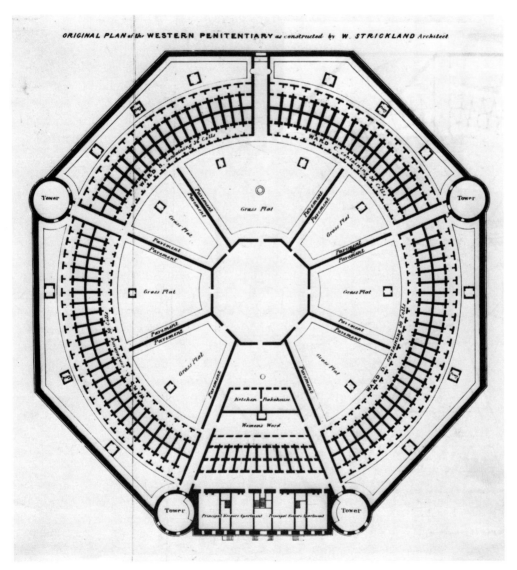

170. First Pittsburgh Penitentiary, William Strickland, 1818–27,
ground plan.

was, in any case, reconsidering its penal policies. The lessons of Auburn had been learnt, but solitude was not to be given up. A second Pennsylvania Penitentiary, at Cherry Hill in Philadelphia, was also now under construction. This too was provided with separate cells. The state had thus already invested a considerable sum of money in solitary prisons; consequently the regime was maintained but adjusted by an Act of 1829 allowing the intolerable burden of total solitude to be mitigated by the provision of work in the cells, and by the appointment of lay visitors, whose mission was to enter the prison as agents for morality. The only persons permitted to undertake this work, apart from certain high-ranking state officials, were the Acting Committee of the Philadelphia Society for Alleviating the Miseries of Prisons. It was their task to confront the prisoner in his cell with virtue while offering solace for his despair.

But the mitigation of solitude made no appreciable difference to the construction of Cherry Hill (Fig. 171). William Strickland, an established figure in Philadelphia, had been ousted from his post as architect for this, the second Pennsylvania Penitentiary by a young immigrant, John de Haviland, who had arrived in 1816.[5] Haviland introduced the radial plan from England and succeeded where Strickland had failed. So conspicuous was his success that in 1829 he was given the job of demolishing Strickland's Pittsburgh Penitentiary, completed only two years before, so that it could be rebuilt on the lines of his own Cherry Hill (Fig. 172).[6] By 1842 he had been commissioned to design at least ten other American penitentiaries.[7]

Haviland's Cherry Hill was destined to become the focus of international interest. In 1831 de Beaumont and de Tocqueville reported their favourable impressions of both the 'separate' system at Cherry Hill and the 'silent' system at Auburn to the French government, but in the United States the respective merits of the two were hotly debated on practical and theoretical grounds. Sides were always taken. To the advocates of separation Cherry Hill was 'more philosophical in its principle, more practical and easy in its application, more charitable in its whole spirit than the Auburn system'.[8] To the advocates of silent association it was a vastly expensive testament to the folly of philanthropists and reformers (the final cost was $785,000 for 400 cells).[9] Cherry Hill soon became identified with reformative imprisonment, Auburn with retributive imprisonment; Cherry Hill with humanity,

171. Philadelphia Penitentiary, Cherry Hill, John de Haviland, 1821–9. The original design was for 250 cells, all on ground level. The decision to increase the number of cells to 400 forced Haviland to add the second storey.

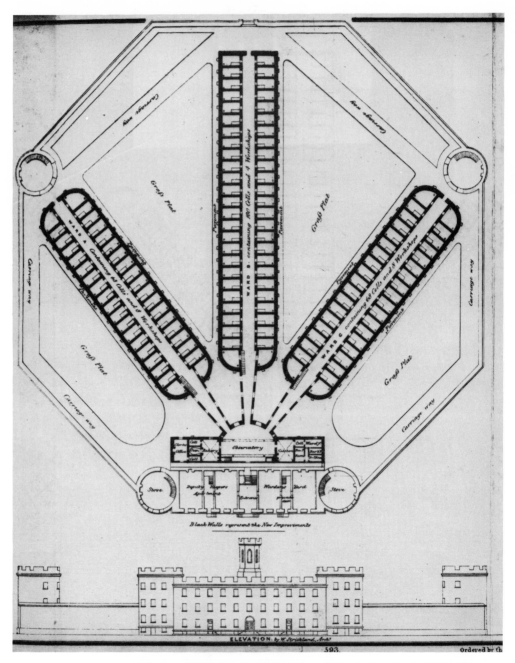

172. Second Pittsburgh Penitentiary, John de Haviland, 1829–32, ground plan.

Auburn with economy; Cherry Hill with idealism, Auburn with realism. These were the dimensions of a controversy that was afterwards exported to Britain. In America the silent Auburn system was the more influential, but European envoys viewed the separate Cherry Hill system with unalloyed enthusiasm. William Crawford and the Rev. Whitworth Russell praised it fulsomely in their report to the Home Department in Whitehall,[10] and dismissed the Auburn system as inconvenient, impractical and cruel. Auguste Demetz, an administrator, and Abel Blouet, an architect, did likewise in their report to the French Minister of the Interior,[11] and the renowned expert on prison discipline, Dr Nicolaus Julius, travelled to America a convinced opponent of solitude in 1835 and returned to Prussia as its most ardent apostle.[12]

To de Beaumont and de Tocqueville the separate and silent systems seemed to be two solutions to the same basic problem of preventing communication; in the one walls were used to enforce solitude, in the other it was enforced by a phalanx of vigilant guards. At Auburn the prisoners, though in close association with one another, were as separate as those in the solitary cells at Cherry Hill, for 'their bodies are together, but their souls are separated . . . they are really isolated, though no wall separates them'. But the philosophical superiority of the Cherry Hill system had to be admitted, because seclusion by walls — that is, seclusion through architecture — overcame the need for communication to be suppressed by naked force and intimidation, as it had to be at Auburn. The separate system maintained isolation with the passive instrument of the prison building itself. The administrative advantages of this were of less consequence than the fact of passive control — a form of constraint transcending the need for human intervention and thereby avoiding violence. As Rev. Daniel Nihil later put it: 'Let the hindrances to enjoyment consist of passive and inanimate obstacles, which cannot be made subject to hostility.'[13]

When Crawford and Russell brought information of the American experiment in solitary confinement to Britain it was greeted as if it were a novel and untried thing. In some ways it was, yet, as has been shown in chapters 2 and 4, solitude had been a major component in reformed prison discipline during the eighteenth century. Although in abeyance for some years, it had never been entirely abandoned. Early-nineteenth-century prisons were always built with refractory cells, designed especially to subdue the animated and disruptive spirits amongst the inmates. These were normally dark but ventilated rooms into which offenders against prison rules were put for a day or two on bread and water. Sometimes the power of solitude to pin the mind on any available image was consciously manipulated by the architect, as it was by Richard Ingleman at Folkingham House of Correction (1807), where the 'cell for strict solitude' was placed next to the chapel so that the only source of illumination was a narrow slot giving a framed view of the pulpit (Fig. 173). At Southwell, also by Ingleman, a similar slot in the refractory cell was aimed at the staircase wall, 'on which it might be advisable to inscribe some religious sentences'.[14] In 1819 Thomas Brutton, the governor of Devizes, where penitential solitude was still enforced, said that he had confined three or four prisoners in solitude for up to a year, until their behaviour merited promotion to an associated ward. Though more obedient, Brutton noticed a 'dullness and constant heaviness' in the prisoners so treated.[15] In 1821, C.C. Western, regarding classification as a mere crutch, suggested that either a congregate regime of hard labour or solitary confinement should take its place. If reformation of character was to be the objective then solitude should be reintroduced 'to give the culprit time for his passions to subside, and the better feelings of his nature to resume their influence [and] exhaust

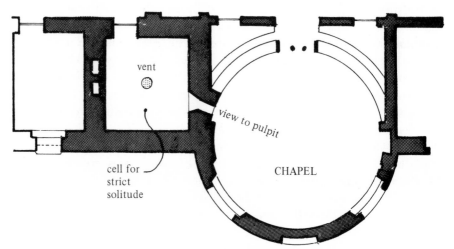

173. Dark cell and chapel at Folkingham House of Correction, Richard Ingleman, 1807.

the animal spirits which supply him with fortitude'.[16] In 1823/4, at Glasgow, a new bridewell was built by John Herbertson with 106 cells for complete solitude.[17] Occasionally other odd items turn up, such as the plan received by the Oxford Magistrates in 1830, for 60 solitary 'dinner cells' for the county gaol.[18] But these piecemeal evidences were a very small corner of the prison system; perhaps little more than residues of eighteenth-century practices and doctrines.

With the appearance of Crawford's *Report on the Penitentiaries of the United States* in 1834 there began a rediscovery of the profound transforming effects of solitude — solitude not as part of the system, not as the pure extremity of the system, but as the very basis of all imprisonment. His partisan account of the American separate prisons proclaimed a new faith that seemed on the face of it no more than a reiteration of an old doctrine. The Philadelphians had not invented a new process of reformation, all they had done was to solve certain technical problems which now made it possible to create an artificial environment in which solitary reformation could be practised. An architectural difficulty had been overcome. Thus the new faith was not so much in a process as in a method of effecting a process.

Solitude was in a way the most perfect form of classification. If there was any distinction between the two it was that classification had, by this time, been limited to the prevention of moral contamination while solitude held out the promise of moral reformation once again. As classes were multiplied in a futile attempt to compartmentalize and contain vice, the hope of reformation had been overshadowed by the search for a conclusive scheme of categories. Prevention took precedence over cure. The reintroduction of solitude provided the final answer. It was suddenly clear that there were as many 'degrees of moral debasement and criminality' as there were criminals; these distinctions were 'as numerous and varying as the individuality of the human soul'.[19] Such being the case, the ultimate in classification was to set every prisoner apart from every other, each in his own category.[20] So, what appears to be the breakdown of the classification system was, from another perspective, the raising of it to the highest level of generality. At the same time individual separation guaranteed absolute uniformity of treatment, a matter of considerable interest to the French, who were fascinated to find that the new prisons had achieved what they took to be perfect equality when free society had been unable to do so.[21]

The three attributes of penal solitude in this second wave were precisely the same as they had been during the first wave of reform in the eighteenth century, that is: reformation through reflection, resistance to the spread of corruption through the prevention of communication, and deterrence through terror.

Fear of solitude was still held to be a function of guilt. The more culpable a man the greater his terror at the prospect of seclusion. Solitude was regarded as an exact recompense for this reason.[22] A prominent prison chaplain cited Archbishop Tillotson as authority for this view: 'If God should leave sinners to themselves, and to the lashes of their own conscience, a more severe and terrible torment can hardly be imagined.'[23] Despite the universally precise distribution of its justice, the degree and duration of solitude would determine its deterrent value. On his return from America Crawford thought unmitigated solitude of the type first practised at Auburn had an undeniably beneficial influence on morals, but its harmful effects on mental and physical health would make it unacceptable to the British public.[24] It was not long before the varieties of solitary regime were being researched on this side of the Atlantic. The subject was fully explored by the Duke of Richmond in the House of Lords enquiry of 1835.[25] Many interesting facts were unearthed. John Howard, it transpired, had all the time believed in separate confinement, although this was not generally known — at least, so the committee was told by Sir James Williams, an ancient Middlesex Magistrate who claimed personal acquaintance with the great reformer: 'Mr. Howard's idea was, that the more solitary it was made, the better.'[26] Outside the penal establishment solitary confinement was practised in a number of schools, notably the Chelsea School of Discipline for vagrant or recalcitrant girls, where being 'put alone to think' had been substituted for corporal discipline; a miniature of penal reform. The school secretary, Mrs Shaw, was very confident of its good effects. From half an hour to two hours usually sufficed, but for more adamantine wickedness confinement was stretched to a night or two. Only once had complete solitude been kept up for any length of time — for over two months — on the perpetrator of an attempted arson. The girl was 'sent into solitary confinement and it answered completely. She left us with a good character, and is still living . . . or is in service in the neighbourhood, to the great comfort of her mother.' During her reformation she was visited at least three times a day by the Matron.

'She was at first very cheerful, and used to sing aloud, and at last she became silent and thoughtful, and before she left I had a very good hope of her.'[27] The transition was characteristic. According to Samuel Hoare the longest it had ever taken to obtain this 'capitulation' under a temperate prison regime with daily attendance from chaplain and governor was 40 days.[28] It seemed unlikely that any prisoner would be able to hold out against it for months or years, even in this alleviated, socialized form, distinguished from solitary confinement by the more gentle title of separate confinement. The two were not to be confused, as the Secretary of State for the Home Department made clear in a circular to local authorities encouraging them to adopt the separate system:

> It is generally understood that solitary imprisonment implies confinement in a gloomy and narrow cell, without occupation and with a diet of bread and water only. Separate confinement . . . means on the other hand, confinement in a large, airy, light, well-warmed and ventilated cell, with moral and religious instruction, regular employment, and the daily visits of the chaplain and officers of the prison, as well as those engaged in the instruction of the prisoners.[29]

Solitude was a force unleashed, separation was the same force in check. The main difference between them was the physical and mental healthiness of the locations in which they were practised.

Philadelphia, where a balance had been struck between oppressive incarceration and comfortable indulgence, was the model. If the reflection that came with unmitigated solitude was thus disturbed, it was not too serious, for those who would now enter the prisoner's cell would be of a rational and calm temperament. Their presence would be remedial, not damaging. Thus under separate confinement a criminal would be cut off from viciousness, profanity and others of his own class, but he would not be denied social intercourse, and in intense solitude merely looking at a good man's face could be construed as a kind of intercourse, and could be a distinct influence for the better, according to Dr Julius: 'Is it not more advantageous to him [the prisoner] to behold the cheerful countenances of a limited number of honest men, than the dark and daring looks of persons excited by the worst passions, and actuated by the worst vices?'[30] The question was rhetorical, not inquisitive. From now on solitude was always combined with the 'moral influence' of the chaplain, governor and subordinate officers.

The chaplain in particular was to carry out personalized missionary work on each prisoner in his separate cell. For all the piety of the eighteenth-century reformers, the professional practice of religion in the new prisons of the 1780s and 1790s was limited to the performance of divine service in the chapel on Sundays, for which the chaplain was generally paid about the same salary as the first turnkey.[31] He played no part at all in the day to day running of the prison. Yet by the 1840s, the chaplain enjoyed a status almost equal to that of the governor; a distinction being made between the active, temporal authority of the one and the inquisitorial, spiritual authority of the other. Relations between governors and chaplains were not always cordial, but it would be hard to prove that the elevation of the chaplain compromised the executive power of the governor, though it often seemed that way at the time. The two were intended to act in concert performing distinct operations in a single process, a state of affairs already acknowledged by George Holford who, in the 1820s, was insisting that the governor should keep his distance from prisoners to ensure complete impartiality in the execution of his duties, while the chaplain, on the other hand, should forge personal relationships with them. The intimacy of the chaplain's approach to the stranded soul gave solace to those suffering cellular confinement and fulfilled an important administrative purpose as well. He was to record his impressions of the inmates in a 'character book', the contents of which were to be read in conjunction with the very different contents of the governor's journal listing infractions and disciplinary measures. 'The chaplain's business', said Holford, 'is to observe the effects of punishment upon prisoners; not to inflict it.' He must read all the letters to and from prisoners and screen all visitors before admission, but 'in giving efficiency to the chaplain we must take care to avoid all collision of authority between him and the gaoler or governor of the prison: all direct power must continue in the hands of the latter'.[32] The chaplain's role was to reach the hearts of men undergoing penal discipline and then to assess them, reporting back his findings to governor and magistrates so that prisoners would be subject to two levels of scrutiny: first of conduct, then of conscience.

In the late 1820s the Rev. John Clay was fashioning just such a binary system of military enforcement and probing religious investigation at Preston House of Correction, which established a pattern of practice generally adopted after the demise of the Rev. Nihil as combined chaplain-governor of Millbank in 1843.[33]

The chaplain's authority to examine character was dramatically increased by the reintroduction of solitary confinement. As it happened Clay was only moderately enthusiastic about the new discipline and refused to place barriers dividing the prisoners, even between men and women, in his chapel at Preston. At Millbank, however, an early version of separate confinement had been imposed when Nihil took office in 1837 and it was clear to many that the kind of complicity sought between prisoner and chaplain could only be fostered in the quiet privacy of the cell. It was here that inner character revealed itself out of reach of inmates and staff alike; here that the crucial judgement could be made — judgement of a man's state of mind — because, even if his acceptance of discipline and regulation were complete, his superficial conduct exemplary, this did not in itself indicate reformation. So the new style of governorship that took shape in the first two decades of the nineteenth century was matched by a new style of chaplaincy in the 1840s: the governor as executor, the chaplain as monitor. In the separate prisons, all modelled on Pentonville, the governor's eye would survey the prison from its internal centre; as in the Panopticon, the interior was thrown open to him, but significantly his gaze could no longer penetrate the cell. The cell was too sacred. A wholesale incursion of this kind would have destroyed its motionless silence, and in any case its secrets — the desperate mental secrets of its occupant, that is — would not be discernible from such a distance. In this blind spot stood the chaplain with his character book and journal.[34]

Separate confinement, humanized but sufficiently fearful, was recommended by a majority of witnesses to the Duke of Richmond's enquiries. Lord John Russell, as Secretary of State for the Home Department, added his official approval, and in 1836 created a new government body, the Inspectorate of Prisons. William Crawford, implacable enemy to classification, and the Rev. Whitworth Russell, the 'dogmatical and arbitrary' opponent of the silent system,[35] were appointed as the Inspectors of Prisons for the Home District. The new Inspectors announced their earnest hope that 'whenever a new prison is to be erected, or an existing gaol enlarged, the principle of individual separation will be carried into effect'.[36] In November 1837 Captain Joshua Jebb, an experienced but little known military engineer, was appointed on the recommendation of Crawford to the complimentary post of Surveyor General of Prisons.[37] Within a year Jebb had published designs for a separate prison on a new principle of construction (Fig. 174).[38] In

the meantime Crawford and Russell had discovered that there were certain legal obstacles in their way. The New Gaol Act of 1839[39] removed
these by explicitly prescribing separate confinement and proscribing
solitary confinement of the old unenlightened kind. The Home Office
and Parliament endorsed the separate system though dissenting voices
were still to be heard. As prison inspectors, Crawford and Russell
regarded themselves as full-time promoters of the system and inspected
prisons in their circuit more with a view to converting governors and

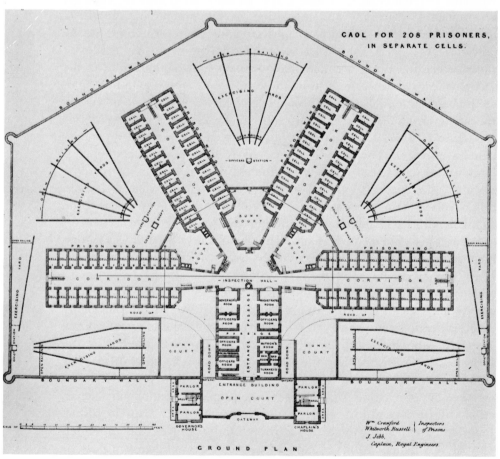

174. Prison for separate confinement, Joshua Jebb, 1838, ground
plan.

magistrates than anything else, an attitude which those who did not subscribe to their views found galling.[40]

It had taken six years to confirm the validity of separate confinement in law. The Home Department had not acted peremptorily, although there were plenty of allegations to that effect. They had considered the matter very carefully. There had been voluminous discussion on all sorts of obscurities, yet the discussions had taken place in a limited arena. It was really more of a dialogue between the prison authorities and Whitehall. The questions were asked, but they were asked of governors, keepers, administrators, prison chaplains and professionals. The magistracy were less in evidence now than they had been during the eighteenth-century reforms, there were few amateurs or outsiders and even the S.I.P.D.'s influence was on the wane. So indeed was the membership; Bullar admitted that the society could boast only about 100 subscribers in 1835. 'They have fallen off very much of late years', he said.[41] The axis between the Home Department and the prisons had created its own hermetic zone of expertise which became steadily more difficult to penetrate.

The prevention of evil communication had been attempted in the Howardian prisons and in the improved prisons of the early nineteenth century (Fig. 175) and was the foundation of every reformative scheme from Thomas Bray's Newgate onwards. It retained that position in separate confinement. Those who could not bring themselves to believe that separation was a reformative panacea could nevertheless believe that it succeeded where classification had failed; that it 'entirely prevents the growth of vice'[42] — a negative but fundamental function made much of by the increasing body of articulate prison chaplains. The Rev. John Field, of Reading County Gaol, believing that sin was infectious, devoted a whole pamphlet to an elaborate but familiar comparison between bodily and spiritual disease. Afflictions, of whatever kind, were the result of sin. In times gone by the corrupt were visited with leprosy. Those sent into exile because of their leprosy were purified spiritually if not physically by their isolation. Thus it was that 'our legislators have learnt the method of correcting criminals which the laws concerning leprosy . . . might suggest'.[43] The same analogy of moral and physical contagion was employed by the Rev. Nihil of Millbank. There would always emerge, he said, a surreptitious society in

Lamina XII

POSTIGOS DE LA GALERIA CENTRAL DE INSPECCION
EN LA PENITENCIARIA DE GINEBRA

every prison aimed against the established order. 'Every bad place has an atmosphere peculiar to itself', spreading an almost corporeal virulence. 'To all external appearances, the institution may be well ordered; a stream of religious influence may flow regularly through its channels, but a dark infernal current rolls beneath.'[44] Prison discipline must aim to dam it. The prison being a place where all evil was brought together had an enormous power to generate corruption. Prison plans were thus nothing more nor less than 'efforts to grapple with the evils of concentration'.[45]

The spontaneous spread of evil through association and communication was acknowledged by every writer on separate prison discipline, whether for the new system or against it (Fig. 176), from Charles Dickens to Whitworth Russell. The conventional analogy with disease might occasionally be mixed with newer stuff, as it was by the magistrate Benjamin Rotch who held that moral contamination in prisons was 'almost electrical . . . so rapidly does it take effect',[46] but whatever the speed of its transmission, the process of dissemination was always seen to follow the same path from the vicious to the more innocent. The gradient was irreversible.

It will be thought that no harm can accrue from a signal, a word or a knock . . . but . . . I am satisfied that such violations of the discipline do obstruct reformation. It has happened more than once when the altered or unsatisfactory state of the prisoner's mind has led me to suspect such practices, these suspicions have been verified.[47]

So warned the assistant chaplain at Pentonville. These feeble signals broke the hold of separation over the prisoner's mind by reviving 'demoralizing and criminal ideas':

It is the singular merit of separate imprisonment that it break off, so far as it can be broken off by human agency, the former habit of thought and feeling. But by interdicted communications with fellow prisoners those old associations are revived. They play upon the soul like a galvanic battery of vice.[48]

In separate prisons the evils of communication were stanched by a method of construction. The cell had to confine a prisoner, not just in

175. *Opposite.* Geneva Penitentiary, door to central inspection gallery: 1, Receptacle for introducing objects without entering; 2, Bell-cord to call guards; 3/4, Windows for seeing without being seen; 5/6 Inspection windows (open and closed); 7, Bell-cord from workroom to gallery guards; 8, Bell to cook; 9, Bell to department A; 10, Bell to department B; 11, Speaking trumpet for silent communication between the director and his employees.

176. George Cruickshank, Newgate Prison Discipline, 1818: the ugliness of unregulated association in caricature.

334

body but had to confine all evidence of his person as well. Images and sounds had to be caged. The sanguine hopes of earlier reformers came to nothing because they had been unaware of, or had grossly underestimated, problems of engineering; their philosophy had been correct, their technology had been inadequate. Entries such as the following were frequently to be found in governor's journals: Maidstone County Gaol, 23 January 1822 — 'Thomas Ellingham, a solitary confined soldier, confined to a dark cell for 3 days for putting his hand out of his cell window and calling out to the females in ward 17.'[49]

Sound was the principal difficulty — how was it to be contained? The first systematic attempt to answer this question was made in 1836. At Millbank, in place of a number of rooms destroyed by fire, experimental cells were built under the direction of Robert Smirke. These transmitted sounds through the vent gratings, and even when the vents were blocked, voices could still be heard through the solid party wall. So Abel Blouet, the French architect who had accompanied Demetz on his tour of American prisons, Michael Faraday, the celebrated scientist, Dr David Boswell Reid, and G.T. Bullar, who was both architect and Secretary to the S.I.P.D., were brought to Millbank to build walls through which no message could pass.[50]

Acoustics was a new science. Some advances had been made in the design of auditoria and concert halls where the aim was to transmit sounds as far and as clearly as possible. Both Reid and Faraday had played their part in this,[51] but their commission at Millbank was to discover the rules of a technology exactly opposite to that so far studied in acoustics, 'a subject that has received little attention, and which had not before been studied with care'.[52]

Twelve walls of varying specifications were built, demolished and rebuilt between the same two cells. The experimentors made attempts to communicate with one another from one sealed cell to the other, and differences in performance were carefully recorded for a range of pitches and volumes, speaking and shouting (Fig. 177). Faraday imagined that sound waves in transit through materials of different densities would behave much as light waves. The walls were therefore designed to provide as many irregular interfaces between emission and reception as possible in order to diffuse the pattern of sound as it passed on its way. Interestingly, the results seemed to confirm his assumptions. The first test (1) reduced the volume of the sound, but high pitched words could

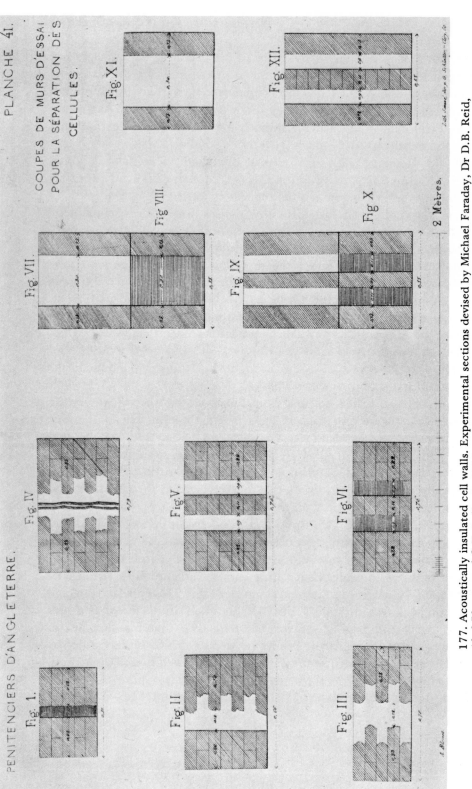

177. Acoustically insulated cell walls. Experimental sections devised by Michael Faraday, Dr D.B. Reid, Abel Blouet, and G.T. Bullar in 1836.

penetrate quite distinctly to the other side. Broken brick cavities (2 and 3) worked much better and when loose canvas sheets were interposed (4) the result was so good that the experimenters 'had the satisfaction of knowing that nothing intelligible could ever be transmitted'.[53] Even the most violent shouting was reduced to a meaningless confusion of sound. The important thing to note is that the Millbank walls were not meant to reduce the transmission of noise; they were meant to eradicate the transmission of information. Noise reduction was found to be greatest with the wall section shown in 10, but it was still possible to hear words through it, consequently it was less favoured than the broken brick and canvas wall through which any word was transposed into a muddled blur by the time it reached the other side.[54] The object had been to suppress the meaning in sounds. It was less a question of acoustics, more a question of the scientific destruction of information.

A yet more imponderable problem was the escape of sound through ducts, pipes, windows, ventilators and doors. At Cherry Hill Haviland had been confronted with the difficulties that would henceforth bedevil all prison designers. The lavatory and water pipes were bound to be used by prisoners trying to contact one another in their isolation. Water traps for the lavatories in each cell, all on separate soil stacks, and water distribution pipes that wove in and out from the cells to the surveillance corridor so that any tapping would be transmitted to the guards as well as to other prisoners, all helped to increase the power of the cell over the mind of the prisoner.[55] But intercommunication, though made more and more difficult, was never made impossible, either in the American penitentiaries or in the English separate prisons. The authorities were later to find this out from prisoners who confessed to them that there was a secret tapping code, known to the criminal fraternity, which would be understood in any separate prison from one end of the country to the other. The Rev. J.T. Burt published this code as divulged to him by an informer. It was simply one knock for *A* and 26 knocks for Z.[56] Although a more clumsy way of spreading evil could hardly be devised, Mayhew and Binney described the same code — 'the prisoner's electric telegraph' — in 1862 amongst a host of other subterfuges for making contact.[57]

Visual communication was easy enough to prevent in the cells, but was very difficult to prevent as soon as the prisoner emerged to take exercise, work or attend chapel. At Cherry Hill, therefore, they did not do so. On Sundays the preacher stood in the central observatory and delivered his sermon as loudly as he could down each of the surveillance corridors, one after the other.[58] It seems to have been accepted early on that the liturgy of the English church required a more intimate presence. In 1835 Rev. Whitworth Russell presented the Duke of Richmond with a plan for a communal chapel for a separate prison — a bold, stark piece of functional engineering by James Savage containing 432 cellular cubicles all oriented towards the pulpit (Fig. 178). The prisoners, once they had climbed down into their cubicles from the access platforms above, could see and be seen by the clergyman 'yet not see or communicate with each other'.[59] It was a type of Panopticon answering very well to the needs of the church and the administration,[60] and was later taken up by Jebb, modified, and incorporated into the Model Prison.

As with religion, exercise was practised in the cell at Cherry Hill. Individual walled yards were appended to each ground level cell (Fig. 171) while on the upper floor two cells were thrown into one so that every prisoner had access to a distinct area in which to walk. This arrangement was not uncommon in the eighteenth-century English prisons (pp. 177–81) but never had it been so extensively or so uniformly applied. Be this as it may, few prisons followed the example, and after Cherry Hill even Haviland gave it up.[61] The earliest English separate prisons either made use of cell corridors to exercise their inmates (as at Glasgow and Springfield County Gaol in Essex, where Thomas Hopper's plan had been hurriedly converted to the new system in 1834)[62] or provided a number of larger yards in which the prisoners were to be aired individually or in small, well-guarded contingents (as in Lieutenant John Sibly's 1835 plan for a separate prison).[63] In 1847 a regulated labour machine was invented by Gibbs which made it possible to transfer useless work from the congregate treadwheel or hand-crank into the individual cell.[64]

Having restricted each prisoner to his own domain so carefully it became necessary to provide a range of facilities within that domain which otherwise would have been quite unnecessary: a measured supply of air, heat, artificial lighting, water and sanitation. It was difficult to heat and ventilate acoustically isolated cells. A combined system of warming and airing was tried at Cherry Hill but it proved most unsatisfactory, with some cells always tropical and others always arctic. One

Appendix N.° 29.

DESIGN FOR A PRISON CHAPEL
BY JAS SAVAGE ARCHT UPON A PLAN
PROPOSED BY THE REVD WHITWORTH RUSSELL
CHAPLAIN TO THE GENERAL PENITENTIARY
MILLBANK IN WHICH ALL THE PRISONERS
CAN SEE THE CLERGYMAN AND BE SEEN BY
HIM AND YET NOT SEE OR COMMUNICATE WITH
EACH OTHER.

SECTION OF CELLS.
to a Scale of 1 inch to 5 feet.

ELEVATION

SECTION

PLAN

ELEVATION OF THE FLANK.

339

178. Chapel for a separate prison, James Savage and Rev. Whitworth Russell, 1835.

in twenty of the prisoners had been found, at one time or another, in a state of advanced asphyxiation owing to the inadequate passage of air through the distribution channels.[65] After a few years a gravity-fed hot water system replaced it.[66] Blouet recorded that the newer English prisons were served by similar gravity-fed water heating,[67] but unless a practical system of combined 'thermo-ventilation'[68] could be devised, doing away with vent gratings and open windows, solitude would be compromised. Crawford and Russell had arrived at this conclusion before Jebb came on the scene, and pointed to the 'uniform and complete' success of the rather more simple thermo-ventilation plant in the House of Commons, and mines and factories.[69] The House of Commons had first been fitted up with an apparatus for air heating by Sir Humphrey Davy in 1811[70] (not very different from that proposed by the Bentham brothers for the Panopticon in 1791). In the early 1830s Dr D.B. Reid and others were experimenting with more adaptable systems that allowed cold fresh air to be introduced as well as hot.[71] However, it was Jebb who brought thermo-ventilation back into the prisons. His plant at Pentonville, built by Messrs Haden of Trowbridge, was no great innovation, but it was a more complicated and wonderful piece of engineering than was necessary in other types of building, due to the peculiar requirement of absolute quarantine for each cell. It too had its failings and its critics but it does seem to have worked marginally better than Cherry Hill at least.[72] Haviland himself felt it worth a visit to England in 1849/50 'with a view to securing the most approved method of warming' for institutional buildings.[73]

Contact by sound or vision, within and outside the separate cell, was now far more carefully guarded against than it had been in any of the solitary prisons of the eighteenth century. Contagious vice was limited by this segregation but, of course, the value of solitude was not just precautionary. As isolation increased, so also did its power to penetrate the heart and mind. Seclusion was simultaneously a preventive and a cure. In the 1830s and 1840s expectations of reform were still high amongst the proponents of separation, yet were somehow less emphatic. The system had a 'tendency' to reform character but perhaps it did not do so inevitably. The most that could reasonably be expected was 'an average standard of virtue, under an average pressure of temptation'.[74] However, the picture of the reformed character had not itself changed.

Separation promoted reflection — it gave prisoners an opportunity to 'converse with themselves'.[75] It acted 'more directly on the mind' than other punishments.[76] On this theme the Rev. Field was able to extend his analogy between lepers and criminals a little further: 'Secluded and alone they can see their folly, feel ashamed, and with sorrow confess their sin. The plague in his own heart, now known, prompts the language of the leper, "I am unclean, unclean!" '[77] Lieutenant Sibly compared the mental effects of the old system of treadwheel labour to that of solitude. All bodily exertion, he explained, must inevitably create a great deal of 'irritation and excitement in the mind', and this was why hard labour, 'from which such signal advantages were expected, has been confessed to have totally failed'. The treadwheel destroyed reflection.[78] For the prison to reform character it must reduce stimulation, not add to it:

A majority of mankind, by yielding to the seductions of the social appetite, and neglecting the exercise of reflection, fall into many evils, and this is the common case of convicts. They are persons who have starved the reflective quality, while they have abandoned themselves to the dissipation and excitements of perpetual mixture with companions.[79]

The 'upsurge of intemperance and violence' recognized by so many during the 1840s amongst the urban poor was portrayed in a very menacing light by William Crawford.[80] It could only be aggravated in prisons, unless they were rebuilt yet again on the separate plan so that the effects of indiscriminate poor relief, unemployment and alcohol which threatened 'to change the moral character of the labouring population of large towns'[81] could be countered and opposed by the reforming influence of the prison. Although English prisons had been improved consistently since Howard's time, they were now no match for the new boldness of the lower orders. In opposition to violence, intemperance and boldness were submission, meekness and quiescence, which were themselves identifiable with reflection, so 'persons confined in a prison should, if possible be reduced to a quiet and submissive state'.[82] No effort was made to divorce the morality of separation from the convenience of management that came with it, because any attendant convenience was taken to be a local demonstration of the benefits of reforming character.

The Inspector General of French prisons, M. Morreau-Christophe, considered that the English would be most unlikely to rebuild their prisons on the separate system because they already had the most complete and impressive prison system in Europe. True, it was not *the* system, but it was admirable in its uniformity, orderliness, healthiness, discipline and cleanliness nevertheless.[83] Even Crawford in the early years thought the prospect of a complete rebuilding on the Philadelphia model would be unlikely to cull much favour in Britain.[84]

The turning point was undoubtedly the publication of the Richmond Commission Reports in 1835. The Committee drew no conclusions — the evidence of experts was simply amassed, and it was overwhelmingly in favour of a more perfect system; that is, a system in which communication would be interdicted more perfectly. With the weight of Lord John Russell behind separation its future looked brighter; with the formation of the Inspectorate in 1835, brighter still; after the passage of the 1839 New Gaol Act it was virtually assured. It would be easy enough to ascribe its success to a Home Office fiat. Certainly the Inspectors and the Surveyor General of Prisons brought the increasing power of their office to bear on errant local authorities, but, as Heather Tomlinson has discovered, some of these, quite independently of government decree, displayed an unexpected eagerness to put separation into practice.[85]

By the time of Joshua Jebb's appointment as Surveyor General the need for an experimental prison to test and, more importantly, to demonstrate the potential of separation had already been agreed.[86] In 1837 Crawford and Russell had published a set of seven ideal plans for county gaols, based, they said, on plans supplied to them by Haviland in Philadelphia,[87] yet the sectional form of these prisons was quite different from Cherry Hill (Fig. 179). There were no corridors. Iron catwalks connected the various storeys of cells on either side of a wide vaulted gallery. The arrangement, not unlike Carlo Fontana's Rome House of Correction (1704; Figs. 24, 25), had the great advantage of unifying the whole prison vertically as well as horizontally. Internal passages, galleries and observatory were thrown into one integral space, as had also been done in Bentham's Panopticon. The form was different but the purpose was the same: everything could be seen at once from the centre. It was the first time that radial planning and open gallery access had been combined in this kind of prison, although Thomas Ustick Walter at Moyamensing County Prison, Pennsylvania,[88] and George Thomas Bullar in his 1836 plan for the remodelling of Newgate,[89] had made use of the same section in single ranges of building

(Fig. 180). The reintroduction of internal galleries seems to have developed not from the Philadelphia separate prisons but from the New York silent prisons where unremitting and universal surveillance was an essential part of the administration. At Auburn, Sing-Sing and Wethersfield — all silent prisons — internal galleries surrounded multi-storey

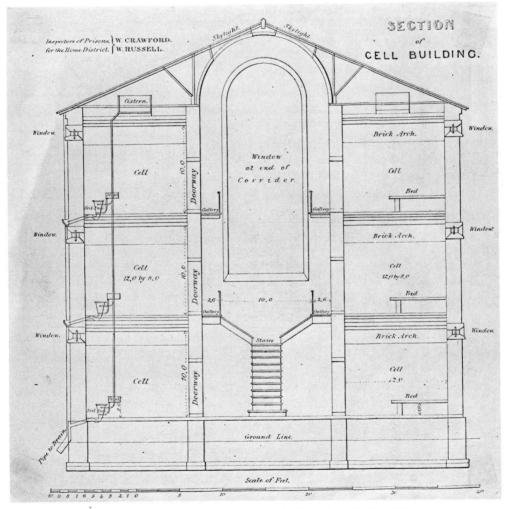

179. Section for a galleried prison wing, William Crawford and Rev. Whitworth Russell, 1837.

ranges of back-to-back cells. At Kingston Penitentiary (Canada) — also silent — the cells were not back-to-back but in single lines piled four storeys high. Eight islanded ranges of cells with access galleries on one side, surveillance galleries on the other, were cased within the cruciform prison building (Fig. 181).[90]

Jebb adopted the radial plan with galleried section for his Model Prison, as vessel of the governor's authority, but it was the model cells within that demonstrated the increasing power of architecture to suppress communication.

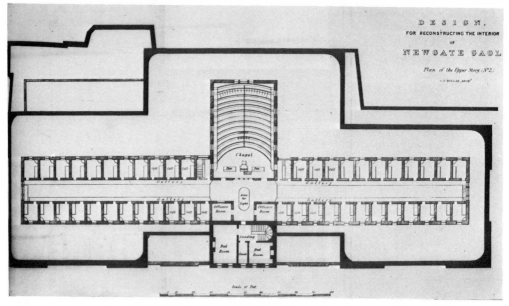

180. Project for the internal reconstruction of Newgate, George Thomas Bullar, 1836, upper floor plan.

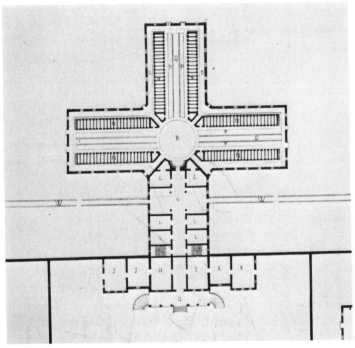

181. Kingston Penitentiary, Canada, Judge Powers, ground plan.

8 The Model Prison

Practical men, and men of science, who had fully examined the question, had allowed that the details of the Pentonville system as at first established were soundly deduced from unquestioned laws of our moral nature.

J.T. Burt[1]

The design of Victorian penal institutions achieved its most comprehensive expression at Pentonville Model Prison, in north London. By the time the new building on the Caledonian Road was filled with convicts it had become something of a national monument. Prince Albert, always interested in improving schemes, had been shown the marvels of its intricate machinery, and so had the King of Prussia, the King of Saxony, the Grand Duke Michael of Russia, Prince William of Prussia, Prince Alexander of the Netherlands, the Archduke of Austria and the Commissioners for a dozen or so European governments. Many other envoys and representatives were to follow, curious to see how the prison worked. All were reportedly impressed, the King of Prussia going so far as to exclaim his admiration aloud, resolving then and there to rebuild the prisons of his own country on the new plan.[2]

Despite the monolithic structure of its carcass Pentonville was erected quickly. The first stone was laid in April 1840 and the works were completed by late 1842. While under construction a puzzled reporter from *The Times* could find no more to say of it than to tell of its immense size and 'curious internal arrangements',[3] but as the works progressed it became evident that these were by no means its most peculiar characteristics. There were bigger prisons in London, and the plan and sectional form had been borrowed in large measure from the influential American penitentiaries.

Pentonville was but the second penal prison built by the Home Department. That it should be an exemplar to local authorities, who built and ran all the other gaols and houses of correction in the country, was taken for granted. Nevertheless, its predecessor, the Millbank Penitentiary, had not achieved that distinction. Millbank had been enormously costly, and even before it was complete there were bread riots among the prisoners, followed by mysterious, undiagnosed epidemics which did nothing to encourage further imitation by central government or local authorities. The conviction had grown up that, at Millbank, the Home Department had sponsored slipshod execution of a dubious design based on imperfect principles.[4] At Pentonville things were to be different. Everything from beginning to end was chosen with scrupulous care, and detailed with infinitesimal precision. Even the inmates had been carefully selected, as the purification they would have to undergo was understood to enervate the mind and sap the body of its vigour. So only the most amenable and healthy, usually first offenders, were picked from amongst those who had already been sentenced to transportation — a policy explained by Sir James Graham, Secretary of State for the Home Department, in the following terms: 'Considering the excessive supply of labour in this country, its consequent depreciation, and the fastidious rejection of all those whose character is tainted, I wish to admit no prisoner to Pentonville who is not sentenced . . . and doomed . . . to transportation.'[5] The reputation of the Model Prison was not to be jeopardized by putting those who passed through it in the false situation of being turned out into a depressed labour market as known criminals. The results of the new system of discipline were going to be tested in the colony of Australia, 'where the stain of tarnished character is not quite indelible',[6] rather than in the streets and alleys of industrial England. Everyone concerned seemed optimistic as to the results of the new system when the first 16 convicts arrived from Newgate to serve 18 months under the model regime before being shipped to Van Diemen's Land for seven or ten years.[7]

The Model Prison filled a 6¾ acre site, contained cells for 520 prisoners and cost £82,271. Each cell-place had therefore cost £158,[8] an amount of money which at the time would purchase a commodious new artisan's cottage for an entire family, yet the building had not exceeded its budget. Indeed, by comparison with Millbank, which had cost the government almost half a million pounds between 1812 and 1822, it was an inexpensive venture (Fig. 182). Jebb emphasized that he had been wielding the razor of economy wherever the aims of the institution were not being furthered by the design,[9] and it is true that

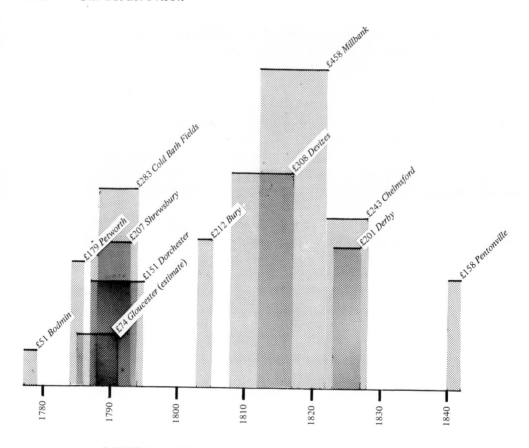

BUILDING COSTS PER PRISONER PLACE

182. Building costs per prisoner place. Dividing the total cost of a prison by the number of cell-places gives this chart of costs over the period of reform. Prisons built after Pentonville maintained costs within fairly narrow limits which were generally lower than those for classified prisons built in the earlier part of the century. The following figures were quoted by Sir Edmund Du Cane: Manchester, £140 per prisoner; Birmingham, £157; Reading, £197; Wandsworth, £198; Holloway, £209 (Du Cane, *The Punishment and Prevention of Crime*, London, 1885, p. 100). The common allegation that separate prisons were more costly to build than other types of prison is not borne out by these figures; indeed, exactly the opposite seems to have been the case.

as a piece of engineering the construction was economical in the abstract sense that no part of it was without its utility. Nothing was redundant, but then again, few other buildings had been required to perform so many operations so exactly, or expected to produce such quantities of virtue from bricks and iron.

The boundary of the Model Prison was defined by a chain of six warders' houses linked together with long stretches of plain wall. Contained within were the four large converging wings, which formed the body of the prison and housed all the prisoners (Figs. 183, 184). Each was made up of a nave-like, barrel vaulted space 16 feet wide and 40 feet high, lined on either side with three storeys of cells reached from a network of light iron galleries and catwalks (Fig. 185). Where the four wings met was an ample central hall commanding a sequence of panoramic views down each of the succeeding galleries. Every door to every cell could be seen from this one point. Mayhew and Binney likened the vista to looking down 'a bunch of Burlington Arcades, that had been fitted up in the style of the opera box lobbies with an infinity of little doors'.[10] Glazed bays jutted out from the Commissioners' and governor's office into the central hall, allowing them this all-encompassing view of the rest of the prison interior (Fig. 186).

There had been hardly any inflammable material used in the construction of the Model Prison, the cells being of vaulted brick with concrete fill. The stairways, bracket supports and balustrades for the galleries were all of iron. The heavy indestructible brick shell served three ends. It was impossible to burn and difficult to escape through, but its most recently discovered attribute was the most significant: it impeded the transmission of sound from cell to cell. According to a visitor in 1864, the silence within Pentonville was so complete — so uncannily still — that he felt it necessary to look into several cell spyholes to make sure that the prisoners were really there.[11] The rules of English prisons had for a long time vainly forbidden 'unnecessary communication' between warders and prisoners, while all talking, whispering, signs or noises between inmates was construed as resistance to amendment.[12] But these rules could not be properly enforced unless the whole prison was undisturbed by sounds. Silence was a necessary blank backcloth against which any minor infringement could be perceived. This is why the warders' uniform at Pentonville included a pair of thick felt overshoes to mask the sound of their footfall as they

183. The Model Prison, Pentonville, Joshua Jebb, 1840–2, ground plan.

ISOMETRICAL VIEW OF PENTONVILLE PRISON.

184. The Model Prison, aerial view.

185. The Model Prison, galleried cell block.

186. The Model Prison, observatory.

patrolled the galleries. Wearing these they could approach unheard as well as unseen without disturbing the pervasive quietness.

The convicts spent almost the whole time isolated in their cells, all 520 of which were exactly the same (Fig. 187). Care had been taken to orient the building in such a way that every cell, during some part of the day, received sunlight, so that even in this way they were equal.[13] The immense side walls were 18 inches thick from the foundations to the roof and the vaults above and below the cells were at least one foot thick at the crown. The major difficulty facing Jebb was that every one of this numberless recession of identical enclosed compartments, measuring 7 feet by 13 feet and 9 feet high, had to contain all that was necessary to sustain a human life.

Jebb had brought the art of designing the solitary cell to a new perfection. At Pentonville it was the key to the whole institution, a kind of chrysalis within which the transmutation of the criminal mind was to take place. In order for this operation to be successfully carried out the crucial connections that linked the cell with the rest of the building and the world at large had to be carefully engineered, and that is why Jebb's Model Prison was among the most grandiose of early Victorian experiments in what is now called environmental control.

Every cell had a water supply, distributed through a complex of carefully designed balancing tanks to ensure that pressure was maintained throughout the system. In the corner of each was a compact ablution unit (Fig. 188) with a tap feeding into a copper washbasin and a glazed earthenware lavatory. There was a night light supplied from a gas factory within the prison to enable the convicts to read during winter evenings, but by no means everything in the cell offered the possibility of use. The window, for example, was located just high enough to be difficult to see out of.[14] It was made up of heavy iron bars on the outside supplemented by a lighter frame of mullions and transoms enclosing small panes of fixed, fluted glazing. It allowed a dose of sunshine through, but could not be opened. The fluting destroyed the image of anything beyond the cell so that even if the convict had managed to raise himself up to see through he could not have gained much satisfaction. The cell was blind: the form and content of the exterior world were obliterated.

The work of a window is normally to ventilate and to light, but at Pentonville these two functions had been separated. The window was

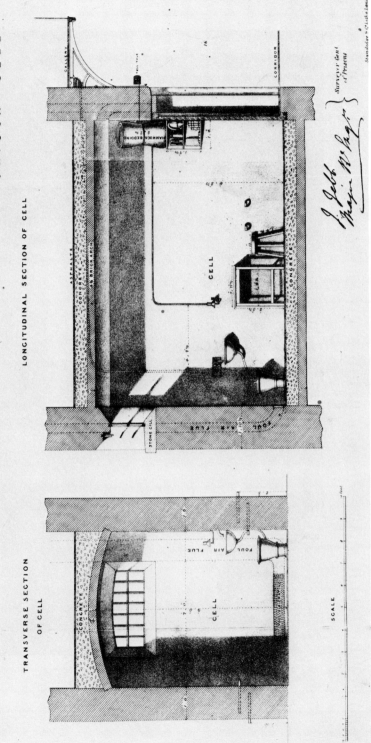

187. The Model Prison, sections of a separate cell.

188. The Model Prison cell, tap, basin and lavatory.

simply to let in a formless smudge of daylight. Ventilation had been integrated with a system of air heating instead. The most remarkable of the extraordinary web of invisible life-lines feeding the cells was this system of combined warming and ventilation known as thermo-ventilation. 'The necessity of resorting to an artificial system for a regular supply of fresh air at all times and seasons', said Jebb, 'will be apparent when it is considered that, in order to prevent communication between prisoners in adjoining cells, it is necessary that the windows should be fixtures.'[15] Sound as well as vision was to be blocked by the window; a disarmingly simple reason that gave rise to an enormous and complicated machinery. Warmed fresh air was supplied through a duct above the door. Foul air was evacuated through a duct at floor level on the opposite side of the cell. The replication of this arrangement 520 times within one building would not, in the best of circumstances, have been an easy matter. There had to be eight heating appliances in the basement beneath the cells. Fresh air, drawn in by convection, passed over an extended surface of metal fins projecting from the stoves. Now warm, it passed into a main horizontal distribution corridor and thence up to each cell. The extraction system was an inverted version of the supply system, all the foul air being drawn out through a vent stack in the middle of each cell block. All this to prevent communication, but the problem had not yet been solved, for ducts would have provided a perfect channel of secret correspondence between the cells had they been planned in the normal trunk-and-branch pattern. To prevent this happening, Jebb had heavy grilles fixed to the duct openings and isolated each supply and extract duct from all the others. The quiet sanctity of the cell was in this way preserved by a costly multiplication of ducts which turned the inner and outer walls of the cell blocks into a warren of intertwining but independent cavities (Fig. 189). It was for the same reason that the waste pipes from the lavatories had water sealed traps added, an earlier flap-trap design having been discarded.

The cell doorway was a narrow low slot, and the door itself was timber with a protective facing of sheet metal. In it there were two subsidiary openings, one a spy-hole designed to be looked into but not out of, the other a trap door which, when opened, made a tray for meals put through it by the warders (Fig. 190). These meals were delivered by a process that was both mechanical and military in its precision. This is

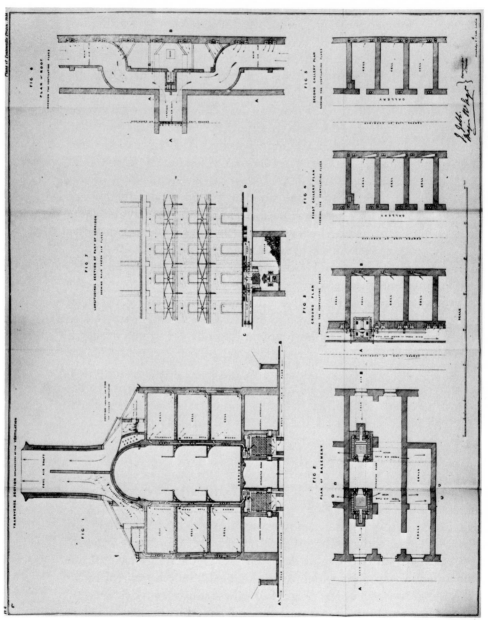

189. The Model Prison, thermo-ventilation plant, ductwork and extract shaft.

358

190. The Model Prison, cell doors and door furniture.

how breakfast was served:

> The brass hand bell was rung once more, to announce that the prisoners' breakfast hour (half past seven) had arrived; and the bell had scarcely ceased pealing before the two oaken flaps let into the asphalte pavement at the corners of the central hall, so that each stood between two of the four corridors, raised themselves as if by magic, and there ascended from below through either flap a tray laden with 4 large cans of cocoa and two baskets of bread. These trays were raised by means of a 'lifting machine', the bright iron rods of which stretched from the bottom to the top of the building, and served as guides for the friction rollers of the trays. No sooner were the cans and bread baskets brought up from below, than a couple of warders, and trade instructors, two to either of the adjoining corridors, seized each half of the quantity, and placing it on the trucks that stood ready by the flaps, away the warder and the instructor went . . . This is done almost as rapidly as walking, for no sooner does the trade instructor apply his key to the cell door than the little trap falls down and forms a kind of ledge on which the officer may place the loaf, and the prisoner at the same time deposit his mug for cocoa.[16]

This was repeated floor by floor, the trucks guided in their flight down the galleries by the top rail of the balustrades. The whole operation, filling the prison with the racket of machinery, rumbling wheels, bells and the slamming of trap doors, was accomplished with immense speed. The feeding of the whole prison took less than ten minutes with this intense combination of engineering skill and the disciplined division of labour, during which not a word was spoken. Dinners were distributed in exactly the same way.

Finally there was a small handle above the cell door which when pulled rang a bell to alert the staff and at the same time raised a number plate in the gallery indicating from which cell the entreaty had come. This was the 'label and gong', an item required by an Act of Parliament which had stipulated that a prisoner kept in solitary confinement must at all times have access to the staff.[17]

These then, were the systems that penetrated the barrier between the inside and the outside of the cells; that filtered the passage of every conceivable form of traffic between the two worlds. They were the very heart of Jebb's model system of prison construction. No other prison or penitentiary had ever been so meticulously contrived. All services and transactions had been depersonalized, mechanized, centralized, and integrated within a form of building which seemed designed to inhibit this very process: a building which, because of what was to go on inside it, had to be considered as 520 separate buildings for all practical purposes.

Jebb's detailed, sophisticated and ingenious designs for the accomplishment of confinement and control spread beyond the cells to encompass the whole prison. The convicts had to leave their cells at certain prescribed times for outdoor exercise or for instruction in the chapel. This presented the Commissioners with a grave problem. A convict might recognize someone he knew, or he might even strike up some sort of furtive acquaintance within the prison. All means of conveying personal identity had therefore to be abolished. Convicts, divested of their names, had numbers emblazoned on uniform and door. It was made an offence for an officer to utter a convict's name, while that most individual and recognizable of human features, the face, was always to be covered with a mask of brown cloth with slots only for the eyes. As with the cells, the architecture was enlisted in support of the ever more profound isolation of the convicts. Between the outspread fingers of the four cell blocks, areas of ground were demarcated with 108 wedges of walled space with open railings at the ends, but partitioned from one another in such a way as to make each a private enclosure. These were to be the exercising yards, where, once a day, every prisoner spent one hour walking to and fro. At the centre of the neat circles of yards would be a covered inspection lodge, from which an inscrutable warder, screened from the view of the convicts, could survey what was going on around him at a glance (Fig. 184). In the event these were not constructed as designed. Instead circuits of concentric stone paths were laid, around which the masked convicts were marched, holding taut a rope knotted at 15 foot intervals (Fig. 191).

While the inmate's physique was sustained by brief spasms of activity in the exercise yards, his moral condition was nurtured by brief episodes of instruction in the chapel, a raked auditorium situated above offices in a subsidiary block of buildings off the central hall. Daily schooling as well as religious service took place here,[18] and in so far as it was here that the convicts were most closely associated and therefore most likely to recognize and signal to one another, Jebb gave more attention to the intimate details of the design. The particular functions of the chapel within the dictates of the model system of discipline made it necessary to 'devise the means by which every prisoner should be effectually separated from his fellow, whilst at the same time, he should see and be seen by the chaplain and also be exposed to the inspection and control of the prison officer'.[19] A rather more precious and condensed version of the technology of compartmentalization was therefore to be found here.

The convicts were sequestered in wooden stalls with open tops through which they could see the raised figure of the preacher at his pulpit (Fig. 192), while guards were strategically distributed around the edges in high-level seats from which they could see into the stalls. After filing in, the convicts closed their stall doors one after the other. When the last door was closed a handle at the end of the row was pulled to lock the whole line of cubicles shut simultaneously, through a series of linked catches, until the service or instruction was over. The same procedure was then conducted in reverse (Fig. 193).

The behaviour of both staff and inmates was further regulated by additional timing instruments distributed throughout the prison to supplement the already inescapable co-agency of rigid rules and vigilant surveillance combined with the passive power of the building itself. One such was to be found in the chapel, used to synchronize the noiseless

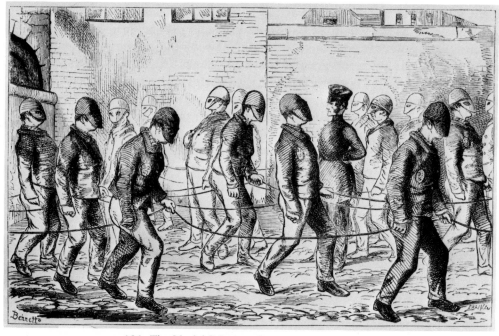

191. The Model Prison, prisoners exercising, 1856.

assembly and dispersal of the convicts. It consisted of a stand with dials marked with letters and figures manipulated by an officer to indicate which stall in which aisle was to be vacated at a given point in time. Jebb calculated that with it the chapel could be filled or emptied of a full complement of prisoners in just seven minutes (Fig. 194).[20]

The warders did not escape the same attention. For them there were a number of tell-tale clocks located in various parts of the prison. Projecting pegs on a revolving dial denoting quarter-hour intervals could be pressed down only by use of a lever fixed to the body of the tell-tale. If an officer did not proceed on his rounds in the right order and at precisely the right time of day, he would be unable to press down the correct peg. His omission was thus recorded and disciplinary action followed, usually in the form of a deduction from his wage.[21]

Pentonville was more impressive for its complexity and perfection than for its originality. It was the outcome of a process of historical development — the end of an evolutionary chain — which it is perhaps worth attempting to define. In terms of its architecture the Model Prison represented a rather specialized form of eclecticism. Each of its components can be traced back: the radial plan, the galleries, the cellular compartmentalization, the ventilation and servicing, the observatory, the chapel; all had emerged from the recent practice of prison building, serving many different systems of discipline. From the Rome House of Correction, Blackburn's concentric designs, the Panopticon and Cherry Hill, elements were brought together to define a second genotype of the prison more perfectly adapted than Bullar's generic radial plans of the 1820s. Yet this says very little, and makes it sound as if the history of the prison was the history of an accumulation of parts. More than this had been involved. The fundamental aim of all these institutions had been to reform corrupted character. Previous chapters have shown how prison architecture was developed quite consciously as a means to this end. Increasing technical sophistication was a consequence of successive failures to achieve reformation, which were frequently seen as failures of *performance* in the prison building. The critical link, then, was the link between reformation of character, which held out a possibility, and the technology of the prison through which that possibility was to be realized. At Pentonville Jebb had finally turned an issue of psychology into an issue of mechanics, and in this respect the

THE CHAPEL ON THE "SEPARATE SYSTEM," IN PENTONVILLE PRISON, DURING DIVINE SERVICE.

192. The Model Prison, the chapel as seen from the pulpit, 1856.

364

193. The Model Prison, stalled chapel pews and the device that locked a whole row shut.

194. The Model Prison chapel, stand and dial to facilitate noiseless assembly and exit of convicts.

Model Prison was not only the most advanced prison, but the most advanced building of its time.

In 1840 there were, it seems, only two projects in England where anything like the same scale or degree of sophistication in mechanical servicing was to be found: first, the Reform Club in Pall Mall of 1837, and second, the project for the Houses of Parliament at Westminster, both by Sir Charles Barry.[22] With the Reform Club so small by comparison and the Westminster designs enlarged but hardly under way, Pentonville may have some claim to pre-eminence, but rather than dwell on this it is more instructive to compare the two kinds of public building deemed worthy of such appurtenances in these early years. On the one hand a prison — the very best prison to be sure, but still a prison — whose inmates were regarded as despicable; on the other hand, the most revered of British institutions, embodying all that passed for democracy and designed to serve the Lords and elected representatives of the realm — establishments which served to define the upper and lower limits of society; an unexpected, if picturesque juxtaposition.

The concert of architecture and engineering at Pentonville had nothing whatever to do with the provision of comfort or with convenience, as it had at the Reform Club and Westminster. It was, instead, a necessary part of the war against communication. Item by item, detail by detail, the entire institution was, as the Rev. Burt put it, 'Soundly deduced from unquestioned laws of our moral nature.' From his point of view, the Model Prison was not an affirmation of our moral nature so much as a recognition of its weakness and an attempt to establish moral nature against the general drift of human nature.

The second rebuilding

After 1839 all new plans had to be approved by the Surveyor General of Prisons, and Jebb took this opportunity to press his model onto any local authority wishing to build. Even without this extra leverage Pentonville would probably have served its purpose, for, after only six years, more than 50 new buildings and additions based on Jebb's plan had been undertaken.[23]

A second, more comprehensive and uniform rebuilding of the English prison system was now underway; a prodigious reconstruction that, by the 1860s, would be practically complete. Model prisons proliferated.[24] Some were hardly distinguishable from Pentonville in plan (Fig. 195), others were single blocks, three wing radials, or five or six wing radials. In some, gothic vaults with clerestory lights were raised above the galleries, complete with tracery.[25] In others improved heating plant was tested.[26] Occasionally an old prison would simply be modified by more complete cellularization and nothing more, as at Devizes House of Correction,[27] or an old Howardian interior would be gutted and then remodelled with open galleries, as at Hereford County Gaol, where Nash had built unusually wide corridors (Fig. 196).[28] There were many variations but change was always in the direction of Jebb's model, with

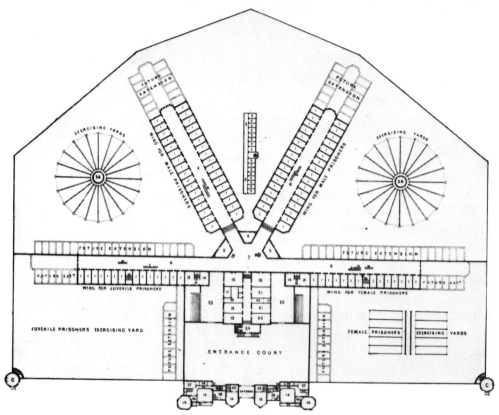

195. Armley Gaol, Leeds, Perkin and Backhouse, 1843–7, ground plan.

196. Hereford County Gaol, John Nash's prison remodelled.

its unmistakable sectional form and patent mechanical contrivances (Figs. 197, 198). The most notable departures were sponsored by Jebb himself for the convict prisons at Dartmoor, Portland and Brixton, special cases where the cells were only for sleeping (Fig. 199).[29] In the local prisons there was little deviation. Jebb could maintain, with some self-satisfaction, in 1854 that 'no alteration of any importance suggested itself for improving the construction of prisons',[30] and certainly, none had. The model had become the norm.

Architects accepted the superior wisdom of Jebb's prison engineering — they had no choice. Sir Charles Barry, sometimes recorded as the architect of Pentonville, was employed merely to apply an Italianate frontage of machicolations and pilasters towards Caledonian Road when Jebb had already completed his designs for the prison interior (Fig. 200). In these same years Barry was employing Pugin to manage the appearance of his proposal for the Houses of Parliament[31] — a reverse of the situation at Pentonville.[32] After this it was the fate of every prison architect to do little more than Barry had done, as the construction, detailing and dimensioning of prison buildings were pre-ordained.

The sequence of events that led to the partial rebuilding of Essex County Gaol gives a fair indication of the manner in which the architect's area of competence was narrowed. During 1843/4 the Essex Justices were discussing the possibility of remodelling Thomas Hopper's Springfield Gaol, built between 1822 and 1826, following complaints from the Inspectors of Prisons that the cells were ill-ventilated, inspection imperfect and the chapel too small. It had been hastily adapted to the separate system in 1834, when reports of the novel American discipline were first reaching this country. The alteration proved insufficient. Model Rules, issued by the Home Office in 1840, required the imposition of either separate confinement in large cells, or total silence with universal officer surveillance.[33] The staff at Springfield declared that neither system was enforceable as there were only seven keepers in the existing prison, compared with 49 at Pentonville, and that, due to defective construction, the inmates could easily hold conversations from one end of a cell block to the other using vent-gratings as mouth-pieces. Besides all this the old cells were too small.[34] So Hopper, still the County Surveyor and now a man of some reputation, dutifully, if not with good grace, prepared a sequence of six different

197. Surrey House of Correction, Wandsworth, D.R. Hill, 1849, galleried cell block.

plans exploring ways to convert the existing cell blocks into galleried sections of the approved type,[35] though he informed the magistrates that the 'model' was not Pentonville but Reading, which had cost less. Some of the plans were complete rebuildings (Fig. 201), others more or less extensive conversions (Fig. 202), and there were many variations of detail. At this point Sir Joshua Jebb made his appearance, travelling from London to attend a meeting of the Gaol Committee in December 1843.[36] Still the magistrates were unable to reach a decision. During the next 18 months Jebb maintained contact by letter and submitted his own sketch scheme of three model wings to the Committee as a guide in their deliberations. After considering eight further proposals from Hopper and one from another hand, the magistrates agreed on a

198. Hull Prison, David Thorp, 1865–70, galleried cell block.

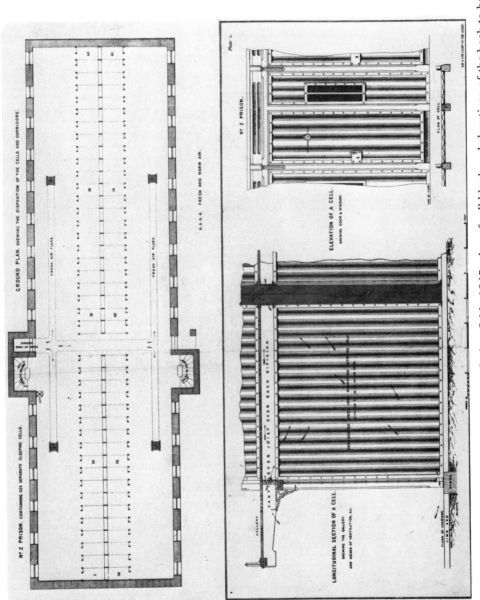

199. Dartmoor Convict Prison, Joshua Jebb, 1847, plan of cell block and elevations of the back-to-back cells partitioned with corrugated iron.

200. Water colour by Thomas Shepherd of the Model Prison, view from the Caledonian Road, 1850.

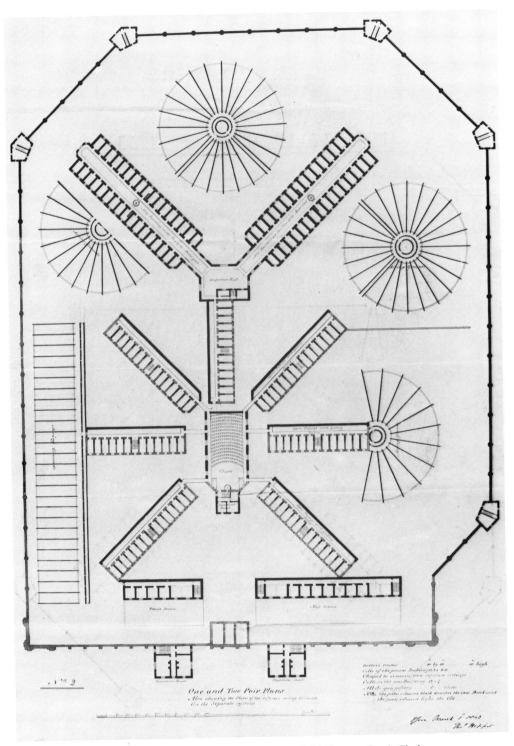

201. Designs for the remodelling of Springfield County Gaol, Chelmsford, Thomas Hopper, 1843.

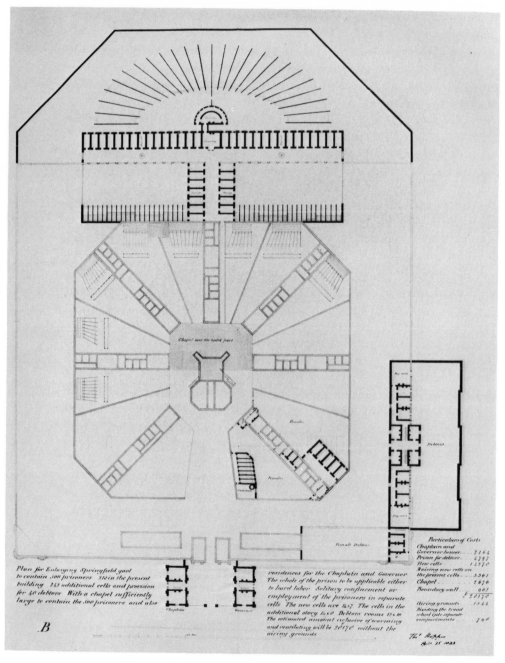

202. Springfield County Gaol, Hopper, 1843.

plan in December 1844, and in April 1845 the alterations, now sanctioned by Jebb, were begun. By 1848 one addition of two galleried wings, in closer conformity with Pentonville, was completed. The result appears meagre. Jebb's interference only seemed to delay matters by insisting on details of the mechanical installations, heating, ventilation and so forth. But this was exactly the point. Hopper's declared preference for Reading was, from Jebb's point of view, preference for an under-serviced prison in which subverting communication would flourish, and the proceedings, protracted as they were, had gone some way to rectify his original omissions.

Up and down the country, Jebb employed similar tactics, insisting on the observance of particulars, harrying or encouraging architects and magistrates by turns.[37] Once resistance to interference had been overcome there was nothing for the architect to do except fit the Jebb wings onto a site and then devote attention to the appearance of facades and entrances which became increasingly mediaeval, ornamental and meretricious (Figs. 203–207), fuelling the wrath of contemporary commentators like William Hepworth Dixon, who railed at the recent 'mania for making our prisons picturesque' along with railway stations, hospitals, provident societies and every other variety of building: 'It would be absurd to build a brewery on the model of St. Paul's . . . but would it be less absurd to do this, than to erect a prison at Reading — the handsomest building in Berkshire — on the model of an Elizabethan palace?' Dixon believed in the improver's maxim that 'repulsive appearance' was a better deterrent to the population than the 'mere restraints and regulations' of prison discipline,[38] but for the majority of architects a commission for a gaol meant a grand opportunity for a free exercise of talent in the composition of secular gothic or Norman facades, behind which loomed the inevitable model cell blocks. The conditional division between facade and plan, evident for so long, had finally been broken into two unconnected tasks presided over by different interests: a technology of moral purpose prescribed and enforced by the Home Office and an architecture of external appearances, within the competence of the individual architect to decide. The more florid treatment of the exterior cannot be attributed to this division — it could be observed in many other kinds of building around the middle of the century — but it did underline it.

The so called prison palace at Reading, designed by Gilbert Scott and

William Moffat (Fig. 203), was an influential facade in so far as it affected other architects' designs in the 1840s. It was also cruelly abused by critics. When, in 1857, the notable M.P. and campaigner for metropolitan improvements, Charles Pearson, held it up to ridicule in *What is to be Done with our Criminals?*, he provoked a characteristic reply from *Building News*, eager to justify the architects.[39] But the vindication of Scott and Moffat's domesticated, toyish castellation could only be accomplished by acknowledging the complete divide between the realities of conditions inside the prison and the illusions of the facade, at the same time taking it for granted that this was a satisfactory state of affairs. Pearson's mistake was to carry on 'as if the

203. Reading County Gaol, Gilbert Scott and William Moffat, 1842–4, entrance.

204. Armley Gaol, Leeds, Perkin and Backhouse, 1843—7, entrance elevation.

205. Birmingham Borough Gaol, D.R. Hill, started 1847, entrance elevation.

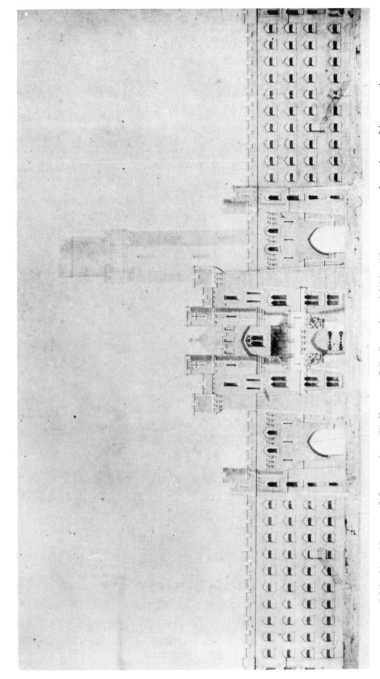

206. City House of Correction, Holloway, J.B. Bunning, 1848–52, entrance elevation of inner prison.

381

palace prison of Reading . . . affected the discipline'. It did not. 'The style and form of Reading prison have been influenced by causes altogether remote from prison discipline, and as they do not contravene any essential of prison discipline, it is in very bad taste', complained *Building News* lamely, 'to make this sneer at Reading.'

It was the idea of the prison, not the fact of the prison, that was to engage the architect's imagination, and the idea of the prison was built up from historical associations. Reading looked like a castle, and the castle, 'in the ears of the people stood for prison for many a hundred years'. The *Building News* then went on to claim that the bare, un-decorated carcass of penitentiary and Panopticon, the eyesores recom-

207. City House of Correction, Bunning, view of entrance.

mended by Pearson, 'have not such a look of dread as these time feared ramparts and towers', which also owned a peculiar beauty. The article concluded with a comparison of Dance's neo-classical Newgate and Scott and Moffat's castellated design, to the effect that Newgate too was architecture only in so far as it comprised 'details of adornment'. Newgate was nevertheless so powerful an image of dread that now 'the word NEWGATE carved on any wall would be significant enough'.

These familiar arguments, in which words and images refer interchangeably to a remote past, were weakened by the questionable assertion that the giant spread-eagles of cell building clearly visible behind the walls of any separate prison were less potent as images than the facile archaeological pretension of portcullis and lodgings in front. Still, the idea that the new prisons signified less to the public than their architectural frontispieces was a consoling one, given that the architect was obliged to 'appeal to recognised associations, instead of attempting to create new ones'.

The truth was probably otherwise. Architects were in considerable danger of losing their last remaining claim on the prison — its imagery — which now belonged to the separate prisons as they stood, as much as to recollections of the dungeon. Neither mediaeval baileys, nor seventeenth-century Newgate for that matter, were conceived as expressive of imprisonment, yet had been precipitated into symbols of confinement by force of events. Already in the 1850s the converging model cell blocks lined with squinting windows were, likewise, universally recognizable for what they were. But from the architect's point of view it was safer to deny the irresistible tendency for a place to represent the events that occurred within it, for object and act to become indistinguishable, because once this fusion had taken place, once signifier and signified were one and the same, the language of architecture would be needed no more.

This awkward situation could not have been eased by the raising of gothic from an essentially theatrical style which could encompass the fearful in its expressive range, to an essentially moral style which could not easily do so. The more that mediaeval styles were mingled with goodness, and the more appropriate they were deemed for general use, the less obviously appropriate they became for prisons. The grandiloquence of J.B. Bunning's Holloway (Figs. 206, 207) may have been an attempt to recapture a sense of primitive intimidation from a gothic that was becoming too tranquil, and Alfred Waterhouse's soaring Venetian ventilation towers at Strangeways, redolent of Ruskin, show how ambiguous prison gothic could be in the 1860s.

Separate confinement spread all over Europe in the 1840s and 1850s. In 1841 the architects Abel Blouet, Harou Romain and Hector Horeau published an atlas of cellular prison designs for the Ministry of the Interior as part of the Projet de Loi, introducing mitigated solitude into France.[40] By 1846, 30 new French prisons were said to be in progress.[41] In Belgium the Inspector General of Prisons, Ducpetiaux, had put separation into practice in 1835, and in the forties a large prison at Liège was constructed on the lines of Cherry Hill. In Sweden the philosophical King Oscar implemented separation in 1846 and built galleried radials with thermo-ventilation and cavity construction.[42] In Amsterdam a prison on the Pentonville plan was commenced and national reforms followed in 1851. In Prussia Frederick William IV raised an exact replica of Pentonville at Moabit (Fig. 208).[43] Tuscany, Norway, Denmark and several German States were also building separate prisons. This was no mere administrative revision; it was a phenomenal burst of constructive energy, the products of which are still at the core of the penal system.

With such precipitate and wide-ranging change came the internationalization of expertise and experience, a development that was formalized in 1844 when the Inspector General of French prisons, Morreau-Christophe, announced the preparation of a quarterly journal, the *Revue Penitentiare*, for which he had sought the co-operation of de Beaumont and de Tocqueville in Paris, Dr Cattaneo in Milan, Crawford and Russell in London, Dr David in Copenhagen, Edouard Ducpetiaux in Brussels, Frederick Hill in Scotland, John Haviland in Philadelphia, Dr Nicolaus Julius in Berlin and Mompiani in Brescia.[44] Two years later the first International Penitentiary Congress was held in Frankfurt-am-Main, at which it was resolved that separate confinement should be applied generally to all convicts.[45]

There can be no doubt that separate confinement appealed to governments and administrators, but its appeal was by no means universal. Enthusiasts portrayed it as a work of humanity; humanity tempered with a reasonable dose of severity. For them the separate prison was 'an institution suggested by the most enlightened and active benevolence . . . calculated to produce the happiest results on the moral

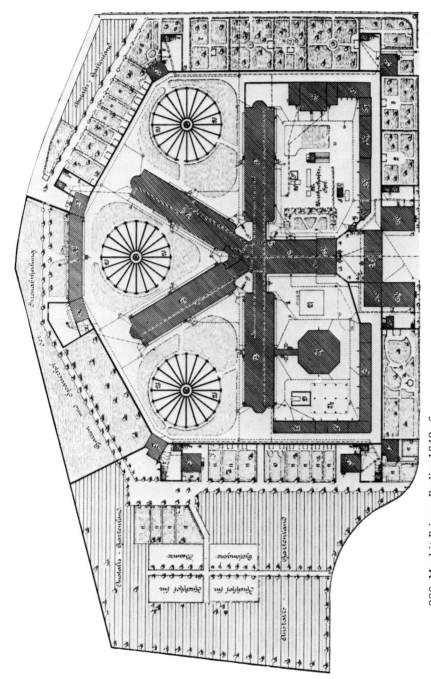

208. Moabit Prison, Berlin, 1842—6.

character and condition of society',[46] which was all very much in the
framework of philanthropic penal reform. However, the alleged benevolence of separation elicited an ambiguous response from critics. Was it
proof of too great a tenderness or a veil for awful severity? It is rare to
find an unequivocal statement of either view. The two passages quoted
below, from a waspish pamphlet written by Peter Laurie to put the lie
to Crawford and Russell's First Report, typify the extraordinary but
very common oscillation between one pole of condemnation and its
apparent opposite. First he derides the ill-directed magnanimity of
reformers:

There is a comedy written by a friend of mine, on an entirely new plan. You see it
is called 'The Reformed Housebreaker', where, by the mere force of wit and
humour, housebreaking is put in so ridiculous a light, that if this piece only has its
proper run, bolts and bars will become useless by the end of the season.[47]

But then only 'amiable philanthropists and enlightened philosophers'
would contemplate putting people away in total seclusion with a smile
on their faces. Laurie, turning tail on himself, said he could think of no
other source for such a doctrine than the *New Angler*, where he had
come across the following advice on the subject of preparing live frogs
for bait: '*Sew up his mouth*, and with a fine needle and silk stitch the
upper part of his leg to the arming wire of your hook, and in so doing
use him as though you loved him.'[48] Laurie took the view that the
model prison was at once too well-appointed to deter, and too dreadful
to reform. Many others agreed. Accusations were most commonly made
in connection with the appearance of insanity in the new prisons. The
softness of the model was said to pamper the body; its severity was said
to attack the mind. On 2 December 1843, *John Bull* disclosed that
several prisoners at Pentonville had already succumbed to madness. The
first, John Reeve, had been transferred to Bedlam on 24 June.[49] He was
followed by a steady stream of convicts unable to stand up to the
mental strains of separate confinement. In the first eight years the authorities declared 22 insane, found 26 suffering from delusions and
recorded three successful suicides.[50]

The propensity for solitude to break down the structure of the mind
had been attested by the eighteenth-century reformers. It was a hazard
which some were now, as then, prepared to take in their stride. The
Rev. Burt and the Rev. Nihil for instance felt that mental breakdown
was an inevitable danger of a system in which the will of a convict was

'subdued . . . bent or broken' and the moral character 'made plastic by the discipline'. The good effects of separation stemmed from this very same forcing open of the mind: 'It is not that the faculty of volition is enfeebled, but that the bad influence by which the will has been previously actuated is withdrawn or abated and the will is bent in its direction; it is broken in its resistance to virtue.'[51] Some violence had to be done to the mental faculty if reformation was to succeed. Was it not reasonable to expect casualties during such a struggle? The question was not whether the model prison produced madness and dementia, but whether the risk was excessive. Nihil, Burt and Adshead maintained that it was not, adding that there was some reason to believe the criminal classes as a whole were, anyway, prone to mental aberrations.[52]

Later on Mayhew and Binney, Griffiths and Hepworth Dixon looked back with the benefit of hindsight, and remembered how desperate was the plight of prisoners in solitude. We hear of Julia Newman who, under Nihil's rule at Millbank, drove herself mad in a very methodical way,[53] and of a gentle soul whose pretence at insanity was magnified in the dark cell until he too was dispatched to Bedlam,[54] and we learn that Pentonville produced *upwards of ten times more lunatics* than should be the case according to the normal rate'.[55] Outside of the prisons this 'tampering with the mysteries of the brain', as Dickens called it,[56] was challenged on a broad front. At one end was the odd Chartist calling for the immediate demolition of the 'Pentonville Bastille' ('every idiot being a proof of the maddening effects of the solitary system')[57] together with universal suffrage. At the other end was a sizeable group against the 'starched inveteracy of hyper-morality'[58] — against, that is, the silly prejudices of reformers. They had no time for reform and no time for criminals either. Carlyle, Dickens, Laurie, Chesterton and *The Times* were the most notable antagonists from this vantage point. The one crucial issue upon which they were all agreed was this: that prison could not reform character. They did not simply criticize the efficacy of the model prison, racing to propose some new and better scheme in its place. Their scepticism was more deep rooted. They denied the very possibility of wholesale reformation through imprisonment.

9　The uncoupling of architecture and reform

As the specification of English prisons approached the limits of technical perfectibility, so the reformers' doctrine was put to the final test. No longer could failure to transfigure the criminal character be put down to 'defects in construction'. It would, perhaps, be possible to fortify every model cell against the infiltration of evil a little more completely, but such improvements were, after mid-century, regarded as of little practical use. With the building of Pentonville a decisive point had been reached after which the notion that imprisonment could redeem criminals evaporated from penal theory with astonishing speed, giving way to a vacant scepticism or positive disbelief. Rothman, Foucault and Ignatieff have recorded this important event in prison history from different perspectives, but the change was a change of opinion with no significant correlative change in practice. The prison itself, which had grown out of a kind of optimism, with the authorities regarding the punished as more malleable than they turned out to be, changed hardly at all. Instead, administrative procedures, management, regulation, construction and detailing were ossified in the name not of universal reformation, but of national uniformity.

Deprived of its power to transform, the prison was reassessed and redefined as a tried and convenient method of exacting punishment and deterring from crime; its form and substance was preserved while its original purpose as an institution was lost to view. It is this disjunction between doctrine and practice, the uncoupling of architecture and reform, that will be briefly examined here.

The first signs of it were manifested in the 1830s, with the polarization of penal doctrine into two inalienable camps: the separate school and the silent school. This dispute over prison discipline — the most celebrated event in nineteenth-century penal thought — opened the divide between sceptics and believers. Those who believed in the ultimate efficacy of reformation by imprisonment pinned their hopes on the separate system; those who regarded any further investment in yet nicer forms of prison construction as futile opposed the separate system and supported the silent system. In Britain at least, the advantage of the silent system was that it could be practised in old prisons, while the separate system was to be practised in specially constructed new institutions which, so the silent school maintained, 'taxed and drained' honest men in order to finance 'the chimerical whims of enthusiasts in systematic perfectability'.[1] It was, from their point of view, no use to pursue perfection if it did not give results. In response to their accusers the acolytes of the separate school published accounts of prisoners whose character had been reformed in model prisons, which the silent school consequently demolished with derisive and scornful commentaries on gullible, devout prison chaplains who 'mistake a fit of the "megrims" [migraine] for a religious frame of mind', confused the bilious with the pious,[2] and who were consistently hoodwinked by prisoners eager to feign the most unexpected moral conversions.[3]

In 1834 Captain George Laval Chesterton instituted the silent system at Cold Bath Fields. After five years of trying to enforce classification he was convinced that discipline should be more rigorous. He was also convinced that imprisonment did not reform but only served to deter. Cold Bath Fields was by this time one of the older surviving prisons. The main block, designed in 1788 on a typically Howardian courtyard plan (Fig. 77), had recently been supplemented with two five wing radials within the old walls, designed by William Moseley and occupied in 1830 and 1832 (Fig. 209). No architectural modifications to this piecemeal development were considered necessary when the silent system was imposed. The enormous bridewell at Tothill Fields, also under the jurisdiction of Middlesex, soon followed suit with Lieutenant A.F. Tracy as governor. Neither the Middlesex Magistrates nor Chesterton, whose prison was always considered the exemplar of silent discipline,[4] were impressed by the zeal of the Inspectors of Prisons in evangelizing separation, and the silent system was maintained by that county until the mid sixties.

Few stood up so well to the pressures exerted from the Inspectorate. The separate system prevailed, but after its general adoption belief in criminal reformation declined all the more steeply. The deaths of William Crawford and Whitworth Russell in 1847 simply made this extensive disillusion more obvious by removing the most influential of

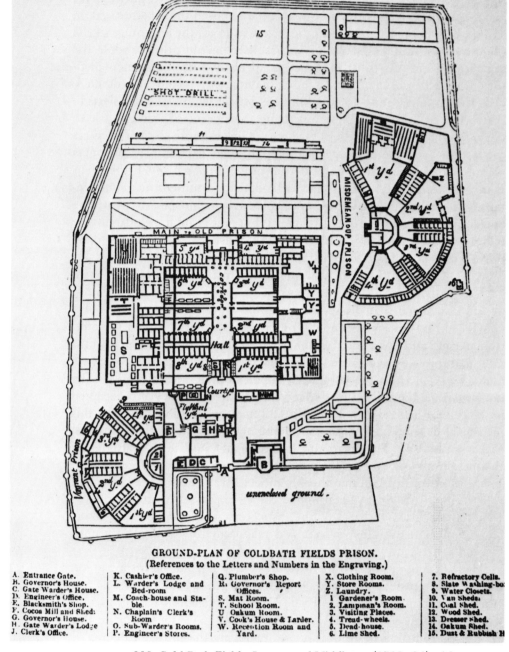

GROUND-PLAN OF COLDBATH FIELDS PRISON.
(References to the Letters and Numbers in the Engraving.)

A. Entrance Gate.	K. Cashier's Office.	Q. Plumber's Shop.	X. Clothing Room.	7. Refractory Cells.
B. Governor's House.	L. Warder's Lodge and Bed-room	R. Governor's Report Offices.	Y. Store Rooms.	8. Slate Washing-box
C. Gate Warder's House.			Z. Laundry.	9. Water Closets.
D. Engineer's Office.	M. Coach-house and Stable.	S. Mat Room.	1 Gardener's Room.	10. Van Sheds.
E. Blacksmith's Shop.		T. School Room.	2. Lampman's Room.	11. Coal Shed.
F. Cocoa Mill and Shed.	N. Chaplain's Clerk's Room	U. Oakum Room.	3. Visiting Places.	12. Wood Shed.
G. Governor's House.		V. Cook's House & Larder.	4. Tread-wheels.	13. Dresser Shed.
H. Gate Warder's Lodge	O. Sub-Warder's Rooms.	W. Reception Room and Yard.	5. Dead-house.	14. Oakum Shed.
J. Clerk's Office.	P. Engineer's Stores.		6. Lime Shed.	15. Dust & Rubbish H

209. Cold Bath Fields, Leroux and Middleton (1788–94) with additions by William Moseley (1830–2).

its partisans. In 1854 the Surveyor General of Prisons — the man who had designed and built Pentonville — went on record upholding Lord Denman's contention that 'the only legitimate end of punishment' was to 'deter from crime';[5] reform was disavowed even from this unlikely quarter. A decade later the Carnarvon Committee, formulating government policy, was equally blunt in its repudiation of reform as the purpose of imprisonment, and equally firm in its espousal of punishment as an end in itself.[6]

However strong this rejection was, and it was certainly a broad shift of informed opinion evident in practically every announcement on prison discipline after 1850, it was not total and unequivocal. It is more true to say that the scope of reform was limited and diminished without being eliminated from penal theory. Indeed it retained a particular place in the system. Reformative discipline was henceforth the privilege of the innocent and the young,[7] and was no longer associated with the newly built prisons at all but with other types of institution. Once an offender had suffered due punishment he might be eligible for improvement, but not before retribution had been exacted. Sir Walter Crofton's Irish Penitentiary System, which in the 1850s and 1860s was praised by those who had not entirely recanted their belief in reform, subjected prisoners to an initial spell in solitude followed by congregate labour in an intermediate establishment. Unlike the solitude of the separate system, Irish solitude — almost unmitigated at Mountjoy, Grange Gorman, Cork and Dublin Newgate — was practised with the sole intent of producing discomfort so that 'each convict may practically feel the result of his offence'.[8] Only outside the prison, in the intermediate farming and quarrying establishments, was reform attempted. When, in this same period, Captain Alexander Maconochie tried to introduce a revised version of character reform into the English prisons, replacing the disputed influence of architecture with his Marks System, he failed miserably. Here just one class of offenders was accorded the privilege of reformation: juveniles. As the prison reform movement began so it ended — with children, who were, once again, moved out of the prisons into reformatories.[9]

The first of the new child reformatories was the Colonie Agricole at Mettray, conceived by Auguste Demetz in 1839 and designed by his colleague Abel Blouet with whom he had visited the American penitentiaries (Fig. 210).[10] It was not exactly a prison.[11] Central supervision

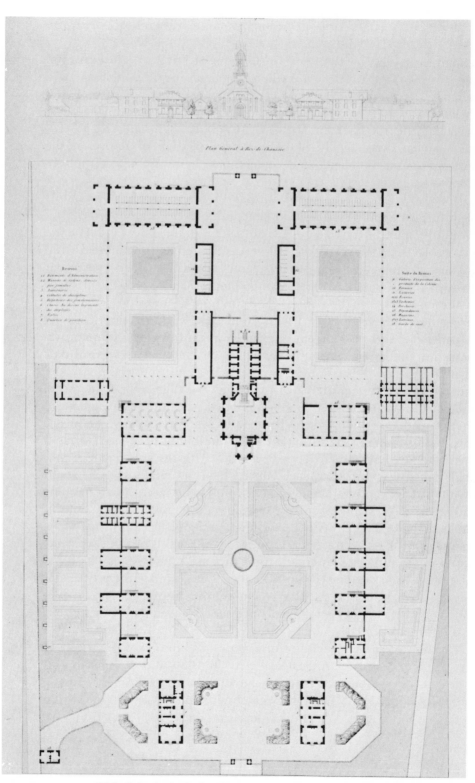

210. Colonie Agricole, Mettray, Abel Blouet, 1839–50, plan and elevation.

was given up and replaced with 12 independent but still autocratic family units, planned to appear as part of a small rural village. The mysterious but mechanical morality of solitude was supplanted by the instruction and example of 'parents', the cell by the 'home'. Authority had been given another structure, equally severe yet more domestic, in which architecture, though still a force, was less central to the process of reformation.[12]

These institutions spread throughout Europe as rapidly as had the separate prisons. By 1879 there were 52 agricultural colonies for criminal children in France, all on the lines of Mettray.[13] In England Parkhurst was planned specifically for juvenile convicts, also in 1839, but it was in the 1850s that there followed a string of reformatory farm schools, 65 of which were occupied by 1870. There was, said the American penologist Enoch Wines, 'nothing of the prison about them — no walls, no spies, no guards; family influences are made prominent and predominant'.[14] Children had always held pride of place as subjects for reformation,[15] so the concern over juvenile welfare after 1850 was not in itself notable. What makes it interesting is that children now had to be taken out of the prisons to be made virtuous, whereas it was precisely for that reason they were put there during earlier phases of reform.[16]

The prison was losing its powers — powers that had hitherto been regarded as almost thaumaturgical in their capacity to heal the corrupted — and so the more innocent had to be evacuated from it. The doctrine that had given rise to the prison system also came under critical scrutiny. The catenary of causes that led down from amusement to passion to crime and thence up through prison and solitude to virtue had been formulated as a kind of equation by the eighteenth-century philanthropists. If one side of that equation was discovered to be in error the other side must surely also be wrong. As the reformed prisons were found wanting, so too was the reformers' aetiology of crime. The notion that criminals should be systematically reformed belonged to the late eighteenth and early nineteenth century. It was not entirely a product of Christian piety or of rationalistic psychology, nor a simple translation of industry's new requirements into ideology, but an amalgam that could flourish only as long as a particular moral sensibility prevailed. From this sensibility issued a cluster of ideas about crime and society, at the centre of which was belief in the neutrality of human nature — a common but in the end rather fragile belief that when all was said and done the criminal was 'neither a brute nor a saint',[17] but an emanation from causes that were outside himself. The habits and associations of a lifetime converged to define a man's character, but that character — evil or virtuous, mild or passionate, criminal or law abiding, submissive or bold — was not of his making. Vice was not integral to the human condition, nor was goodness; both were manufactured by civilization.

The reforming structure that was advanced almost to the point of finality in the prisons, evident too in the design of schools, lunatic asylums, barracks, factories, workhouses, hospitals, model farms and model villages, was to counteract the degeneracy of existing society. These new varieties of institution were built in the hope that mankind could be raised toward perfection by a form of administration channelled through a carefully distributed architecture. It was for this reason that, speaking of prisons, Abel Blouet could hold that 'to persist in the ancient mode of construction, will be to perpetuate the abuses that are inherited with it'.[18] He did not mean by this that there was some analogical relationship between style and civilization; he meant that there was a causal bond between the form of the prison and its effects on conduct. The idea was of an exact consequence, not of a vague parallelism.

The petrified relics of darker ages had been destroyed and, in the rebuilding, a new shape, both physical and moral, had been given to society. In this presumptuous, overweening spirit the prisons had been conceived, but towards the middle of the nineteenth century there were many commentators to be found comparing their own more productive society unflatteringly with its medieval antecedent. Two well-known examples will suffice to show how these views were applied to prisons and criminals.

Amongst architects Augustus Welby Northmore Pugin was advocating a return to faith and gothic building. His contentious and polemical *Contrasts* were propaganda against classicism in architecture and against Utilitarianism, the two identified as aspects of the same malaise. The crowning contrast, which only appeared in the second edition of 1841, was the contrasted town — the nineteenth-century town shown changed beyond recognition from the fifteenth-century original (Fig. 211), with only a few remnants of its past glory to be seen. Pugin filled the immediate foreground of this picture with four modern enterprises: a gothic church rebuilt in the classical style, a lunatic asylum, a gas works, and, right in the very centre, a new gaol, with central inspection, classification and unproductive labour to epitomize the age. Directed at institutions — prisons, asylums and workhouses[19] — Pugin's strident nostalgia turned the enlightenment diagram of progress upside down and pointed backwards from the cruelties of the present to gothic gentleness. This was an inversion in which only the ideal of leniency was preserved intact, and was one of several attempts between the late eighteenth and the early twentieth century to devise a picturesque social landscape to correspond with the art of good building (Repton, Morris, Unwin). But this nostalgia for peaceful piety had a counterpart, less evident in architecture, more in journalism: a nostalgia for good and evil, which was employed to great effect by Thomas Carlyle in one of his *Latter Day Pamphlets*; the subject: model prisons.[20] Far from imputing harshness to the contemporary authorities as Pugin had been prone to do, Carlyle dismissed them as tender minded obscurantists

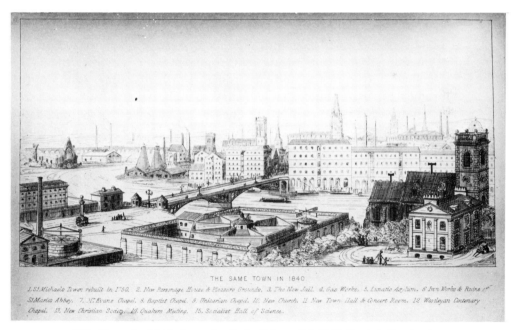

211. Town in 1840, from the 2nd edition of A.W.N. Pugin's *Contrasts*.

determined to extinguish the difference between good and evil. The model prisons were almost heavenly in their orderliness, so what right had 'the soldiers of . . . the genius of darkness' to such territory? Howard he charged with having attempted the 'abolition of punishment' in the cause of philanthropy when what was needed was a 'hearty hatred for scoundrels'. Still, such divergent interpretations of the old ways should not obscure an obvious similarity. With Carlyle and Pugin, and Dickens too for that matter, it is not the virulence of their feeling against criminals that sets them apart from earlier critics, but the virulence of their feelings against contemporary methods of reform. The motives for punishing were conceived differently now; punishment was no longer meted out as a kind of medicine.

These pundits, influential though they and their followers may have been, attacked reform from outside the prison system. Until the 1840s the only reaction from within had been the negative scepticism typified by G.L. Chesterton and the silent school. However, the science of penology, invented as an appendage to reformative imprisonment,[21] was eventually to define concepts of criminal treatment that would dispense with the idea of reformation altogether.

This point had certainly been reached by 1876, when Cesare Lombroso published *L'Uomo Deliquente*, a work generally accepted as laying the foundation of the anthropological or positivist theory of criminal development, and according to which crime was not the product of circumstance, habit or exacerbated passion but of *criminality* (a noun very rarely used in the English language before the middle of the nineteenth century).[22] Criminality was an inherent quality distinguishing those who committed crimes as by and large psychologically different from the normal human being; an inferior type that not only possessed primitive and ferocious instincts, but could be identified by raised cheek bones, deep set eyes and prominent brows. There had been many references to the connection between anatomy and crime, but in making it account for criminal behaviour in general and linking it with heredity, Lombroso provided a suitable intellectual receptacle for the continuing reaction against reform; a reaction that until then had been emotional and pragmatic by turns.

Certainly, the same could not be said of an earlier science which had attempted to define the criminal type — phrenology[23] — though even phrenology was able to claim one significant convert from the prison establishment in England. In 1852 Captain George Laval Chesterton, the governor of Cold Bath Fields who had explicitly denied the reforming effects of imprisonment, was introduced to Monsieur Leger, a member of the Medical Institute of Paris. Leger wanted to conduct an experiment in what he called electro-phrenology on Chesterton's prisoners. Using the magnetoscope (an instrument invented by Mr Rutter of Brighton to test the quality of metals) he was able, or so he said, to 'delineate the extent and character of mental organs'. Though Chesterton first regarded the whole thing as a waste of time, he changed his mind when Leger demonstrated the unerring accuracy of his diagnosis by practising it on Chesterton himself. Thereafter some 100 prisoners at Cold Bath Fields and another 60 at Tothill Fields were subjected to it. Their proclivities and propensities were shown up to such good effect that Chesterton declared his complete reliance on these 'remarkable tests' where he had no previous knowledge of a prisoner's character.[24] Of all those prominent in the field of prison discipline during the 1830s and 1840s only Chesterton in this country and Edward Livingstone in America were swayed by the claims of phrenology. Livingstone, like Chesterton, denied the possibility of reform through imprisonment.[25]

Phrenology, together with other physiognomic explanations of crime advanced at the time,[26] helped undermine the edifice of reform only after it had begun to collapse. The timely arrival of criminal anthropology hastened demolition by removing its foundation on criminal psychology. Criminals were born and not bred; at the very least there was a dynamic interplay between innate instincts and acquired habits. It would seem then that the prison population was composed largely of degenerates, either suffering some pathological, congenital defect, or representing a regressive sub-species from an earlier stage in evolution. The criminal was still described with the aid of medical terminology, yet while the criminals of the eighteenth and early nineteenth centuries were suffering a remedial infection, those of the later nineteenth century were victim to what was considered by some to be the most 'radically incurable of all natural defects'.[27]

The prison could no more reform the character of 'a class of fools whom even experience fails to teach'[28] than it could transform lead into gold. Character was a natural endowment that might be modified but could not be essentially altered and the prison therefore became a place in which to restrain a potentially dangerous, perhaps half-savage race of beings. It served a purpose but it could not possibly amend or rectify. It was not only theorists who would argue so, for this was also the opinion of Sir Edmund Du Cane, who succeeded Jebb as Surveyor General of Prisons, was later Secretary to the Prison Commission and who, after 1874, had directed the building of Wormwood Scrubs, the last major prison of the nineteenth century. Wormwood Scrubs was on a plan that relinquished central inspection but in all other respects was hardly distinguishable from the separate prisons of the forties and fifties (Figs. 212, 213), which indicates, as well as anything could, the severing of the prison from the idea of reformation, allowing its fabric

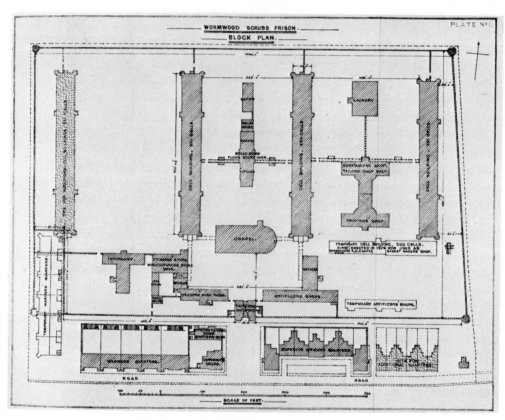

212. Wormwood Scrubs, Sir Edmund Du Cane, 1874–91, block plan.

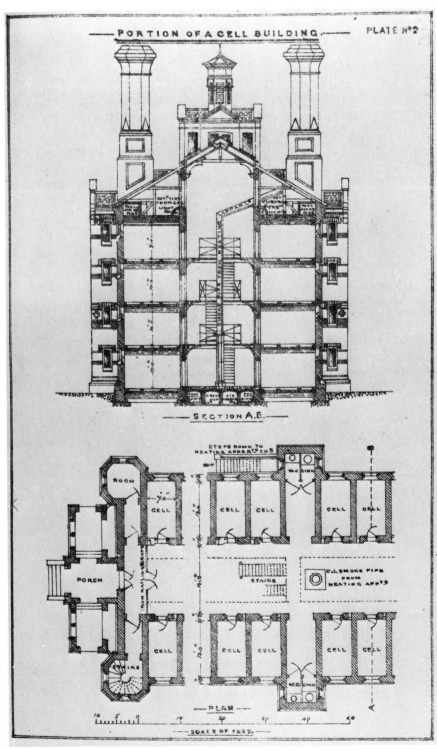

213. Wormwood Scrubs, Sir Edmund Du Cane, section and part plan of cell block.

to stand untouched while the intellectual construction which had given rise to it lay in ruins round about.

Even those who disapproved of this theory with which vice was 'explained away . . . by referring it to a survival of brutal and primitive savagery' did not draw on the old doctrine of universal reformability, but regarded crime instead as an 'essential element of human nature' that could never be rooted out though it might perhaps be suppressed.[29] The same was true of those who saw crime as a social phenomenon.[30] Whether the cause of crime lay bonded in the structure of society as Quetelet, Durkheim and Marx held, or whether it was fixed in the genetic constitution of mankind, it was beyond the scope of the prison to erase it.

After all this the prisons began to be seen in a different light. Orderly and solitary they still were, but drained of all purpose these qualities became inexplicable and timeless. From those who for one reason or another had witnessed their inner workings — Doré, Kropotkin and Wilde — came an image as vivid as that of the reek and violence of unreformed gaols. Where there had been disorder, licence and corruption through intercourse there was now an unrelenting repetition of futile tasks performed within the close, bleak perspective of converging walls.

214. Illustration published in 1907 for Charles Dickens' essay on prisons in *American Notes*.

10 Architecture limited and unlimited

So the edifice of the prison remained intact, hardly touched by the shifts in penal thought. No intellectual movement proved capable of seriously disturbing the ineluctable procedures of imprisonment or of displacing the lifeless, durable forms of prison building, both held in place by the overwhelming fact of their existence. In the meantime, the powers of prison architecture had been limited by consensus; by an agreement that it was ineffective as an instrument of reformation.

It would be quite wrong though to give the impression that the issue was laid to rest in this mood of jaded disillusion, the prison being regarded as redundant apparatus of a fruitless experiment. By some lights the separate prisons were immensely successful. Not only did they remain the keystone of penal practice in Britain and many other countries, and not only did they become the paradigm of institutional building during the nineteenth century, they also effectively remodelled the nature of reality within their walls.

If, from Howard's time onwards, the vindication of the prison has been sought outside it − in its after effects on conscience, in its influence on recidivism, in its value as a deterrent, then it is surely time to focus attention within, for within the prison nothing remained the same. During one century its topography, economy and society had altered beyond recognition. This altered internal constitution of the prison existed more for itself than for any extraneous purpose. However much it was dragged into debates about the world at large it remained essentially separate and self-sufficing. The reformers had tried to establish within the new prisons a geography of innocence, subtracting everything from the field of knowledge of the inmate, and removing from his influence everything that could evolve into vice. The prison administration, looking at things differently, were prone to interpret the resulting situation in terms of blatant power relations: magnifying the authority of the governor, increasing the executive effect of the

402

officers and diminishing the capacity for reaction amongst the prisoners. But either way the intended effects could be relied upon only within the precincts of the institution.

To read the prison literature of the 1840s and 1850s one would think this limitation of effect had rendered architecture completely useless in the cause of reform. But if the perspective is broadened sufficiently another possibility comes into view. Since the effects of imprisonment were local to the prison and proved difficult to export, was it not all the more urgent to inscribe a larger territory with the hall-marks of morality? If the effects were local to the architecture then perhaps the architecture should be more universally applied.

The purpose of this final chapter is to investigate the ambiguous position of prison architecture during this odd period of triumph and failure. The ambiguities quickly multiply. For instance, if strictly architectural parallels with different kinds of building are sought, they are easily enough found in other institutions; but if instead the locus of reform, rather than the shape of plans, is traced, if we search for equivalent intentions rather than comparable structures, then the effects of prison architecture are indeed found to spread widely during the nineteenth century. The role of the architectural profession in the development of the prison was also ambiguous. Architecture was undoubtedly crucial to the reformed penal institutions but it was a variety of architecture that flourished at the periphery of the profession; indeed prison architecture was distinct enough from that taught in academies and normally practised in offices to be disengaged altogether from it by the 1840s.

Even so, the prison's development had been fuelled by converting principles of neo-classicism into principles of institutional formation, and, as we shall see, there may have been deeper reasons for the sucesss of the conversion.

The shifting locus of reform

During the later nineteenth century the English prisons appeared to be remnants of a spent force and were being reinterpreted by commentators as products of another age, curious and incomprehensible. The revised position of the separate prisons in the scheme of things was not now so very different from that of the unreformed prisons of the eighteenth century. The separate prisons reflected a tradition rather than a policy. They were no longer able to eradicate crime and had become instead the breeding ground of villainy and the proper abode for the criminal type. They had also become fixed elements in the popular drama of crime and its recompense, as the wards of Newgate had been before.

What is more, the separate prisons were becoming increasingly like the world in which they were situated — or rather the world was becoming like them. Just as the unreformed prisons of the eighteenth century had provided a perverted microcosm of everyday reality within buildings that were merely fractions of the town or city, so too did the prisons of the late nineteenth century. But this time, instead of the prisons condensing and distorting the wider world, the wider world began to borrow characteristics from the prisons. Similar sensibilities were brought to bear on issues that seem, at first sight, distant from imprisonment, while in architecture the same underlying principles were applied with the same intention of shaping experience through the medium of building. Others have pointed to the similarity between the prisons and the factories,[1] seeing the former as seminaries for an industrial work force in which the alienation between labour and production was nearly absolute. Yet it was not the workshop but the cell which was the fundamental space of the prison. In terms of planning, the separate prisons were comprised of a marriage between the static, shrouded, contemplative, individualized space of the cells and the generalized connective space of the galleries converging on the central observatory. This marriage between open and closed space was echoed more directly in housing than in the factories, and this is not the only connection between the prisons and housing.

The intimate charms of family life were recognized in the eighteenth century. By the middle decades of the nineteenth domesticity was seen not just as the proper condition of families but, often, as superior to all other varieties of social experience. In the dwellings of the upper strata of English society, between 1770 and 1820, the distribution of rooms, the organization of access and the arrangement of furniture had undergone considerable transformation in the cause of intimacy in general and domesticity in particular.[2] But it was not until the 1840s that similar attention was given to the homes of the labouring classes. In

1842, the year that Pentonville was completed, Edwin Chadwick published his *Report on the Sanitary Condition of the Labouring Population*, marking the inception of the housing reform movement in England. In the 1850s, 1860s and 1870s, just those years when reform was retreating from the prisons, another campaign was being mounted in the slums. There was no noticeable migration of reformers from prisons to housing, no transferring or sharing of allegiances, as had been the case with the anti-slavers and the penal reformers after the 1780s. The subjects did not overlap in this way, yet, in the 1857 *Prospectus* of the Society for Improving the Condition of the Labouring Classes, by far the most influential body in the early development of model dwellings, it was still the 'illustrious Howard' to whom homage was paid, as he was held responsible for 'the removal from our prisons of evils similar in character, though more concentrated and intense in degree' than those now witnessed in the slums.[3]

Prison reform had begun with a fever scare, and so had housing reform. The same causes were also observed and the same remedies propounded in the 1840s as in the 1770s, although it was not typhus but cholera that threatened to break out of the slums to infect the population at large. Filthy, overcrowded tenements and hovels in narrow, airless alleys generating and protecting putrid, contagious miasmas were to be destroyed and replaced with well-spaced, well-ventilated buildings at a lower density of occupation. The analogy between the spread of vice and the spread of disease was still commonplace, and when the reformers ventured into the heart of the rookeries, those most abandoned haunts of low life, they recorded the details of an immense, teeming, mixed and, to them, formless population, whose violent, promiscuous, disordered lives were lived out in a correspondingly amorphous terrain in which no distinction between persons or events, public or private, was possible and in which, as an inevitable consequence, vice flourished like disease. All of this was very close in tone and content to the complaints and investigations of penal reformers half a century earlier.

Side by side with a meticulous language of factual description there existed a rhetoric of housing reform that employed a familiar range of colourful metaphors, analogies and contrasts: infestation, the ubiquitous smell of decay, the bodies of the dead among the living, hellish habitations, loathsome corrupt flesh in contact with the fresh and innocent, labyrinths, remnants of gothic barbarity, the subterranean, the primitive and the chaotic. These belonged to a form of literary expression that, like the rhetoric of penal reform, had an effective political cutting edge. There is also reason to believe that certain of the rookery dens and backlands described with the aid of this heavy barrage of allusion were less exotic, less phantasmagorical and altogether more plain than they were made out to be – again, just as in the case of the unreformed prisons.[4]

What this descriptive technique made possible, however, was an ultimately vivid contrast between the unfathomable degeneracy of the rookery and the idealized, gentle propriety of the well-ordered domestic dwelling. If the rookeries were characterized by their formless, indecipherable confusion, if their human and physical geography could be described only in terms of the violence done to expectations as in some kind of nightmare, then the new varieties of reformed housing that were to replace them set out to divide and specify space. But, as with penal reform, the mere description of disorder was not in itself sufficient to define a superseding structure.

In the separate prisons the condition that gave purpose to the organization of space was solitude; even surveillance was subservient to this. In the model dwellings constructed in the cause of housing reform domesticity was to be the agency of deliverance. There was obviously a vast difference between the dismal, enforced isolation of the cell and the intimacies, however restrained, cultivated by the new domestic architecture. Yet while they represent two distinct varieties of privacy, the means employed to give them definition were markedly alike. For instance, prisons and housing both employed a radical and consistent division between servicing space and private, occupied space. In both cases private space was identified as the locus of morality. In model housing this tended to reduce public spaces (the street, courtyard, access staircases, landings and walkways) to the status of mere channels for ventilation, policing and traffic, judged successful in so far as they were used for nothing else. There was a similar insistence on the sequestration of the unit; in housing, services previously shared (privies, water supply, ovens, washing places) would be replicated within each flat, providing a more variegated scheme of occupations in the home, but at the same time emptying public space of all purposeful activity. Finally, both prisons and housing attempted the designation of moralized social relationships via architecture. The model dwelling, as receptacle of the nuclear family, would, wherever economically feasible, promote the nocturnal separation of the sexes amongst children, as well as dividing parents and children to preserve the latter's innocence. This was done by providing three or four major rooms instead of one as the theatre of family life, an arrangement that would further aid modesty by allowing dressing, washing and so forth to be undertaken in private. The tendency in such a household would be to define certain levels of propinquity, to fix certain ranges of common and solitary experience, between the members of a tiny, islanded society.[5]

In the model dwellings architecture was neither as inescapable nor as prominent as in the model prisons, and it was applied to different ends. In three respects, however, the resemblance is striking: firstly, as a pattern of historical events; secondly, as a method of architectural prescription; finally, as a close alliance between architecture and reform. One major difference also worth considering is that the prison existed at the edge of everyday life whereas the house was at its centre.

In the late eighteenth century and the first decades of the nineteenth, the alliance between reform and architecture was producing a series of new building types — the hospital, the orphanage, the prison, the lunatic asylum, the workhouse — which set out to quarantine and correct abnormal conditions. As the nineteenth century progressed, other reforms, similarly sporadic and under no one banner, began to move steadily towards the middle of society. Street improvements, model dwellings, public baths, and Board schools were probably the most notable of a variety of places and landscapes into which a geography of moral values was likewise to be inscribed. Thus it seems there were two phases of reformed architecture, the one flourishing before 1840, the other after that date. The first set out to rectify aberrations, the second to define the commonplace, and in doing so the approach became less single minded, the situations more complex, the authority of architecture less complete, and the results more compromised. It must be borne in mind, though, that the intentions were considerably more ambitious. This was no longer the reforming of those beyond the pale of society but a sizeable section of the labouring classes. The institutions and facilities touched by reform share a common architecture. They have a common root too in a particular sensibility that saw existing conditions in terms of filth, brutality, contamination and degradation, and dreamed of delicacy, decency and quietude. The architecture that developed out of this sensibility may seriously be considered as a mutation of conventional architecture.

Neo-classicism and the architecture of reform

What did this new kind of architecture have to do with the architecture about which most books are written: the architecture of taste, sensibility, patronage and style, and to what extent was its development related to the changes that were taking place in the profession of architecture during the same period? In particular regard to the prison, the evidence amassed by Colvin and his collaborators tells a good deal.[6]

Clearly, those whose greatness belongs to the conventional histories were not above applying themselves to the design and construction of reformed prisons. Dance the younger not only rebuilt Newgate, he provided designs for the Southwark Compter, Giltspur Street Compter and Whitecross Street Debtors' Prison. Robert Adam built the Edinburgh Bridewell (1791–4), and James Wyatt the Petworth House of Correction (1785–8). John Nash in his early Welsh years built county prisons at Carmarthen (1789–92), Cardigan (1793), and Hereford (1795–6). John Soane submitted a design for the first National Penitentiaries competition in 1782 and later rebuilt Norwich County Gaol (1792–3). Robert Smirke took over both the construction of Millbank Penitentiary and Maidstone County Gaol in 1817, reconstructed Lincoln Castle Gaol (1823–30) and made designs for a prison in St John's, Newfoundland (1831). William Wilkins produced an ideal prison plan in collaboration with the gaoler, John Orridge, and the penal reformer, Thomas Fowell Buxton (1818), made additions to Bury St Edmunds Gaol (1819) and built Huntingdon Gaol (1826–8). These six men produced a good proportion of the major landmarks of British neo-classicism.

Many who would be remembered as minor masters of style and composition also handled such work: John Carr (York Castle Women's Prison, 1780; Northallerton House of Correction, 1784–8), Thomas Harrison (Chester Castle County Gaol, 1786–1800), James Gandy (Lancaster Castle Gaol, 1818–21), John Dobson (Carlisle County Gaol, 1822–5; Morpeth County Gaol, 1823–8), David Asher Alexander (Dartmoor, 1806–12; Maidstone County Gaol 1810–17), Thomas

Hopper (Fisherton Anger County Gaol, 1818; Springfield County Gaol, 1822—48; Ilford House of Correction, 1828—31), and Francis Goodwin (Derby County Gaol 1823—7) were perhaps the most notable of this group.

By the end of the Napoleonic Wars not even the most remote local authorities were employing carpenters and artisans to build their prisons without the guidance of an architect. On the face of it the architects' mandate was clear; they had expanded their field of action, had performed valuable service in the eyes of their new clients, the magistracy, and had developed novel arrangements for equally novel institutions. The advantages of their increasingly professional methods of work, more thorough, more careful and more disengaged from the act of building, were apparent.

There was a close temporal coincidence between the reform of the prisons and the formation of the profession of architecture. The Royal Academy was founded in 1768 and John Howard published *The State of the Prisons* in 1777; the Institute of British Architects (I.B.A.) received its Royal Charter in 1837 and Pentonville was completed in 1842 — pairs of dates that bracket the major developments in both fields. Three of the seven-man founding committee of the I.B.A. were involved in prison design. H.E. Kendall had built three houses of correction in Lincolnshire; P.F. Robinson had just completed the rebuilding of York Castle County Gaol and James Savage was collaborating with the Rev. Whitworth Russell, campaigner for separate prisons, in designing the first solitary stalled prison chapel (Fig. 178). James Elmes, one of the most tireless advocates of professional organization, who helped to establish the London Architecture Society in 1806 and twice attempted to set up professional associations, in 1810 and 1819, was the author of the first monograph on prison architecture published in 1817.[7]

Such circumstantial evidence might imply a deeper concordance between the professionalization of architecture and the development of prison design, but there are reasons for resisting so tidy an interpretation. Elmes' book on prisons, for example, was a thoroughly unsatisfactory work, both derivative and outmoded. One year before its appearance the Society for the Improvement of Prison Discipline had been constituted, a body that would successfully challenge the authority of architects to design prisons unaided. After 1839, when the engineer Joshua Jebb was given power to authorize all future projects, the architect became hardly more than the executor of pre-ordained forms. So while the prisons and the profession both arose between the 1770s and 1840s, the influence of architects over the development of prison design was on the wane after 1820. What is more, the involvement of the entire breadth of the profession from the distinguished to the humble, while it indicates the general acceptance of the prison as worthy of attention, does not suggest any great enthusiasm for the subject. Neither the big names nor the middle ranges within the profession had much effect on the evolution of the reformed prison; those who did were thoroughly obscure.

William Blackburn, the most significant of all prison architects, obtained a silver medal from the Royal Academy, but afterwards did little else than build his 19 prisons. The only other works listed by Colvin are the Watermen's Hall in London, a house on Denmark Hill, a Unitarian Chapel in Bristol and some alterations to Guy's Hospital. George Byfield, perfecter of the early-nineteenth-century radial, and a pupil of Robert Taylor, exhibited at the R.A. after 1780 (drawings of Canterbury Gaol were hung in 1806) and ran a comfortable practice on mainly domestic commissions, added to which were a brewery, a chapel, a guild hall, a house of industry and of course prisons at Worcester, Bury St Edmunds, Canterbury and Cambridge. But his two applications to become an associate of the R.A. were both turned down. Richard Ingleman, partisan of the polygonal prison, was son of a surveyor, from whom he presumably received his training. He built lunatic asylums at Nottingham, Lincoln and Oxford, and prisons at Southwell and Devizes. Otherwise his practice was small and parochial. George Thomas Bullar, architect and secretary to the S.I.P.D., is otherwise entirely unknown, probably never built anything except Parkhurst juvenile prison and does not even warrant inclusion in Colvin's *Biographical Dictionary of British Architects*. Elmes' pupil John de Haviland, who emigrated to the United States and designed the first separate prison at Cherry Hill, was, like Blackburn, known as a good prison architect rather than as a good architect. Of course, Jeremy Bentham, philosopher and author of *Panopticon*, and Joshua Jebb, the military engineer responsible for the Model Prison, stood outside the ranks of the profession, but those who changed the nature of the prison from within it were essentially specialists; Byfield, for example, who handled a relatively wide range of commissions, was described by an obituarist as 'an eminent architect who has built several gaols, and for many years has made this branch of his profession his particular study'.[8]

The famous were happy to take on reformed prisons, which were, after all, quite sizeable and profitable, but did so as if these institutions were the final, lowly beneficiaries of principles derived from temple and palace. While there was some truth in the idea, it did not enable them to come to terms with the singular character of the task they undertook with so patronizing an attitude. These leaders of taste would, on the other hand, take note of the advances made by Blackburn, Byfield and Bullar, imitating and adapting them to the purpose in hand; it was as if the professional pyramid had been inverted. To figures at the outer rim of the architectural profession a commission for a county gaol or even a bridewell represented a major achievement, as it certainly would not for Adam, Soane, Nash or Smirke, whose interests and fortunes lay elsewhere. Less considerable men gave the prison its due by forging the specific connections between architecture and the intentions of reformers; devoting themselves to the search for an exact correspondence between the distribution and detailing of fabric and the forming of a silenced, segregated, supervised population.

It seems that architects — obscure ones at that — were most influential in shaping the reformed prison during the early years, and less so as time went on. The only obvious conclusion to be drawn is that, having claimed and then lost the prison to superior agencies (the S.I.P.D. and the Home Department), architects would be made even more keenly aware of the need to protect their interests with some countervailing concentration of authority. Perhaps then, as Mordaunt Crook suggests, the quest for professional status was more the product of insecurity than of confidence.[9]

Even in the early years the working techniques employed to such effect by architects had as much to do with academic training as with professionalism. As mentioned in chapter 1, the production of scaled plans, elevations and sections, the latter rendered boldly and realistically to reveal the inner workings of the institution, helped deliver control of the prison from the keepers by giving the magistrates an opportunity to impose their will on the shape of the prison from a convenient distance. The thoroughness of some of these representations, with everything itemized, annotated and costed, was surely an aspect of burgeoning

professionalism, but the method of representation — the way of drawing the building — was academic in character. By the eighteenth century
realistic orthographic projection was being propagated in academies
throughout Europe as the convention for illustrating monuments,
palaces and ecclesiastical buildings. At the Royal Academy under
William Chambers and his successors, any aspiring pupil had to master
the technique if he wished to exhibit. A fair proportion of prison architects had attended lectures at the R.A. and many had exhibited there.
Some, like Blackburn, had even received medals. It is therefore hardly
surprising that they drew the way they did, but what should be emphasized is the change of subject matter to which that kind of drawing was
applied, and the new relationships that were made possible by the change.

The transition from academic planning to prison planning is touched
on in chapters 4 and 6. The visual properties of the neo-classical, centralized plans favoured at the Royal Academy were gradually trans-
muted into blind, instrumental geometries that would finally result in
the prison becoming an indispensable vehicle for the authority and
order that earlier plans had set out only to symbolize. The difference is
well displayed in Robert Adam's plans for the Edinburgh Bridewell
before and after his correspondence with Jeremy Bentham (Figs. 115–
117), yet there is something also to be gleaned from the ease with
which the transition took place. There was, after all, more than a passing
parallelism between the ways in which the art of architectural composition treated the arrangement of iconographic and representational
elements and the way in which reformed institutions treated the organization of staff and inmates. If that contention seems overstated, one
final example might help to localize it and give it substance.

In 1800 and 1801 two designs by the otherwise unknown Arthur
Brown, who described himself as an amateur but had, nevertheless, a
reasonable grasp of contemporary practice, were published in the
Gentleman's Magazine. The first was for a Temple of Naval Victory
(Fig. 215), a monumental three-tiered construction approaching
200 feet high, that was to commemorate the recent performance of the
English fleet against the French.[10] The temple was a conventional
enough piece of neo-classical grandiloquence, piling up and rearranging
basic classical formations, applying to them the proportional and decor-
ative scheme of the Corinthian order, and adding swags, cinerary urns
and other direct allusions to classical antiquity.

413

Elevation of
a Design for
A TEMPLE
OF VICTORY;
or British
Pantheon?

Section

Ground Plan

215. Design for a Temple of Naval Victory, Arthur Brown, 1800.

A year later, perhaps to demonstrate his versatility, Brown published another of his designs, this time for the prison at Bury St Edmunds (Fig. 216).[11] These two centralized buildings, produced by the same hand within a year or so of each other, illustrate the properties of two fundamentally different kinds of architecture, constituted differently, expressed differently, and to which had to be applied different standards of judgement, yet which shared more than is at first apparent.

Comparing them to see exactly how neo-classical and academic characteristics were brought into play in the prison, three levels of similarity can be discerned. First and most superficial were the residual elements of classical decoration seen in the prison project.[12] These architect's indulgences, reduced to the most abstract and sparing marks, were little more than vestigial indicators of paternity. A second inheritance, more integral to the functioning of the prison, was to be found in the plan geometry. Both projects employed concentric geometry and both, as Brown noted in his descriptions of them, were based on the circle. In the temple the circle was used for its symbolic perfection and to provide, within the domed interior, an encompassing panorama of architecture, sculpture and painting to be contemplated by the observer. In the prison, however, the properties of the circle were employed otherwise, establishing the authority of the gaoler by displaying not the architecture and its decoration, but the inmates and their activities. In the light of events there can be no possible doubt about this, but Brown himself did not apparently recognize the distinction, writing of the prison's plan:

I have chosen a circular form because I am sure it could be erected cheaper than any other; for of all the figures which are bounded by a given perimeter, none is so spacious or contains so large an area as the circle: it is, besides, more simple, uniform and strong, than any others.[13]

The formal perfection of the circle was translated directly into practical properties — economy and strength — yet while this transition from the symbolic to the prosaic seems fully in accord with the nature of the project, Brown's explanation had little to do with the plan's effects on prison life. Perhaps as a result of his vagueness in this matter, the principle of inspection was planted into it in a rather indecisive way.[14]

The third similarity has to do with the placing of human figures in an architectural context. Here one might say that it is a contrast rather than a likeness, for the differences are as significant as the similarities.

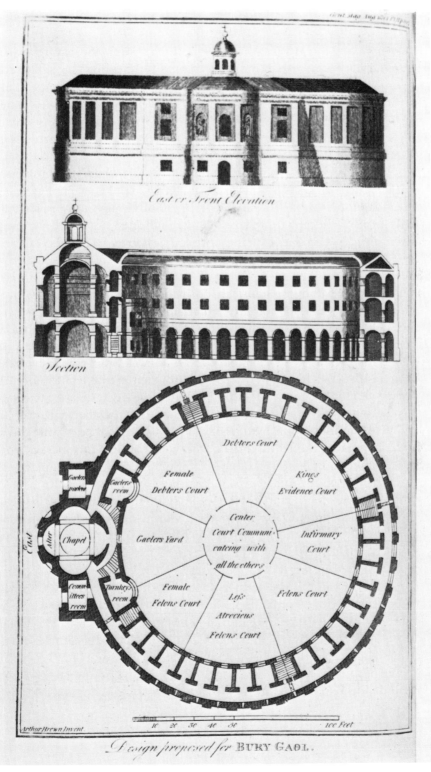

East or Front Elevation

Section

Debtors Court

Female
Debtors Court

Kings
Evidence Court

Gaolers
parlour

Gaolers
room

East

Alter

Chapel

Gaolers Yard

Center
Court Communi-
cating with
all the others

Infirmary
Court

Comm-
ittees
room

Turnkeys
room

Female
Felons Court

Less
Atrocious
Felons Court

Felons Court

Arthur Brown Invent.

10   20   30   40   50   100 Feet

Design proposed for BURY GAOL.

216. Design for Bury St Edmunds Gaol, Arthur Brown, 1801.

Brown made it clear that the Temple of Naval Victory had a programme even more exacting than that of the prison. The appropriate-
ness of his design with its concentric plan and vertical tiering was in its
capacity to structure representation. At the very apex of the monument,
surmounting an octagonal lantern, was to be fixed a statue of George III,
in whose reign the victories were achieved. Below, in four aedicular
frames around the tower were niches in which were to be placed statues
of 'our four most victorious admirals', with inscribed tablets and
emblematic trophies: 'By this arrangement, each of the grand entrances,
having a statue of one of our four great admirals placed over it in front,
will form a triumphal arch peculiarly dedicated to him by a proper
inscription in the frieze of the portico.'[15] Brown went on to describe
how the dome set within these four triumphal gateways was to be
frescoed with battle scenes from the campaigns, and then returned to
the question of how the abstract formations of structure were to provide proper homes for statuary 'correspondent with the architecture of
the building'. A further 28 niches around the lower part of the structure
were to receive statues of lower ranks of naval and government officers.
The temple had two occupied centres, an elevated symbolic centre
occupied by the image of the King and a terrestrial centre under the
dome which was accessible to all. Visitors could insinuate themselves
into this privileged position, but they were not entailed into the hierarchy of representation by doing so. It was a vantage point that did not
materially alter the status of the observer. In Bury prison exactly the
same concentric, hierarchical distribution of figures took place. The
equally ambiguous centre, vacillating between literal centrality (the
central surveillance court) and visible symbolic centrality (the chapel
and staff accommodation prominent within the ring of building), was
occupied at both points by the gaoler and his deputies. At the perimeter,
in abject equality but divided into separate classes, were the prisoners in
their cells, at work or taking exercise. The circles of authority extended
out from a common centre in both cases: the King, admirals, captains
and officers; governor and prisoners — the basic geometry of their
relationships were the same. In purely architectural terms there was also
an equivalence between the niches and the cells as receptacles for the
human figure: in the niches sculptured representations of the exalted,
idealizing their appearance, memorializing their fame and their
exploits, were placed for the world to see, while in the cells living

subjects were treated to a quite different kind of observation and scrutiny.

In the temple the construction of the building was analogous to a social structure based on gradation of status. Into this relatively abstract vessel were inserted figures and events belonging to a particular historical moment. They were images; they were fixed in perpetuity; they were objects of adulation. In the prison the building adopted a similar general configuration, supplanted images with flesh and blood and, instead of representing authority, helped to implement it. Except in so far as it harked back to classicism, it did not portray anything at all. The Bury prison project was drifting away from representation, a movement characteristic of prison architecture generally. It relinquished imagery and symbolism, and was on the way to defining the shape of society, and the very texture of experience by an act of mute force. But this seems to have been a process of conversion rather than the making of something new under the sun. In the temple, architecture, itself containing much that was representational (from its grandeur to its acanthus leaves), was populated with a host of figurative forms. The arrangement of the building was not meant to affect conduct directly. By contrast the architecture of the prison engaged directly with those who occupied it and converted an ordered, idealized representation of events into a similarly ordered fabrication of events. In the process the conventional content of architecture had undergone a double transition: images were supplanted by living subjects and the famous were replaced by the obscure. As architecture became more powerful its subject matter became the powerless.

While monumental architecture, like that of the temple, was concerned to provide a framework for the composition of statuary, pictures, emblems and inscriptions into a definitive iconography, the new institutional architecture worked in the same way with a different material. The eloquence of this mutant architecture was no longer in its appearance; it was no longer in the architecture itself at all but in its effects on those who occupied it. Architecture was now an active agency in the world rather than a representation of it, and would have to be judged by results. Thus, while architecture seemed to be in retreat in so far as it had to do with visible form, its orbit was made capable of extending indefinitely over the lower reaches of society. On the one hand architecture had suffered decisive limitation; the old rules did not apply. The superior, analogical order made visible in architecture for thousands of years had been displaced by local forms derived from particular institutional structures and devoid of representational intention. On the other hand it was now being directly applied to issues of human conduct. It seems likely that the skills required to fix a scheme of images within an architectural structure were usefully diverted to the comparable task of constructing a geography of occupied space at first for inmates, and latterly for a wider population. This was surely architecture unlimited.

It should nevertheless be clear from earlier chapters that the architecture of reform was adaptable within only a narrow spectrum. Although it was applied to a wide range of issues affecting a wide range of building types, the basic repertoire of techniques was small, tending always towards compartmentalization, sequestration, classification, dividing always between generalized space and particular space, channelling transactions and communications. And so the architecture of reform stood not for all conceivable authority, morality and order, but for a narrow band of each; it could not model all social relationships but only certain varieties.

The frequent references to the mercy of the reforming mission and to the archaic barbarity of existing eighteenth-century practices gives a clue as to why, despite its limitations, architecture should have appeared to provide so universal a remedy. In practically every sphere of life, national, civic or domestic, prior to the eighteenth century, patriarchal authority prevailed. Patriarchy required that authority be vested in persons: the father, master, lord or king. Punishment had also to emanate from the same source. Floggings proliferated. Personification bred violence, although attempts were made again and again to make love and fear flow in the same channels. Erosion of personified authority, with its attendant discipline and enforced veneration, took place slowly, but by the time Howard began the campaign for penal reform, patriarchal institutions were under attack. It was with feelings of revulsion that he and other reformers turned away not so much from patriarchy as from its degenerate remains: all that energy and emotion spent on domination and submission, every kind of human interchange subjected to the same distortion, all social acts shot through with the same greeds and tyrannies. No wonder association seemed so inevitably corrupting; no wonder either that the reformers vigorously denounced floggings and tortures and also made every effort to divest the gaolers of their customary powers, for the eighteenth-century gaoler as described in the annals of reform was a caricature of the patriarch, intemperate, tyrannical and self-interested. In this climate of opinion the kind of authority that could be established with the aid of architecture had to be contrasted with the authority associated with corrupted patriarchy.

The effects of reformed architecture were essentially passive and preventive. Even surveillance was construed as primarily a means of avoiding disorders, riots and escapes. Classification was to prevent the spread of vice. Solitude was to create the preconditions for introspection by obliterating the rest of the world. Instead of violence, there should be calmness of a kind; instead of the personification of authority, its depersonalization. Personification breeds violence, but the walls of a reformed prison breed only despair, replacing the terror of physical pain with the bewilderment of solitude. The major agencies of compulsion were not the governor, the chaplain or even the officers, but the building itself, inescapable, all-encompassing and, as the Rev. J.T. Burt so well understood, 'not subject to hostility', for bricks and stones, blameless in themselves, absorb passion and hatred endlessly. The reformed prison was, from this point of view, a subtle and brilliant retribution that vested in a place properties that had hitherto been vested in persons.

The architecture of the reformed prison was born out of a widespread perception of the evils of unmediated intercourse and a concomitant belief that goodness could only flourish in its own space. The principal ingredient of the nineteenth-century prisons, separate confinement, originated in a specific revulsion against a type of gregariousness that consumed itself in passion, jealousies, tricks and frauds, a kind of amusement that fed on weakness and violation. The cell offered a deliverance from this brand of society and its illusory enjoyments. Later, the model tenements offered a different sort of sanctuary from the same exacerbating intercourse.

Suppose that such reforms were effective enough in their way, and that we are now, most of us, used to living in the wake of reform. The question then remains as to whether this mutant architecture, which throws us inward on our own resources and reduces contact, enables us to replace the disgust once felt for others with a renewed longing for their presence. This then would be an outline of the situation:

an architecture, devised by those who were appalled at the cruelty and lust engendered by association, that was so successful in suppressing the darker aspects of human intercourse that it obliterated its own origins, purchasing for us the luxury of believing that the true expression of goodness is to be found in some indefinite blissful communion with others and not in the deeper recesses of the soul. If so, such innocence has been expensively bought.

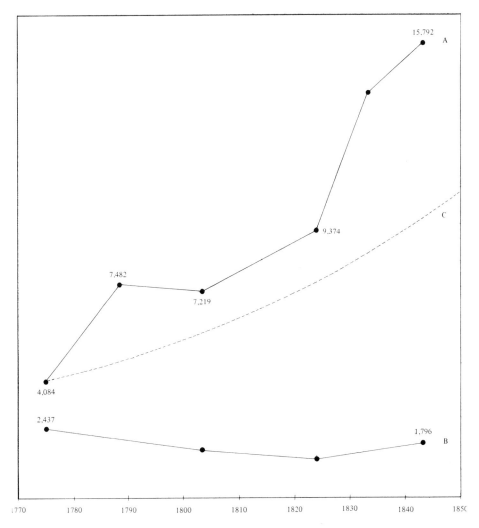

217. The prison population, 1775–1843: A. The number of persons
imprisoned at a given point in time throughout England and Wales;
B. The number of debtors imprisoned at a given point in time in
England and Wales; C. The population growth curve.
    Sources: circa 1775, Howard, *State of the Prisons*, 1st edn; for
1788, *ibid*. 4th edn; circa 1803, Neild, *General State of the Prisons*;
for 1823, 1833 and 1843, *P.P.*, Annual Gaol Returns, Schedule B.
Although there were undoubtedly inaccuracies and omissions in
these early statistics, the rapid and consistent development of the
prison as the major legal sanction for crimes and misdemeanours,
together with the dwindling of the debtor population, is reflected
clearly enough.

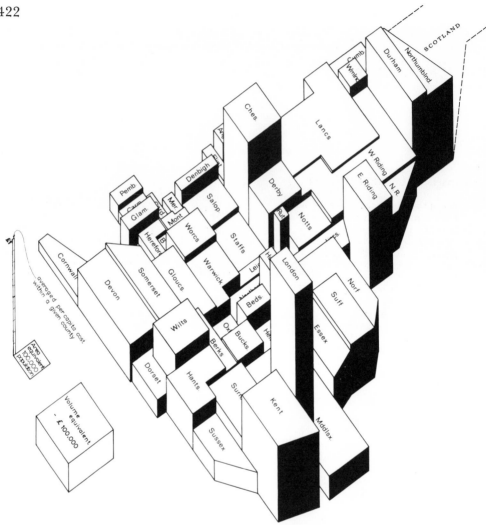

218. Expenditure on prison building, 1800–30. The base map is of England and Wales. The area of each county represented on the map is proportional to the population of that county in the 1811 census. The volume of the blocks projected up from the base map are proportional to the total expenditure of local authorities (Boroughs and Cities included) within that county between 1800 and 1830. The height of the blocks thus represents the per capita expenditure in each county. Unexpectedly, considering their lowly reputation as regards reform, London spent more per head on prisons than any other local authority. Counties that had reformed their prisons in the eighteenth century, such as Sussex, Gloucester, Middlesex and Dorset, tended to spend less than other authorities in this period. Constructed from information in *P.P.*, 1831, vol. XV, 'An Account of the Total Expenses Incurred in Building, Repairing etc. Gaols and Houses of Correction'.

Notes

1. Another world, yet the same

1 The opening sentence of Rev. Walter Lowe Clay, *The Prison Chaplain*, London, 1861.
2 John Howard, *The State of the Prisons*, 4th edn, London, 1792, pp. 303, 339.
3 John Howard, *An Account of the Principle Lazarettos*, London, 1791, p. 2.
4 He used the word to describe a room recessed into the ground whether inhabited or not. Hertford Bridewell, for example, had a dungeon which was reached by seven steps and had side windows. Howard, *State of the Prisons*, p. 256.
5 *Ibid.*, and James Neild, *The General State of the Prisons*, London, 1812.
6 According to R.B. Pugh the widespread use of castles stems from an edict to sheriffs in 1166 giving them the choice of using the King's Borough or the King's castle as the location for a prison. See R.B. Pugh, *Imprisonment in Medieval England*, Cambridge, 1970, p. 59. According to L.O. Pike the laws against wanderers and strangers of Henry III tended to push gaols towards the city gates, where such persons were apprehended. See L.O. Pike, *A History of Crime in England*, London, 1873, vol. I, p. 219.
7 Middlesex R.O., 'Inventory of Goods & Utensils Belonging to the House of Correction in Clerkenwell', 31 May 1765, MJ/OC/8.
8 G.L.C. Archives, plan taken in 1686, ref. r.p.h. 10.6.2.
9 Wilts. C.R.O., plan for enlargement of Marlborough Bridewell by John Hammond (called a carpenter in an accompanying letter), 1786, Q.S. Prisons (plans).
10 Wilts C.R.O., plan of Devizes Bridewell by E. Reynolds, July 1775, Q.S. Prisons (plans). Reynolds' remodelling involved the construction of three brick fireplaces and 'making secure' the rooms by lining them with boards. See also Howard, *State of the Prisons*, p. 377.
11 Clifford Dobb, 'Life and Conditions in London Prisons 1553–1643, with special reference to contemporary literature', unpublished thesis, Oxford, 1952, pp. 426 et seq. Dobb traces this kind of description through the numerous character books to Dekker's *Lanthorne and Candle Light*, 4th edn, 1616, which contained six chapters on prisons and prisoners.
12 Geffray Mynshull (Garffeg Lluhnsynm), *Certain Characters and Essayes of Prison and Prisoners*, London, 1618 (no pagination).
13 Jacob Ilive, *Reasons Offered for the Reformation of the House of Correction at Clerkenwell*, London, 1757, p. 10; and R.H. Condon, 'The Reform of the English Prisons, 1773–1816', unpublished thesis, Brown University, 1962. The item was taken from the *Annual Register*, vol. XXXII, pp. 31–3.
14 The convergence has been well described by Sidney and Beatrice Webb, *English Prisons Under Local Government*, London, 1922.
15 This trend is not presented as an established historical fact but as a reasonable inference drawn from the sources cited in this chapter. It must also be added that after the Black Act of 1723 the number of capital statutes increased

dramatically, the effects of which were, however, mitigated by more frequent resort to transportation.

16 Webb, *English Prisons*, p. 5.

17 Eric Stockdale, *A Study of Bedford Prison 1660—1877*, Bedford, 1977, ch. 3 and Appendix 2, p. 220.

18 Extract from Orders of the Shropshire Quarter Sessions, kindly supplied to me by M.F. Messenger, the Shrewsbury Borough Librarian. Almost identical complaints had been made by Alexander Harris, warden of the Fleet, regarding the disturbances of 1619. See Alexander Harris, *The Oeconomy of the Fleete*, ed. Augustus Jessopp, London, 1879, p. xxi.

19 John Earle, *Microcosmographie: The World Displayed*, London, 1629, pp. 193 et seq. Ludgate's 'Domestick government' involved the choice of Reader of Divine Services, the Upper Steward, Under Steward, seven assistants, a running assistant, two church wardens, a scavenger, a chamberlain, a running post, and six criers. The Reader was chosen by the stewards and the keeper, the rest by 'general election'.

20 W.J. Sheehan, 'Finding Solace in Eighteenth-Century Newgate', in J.S. Cockburn (ed.), *Crime in England 1550—1800*, Princeton, 1977, p. 134. The rules were re-established at Newgate in 1730.

21 Howard, *State of the Prisons*, pp. 449, 414, 429, 416, 347, 312. The same was probably true of many more. Howard tended to describe prisons room by room, but rarely gave a clear indication of the relationship between rooms or between parts of the prison.

22 Ilive, *Reasons Offered*, p. 23.

23 Sheehan, 'Finding Solace', p. 237.

24 William Fuller, *Mr. William Fuller's Trip to Bridewell*, London, 1703, p. 17.

25 Walter Besant, *Survey of London*, vol. VIII, London, 1902, p. 538.

26 Marmaduke Johnson, *Ludgate: What it is, Not What it Was*, London 1759, p. 51.

27 'B.L.', *An Accurate Description of Newgate*, London, 1724, p. 40.

28 For Exeter see Neild, *General State of the Prisons*, p. 209. For Beccles and shackled prisoners outside Fisherton Anger see Howard, *State of the Prisons*,

pp. 303, 376.

29 'B.L.', *Description of Newgate*, pp. 4, 35, 40.

30 *A Description of the King's Bench, Fleet and Marshalsea Prisons*, London, 1828, pp. 7—11.

31 Howard, *State of the Prisons*, p. 366.

32 Dobb, 'Life and Conditions in London Prisons', p. 100.

33 Harris, *The Oeconomy of the Fleete*, p. xiii, p. 59.

34 *Ibid.*, p. 143.

35 *Ibid.*, 'The Forme of the Table that shall Hange in the Hall in the Fleete'.

36 R. Ackerman, *Microcosm of London*, London, 1808—11, vol. II, pp. 55, 56.

37 W. Paget, *The Humours of the Fleet: an Humourous Descriptive Poem written by a gent. of the College*, London, 1794, p. 15.

38 Simon Wood, *Remarks on the Fleet Prison, or The Lumber House for Men & Women*, London, 1733, p. 15.

39 Henry Ellis, 'Plan Projected for Building a House of Correction in Westminster', reproduced in *Archaeologia*, vol. XXI (1826), p. 4.

40 E. Gayton, *Wil Bagnal's Ghost: or the Merry Devill of Gadmunton in his Perambulation of the Prisons of London*, London, 1655, p. 38.

41 Humphrey Gyfford, *A Second Account of a Publick Design for the Accommodation and Relief of the Prisoners of the Compter in Poultry*, London, 1670, p. 1.

42 Earle, *Microcosmographie*, p. 23.

43 Dekker, *Lanthorne and Candle Light*, ch. 14.

44 W.J. Pinks, *History of Clerkenwell*, London, 1881, p. 81.

45 Ilive, *Reasons Offered*, p. 32.

46 C.L.R.O. Surveyor's Justice Plans, vol. I, Plans drawn up for the Clerk to the 1756 Committee to Rebuild Newgate.

47 It was the keeper, Robert Ackerman the Younger who so described it. See R.B. Pugh, 'Newgate Between Two Fires' in *Guildhall Studies in London History*, Oct. 1978, p. 139.

48 William Maitland, *History of London*, vol. I, 1756, pp. 22—31. Cripplegate had been a debtors' prison in the Middle Ages but was rebuilt as the Bailiff's

accommodation.
49 'B.L.', *Description of Newgate*, p. 41.
50 *Ibid.*, p. 11.
51 *Ibid.*, p. 12.
52 Bernard de Mandeville, *An Enquiry into the Causes of the Frequent Executions at Tyburn*, London, 1725, p. 17.
53 Harris, *The Oeconomy of the Fleete*; and Ilive, *Reasons Offered*, p. 32.
54 *The Humble Petition of the Poor Distressed Prisoners in Newgate*, London, 1676, printed as heading.
55 Royal Commission on Historical Monuments (England), *York Castle*, H.M.S.O., 1973, pp. 78 et seq. R.B. Pugh (ed.), *Victoria County History, City of York*, London, 1961, p. 526.
56 Neild, *General State of the Prisons*, p. 154; and Stephen Glover, *A History of the County of Derby*, Derby, 1833, pt 1, vol. II, p. 469.
57 Howard, *State of the Prisons*, p. 262; and Essex C.R.O. Plan, ref. Q/AGb/6.

58 H.M. Colvin, *Biographical Dictionary of British Architects*, London, 1978. For description of Hertford see Howard, *State of the Prisons*. A plan of Bath is reproduced in T.A. Markus, 'The Pattern of the Law', *Architectural Review*, vol. CXVI (1954), p. 251.
59 Colvin, *B.D.B.A.*
60 Martin S. Briggs, *The Architect in History*, New York, 1974, p. 326.
61 Bedford C.R.O., Q.S. catalogue. Archivist's notes on St Mary's Bridewell; and Stockdale, *Bedford Prison*, p. 43.
62 Middlesex R.O., MJ/SBB/272, p. 39.
63 Elizabeth Melling, *Kentish Sources, VI: Crime and Punishment*, Maidstone, 1969, pp. 213, 216.
64 Ackerman, *Microcosm of London*, vol. II, p. 61. For earlier examples see Pugh, *Imprisonment in Medieval England*, pp. 339–41.
65 Howard, *State of the Prisons*, p. 262.

2. From correction to reformation; from dungeon to cell

1 John Howard, *The State of the Prisons*, 1st edn, Warrington, 1777, p. 5.
2 Thomas Dekker, *The Honest Whore*, pt II, London, 1630, Act V, scene II, lines 51–3.
3 *Parliamentary Papers*, 1778–9, vol. X, 'Observations on the Bill to Punish by Imprisonment and Hard Labour', sect. 5.
4 19 Hen. VII c. 2.
5 22 Hen. VIII c. 12; 27 Hen. VIII c. 25; 1 Ed. VI c. 3 respectively.
6 Robert Seymour, *Survey of the Cities of London and Westminster*, London, 1734, vol. I, p. 35.
7 Alfred James Copeland, *Bridewell Royal Hospital, Past and Present*, London, 1888, p. 23.
8 *Ibid.*, p. 40.
9 Juan Luis Vives, 'De Subventione Pauperum' in F.R. Salter, *Early Tracts on Poor Relief*, London, 1926, p. 12.
10 Sidney and Beatrice Webb, *English Poor Law History*, London, 1927, p. 49.
11 Fynes Moryson, *Itinerary*, London, 1617, p. 155; Dekker, *The Honest Whore*, pt II, act V; and Ned Ward, *The London Spy*, London, 1704, p. 36.

12 Lawrence Stone, *The Family, Sex and Marriage in England, 1500–1800*, London, 1977, pp. 152 et seq.
13 Copeland, *Bridewell*, pp. 40, 43, 50.
14 For the Tun see R.B. Pugh, *Imprisonment in Medieval England*, Cambridge, 1970, p. 112. The punishment for idleness laid down in 1426 was to put the culprit in the stocks for anything up to three days (11 Hen. VII c. 2).
15 A.J. Copeland, 'Extracts from the Old Court Books at Bridewell Hospital', *Under the Dome: Bethlehem Royal Hospital Quarterly*, vol. XII, no. 45 (1902), p. 4.
16 Copeland, *Bridewell*, p. 65.
17 Copeland, in *Under the Dome*, vol. XI, no. 43 (1901), p. 80; no. 44 (1901), p. 112.
18 *Ibid.*, vol. XII, no. 45 (1902), p. 38. See also John Howes, *Being a Brief Note of . . . the first Erection of the 3 Royal Hospitals*, London, 1904, p. 73.
19 18 Eliz. I c. 3; 39 Eliz. I c. 4; 7 James I c. 4, respectively.
20 5 Anne c. 6, and then 6 Geo. I c. 19.
21 S.A. Peyton, 'The Houses of Correction

at Maidstone and Westminster', *The English Historical Review*, vol. XLII (1927), p. 251.

22 Copeland, *Bridewell*, p. 48.

23 Thorsten Sellin, *Pioneering in Penology: The Amsterdam Houses of Correction in the 16th and 17th Centuries*, London, 1944, pp. 69–70.

24 *Ibid.*, p. 71.

25 Henry Fielding, *A Proposal for Making an Effectual Provision for the Poor, for Amending their Morals and for Rendering them Useful Members of Society*, London, 1753, p. 58.

26 *Ibid.*, p. 28.

27 Dom Jean Mabillon, 'Reflexions sur les Prisons des Ordres Religieux', *Ouvrages Posthumes*, vol. II, Paris, 1724, p. 321.

28 *Ibid.*, pp. 334–5.

29 David Knowles, *Monastic Orders in England*, Cambridge, 1963, pp. 376–8.

30 Dr L. Pastor, *History of the Popes*, trans. Dom Ernest Graf, vol. XXXIII, London, 1957, p. 493.

31 Allan Braham and Helmut Hagar, *Carlo Fontana: the Drawings qt Windsor*, London, 1977, figs. 334–8; and John Howard, *The State of the Prisons*, 4th edn, London, 1792, p. 114.

32 The full text in French can be found in M. Morreau-Christophe, *Rapport sur les Prisons d'Angleterre*, Paris, 1839, pp. 75–8.

33 This was the inscription over the outside door; see Howard, *State of the Prisons*, 4th edn.

34 Braham and Hagar, *Carlo Fontana*, p. 143.

35 *Ibid.*

36 Howard, *State of the Prisons*, 4th edn.

37 Rev. J. Field, *Correspondence of John Howard the Philanthropist*, London, 1855, p. 55.

38 The remark was made by Remacle, a Senior Magistrate. See Morreau-Christophe, *Rapport sur les Prisons d'Angleterre*, p. 51.

39 Sion College Mss, London. See H.P. Thompson, *Thomas Bray*, London, 1954, pp. 24–5.

40 The whole text of the Ms. from the S.P.C.K. archives was reproduced in William Hepworth Dixon, *John Howard and the Prison World of Europe*, 3rd

edn, London, 1850, pp. 4–11.

41 Bray's catalogue of evils at Newgate is comparable to another, made 100 years earlier, in 1617, by the Mayor of London (John Leman?), *Proclamation for the Reformation of Abuses in the Gaol of Newgate*, C.L.R.O., Printed Bill, P.D.–10–26. Characteristically the 1617 Proclamation was concerned with the abolition of shameful comforts and did not stretch the idea of reformation to include the character of prisoners.

42 Thompson, *Thomas Bray*, p. 25.

43 Dixon, *John Howard*, p. 11.

44 *Ibid.*, p. 5.

45 *Ibid.*, p. 9.

46 Michael Ignatieff, *A Just Measure of Pain*, London, 1978, pp. 58–66.

47 See for example, George Wither, *An Improvement of Prison into Real Freedom*, London, 1661, pp. 23–4; Samuel Speed, *Prison Pietie*, London, 1677, p. 143; 'B.L.', *An Accurate Description of Newgate*, London, 1724. See also Clifford Dobb, 'Life and Conditions in London Prisons 1553–1643', unpublished thesis, Oxford, 1952, p. 473.

48 Geffray Mynshull, *Certain Characters and Essayes of Prison and Prisoners*, London, 1618 (no pagination).

49 *Hell in Epitome: or a Description of the Marshalsea*, London, 1718.

50 E. Gayton, *Wil Bagnal's Ghost: or the Merry Devill of Gadmunton in his Perambulation of the Prisons of London*, London, 1655, pp. 1, 16, 18, 36, 37.

51 Anon., *A Charitable Visit to the Prisons*, London, 1709, p. 48.

52 Robert Denne, *A Letter to Sir Robert Ladbroke*, London, 1771, p. 19.

53 D.P. Walker, *The Decline of Hell: Seventeenth-Century Discussions of Eternal Torment*, London, 1964. Esp. ch. 1, sect. ii, ch. 3, sect. iii and ch. 4.

54 John Brewster, *On the Prevention of Crimes and on the Advantages of Solitary Imprisonment*, London, 1792, p. 3.

55 Dixon, *John Howard*, p. 8.

56 For example, Tobias Swinden, *Enquiry into the Nature and Place of Hell*, London, 1727. Swinden reasserts the reality of hell but considers the old sadistic tortures to be 'light airy and fantastic stuff'. He felt it was only

necessary to give hell a position in the universe — a boundary. Its internal geography was no longer of any consequence.

57 Walker, *The Decline of Hell*, p. 39. The integrity of this connected pattern of ideas can be illustrated by the opinions of Jacob Ilive, prisoner and reformer of Clerkenwell House of Correction. Though a minor figure in the reform movement his work is a rich source for its ideology. He was an outspoken opponent of eternal punishment and had declared that 'hell-fire' would not be a physical affliction but an 'immaterial' one. J. Ilive, *The Oration of John XIV, 2. Spoke at Joyners Hall*, London, 1733.

58 Jean Jacques Rousseau, *Emilius and Sophia*, trans. Kenrick, London, 1763, vol. III, pp. 67–8.

59 Brewster, *On the Prevention of Crimes*, p. 4.

60 Jonas Hanway, *Distributive Justice and Mercy*, London, 1781, p. xv.

61 Sir William Eden, *Principles of Penal Law*, London, 1771, p. 178.

62 John Howard, *An Account of the Principle Lazarettos*, London, 1791, p. 221.

63 Vicomte Vilain XIII, *Memoire sur les Moyens de Corriger les Malfaiteurs*, Brussels, 1841 edn. See also Howard, *State of the Prisons*, 1st edn, p. 142; Society for Diffusing Information on the Subject of Capital Punishment and Prison Discipline, *An Account of the Maison de Force at Ghent*, London, 1817; Thomas Fowell Buxton, *An Inquiry Whether Crimes and Misery are Produced or Prevented by our Present System of Prison Discipline*, London, 1818, p. 48.

64 Denne, *A Letter to Sir Robert Ladbroke*, pp. 11–12. The source for this information was *The Modern Universal History*, vol. VIII, p. 177, and vol. IX, p. 91.

65 This is what B.L. had to say of common side felons at Newgate, a place he was concerned to present in a generally favourable light: 'The common side is a most terrible, wicked and dreadful place . . . Solomon says, *The curse of the Lord is in the house of the wicked*, Prov. ii, 33. And this is too much verified amongst these poor unfortunate wretches: who, instead of humbling themselves to Almighty God, and beseeching him to give them his Grace, and to pardon their horrid Sins, continually augment the same, and in the most sinful and wicked manner they possibly can contrive, accelerate their own destruction.' 'B.L.', *Description of Newgate*, p. 42.

66 *O.E.D.* Benign effects of passion were recognized in more general discussions. Francis Hutcheson for example saw them as the basis of all social intercourse, but only Beccaria explicitly extended this ambivalence to the passion of criminals. J. Heath, *Eighteenth-Century Penal Theory*, Oxford, 1963, p. 83; Cesare Beccaria, *Essay on Crimes and Punishments*, London, 1775, p. 128.

67 Denne, *A Letter to Sir Robert Ladbroke*, p. 59.

68 *Ibid.*, p. 45.

69 Jonas Hanway, *Solitude and Imprisonment*, London, 1776, p. 12, and Brewster, *On the Prevention of Crimes*, pp. 24–6.

70 Hanway, *Distributive Justice and Mercy*, p. 45.

71 Wolfgang Liebenwein, *Studiolo*, Berlin, 1977; Ariane Van Buren, 'Rooms Designed for One Person: Three Italian Renaissance Studioli', unpublished thesis, Brown University, 1976.

72 Alexander Pope quoted in John Dixon Hunt, *The Figure in the Landscape*, London, 1976, p. 78.

73 Mark Girouard refers to the eighteenth-century country house as the social house (*Life in The English Country House*, London, 1978, ch. 7) but this sociality existed on the major floor of the building and only rarely penetrated the more intimate and private territory above. For examples showing plans of upper floors see: James Paine, *Plans, Sections and Elevations of Nobleman's and Gentleman's Houses*, London, 1783; John Carter (ed.), *Builder's Magazine*, London, 1777 *et seq.*; George Richardson, *A Series of Original Designs for Country Seats*, London, 1795; and Richardson's edition of *Vitruvius Britannicus*.

74 Paul Hazard, *European Thought in the Eighteenth Century*, trans. J. Lewis May, Harmondsworth, 1965, p. 166.

75 Jonas Hanway, *Thoughts on the Plan for a Magdalen House*, London, 1759.

76 John Hutchins, *Jonas Hanway: 1712–1786*, London, 1940, p. 115.

77 Hanway, *Distributive Justice and Mercy*, p. x.

78 *Ibid.*, p. 59.

79 *Ibid.*, p. 96.

80 *Ibid.*, pp. 35, 36. Hanway boasted that Dodds wrote the poem after reading his *Solitude and Imprisonment*.

81 19 Geo. III c. 74.

82 Society for Giving Effect to H.M.'s Proclamation Against Vice and Immorality, *Report Respecting the Improvements which have Lately been Made in the Prisons and Houses of Correction in England and Wales*, London, 1790, pp. 13–14.

83 Hanway, *Distributive Justice and Mercy*, p. ix.

84 Hanway, *Solitude and Imprisonment*, p. 34; Denne, *A Letter to Sir Robert Ladbroke*, p. 51.

85 G.O. Paul, *Considerations on the Defects of Prisons*, London, 1784, p. 334.

86 Howard, *State of the Prisons*, 1st edn, p. 43. The Webbs tell of an incident at Fisherton Anger, where a prisoner sentenced to solitary confinement asked to be hanged instead, recorded by Howard in *Observations, Moral and Political* (1784).

87 Howard, *Lazarettos*, p. 185.

88 Jeremy Bentham, *The Rationale of Punishment*, London, 1830, p. 116. See also *Panopticon Postscript*, London, 1791, pp. 71–6.

89 A.K. Wedderburn, *Observations on the State of English Prisons and the Means of Improving Them*, London, 1793, p. 16.

90 William Paley, *Principles of Moral and Political Philosophy*, London, 1786, p. 544.

91 Hanway, *Distributive Justice and Mercy*, p. 43.

92 G.O. Paul told his fellow magistrates, 'It would indeed be insulting your understanding with a chimera should I presume to offer to your attentions a plan of reform *depending solely for its effects on a principle of construction.*' A 'good arrangement of parts' was just one aspect; with it must go good regulations and a well-chosen police. Two decades later the limitations of good architecture were highlighted by the conditions at Cardigan County Gaol and Bridewell. John Nash's fine new prison had been completed in 1797, but when Neild visited it in 1803 the inspection lodge, instead of housing a vigilant keeper, was being used as a threshing floor for corn. A lunatic and a felon were kept in the same cell together. Geese, ducks and chickens made better use of the airing yards than did the prisoners. Magistrates seldom inspected it, and there were no written rules, as far as Neild could tell. Prison building and prison administration had to work together. The best architecture could not prevent a decline into the old ways under a negligent keeper with lax standards; G.O. Paul, *An Address to the Magistrates of the County of Gloucester*, Gloucester, 1789, p. 3; James Neild, *The General State of the Prisons*, London, 1812, p. 119.

93 Ignatieff, *A Just Measure of Pain*, p. 95.

94 Howard, *State of the Prisons*, 1st edn, p. 40.

95 Hanway, *Solitude and Imprisonment*, p. 113.

96 Denne, *A Letter to Sir Robert Ladbroke*, p. 40.

97 Anon., *Hanging not Punishment Enough*, London, 1701, p. 9; Bernard de Mandeville, *An Enquiry into the Causes of the Frequent Executions at Tyburn*, London, 1725.

98 Mandeville, *ibid.*, p. 28.

99 *Ibid.*, pp. 41–2.

100 W.J. Sheehan, 'Finding Solace in Eighteenth-Century Newgate', in J.S. Cockburn (ed.), *Crime in England 1550–1800*, Princeton, 1977, p. 238.

101 Mabillon, 'Reflexions sur les Prisons des Ordres Religieux', p. 325.

102 Lanfranc's definition of a *carcere* was a windowless and doorless room accessible only by a ladder from the top (Pugh, *Imprisonment in Medieval England*, p. 376). This is Howard's description of Portman Castle prison (on an island

fortress near Toulon): 'The descent is by ladder, through a stone aperture of 4 feet diameter; which, after the ladder is removed and the hole covered, is a secure but dreadful place of confinement . . . this is a prison similar to many in castles, in the *barbarous* ages.' *Lazarettos*, p. 56.

103 Umberto Franzoi, *The Prisons of the Venetian Republic*, Venice, 1966, pp. 15, 18—24, 30—2.

104 Josephus Furttenbach, *Architectura Universalis*, Ulm, 1635, plates 27 and 28.

105 Speed, *Prison Pietie*, p. 126.

106 Daniel Marot, *Das Ornamentwerk*, Berlin, 1892, vol. I, p. 123.

107 Per Bjorstrom, *Giacomo Torelli and Baroque Stage Set Design*, Stockholm, 1961, pp. 235, 236. Bibbiena *carcere* sets were in fact quite shallow, allowing more extravagant illusionistic perspectives by flattening the real space of the stage.

108 Edile Law IX, see F.E. Manuel (ed.), *The Enlightenment*, Englewood Cliffs, 1965, p. 123.

109 Etienne Boullee, *Treatise on Architecture*, ed. and trans. H. Rosenau, London, 1953, pp. 64—5; Helen Rosenau, *Social Purpose in Architecture, 1760—1800*, London, 1970, p. 39; Yvan Christ, *C.N. Ledoux*, Paris, 1961, p. 134.

110 Milizias' recipe for civil prisons in 1785 was to provide the deepest shade, cavernous entrances and terrifying inscriptions. Quoted by N. Pevsner, *A History of Building Types*, London, 1970, pp. 162—3.

111 Paul Bru, *Histoire de Bicêtre*, Paris, 1890, pp. 49—51.

112 Essex C.R.O., Plans for alterations to Moulsham dated 1819, ref. Q/AGb 1/3/1.

113 Carter, *Builder's Magazine* (1778), plates

CLXV, CLXIX, CLXXII. Much the same could be said of Ledoux's prison at Aix produced nine years later.

114 Howard, *Lazarettos*, p. 173.

115 The Society for Diffusing Knowledge Respecting the Punishment of Death, *A Visit to Warwick Gaol*, London, 1816. Society for Giving Effect to H.M.'s Proclamation, *Report Respecting Improvements made in Prisons and Houses of Correction*, p. 5. See also Howard, *Lazarettos*, p. 307.

116 Howard, *State of the Prisons*, 4th edn, p. 445.

117 Dobb, 'Life and Conditions in London Prisons', p. 425. Dobb contrasts two kinds of prison writing, the one pietistic, stemming from Boethius, the other realistic, stemming from Dekker. In many seventeenth- and eighteenth-century authors the two strands are woven together.

118 Josiah Dornford, *Nine Letters to the Lord Mayor . . . of the State of the Prisons*, London, 1786, Letter 2, p. 17.

119 R. Evans, 'Rookeries and Model Dwellings', *Architectural Association Quarterly*, vol. x, no. 1, pp. 25—36.

120 A Gentleman, *Anecdotes of the Life and Character of John Howard*, London, 1790, p. 38.

121 Philanthropos [William Ladd], *Howard and Napoleon Contrasted in Eight Dialogues*, Portsmouth, New Haven, 1830; Society for Diffusing Useful Knowledge, *Chivalry and Charity Illustrated*, London, 1840.

122 Elizabeth Inchbald, *Such Things Are*, London, 1788. For the Monument fund see *Gentleman's Magazine*, vol. LVII (1787), pp. 44, 178, 284, 464, 485.

123 Ignatieff, *A Just Measure of Pain*, pp. 42—52.

3. Gaol fever

1 If the number of prison institutions recorded by Howard in the 1st edn of *The State of the Prisons* (Warrington, 1777) is subtracted from those recorded by Nield between 1800 and 1808, the difference is 72, but some of these were

simply left out by Howard, although they existed at that time. According to R.H. Condon, of the 43 prisons containing more than 20 felons in Howard's time, 24 were rebuilt by 1800 (see Condon 'The Reform of the English

Prisons, 1773—1816', unpublished thesis, Brown University, 1962, p. 124). The figure 45 is mine, based on the material in ch. 5.

2 4 Geo. I c. 11.

3 See Geffray Mynshull, *Certain Characters and Essays of Prison and Prisoners*, London, 1618; Anon., *A Charitable Visit to the Prisons*, London, 1709, p. 93; and John Stow, *Survey of the Cities of London and Westminster*, ed. J. Strype, London, 1720, vol. II, p. 9.

4 Thomas Day, *Some Considerations on the Different Ways of Removing Confined and Infectious Air*, Maidstone, 1784, p. 5.

5 G.O. Paul, *Considerations of the Defects of Prisons*, London, 1784, pp. 24—5, and also Sir S.T. Janssen, *A Letter to the Lord Mayor of London*, London, 1767, Appendix 13.

6 Day, *Some Considerations*; and John Pringle, Letter to S.T. Janssen, Alderman, 15 Oct. 1750, C.L.R.O.

7 The two petitions to Parliament of 1764 (Jan. and March) listed the possibility of a further assize epidemic as the most pressing reason for demolishing the old gate. See *Universal Magazine*, vol. XXXIV (1974), p. 69.

8 John Pringle, *Observations on the Nature and Cure of Hospital and Jayl Fevers*, London, 1750, p. 8. Thomas Day mentions a Dr Munro with Pringle as the discoverers of the true extent of gaol fever; Day, *Some Considerations*, p. 13.

9 Day, *Some Considerations*, p. 9.

10 G.O. Paul, *Thoughts on the Alarming Progress of Gaol Fever*, Gloucs., 1784, p. 7. Howard stated that during the American War 1,000 soldiers were lost this way; see John Howard, *The State of the Prisons*, 4th edn, London, 1792, p. 9. Janssen estimated 2,500 deaths in the British fleet in 1745/6 through a fever transmitted by Newgate transportees; see Janssen, *Letter to the Lord Mayor*, Appendix 13. Both Lynd and Pringle took up appointments as military surgeons and were familiar with the diseases of army and navy. See Charles Singer, *A Short History of Medicine*, Oxford, 1928, p. 169.

11 Stephen Hales calculated the average death rate from fever in the Savoy and Newgate to be over 100 a year. Pro-rata this would give a mortality rate in all the nation's prisons of about 1,000 per annum. This is a very rough surmise.

12 Howard, *State of the Prisons*, 1st edn, p. 17. Day, *Some Considerations*, p. 8; Paul, *Considerations on the Defects of Prisons*, p. 28.

13 This was a common denominator of eighteenth-century penal thought. Montesquieu, Beccaria, Howard, Paley, Blackstone and Bentham were all searching for the correct means to effect such proportionality.

14 If we are to believe evidence given in 1801, fevers of various descriptions accounted for 66% of all deaths in early-eighteenth-century London; see D.M. George, *London Life in the Eighteenth Century*, London, 1966, p. 70. Dr Fordyce in the 1770s thought putrid and inflammatory fevers the greatest cause of adult mortality in the metropolis from his inspection of the Death Bills, but he gives no figures; see William Fordyce, *An Enquiry into the Causes, Symptoms, and Cure of Putrid and Inflammatory Fevers*, 3rd edn, London, 1774, pp. ix—x. Charles Creighton lists the major typhus epidemics as 1685/6, 1694, 1741/2, 1782—5. See his *History of Epidemics in Britain*, 2nd edn, London, 1965, vol. II, pp. 13, 27—9, 160.

15 Creighton, *ibid.*, pp. 27—9.

16 H. Guerlac, entry under Hales in C.C. Gillespie (ed.), *Dictionary of Scientific Biography*, N.Y., 1972.

17 Nathaniel Henshaw's long forgotten *Aero-Chalinos* of 1677, found in the Royal Society archives by Hales, ascribed extensive curative powers to compressed and rarified airs; see Stephen Hales, *Description of Ventilators*, London, 1743, p. xvi. The difference was that Henshaw did not account for these powers.

18 John Arbuthnot, *An Essay Concerning the Effects of Air on Human Bodies*, London, 1733, pp. 11, 17.

19 John Arbuthnot, *Discourse Concerning Fever*, London, 1727, p. 229; Pringle, *Observations*, p. 5; Day, *Some Consider-*

ations, p. 17; Paul, *Thoughts*, p. 5.

20 Day, *Some Considerations*, p. 15.

21 Fordyce, *An Enquiry into the Causes, Symptoms and Cure of Putrid and Inflamatory Fevers*, London, 1773, 3rd edn, 1774, 4th edn, 1777. For a similar interpretation see also J. Huxam, *An Essay on Fevers and their Various Kinds as Depending on Different Constitutions of the Blood*, London, 1750.

22 *Memorial of Dr Ryan*, 1773, Misc. Mss., C.L.R.O.

23 Pringle, *Observations*, sect. V.

24 H.P. Thompson, *Thomas Bray*, London, 1954, pp. 97–8.

25 Hales, *Description of Ventilators*, London, 1743, p. 39. Since 1740 Hales had been involved in a protracted dispute with the Admiralty over the relative merits of his own proposals for ship ventilation and those of Samuel Sutton which had no explicit organic model. Sutton's plan was to induce a through-put of air by inserting two tubes into an enclosed hold and then applying heat to one of them. See A.E. Clark-Kennedy, *Stephen Hales*, Cambridge, 1929, ch. IX.

26 Clark-Kennedy, *ibid.*, pp. 190–1, 194.

27 *Gentleman's Magazine*, vol. XXXIV (1764), p. 17.

28 R.B. Pugh, *Imprisonment in Medieval England*, Cambridge, 1970, pp. 188, 332.

29 Stephen Hales, *An Account of the Good Effects of the Ventilators at Newgate and Savoy*, 1 sheet ms. n.d. (1753), C.L.R.O.

30 *Gentleman's Magazine*, vol. XX (1752), p. 179, and Hales, *Description of Ventilators*, p. 20.

31 John Pringle, *An Account of Several Persons Siezed with the Gaol Distemper*, ms. read 1 Feb. 1752, C.L.R.O.

32 Howard, *State of the Prisons*, 1st edn, p. 45.

33 Pringle, *Account of Several Persons*.

34 Ms. C.L.R.O. (small box 54, paper 8).

35 Howard, *State of the Prisons*, 1st edn, p. 45; Robert Denne, *A Letter to Sir Robert Ladbroke*, London, 1771, p. 7.

36 Pringle, *Account of Several Persons*, and also *Observations*, p. 47.

37 For these contraptions see esp. Day, *Some Considerations*, p. 47.

38 William Smith, *The State of the Gaols in London, Westminster and the Boro' of Southwark*, London, 1776, pp. 6, 12.

39 Dr Sharpe, *Memorials of Newgate Gaol and Sessions House*, Mss. n.d., C.L.R.O., Sharpe mentions the Ware plans. Jones' plans are at the C.L.R.O. Dance the elder's were reproduced in the *Universal Magazine*, vol. XXXIV (1764), p. 69. Janssen, *Letter to the Lord Mayor*, pp. 5–6, and Appendix 1.

40 Pringle, *Observations*, pp. 47–8;

41 This point was brought up by Harold Kalman in his 'Newgate Prison', *Architectural History: Journal of the Soc. of Arch. Hist. of G.B.*, vol. XII (1969), p. 52.

42 The privy blocks in Dance the elder's plans were also integrated into the main building, and were organized round open vent shafts, but they are rather less sophisticated.

43 7 Geo. III c. 37. The coal tax seems first to have been used in the 1670s for the rebuilding of Newgate, the Wood Street Compter and the Poultry Compter after the Great Fire, and was later used to build the Giltspur Street Compter, after 1800. See Condon, 'The Reform of the English Prisons', p. 13.

44 Kalman, 'Newgate Prison', pp. 51–2.

45 Sir John Summerson, *Georgian London*, Harmondsworth, 1962 edn, p. 48.

46 There are many of Dance the younger's early sketches in the C.L.R.O. collection. One of these, a three court plan with an asymmetrical facade, seems to have been designed around the privy/stair details, drawn in larger scale on the same sheet. They are the only firmly draughted items in the drawing. C.L.R.O. Surveyor's Justice Plans, vol. XXIV; also Kalman, 'Newgate Prison', fig. 30a.

47 18 Geo. III c. 48. £15,000 had been spent on the Sessions House out of a total of £40,000 that had been made available, leaving £25,000 extra to be spent on the gaol.

48 Howard, *State of the Prisons*, 4th edn, pp. 213–15, and also Smith, *State of the Gaols*, p. 40.

49 J.C. Lettsome, *Hints Respecting Newgate*, London, 1794, pp. 19–20.

50 Plans at Essex C.R.O.

51 Plans at Essex C.R.O.
52 James Neild, *The General State of the Prisons*, London, 1812, p. 120.
53 *Ibid.*, p. 80.
54 Jonas Hanway, *Distributive Justice and Mercy*, London, 1781, sect. VII.
55 Janssen, *Letter to the Lord Mayor*, Appendix 3. Denne, *A Letter to Sir Robert Ladbroke*, pp. 9 and 12.
56 John Jebb, *Thoughts on the Construction and Polity of Prisons*, London, 1786. Intro. by Capel Lofft, p. xiv.
57 *Ibid.*, p. 6. This device was not adopted for prisons but was used at the Retreat, Tuke's lunatic asylum at Wakefield. See Charles Watson and James P. Pritchett, *Plans etc. and Description of the Pauper Lunatic Asylum*, York, 1819.
58 Smith, *State of the Gaols*, p. 78.
59 Jeremy Bentham, *Panopticon*, London, 1791, part I, Letter xx.
60 Lettsome, *Hints Respecting Newgate*, p. 20.
61 Howard, *State of the Prisons*, 1st edn, pp. 40–1.
62 A Gaol Act of 1532 stipulated that prisons were to be built in towns to ensure a good supply of alms. Pugh, *Imprisonment in Medieval England*, p. 330.
63 Howard, *State of the Prisons*, 4th edn, p. 255.
64 *Ibid.*, 1st edn, p. 42.
65 James Heath, *Eighteenth-Century Penal Theory*, Oxford, 1963, p. 92 quoted from H. Fielding, *Enquiry into the Causes of the Late Increase in Robbers*, London, 1751.
66 Howard, *State of the Prisons*, 1st edn,

p. 20.
67 This was the conclusion reached by the philosopher Thomas Reid, see D.D. Raphael (ed.), *British Moralists*, vol. II, p. 303, extract from *Essay on the Active Powers of man*, 1788; see also Denne, *A Letter to Sir Robert Ladbroke*, p. 59.
68 James Hanway, *Solitude and Imprisonment*, London, 1776, p. 14.
69 A.K. Wedderburn, *Observations on the State of the English Prisons and the Means of Improving Them*, London, 1793, p. 7.
70 The analogy is taken from Pope's *Essay on Man*, lines 217–20.
71 Hanway, *Solitude and Imprisonment*, p. 108.
72 Society for Giving Effect to H.M.'s Proclamation against Vice and Immorality, *Account of the Prisons and Houses of Correction in The Home Circuit* (taken from Howard), London, 1789, p. iii.
73 Papers relating to the Gaol Fever at Chester Castle, 1801, Cheshire C.R.O. Creighton records 1800/1 as the last winter in which there was a general epidemic of typhus in Britain. By the 1820s the proportion of deaths caused by typhus had dwindled. It would be rash to claim that its disappearance in the prisons was entirely due to the effects of penal reform and new building, but it is indicative that during the early years of the nineteenth century its source was being traced back to the dwellings of the poor rather than the prisons. Creighton, *History of Epidemics in Britain*, vol. II, pp. 139, 160.

4. Penitentiaries and reformed prisons

1 S.T. Janssen, *Three Tables: 1749–1771, showing Numbers Committed, Numbers Executed and Numbers Pardoned or Transported*, republished, London 1784; and John Howard, *The State of the Prisons*, 4th edn, London 1792, pp. 478–83. Figures for only the Midland and London Circuits were given.
2 16 Geo. III c. 56.
3 24 Geo. III c. 56.
4 See *Gentleman's Magazine*, vol. L

(1777), p. 447; also printed copy of 1779 Act, Bentham Mss, U.C.L., Box 116(b).
5 19 Geo. II c. 74.
6 For the full list of occupations see section 32 of the Act.
7 19 Geo. III c. 74, Preamble.
8 John Howard, *An Account of the Principle Lazarettos*, London, 1791, p. 222.
9 *P.P.* 1778–9, vol. X, 'Observations on the Bill to Punish by Imprisonment and

Hard Labour'. For Bentham's opinion of the 'Censor', which he visited, see Bentham Mss, U.C.L., Box 119(a) folder 3. He calculated that one in five or one in six died each year. See also section 27 of the Act.

10 *P.P.* 1776–8, vol. IX, Bill 287.

11 *P.P.* 1778–9, vol. X, 'Observations', p. 1.

12 *Ibid.*, sect. 5, p. 5.

13 19 Geo. III c. 74, sect. 25.

14 So described by Hanway in the Advertisement to *Distributive Justice and Mercy*, London, 1781.

15 *P.P.* 1784, vol. XXXIX, 'Report from the Committee Appointed to Enquire into the Execution of the 1779 Act', p. 1040 *et seq.*

16 *Ibid.* Second prizes of £50 for the Male Penitentiary and £30 for the Female Penitentiary went to Thomas Leverton and George Richardson, respectively.

17 Later in life Soane wrote of his involvement with the Commissioners. While awaiting the results of the competition, he was informed of a 'considerable difference of opinion' amongst the three supervisors as to the relative merits of the various schemes. See John Soane, *Memoirs of the Professional Life of An Architect Between 1768 and 1835*, London, 1835, pp. 16–17 (privately printed copy in Soane Museum).

18 19 Geo. III c. 74, sect. 38.

19 Original layout plan in Soane Museum. According to H.M. Colvin, Baldwin was responsible for Bathwick New Town. See *B.D.B.A.*

20 R.I.B.A. Drawings coll. (K9/21) n.d. Newton died in 1790.

21 Society for the Improvement of Prison Discipline, *Remarks on the Form and Construction of Prisons*, London, 1826, p. 69.

22 I am grateful to Janet Smith of the Liverpool Record Office, who supplied this information.

23 I am very much indebted to Ian McIvor, of the N.M.R., Scotland, for drawing my attention to plans by Baxter and Wardrop in the Edinburgh City Architect's Office, and for suggesting a possible connection between Blackburn and the Calton Gaol designs.

24 *A General and Descriptive History of the Ancient and Present State of Liverpool*, printed R. Phillips, Liverpool, 1795, pp. 177–8.

25 This is confirmed from Neild's description, see James Neild, *The General State of the Prisons*, London, 1812, p. 356.

26 Society for the Improvement of Prison Discipline, *Remarks.* The worst fault in Blackburn's design was said to be the *I*-shaped prison blocks, the clustered terminations of which left too narrow a space for the yards to be properly surveyed from the centre. Interestingly, the inner ring of terminal blocks do not appear on either the earliest Liverpool map showing the gaol engraved from the project (1785) nor later drawings.

27 *P.P.* 1784, vol. XXXIX, pp. 104 *et seq.*

28 From the costings, it appears that the reductions were effected by omitting all sorts of fittings and appurtenances, and also by paring down the accommodation to a minimum. The main saving was in the substitution of timber floors for vaulted construction, as timber prices had recently fallen by 50%.

29 Romilly, a well-informed Parliamentarian, agreed with the Commissioners that the insuperable difficulty was cost. James Heath, *Eighteenth-Century Penal Theory*, Oxford, 1963, p. 270.

30 *Proceedings of the Dorset Natural History and Antiquarian Field Club*, vol. XXV, Dorchester, 1904, pp. 42–3; and Dorset C.R.O., Contract for Building a New Prison, 1783. The estimate of £4,000 is Weinstock's.

31 M.B. Weinstock, 'Dorchester Model Prison: 1791–1816', *Dorset Nat. Hist. and Archaeol. Soc. Proceedings*, vol. LXXVIII (1956), p. 94.

32 Dorset C.R.O., Plan and Printed Description of Dorchester County Gaol.

33 West Sussex R.O., Committee Reports on Horsham Gaol, QAP/4/W1; and Howard, *State of the Prisons*, 4th edn, pp. 270, 271.

34 West Sussex R.O., Committee Reports on Petworth House of Correction, QAP/5/WE1. Petition of 2 Oct. 1786.

35 A copy of the Contract for Building Bodmin Gaol, dated 1 Nov. 1777, can be found in Dorset C.R.O. For details of Call's life see *Gentleman's Magazine*,

vol. LXXI (1801), pp. 282, 369. The plan is in the topographical collection, British Museum map room. K.9.32.1.

36 24 Geo. III c. 54 and 55. Michael Ignatieff suggested to me that the country wide epidemic of typhus that lasted from 1782 to 1785 may have been fostered by the rise in prison population. This would have added to the balance in favour of initiating reforms during these years. Certainly Howard noticed that fever was re-emerging into the gaols in 1783; see *Lazarettos*, p. 232.

37 24 Geo. III c. 54, sections 9—11. Building costs had to exceed half the annual assessment before a mortgate could be raised.

38 Normally this propagandizing took place within the restricted enclave of the Grand Jury. Occasionally, as at Oxford and Gloucester, the agitation reached the press. See M. Wall, *Letter to C. Willoughby, Chairman of the Quarter Sessions*, Oxford, 1786. The 12 major projects initiated between 1785 and 1788 were as follows: Oxford County Gaol (W. Blackburn), Shrewsbury County Gaol (W. Blackburn), Ipswich County Gaol (W. Blackburn), Chester County Gaol (Thomas Harrison), Ilchester Gaol (?), Salford New Bayley (W. Blackburn), Winchester County House of Correction (?), Winchester County Gaol (?), Exeter County Gaol and Penitentiary (W. Blackburn), Dorchester County Gaol (W. Blackburn), Cold Bath Fields (Jacob Leroux and Charles Middleton), Lincoln Castle County Gaol (?).

39 Bedfordshire C.R.O., Archivist's abstract of the History of the County Gaol in Ms. catalogue. Also, Eric Stockdale, *A Study of Bedford Prison 1660—1877*, Bedford, 1977, p. 80.

40 *Report from the Committee of Aldermen Appointed to Visit Several Gaols in England*, London, 1816, Introduction.

41 The incident is related by E.A.L. Moir in 'Sir George Onesiphorus Paul', in H.P.R. Finberg (ed.), *Gloucestershire Studies*, Leicester, 1957, p. 221.

42 G.O. Paul, *Considerations of the Defects of Prisons*, London, 1784, p. 5.

43 *Ibid.*, p. 66.

44 *Ibid.*, p. 49.

45 The Gloucestershire C.R.O. holds an almost complete though damaged set of working drawings by Blackburn for all these prisons. See also, Committee Report on Prison Reform, 1783. The brief was as follows:
County Gaol:

Men felons	55	
Women felons	15	
Debtors	40	
Fines	10	
King's evidence	4	
Men convicts	30	
Women convicts	6	
Bridewell	20	
	180	(207)
Dursley (Horsley) Bridewell	50	(46)
Lawford's Gate Bridewell	40	(40)
Littledean Bridewell	40	(24)
Northleach Bridewell	40	(40)

Bracketed figures show accommodation actually provided. Unbracketed figures are from 1783 brief.

46 Paul, *Considerations*, p. 78.

47 Arthur Griffiths, *Memorials of Millbank*, London, 1875, vol. I, p. 10.

48 For Petworth see Sidney and Beatrice Webb, *English Prisons Under Local Government*, London, 1922, p. 54n. For the Gloucester prison population see Neild, *General State of the Prisons*. Lawford's Gate, for example, had never contained more than 24 prisoners, although there was room for 40.

49 A particularly clear record of this process of a committee working to define not just a brief, but a form of building and a method of construction too is to be found in the Middlesex C.R.O., Minutes for the Committee for Building the New House of Correction, 1784—8.

50 This three part formula can be usefully compared with that offered by P.G. Bugniet in the explanation of his Paris prison design of 1765: 'Safety and health are the two essential aims which come to mind when conceiving the idea of a prison.' Reformation was not included. See, *Journal of the Soc. of Architectural Historians* (U.S.A.), vol. XII, pt 2, p. 29.

51 See pp. 104—9 above.

52 Blackburn incorporated these features into all his prisons. The encircling path in Soane's Male Penitentiary did not serve quite the same purpose, as part was used for the fabrication of rope.
53 Lincolnshire C.R.O., Ground floor plan of Kirton Bridewell, n.d.
54 C.L.R.O., S.J.P. portfolio vol. I, scheme for Borough Compter, 1785.
55 This suggestion was made by a Mr M. O'Connor in a letter to Janssen in 1750. See S.T. Janssen, *A Letter to the Lord Mayor of London*, London, 1767, Appendix 1.
56 Jeremy Bentham, *Panopticon Postscript*, 1791, sect. XX. Unfortunately there are no details of Blackburn's prisons that corroborate his use of the drain under the wall. It was not shown at Gloucester, but may have been used elsewhere.
57 Blackburn was consulted on the early plans produced by Harrison. See Chester C.R.O., Letter from Blackburn dated 30 Sept. 1784 on Castle Gaol plans.
58 Again I am grateful to Ian McIvor for showing me these plans. Baxter produced several similar layouts for Calton. The one illustrated in Fig. 70 copies even the elevation details of the Salford New Bailey. Although no plans of Salford exist, we know the outline of it to have been exactly the same as Baxter's. See T.A. Markus, 'The Pattern of the Law', *Architectural Review*, vol. CXVI (1954), fig. 11. The Lord Provost of Edinburgh, so Mr McIvor informs me, had visited Blackburn and a number of his prisons, including Salford. It would seem likely that he made the plans available to Baxter on his return.
59 The best record of this prison is a series of photographs taken in 1930, before its demolition, in Herefordshire C.R.O.
60 For a description of Lancaster Gaol see Lancs. C.R.O., Commissioners' Report on the Management of H.M. Prison at Lancaster, Oct. 1912, pt 2, p. 5 et seq.
61 This was suggested by Howard, who said that the gaoler's house 'should be in or near the middle of the gaol, with windows to the felons' and debtors' court yard'. See John Howard, *The State of the Prisons*, 1st edn, Warrington, 1777,

p. 418.
62 Lancs. C.R.O., Proceedings of the Lancaster Castle committee, 14 Jan. 1794.
63 *Gentleman's Magazine*, vol. LXVI, Supplement (1796), p. 1065, Letter from 'Eugenio'.
64 The word was used by Blackburn in notes on the Gloucester drawings.
65 Neild, *General State of the Prisons*, pp. 81–2.
66 *P.P.* 1819, vol. VII, 'Report of Select Committee on the State of the Gaols', p. 332. John Orridge giving evidence. Orridge solved the problem by stopping the privileges of prisoners discovered sleeping in their cells with the shutters closed.
67 *P.P.* 1800, vol. CX, 'Report of the Commissioners of Enquiry into the State of and Management of H.M. Prison in Cold Bath Fields', p. 9.
68 *P.P.* 1847, vol. XXIX, 'Second Report of the Surveyor General of Prisons' (Joshua Jebb), plate XIV. Jebb designed a manual damper within each cell to control the air flow at Pentonville and Kirkdale. They were not installed at Pentonville and are absent from later designs.
69 John Jebb, *Thoughts on the Constitution and Polity of Prisons*, London, 1786, p. 7.
70 Chester C.R.O., Plans of the Castle Gaol, and Courthouse, by T. Harrison.
71 In 1833 a cholera scare in London led the authorities to inspect the Cold Bath Fields sewers. They found most to have collapsed. Pinks attributed this to shoddy workmanship, but it is much more likely to have been the result of subsidence. See W.J. Pinks, *History of Clerkenwell*, London, 1781, p. 82.
72 14 Geo. III c. 59, where they are referred to as 'sick apartments'.
73 F.G. Emmison, *Guide to the Essex Record Office*, n.p., 1969, p. 13. The magistrates launched an appeal, but the Exchequer dropped the surcharge in 1792, as the County had, by that time, made amends.
74 *P.P.* 1800, vol. CX, 'Report of Commissioners . . . into Cold Bath Fields'.
75 Worcester C.R.O. contains a specification for the County Gaol, circa 1810,

by G. Sandys, in which all these items are shown in detail.

76 John Headlam, *A Letter to The Right Honourable Robert Peel . . . on Prison Labour*, London, 1824, pp. 18–19.

77 Paul, *Considerations*, p. 8.

78 Rev. John Wallis, *The Bodmin Register for 1833*, Bodmin, 1833. This description was kindly supplied to me by W.E. Long, the curator of the Bodmin Museum.

79 Paul, *Considerations*, p. 31.

80 *Ibid.*, p. 32.

81 The Salford dimensions are taken from a comparative list of cell sizes compiled in 1844. See Essex C.R.O., 'Examinations of Prison Discipline taken before a Committee of Magistrates', QAG/p.19.

82 Dorset C.R.O., Printed Plans and Description of the County Gaol.

83 At Horsham and Petworth it was part of the gaoler's house. In later prisons even the gaoler is isolated within his own prison (rules from the early nineteenth century onward always forbade the keeper to have guests overnight without permission). For a typical relation of the procedure of admittance see Rules for Preston House of Correction (Lancs. C.R.O.) 1793, rule 15.

84 Neild, *General State of the Prisons*, p. 528.

85 Dorset C.R.O., Plans and Description of the County Gaol.

86 H.M. Colvin, *Biographical Dictionary of British Architects*, London, 1978, entry under Thomas Johnstone, notes that the Warwick County Museum have a model of a prison chapel by Johnstone (1779) which shows these separations.

87 Middlesex R.O., Clerkenwell House of Correction Sessions Book 1258/67, entry under 4 July 1771.

88 Middlesex R.O., 'Report by Rev. S. Glasse & Mr. Aris laid before the Committee for Building the House of Correction', Sept. 1794, MA/G/CBF 201d.

89 *P.P.* 1816, vol. XVIII, pp. 339 et seq.

90 Howard, *State of the Prisons*, 4th edn, pp. 152–3.

91 Essex C.R.O., Plans QAG/p.4.

92 C.L.R.O., S.J.P. portfolio vol. I.

93 Wiltshire C.R.O. An Address to the Grand Jury of Jan. 1790 stated that the new prison was for solitary confinement. See also E. Lush, 'A Plan for Building 36 New Cells', Wiltshire C.R.O.

94 Neild, *General State of the Prisons*, Liverpool Borough Gaol.

95 Dorset C.R.O., Plans and Description of the County Gaol.

96 It is generally thought that this method of extending the compass of isolation was invented by John Haviland for the Philadelphia East Penitentiary (commenced 1829). It is more probable that Haviland, as an English emigrant, exported the technique to America. Ignatieff records that Reading County Gaol had cells of this kind too. See Michael Ignatieff, *A Just Measure of Pain*, London, 1978, p. 102.

97 Hampshire C.R.O. A plan of the Bridewell was reproduced in the Magistrates' Report on Winchester Gaol 1816–17. See also Neild, *General State of the Prisons*, p. 586.

98 Lincolnshire C.R.O., Plan of Kirton Bridewell, n.d.

99 By law (24 Geo. III c. 54 sect. 4) a prisoner had to be taken out of his cell to chapel once a week.

100 C.L.R.O., S.J.P. portfolio vol. I. These stylistically unexceptional plans are not well known. See also, W.G.G. Hunt, 'The Southwark Compter', Paper delivered to the Guildhall Historical Association, July 1971, C.L.R.O., Misc. Mass. 311.18.

101 The executed plan, completed in 1795, contained no cells at all.

102 So described by William Morton Pitt.

103 He is known to have prepared designs for Bedford County Gaol and Lancaster Castle Gaol, though neither have survived. See Bedfordshire C.R.O. Abstract of the History of the County Gaol in Ms. catalogue, and Lancs. C.R.O., Proceedings of the Lancaster Castle Committee, Lancaster Session, 3 Oct. 1786.

The *D.N.B.* unreliably lists work on an Irish Penitentiary House (said by Bentham to have been a Panopticon), the Tank in Cornhill, Limerick Prison and alterations to Dublin Newgate, omitting to mention any of his English prisons, with the exception of Oxford City Gaol. The Society for the Improvement of Prison Discipline publication, *Remarks on the Form and Construction of Prisons*, attributes Oxford County Gaol (sometimes ascribed to George Moneypenny) and Monmouth Gaol to Blackburn, and lists most of his English works too (p. 7). Colvin in *B.D.B.A.* lists Oxford County Gaol (*c.* 1785), Oxford City Gaol (1786—9), Liverpool Borough Gaol (1786—7), Ipswich County Gaol (1786—90), Salford New Bailey (1787—90), the five Gloucester prisons (*c.* 1785), Preston House of Correction (1789), Monmouth County Gaol (1788—90), Dorchester County Gaol (1789—95), Exeter County Gaol (1789—95), Lewes House of Correction (1789—93), Limerick Gaol (1789) and alterations to Dublin Newgate. Shrewsbury County Gaol was also designed, at least in part, by Blackburn.

104 *D.N.B.*
105 Norfolk C.R.O., Plans of the 1791—2 rebuilding.
106 Leicestershire C.R.O., Plans by G. Moneypenny for County Gaol, 1789.
107 J. Nichols, *The History and Antiquities of the County of Leicester*, vol. I, pt 2, Wakefield reprint, 1971, p. 530, and plate XVIII, which compares all Leicester's public facades.
108 For Walnut Street see Anon., *Some Account of the Prison at Philadelphia*, London, 1816. For French reforms see L. Radzinowicz, *History of English Criminal Law*, vol. I, London, 1948, p. 298.
109 A.K. Wedderburn, *Observations on the State of English Prisons and the Means of Improving Them*, London, 1793, p. 16. See also Ignatieff, *A Just Measure of Pain*, pp. 108—9.
110 Anon., *Gloucester Bastille!!!! Pathetic Particulars of a Poor Boy*, London, 1792.
111 E.P. Thompson, *The Making of the*

English Working Class, Harmondsworth, 1968, p. 192. Dr J.R.S. Whiting has since pointed out to me that Wake did not, as Thompson says, die while in prison.
112 Gloucester, C.R.O., *Kidd Wake Poster*, printed in London, 1799.
113 Francis Burdett, *An Impartial Statement of the Inhuman Cruelties Discovered in Cold Bath Fields Prison*, London, 1800.
114 *P.P.* 1822, vol. II, 'Reports of the Commissioners on the State of Ilchester Gaol'. For a list of the accusations see pp. 745—6.
115 William Godwin, *An Enquiry Concerning Political Justice*, vol. II, London, 1793, pp. 752—3.
116 First published, *Morning Post*, 6 Sept. 1799.
117 G.O. Paul, *An Address to the Magistrates of the County of Gloucester*, Gloucester, 1789, pp. 152—3.
118 *P.P.* 1800, vol. CX, 'Report of the Commissioners . . . into Cold Bath Fields', p. 28.
119 George Moneypenny was the architect for the conversion. See *P.P.*, 1816, vol. XVIII, p. 348. This explanation of events is different from that offered by Ignatieff who, noticing the same tendency to discard solitary confinement, puts it down to the effectiveness and strength of public reaction on the one hand, and the pressure of overcrowding within the prisons on the other. Ignatieff, *A Just Measure of Pain*, pp. 107, 142.
120 R.H. Condon, 'The Reform of the English Prisons, 1773—1816', unpublished thesis, Brown University, 1962, pp. 96—8; Webb, *English Prisons*, p. 468. Edward Mullins in his *Treatise on the Magistracy of England*, London, 1836, claimed that even in 1793 the Counties of England as a whole spent a staggering 44% of their income on prison building and administration.

5. A way of obtaining power

1 Jeremy Bentham, *Proposal for a New and Less Expensive mode of Employing and Reforming Convicts*, printed 1798, Bentham Mss., U.C.L., box 116(b), paper 653.

2 Jeremy Bentham, *A View of the Hard Labour Bill*, London, 1778, Preface.
3 *Ibid.*, pp. 59—62. Bentham suggested a solution of gold in aqua regia, which produced a purplish dye.

4 C.W. Everett, *Jeremy Bentham*, London, 1966, p. 42. The question of why such a project should take up so much of a great philosopher's time has perplexed many of his biographers.

5 Maria Sophia Bentham, 'Memoir of the Late Brigadier General Sir Samuel Bentham', *Papers and Practical Illustrations of Public Works*, London, 1856.

6 J.H. Burns, 'Bentham and The French Revolution', *Transactions of the Royal Historical Society*, 5th series, vol. XVI (1966), p. 95. Bentham, aware of the Empress's visit to the area, nevertheless remained indoors. Apparently he expected her to come to him and request that he compile a rational legal code for Russia.

7 Bentham Mss., U.C.L., Box 119(a), papers 14—16.

8 Bentham Mss., U.C.L., Box 119(a), paper 14. Parnell was approached before September 1790. See also, J. Bowring (ed.), *The Works of Jeremy Bentham*, Edinburgh, 1843, vol. XI, suppl. p. 104.

9 Bentham Mss., U.C.L., Box 117(a), folder 2. Bentham calculated that 11 rotundas would serve the purpose. See also, Burns, 'Bentham and the French Revolution', p. 107.

10 Bowring, *Works*, vol. XI, suppl., p. 98.

11 Bentham, Mss., U.C.L., Box 117(a), folder 6, Examination of J.B.

12 Bentham, *View of the Hard Labour Bill*, p. 4.

13 Cited by Gertrude Himmelfarbe, 'The Haunted House of Jeremy Bentham' in *Victorian Minds: Essays on Nineteenth-Century Intellectuals*, London, 1968, p. 73.

14 'History of the War Between Jeremy Bentham and George III, by One of The Belligerents', 1831; see Bowring, *Works*, vol. XI, suppl., p. 98 et seq. for extracts.

15 Jeremy Bentham, *Panopticon*, London, 1791, Letter I.

16 Jeremy Bentham, *Panopticon Postscript*, London, 1791, pt 1, sect. VIII.

17 Bowring, *Works*, vol. X, p. 564.

18 Bentham Mss., U.C.L., 117a, paper 18.

19 'Outline of the Plan of Construction of a Panopticon Penitentiary', Bowring, *Works*, vol. XI, suppl., p. 96.

20 The original drawings were destroyed by fire previous to printing, and in Bentham's absence an engraver extemporized this plate. See *Panopticon Postscript*, pt 1, sect I. An apology was also engraved on the plate itself.

21 Bentham, *Panopticon*, Letter V.

22 *Ibid.*, Letter XI.

23 Bentham, *Panopticon Postscript*, pt 1, sect. VIII.

24 *Ibid.*

25 Bentham Mss., U.C.L., 119a.

26 Bowring, *Works*, vol. XI, suppl., p. 96.

27 Bentham Mss., U.C.L., 119a, paper 24; Bentham, *Panopticon Postscript*, pt 1, sect. VIII. This item was not incorporated into Reveley's design.

28 Louis Pierre Baltard, *Architectonographie des Prisons*, Paris, 1829, p. 18.

29 Bentham, *Panopticon Postscript*, pt 1, sect. VIII. The idea came from a certain Mr Merlin, who had installed such a system in his own house, complete with a series of manual pointers and bells, for issuing instructions to his servants.

30 Bentham Mss., U.C.L., 119a, paper 23.

31 Bentham, *Panopticon Postscript*, pt 1, sect. II.

32 Bentham Mss., U.C.L., 119a, paper 23.

33 Bentham, *Panopticon*, Letter VIII.

34 Bugniet's Paris Prison design and Luigi Vanvitelli's Lazaretto at Ancona, which were both organized round a central chapel, were of this more common type, as was Philbert De L'Orme's cellularized chapel, for all that its plan and section are very similar to the Panopticon. I am indebted to Joseph Rykwert for pointing out the last two examples.

35 Frances Yates, *The Art of Memory*, Harmondsworth, 1966, p. 161.

36 Gustave Loisel, *Histoire des Menageries de l'Antiquité à nos Jours*, 3 vols., Paris, 1912. For antique aviaries see vol. I, p. 84 *et seq.*; for Le Vau's menagerie see vol. II, pp. 104—6.

37 Bentham, *Panopticon*, title page.

38 Bentham Mss., U.C.L., 119a, paper 12, in a letter to Robert Adam, 28 May 1791.

39 D.D. Raphael, *British Moralists*, Oxford, 1969, vol. I, pp. 160—1. The quotation is from John Locke's *Essay Concerning Human Understanding*.

40 Claude Helvetius, *Treatise on Man*,

trans. Hooper, London, 1777, p. 131.

41 Offray de la Mettrie, *Man a Machine*, trans. (attributed to Marquis d'Argens), Dublin, 1794, p. 38.

42 James Heath, *Eighteenth-Century Penal Theory*, Oxford, 1963, p. 170, from Servan's Address on the Administration of Criminal Justice, 1767.

43 Helvetius, *Treatise on Man*, p. 15.

44 *Ibid.*, p. 20.

45 Rush, a member of the Society of Friends, tried rather disingenuously to reintroduce Sensationalism into the fabric of religion. Free will was reasserted — but only in so far as physical causes were not controlling the production of virtue and vice — but since physical causes had, according to Rush, a virtual monopoly, it made little practical difference.

46 Benjamin Rush, *An Oration Delivered Before the American Philosophical Society*, London, n.d., p. 44.

47 *Ibid.*, p. 42.

48 F.E. Manuel (ed.), *The Enlightenment*, Englewood Cliffs, 1965, p. 115.

49 A point made by J.L. Talmon in *Origins of Totalitarian Democracy*, London, 1952, p. 22.

50 Helvetius, *Treatise on Man*, p. 4.

51 A year after the *Oration*, Rush called for the setting up of a penal system with coassification, labour, indeterminate punishment and individual treatment. See H.B. Gill, 'Correctional Philosophy and Architecture', *Journal of A.I.A.*, vol. XXXII (July 1961), pp. 67–73.

52 Bentham, *Panopticon Postscript*, pt 1, sect. VIII.

53 N. Hans aptly described the Felicific Calculus as a 'merchant's account of profit and loss as the basis of moral philosophy', see 'Bentham and the Utilitarians' in A.V. Judges (ed.), *Pioneers of English Education*, London, 1952, pp. 83–103.

54 Jeremy Bentham, *The Principles of Morals and Legislation*, London, 1789, Preface.

55 Bentham, *Panopticon Postscript*, pt 1, sect. V.

56 Bentham, *Panopticon*, Letter X.

57 *Ibid.*, Letter XV.

58 Bowring, *Works*, vol. XI, Suppl., p. 107.

59 Bentham Mss., U.C.L., Box 117(a), paper 98.

60 Bowring, *Works*, vol. X., p. ?70. Letter from J.P. Garran.

61 M.P. Mack (ed.), *A Bentham Reader*, N.Y., 1969, p. 283.

62 Bentham, *Panopticon Postscript*, pt 1, sect. V.

63 Jeremy Bentham, *The Rationale of Punishment*, London, 1830, p. 354.

64 Most of these uses were listed and explained in the 1787 Panopticon Letters. See also, Bentham Mss., U.C.L., Box 119(a), 24 (Bridewell); 133, paper 1 (orphanages); Box 107(b), paper 21 (magdalen house and infant hospital); Bowring, *Works*, vol. VIII; *Chrestomathia* (school) and *Outline of a Work Entitled Pauper Management Improved* (industry houses).

65 Bentham Mss., U.C.L., Box 107(b), folder 20. Some 20 years earlier, in 1782, Samuel Wyatt had built a semicircular poultry pen for 600 hens with a lodge stretching across the diameter at Winnington Hall for Lord Penrhyn. See John Martin Robinson, 'Model Farm Buildings of the Age of Improvement', *Architectural History, Journal of the Society of Architectural Historians of G.B.*, vol. XIX (1976).

66 Bentham Mss., U.C.L., Box 133, folder 1.

67 *Ibid.*

68 More recently Jean Genet's poetic romances of life in French prisons have described it in terms that could hardly be called utopian, but which nevertheless shows it to have been the perfect location for the timeless struggle between authorities and criminals. For Genet the prison became an ideal setting for a sort of drama, for Bentham it was the ideal container for an exacting process. See Jean Genet, *The Thief's Journal*, trans. B. Frechtman, Harmondsworth, 1965, pp. 70 et seq.

69 Gilbert Geis, 'Jeremy Bentham', in H. Mannheim (ed.), *Pioneers in Criminology*, London, 1961, p. 64.

70 Bowring, *Works*, vol. XI, suppl., p. 107.

71 Bentham, *Panopticon Postscript*, pt 1, sect. XVIII.

72 Bowring, *Works*, vol. XI, suppl., p. 105.

73 Bentham, *Panopticon Postscript*, pt 1, sect. II.

74 *Ibid.*, sect. XIX.

75 Bentham Mss., U.C.L., Box 117(a), folder 6, Notes on Examination of J.B. taken 28 June 1798.

76 Bunce was an architect with the Navy Department who had previously worked with Jeremy Bentham on the 'Frigi-darium' perishable food store. See H.M. Colvin, *Biographical Dictionary of British Architects*, London, 1978.

77 J. Bentham, *Outline of a Work Entitled Pauper Management Improved* (first printed in *Annals of Agriculture*, vol. XXX (1797)), in Bowring, *Works*, vol. VIII, pp. 369—74.

78 There is an uncanny resemblance be-tween the elevation of the 1797 Panop-ticon House of Industry and the Sheer-ness Naval Dockyard Boat Store by G.T. Greene (1858—61). It is tempting to suggest a connection, particularly as Samuel Bentham was a very active Inspector General of Naval Works be-tween 1796 and 1805, and later (1812) designed a dock complex for Sheerness.

79 The comparison was cited by C.K. Ogden in *Jeremy Bentham 1932—2032*, London, 1932.

80 Bentham, *View of the Hard Labour Bill*, pp. 110—12.

81 Bentham, *Panopticon Postscript*, pt 1, sect. VII.

82 Bentham Mss., U.C.L., Box 119(a), folder 9, 'Objections'.

83 Bentham, *Panopticon Postscript*, pt 1, sect. XXIII.

84 Bentham, *Pauper Management Improved*, in Bowring, *Works*, vol. VIII, pp. 375—6.

85 According to Maria Sophia Bentham, Spencer in the same year was approach-ing Samuel Bentham for Naval Semin-aries on the Panopticon plan, so his obduracy over the site must be con-sidered as a matter of self-interest and not a matter of principle. See M.S. Bentham, 'The Panopticon or Inspection Principle in Dockyards and Manufac-tories', *Civil Engineer and Architect's Journal*, vol. XVI (1853), p. 454.

86 Bowring, *Works*, vol. XI, Suppl., p. 108, Letter to Earl Spencer, 16 Aug. 1793.

87 Bentham Mss., U.C.L., Box 117(a), folder 6, paper 98.

88 Bentham Mss., U.C.L., Box 117(a), folder 5, Letters to G. Rose, Feb.—April 1798.

89 Bentham Mss., U.C.L., Box 116(b), folder 4, Letter to Thornton, July 1800.

90 *P.P.* 1810—11, vol. III, 'Reports from the Select Committee on Laws Re Peni-tentiary Houses', pp. 569 *et seq.*

91 Bentham Mss., U.C.L., Box 119(a), folder 2, Letter from J.B. to Reveley, 13 April 1791, complaining that the archi-tect had taken too much upon himself; Letter from J.B. to Robert Adam, 28 May 1791.

92 The Adam plans for Edinburgh Bridewell are in the Soane Museum, London. The courtyard plans are undated.

93 The deviations from the Bentham Panop-ticon were noted in an anonymous tract by A Citizen, *The Gaol of the City of Bristol*, London, 1815, pp. 77 *et seq.*

94 Society for the Improvement of Prison Discipline, *Remarks on the Form and Construction of Prisons*, London, 1826, p. 27.

95 Bentham, 'The Panopticon or Inspection Principle', pp. 453—6.

96 Architectural Publication Society, *Dic-tionary of Architecture*, London, 1853—92, vol. VI, entry under 'Panopticon'. The same volume, under 'Prisons', informs the reader that in 1816 (sic) Havilland erected the first prison on the 'radiating or panopticon principle' at Cherry Hill, Philadelphia. This shows how far the misunderstanding had developed.

6. Classification, inspection and labour

1 The largest gap was in the three years between 1824 and 1828, during which time no major new building was com-menced, as far as I am aware.

2 The Select Committee on Secondary Punishments, reporting in 1831 (*P.P.* 1831—2, vol. VII, p. 559), saw this rise as due, not to an increase in prison build-

ing as did some (e.g. Britannicus, *An Address to the Magistrates*, London, 1819, pp. 34–5), but to the side effects of unemployment following the French Wars, coupled with an unprecedented rise in national population. See also Michael Ignatieff, *A Just Measure of Pain*, London, 1978, pp. 179–87.

3 These statistics were compiled from the local authority gaol returns (Schedule B) for 1832–3 (*P.P.* 1834, vol. XLVI) and James Neild, *The General State of the Prisons*, London, 1812.

4 Richard Ingleman, 'Address to the Wiltshire Quarter Sessions Magistrates on Devizes House of Correction', printed Newark, 1808, Wiltshire C.R.O.

5 Society for the Improvement of Prison Discipline, *Report of the Committee*, London, 1818, p. 10.

6 *Idem*, *Remarks on the Form and Construction of Prisons*, London, 1826, p. iii.

7 Neild, *General State of the Prisons*. For a brief synopsis of Neild's life see J.C. Lettsome, 'A Tribute of Respect to James Neild' in *Hints to Promote Beneficence*, vol. I, 2nd edn, London, 1816, pp. 25 et seq.

8 For Southwell poor relief see S.G. and F.O.A. Checkland (eds.), *The Poor Law Report of 1834*, Harmondsworth, 1974, pp. 127, 339, 352. For Southwell House of Correction see Richard Phillips Shilton, *History of Southwell*, Newark, 1818, pp. 174–5, 181–204; and Richard Ingleman, 'Explanation of the Plans for a House of Correction at Southwell', printed 1807, Wiltshire C.R.O.

9 So described by Neild in his section on Bury Gaol. Neild, *General State of the Prisons*.

10 John Orridge, *Description of the Gaol at Bury St Edmunds*, London, 1819; Thomas le Breton, *Thoughts on the Defective State of Prisons*, London, 1822. For Harris see H.M. Colvin, *Biographical Dictionary of British Architects*, London, 1978.

11 George Holford, *Thoughts on the Criminal Prisons of this Country*, London, 1821, p. 6.

12 Arthur Griffiths, *Memorials of Millbank*, London, 1875, vol. I, p. 34.

13 Henry Mayhew and John Binney, *The Criminal Prisons of London*, London, 1862, p. 236.

14 By 1821 a committee of the S.I.P.D. could observe the anomalous arrangements at Cambridge Town Gaol with some surprise, where 'the gaoler does not reside in the gaol, but carries on the business of a taylor', *Third Report*, London, 1821, Appendix, p. vi. For Devizes regulations see: 'Rules for the Penitentiary House at Devizes' n.d. (1816?), Wiltshire C.R.O.

15 These qualities were demanded in an advertisement for a keeper at Kirton Bridewell in 1821, Lincolnshire C.R.O.

16 See Ignatieff, *A Just Measure of Pain*, pp. 189–93 and Eric Stockdale, *A Study of Bedford Prison 1660–1877*, Bedford, 1977. The gaoler who in 1814 replaced the long line of family innkeepers-cum-gaolkeepers at Bedford was sergeant major in the local militia.

17 George Holford, *An Account of the Penitentiary at Millbank*, London, 1828, pp. 77n.

18 *Ibid.*, pp. 41–7. For the competition see *Gentleman's Magazine*, vol. LXXXII pt 2 (1812), p. 80. None of the entries survive. The other two award winners were Charles Augustus Busby, a pupil of D.A. Alexander (Maidstone County Gaol) who later worked with Francis Goodwin (Derby County Gaol) and Hervey? (perhaps John Harvey who replaced Hardwick as superintending architect at Millbank in 1813); see Colvin, *B.D.B.A.*

19 George Holford, *The Convict's Complaint and the Thanks of the Convict*, London, 1825.

20 Griffiths, *Memorials of Millbank*, London, 1875 vol. I, p. 43. Griffiths had been Deputy Governor at Millbank and made use of the prison archives. Details of its construction are taken largely from this source.

21 George Holford, *A Short Vindication of the General Penitentiary at Millbank*, which includes also the Second Vindication, London, 1825. Second Vindication, p. 9.

22 Society for the Improvement of Prison Discipline, *Remarks*, Appendix 'Minutes of Evidence of the Committee', March

1824, pp. 61–4; Griffiths, *Memorials of Millbank*, vol. I, ch. IV.

23 J.C. Lettsome had suggested that tennis courts be put in the Newgate yards but this is the only other example I have been able to find. See J.C. Lettsome, *Hints Respecting Newgate*, London, 1794, p. 18.

24 The three were Whitworth Russell (chaplain at Millbank), Benjamin Chapman (governor of Millbank) and Orridge. See *P.P.* 1835, vol. XII, 'Select Committee on Gaols and Houses of Correction', General Index and Abstract of Evidence. The quotation is from Sibly, Governor of Brixton, *P.P.* 1835, vol. XI, p. 134.

25 Ingleman, 'Address to Wiltshire Quarter Sessions Magistrates on Devizes House of Correction'.

26 *Ibid.*

27 Society for the Improvement of Prison Discipline, *Remarks*, p. 36.

28 James Elmes, *Hints for the Improvement of Prisons*, London, 1817, p. 14. For Moneypenny's prisons see Neild, *General State of the Prisons*, under 'Exeter' and 'Winchester'.

29 It should be added that in this period many prisons had no facade at all, being tucked away behind the more elegant civic edifice of a sessions house. Harrison's Chester Castle prison designed in 1786 is an early example, combining prison and courts into one unified architectural scheme, but the practice became more common in the first three decades of the nineteenth century; for example at Cambridge County Gaol and Sessions House (1806–10), George Byfield; Durham County Gaol and Sessions House (1810–11), Francis Sandys and Ignatius Bonomi; Knutsford House of Correction and Sessions House (1817–19), George Moneypenny; Lincoln City Gaol and Sessions House (1805–9), William Hayward; Spilsby House of Correction and Sessions House (1824–6), H.E. Kendall, and Morpeth County Gaol and Sessions House (1822–31), John Dobson.

30 Orridge, *Description of the Gaol*, p. 3.

31 *Ibid.*

32 Le Breton, *Thoughts on the Defective State of Prisons*, plate 3.

33 Its consequences and effects were, how-ever, already evident in designs like those for Devizes, 1808; Maidstone, 1813; and Millbank, 1812.

34 Neild, *General State of the Prisons*, p. 207.

35 Society for the Improvement of Prison Discipline, *Rules Proposed for the Government of Gaols, Penitentiaries and Houses of Correction*, London, 1820, p. 43.

36 Le Breton, *Thoughts on the Defective State of Prisons*, p. 12.

37 Stephen Glover, *History of the County of Derby*, 1833, pt 1, vol. II, pp. 478–9.

38 4 Geo. IV c. 64.

39 Thomas Hopper, 'County Surveyor's Report on the State of the Gaols and Houses of Correction in Essex', dated Feb. 1819, Essex C.R.O., QAG/p.4.

40 Society for the Improvement of Prison Discipline, *Report of the Committee*, London, 1818, p. 25.

41 Thomas Fowell Buxton, *An Inquiry Whether Crime and Misery are Produced or Prevented by our Present System of Prison Discipline*, London, 1818, p. 59; and *Gentleman's Magazine*, vol. LXXXIII pt 2 (1813), pp. 32–4.

42 Ingleman, 'Address to Wiltshire Quarter Sessions Magistrates on Devizes House of Correction'.

43 'Report of the Committee of Magistrates for Superintending and Regulating the County Gaol of Norfolk', 16 Oct. 1819, p. 7, Norfolk C.R.O. The Committee included Thomas Beevor who had been responsible for the Wymondham Bridewell in 1787.

44 John Howard, *The State of the Prisons*, 1st edn, Warrington, 1777, p. 16.

45 24 Geo. III c. 54, sect. 4.

46 Society for the Improvement of Prison Discipline, *Rules Proposed*, p. 43n.

47 *Idem, Remarks*, Appendix, p. 60.

48 *Idem, Report*, p. 7. J.T. Becher put the same point to a committee of the House of Commons in 1810 in describing the regime at Wymondham:
'We treat mankind as constituted of habits, and our principle is to eradicate those which are bad, and to implant others that are better. With this intent we frequently receive a man, filthy, diseased, drunken, idle, and profane; and

that man in a short time becomes clean, sober, healthy, diligent, and to all appearances a good moral man: by which I mean to imply, that he does not swear, nor behave inattentively during the hours of devotion, nor invade the little property of his fellow prisoner or quarrel with him, or do any act unbecoming to a man of sound principles.'
P.P. 1810–11, vol. III, p. 606.

49 *P.P.* 1819, vol. VII, 'Report of the Select Committee on the State of the Gaols', p. 323, Orridge giving evidence.

50 Holford, *Account of the Penitentiary at Millbank*, p. 148.

51 See, le Breton, *Thoughts on the Defective State of Prisons*, pp. 8 et seq. The same problem arose in France, where classification was also prescribed by law. See L.P. Baltard, *Architectonographie des Prisons*, Paris, 1829, pp. 20–2.

52 Richard Elsam, *A Brief Treatise on Prisons*, London, 1818, pp. 17–18.

53 Le Breton, *Thoughts on the Defective State of Prisons*, p. 8.

54 Society for Diffusing Information on the Subject of Capital Punishment and Prison Discipline, *An Account of the Maison de Force at Ghent*, London, 1817, p. 9.

55 Society for the Improvement of Prison Discipline, *Remarks*, p. 4.

56 *Ibid.*, pp. 34 et seq.

57 Byfield's plans for the gaols at Cambridge, Canterbury and Worcester are deposited in the respective County Record Offices.

58 Buxton, *Enquiry*, Appendix, p. 11.

59 *P.P.* 1819, vol. VII, 'Report of the Select Committee on the State of the Gaols', p. 323.

60 Shilton, *History of Southwell*, p. 197.

61 Orridge, *Description of the Gaol*, p. 5.

62 Le Breton, *Thoughts on the Defective State of Prisons*, p. 7. Abingdon Bridewell, a prison which had been designed in association with the keeper of Oxford County Gaol, Daniel Harris, was also on a condensed plan with crossing wings, though this may have been for different reasons.

63 *Ibid.*, p. 15.

64 Society for the Improvement of Prison Discipline, *Remarks*, p. 41n.

65 The earliest of Byfield's drawings at Worcester C.R.O. are dated 1801, which is one year earlier than the conventional date for Bury St Edmunds Gaol, but Worcester was not constructed till 1809–14.

66 This includes all the prisons, the form of which has been ascertained either through descriptions or surviving plans:
Polygonals
Devizes House of Correction (1808–17), Richard Ingleman.
Brixton County House of Correction (1818–21), Thomas Chawner.
Bedford Penitentiary (1819), James Elmes.
Addition to Southwell House of Correction (1817), Ingleman.
Kirkdale House of Correction (–1819), Thomas Wright.
Wakefield House of Correction (1821?), radial/polygonal, architect unknown.
Durham County Gaol (1809–11), Francis Sandys and Ignatius Bonomi.
Millbank (1812–22), William Williams and T. Hardwick.
Radials
Bodmin New Gaol (1826), architect unknown.
Exeter County Gaol and House of Correction (1807–10), Geo. Moneypenny.
Abingdon Bridewell, Berks. (1811), Jeffray Wyattville and Daniel Harris.
Guildford County House of Correction (1822), architect unknown.
Maidstone County Gaol (1810–17), D.A. Alexander.
Canterbury County Gaol (–1808), George Byfield.
Dover County Gaol (1818–21), Richard Elsam.
Tothill Fields Bridewell (Westminster) (1829–34), Robert Abram.
Cold Bath Fields Vagrants Wing (–1830), William Moseley.
Cold Bath Fields Misdemeanants Wing (–1832), William Moseley.
Chelmsford County Gaol (1822–8), Thomas Hopper.
Ilford County House of Correction (1828), Thomas Hopper.
St James County House of Correction, Colchester (1832), Thomas Hopper.

Bury St Edmunds Town Gaol (1802–3), George Byfield.

Norfolk County Gaol (1824–8), Francis Stone.

Norwich City Gaol (1824–7), Richard Brown.

Cambridge County Gaol (1807), George Byfield.

Bedford County Gaol (1801), John Wing.

Worcester County Gaol (1801–14), J. Byfield and Sandys.

Leicester County Prison (1824–8), William Parsons.

Southwell County House of Correction (1807–8), Richard Ingleman.

Derby County Gaol (1823–7), Francis Goodwin.

Knutsford County Gaol and House of Correction (1820?), George Moneypenny.

Lancaster Castle female prison (1818–21) (rotunda), J.M. Gandy.

Beverly House of Correction (1804–14), William Watson and J.P. Pritchett?

York City House of Correction (1814), Peter Atkinson (the younger).

York Castle County Gaol (1826–35), P.F. Robinson.

Carlisle County Gaol (1822–6), J. Orridge and J. Dobson.

Newcastle Upon Tyne Town and County Gaol (1823–8), John Dobson.

Spilsby Prison (1824–6), H.E. Kendall.

67 'Plans for a House of Correction on Brixton Hill', signed Bevans, Surrey C.R.O.

68 For Wakefield see Society for the Improvement of Prison Discipline, *Remarks*, p. 30. The Springfield plans are in Essex C.R.O., QAG/b. 1/5.

69 Le Breton, *Thoughts on the Defective State of Prisons*, p. 7.

70 Printed plans for a Bridewell and House of Correction at Devizes, dated March 1808, Wiltshire C.R.O.

71 S.I.P.D., *Third Report*, pp. 80–1.

72 Richard Ingleman, 'Notes on Designs for a County Gaol at Salisbury', 10 Sept. 1817, Wiltshire C.R.O. The plans, he wrote, 'are intended to combine the properties of the windmill and circular forms'.

73 Griffiths, *Memorials of Millbank*, vol. I, p. 33.

74 Ingleman built a prison on the Fisherton plan at Sligo in Ireland, according to his 'Notes'. For the progress of Devizes see R.B. Pugh (ed.), *Victoria County History of Wiltshire*, vol. V, London, 1957, pp. 184 *et seq*; there are only two other examples of circular improved prisons — that submitted to the Bedfordshire Justices in 1819 as a 'House of Reform for Inferior Offenders' by Robert Salmon, Beds. C.R.O., PP/2/3 (unexecuted) and, the earliest, a design submitted to the Norfolk magistrates for Bury St Edmunds Gaol in 1801 by Arthur Brown, see *Gentleman's Magazine*, vol. LXXI (1801), pp. 697–9 (unexecuted).

75 Holford, *Vindication of the General Penitentiary at Millbank*, Appendix, pp. iv–viii.

76 Society for the Improvement of Prison Discipline, *Rules Proposed*, Appendix, 'Description of a Corn and Flour Mill, also of a Pump Mill adapted for the Employment of Prisoners', William Cubitt.

77 *P.P.* 1824, vol. XIX, 'Treadwheels: Copy of Correspondence Between the Sec. of State for the Home Depart., and the Visiting Magistrates of Prisons in which the Treadwheel has been Introduced', p. 165.

78 Society for the Improvement of Prison Discipline, *Rules Proposed*, p. 59.

79 19 Geo. III c. 74, sect. 32.

80 Robert Seymour, *Survey of the Cities of London and Westminster*, London, 1734, vol. I, p. 185.

81 Neild, *General State of the Prisons*, p. 168.

82 It seems to have been well known that Cubitt based his mill on a Chinese model, see K. Briscoe, *A Letter on the Nature and Effects of the Treadwheel*, London, 1824, p. 130; and also a letter from Edward Weir on the Treadwheel, n.d., West Sussex C.R.O., QAP/2/4.

83 Society for the Improvement of Prison Discipline, *Rules Proposed*, p. 62.

84 Briscoe, *Letter on the Nature and Effects of the Treadwheel*. E. Weir was, however, purveying his treadwheels as 'admirably calculated for the employment of the Parish poor'.

85 *Encyclopadeia Britannica*, 4th edn, 1824, entry under 'Prisons and Prison Discipline'.

86 Letter from the Secretary of State Respecting the Use of the Treadwheel, dated 10 March 1823, East Sussex C.R.O.

87 Society for Diffusing Useful Information on the Subject of Capital Punishment, *An Account of the Maison de Force at Ghent*, London, 1817, p. 14.

88 *P.P.* 1835, vols. XI–XII.

89 *P.P.* 1835, vol. XII, p. 463.

90 Daniel Nihil, *Prison Discipline in its Relation to Society and Individuals*, London, 1839, p. 13.

91 *P.P.* 1835, vol. XII, plate 1; see also Papers on Treadwheel, East Sussex C.R.O.

92 For the Devizes wheel see Plans of Workroom and Treadmill n.d., Wiltshire C.R.O.; for the Springfield wheel see Plans of Alteration to Springfield, 1843, Essex C.R.O., QAG b 1/11; for Brixton wheel faults see Briscoe, *Letter on the Nature and Effects of the Treadwheel*, p. 118; for Maidstone faults see *P.P.* 1825, vol. XXIII, p. 576; for Cold Bath Fields see Papers re Death of a Prisoner Entangled in the Treadwheel, MJ SPC.E. 3191, Middlesex R.O.

93 Plan of Brixton House of Correction dated 1821, signed by Cubitt, Surrey C.R.O.

94 John Headlam, *A Letter to the Right Honourable Robert Peel . . . on Prison Labour*, London, 1824, p. 36.

95 Charles Callis Western, *Remarks on Prison Discipline Delivered to the Lord Lieutenant and Magistrats of the County of Essex*, London, 1821, pp. 5, 16.

96 *P.P.* 1824, vol. XIX, pp. 149 et seq.

97 Letter from Secretary of State re Treadwheels, 10 March 1823, East Sussex C.R.O.

98 *P.P.* 1825, vol. XXIII, pp. 567 et seq.

99 John Mason Good, M.D., *Letter to Sir John Cox Hippsley on the Mischiefs Incidental to the Treadwheel*, 2nd edn, London, 1824, p. 4.

100 Briscoe, *Letter on the Nature and Effects of the Treadwheel*, p. 45.

101 H. Drummond, *A Letter to the Justices of the Peace for Surrey on the Cases in the House of Correction at Guildford*, London, 1824.

102 *P.P.* 1831–2, vol. VII, 'Report of the Select Committee on Secondary Punishment', Appendix 1, p. 133. At Knutsford the labour would thus be equivalent to climbing from the bottom to the top of the Post Office Tower, London, 16 times a day on tiptoe in summer, and 11 times a day in winter.

103 In Middlesex C.R.O. MA/DCP/G 191–7. None signed, perhaps also by Abram.

104 Plans for the first scheme are preserved in Derby C.R.O.

105 Glover, *History of the County of Derby*, pp. 476–9.

106 *P.P.* 1819, vol. VII, 'Reports of the Select Committee on the State of the Gaols', pp. 323–34.

107 *P.P.* 1837, vol. XXXII, Second Report of the Inspectors of Prisons for the Home District, p. 14; also, *P.P.* 1835, vol. XI, pp. 139 et seq., Sibly giving evidence; and *P.P.* 1831–2, vol. VII, 'Report of the Select Committee on Secondary Punishment', p. 607.

108 As early as 1827 William Roscoe, the Liverpool antiquarian and philanthropist, published an account of the two new American systems of imprisonment, criticizing both (see N.K. Teeters and J.D. Shearer, *The Prison at Philadelphia: Cherry Hill*, N.Y., 1957, pp. 27–8). The government report of 1831 from the Select Committee on Secondary Punishments was more partisan and enthusiastic, see *P.P.* 1831–2, vol. VII, p. 565.

109 This extraordinary volte-face is nowhere more in evidence than in the 1835 House of Lords Reports from the Select Committee on Gaols and Houses of Correction.

7. Architecture against communication

1 The focus of their attention was the Walnut Street Prison. For a description of improvements see Anon., *Some Account of the Prison at Philadelphia*,

London, 1816, esp. solitary block, pp. 6 et seq.

2 K. Negley Teeters and John D. Shearer, *The Prison at Philadelphia: Cherry Hill*, N.Y., 1957, p. 19.

3 G. de Beaumont and A. de Tocqueville, *On the Penitentiary System of the United States and its Application to France*, trans. F. Lieber, Philadelphia, 1833, p. 5.

4 *Ibid.*, p. 9. See also *P.P.* 1834, vol. XLVI, William Crawford, Report on the Penitentiaries of the United States, p. 357.

5 Teeters and Shearer, *The Prison at Philadelphia*, pp. 35–53.

6 Blake McKelvey, *American Prisons: A Study in American Social History Prior to 1915*, Chicago, 1936, p. 12.

7 Haviland Papers, Somerset C.R.O., H.V. 88, Newspaper cutting dated 1842.

8 Francis Lieber's introduction to Beaumont and Tocqueville, *On the Penitentiary System*, p. xi n.

9 Teeters and Shearer, *The Prison at Philadelphia*, p. 73.

10 *P.P.* 1834, vol. XLVI, Crawford, Report, pp. 349–669.

11 Auguste Demetz and Abel Blouet, *Rapports sur les Penitenciers des Etats Unis*, Paris, 1837.

12 *Ibid.*, p. 41.

13 Beaumont and Tocqueville, *On the Penitentiary System*, p. 24; and Daniel Nihil, *Prison Discipline in its Relation to Society and Individuals*, London, 1839, p. 59.

14 Richard Ingleman, 'Explanation of the Plans for a House of Correction at Southwell', printed 1807, Wiltshire C.R.O.; and Plans of Folkingham House of Correction with Explanation, Lincs. C.R.O.

15 *P.P.* 1819, vol. VII, 'Report of the Select Committee on the State of the Gaols', p. 356.

16 Charles Callis Western, *Remarks on Prison Discipline Delivered to the Lord Lieutenant and Magistrates of the County of Essex*, London, 1821, pp. 8, 13. See also, A Citizen, *The Gaol of the City of Bristol*, London, 1815, in which both reformative solitude and the Bentham Panopticon were commended to the Bristol Magistrates; and A. Wilson,

Outlines of a Plan for the Improvement of Prison Discipline, Dublin, 1830. Wilson, a follower of Hanway, practised solitary confinement in the Richmond Bridewell of which he was governor.

17 *P.P.* 1837, vol. XXXII, Second Report of the Inspectors of Prisons for the Home District, p. 15.

18 Oxford C.R.O., Plans QSE 20.

19 As stated by Oscar, King of Sweden. See Rev. John Field, *The Advantages of the Separate System of Imprisonment*, London, 1846, p. 29. In 1836 a Committee on the Laws Relating to Prisons, chaired by Lord John Russell, resolved that, as classification had gone as far as it could go and still was not effective, more 'discretion' should be allowed to Justices in classifying prisoners by character; *P.P.* 1836, vol. XXI, p. 301.

20 This point was made by A. Wilson in *Outlines of a Plan*, p. 27.

21 Beaumont and Tocqueville, *On the Penitentiary System*, p. 32; Demetz and Blouet, *Rapports*, p. 29.

22 Demetz and Blouet, *Rapports*, p. 43.

23 Field, *The Advantages of the Separate System*, p. 225. There were those, however, who believed that variations in the severity of solitude as experienced did not necessarily correspond to the moral turpitude of the subject, for example see Letter from Sir Robert Peel cited in L.W. Fox in *The English Prison and Borstal System*, London, 1952, p. 35.

24 *P.P.* 1834, vol. XLVI, Crawford Report, p. 360.

25 *P.P.* 1835, vol. XII, p. 716 for 48 entries in the Report's index under Solitary Confinement. None of the witnesses were against it in principle though some — Elizabeth Fry and Samuel Hoare amongst them — urged that it be used with moderation.

26 *P.P.* 1835, vol. XI, p. 123.

27 *P.P.* 1835, vol. XII, pp. 484–5.

28 *P.P.* 1835, vol. XI, p. 19.

29 Lord John Russell, Circular from the Home Dept, reproduced in Rev. John T. Burt, *The Results of the System of Separate Confinement*, London, 1852, Appendix VII, pp. 281 *et seq.*

30 Joseph Adshead, *Prisons and Prisoners*,

London, 1845, p. 90.

31 For example, the new Rules and Regulations for Blackburn's Staffordshire County Gaol in 1793 stipulated that the governor receive £200 p.a.; the first turnkey £30 p.a.; the second turnkey £25 p.a.; the chaplain £30 p.a., and the apothecary/surgeon £25 p.a.

32 George Holford, *An Account of the Penitentiary at Millbank*, London, 1828, pp. 135–8; and *Thoughts on the Criminal Prisons of this Country*, London, 1821, pp. 72–3.

33 J.A. Hoyles, *Religion in Prisons*, London, 1955, chs. 2 and 3.

34 Two entries in the *Regulations for Prisons in England and Wales*, Home Office, 1843, respecting the chaplain should be cited:
'121 — He shall, at stated times, see every prisoner in private, in order to be able to direct his advice and instruction, with reference to the peculiar character and state of mind of each prisoner, and that under circumstances in which the prisoner is likely to be least reserved, and most open to good influence.'
'126 — He shall keep a character book in which shall be entered the names of all prisoners, with such information as he may receive, in his communications with them or otherwise, touching the following particulars:— age, occupation, condition, education and connections of the prisoner; his previous character & habits; when & where received, and with what character; whether previously convicted and how often.'

35 Described thus by George Laval Chesterton, practitioner of the 'silent system' at Cold Bath Fields, in *Revelations of Prison Life*, 2nd edn, London, 1856, vol. I, p. 316.

36 *P.P.* 1837, vol. XXXII, Second Report of the Inspectors of Prisons for the Home District, p. 29.

37 *D.N.B.*

38 *P.P.* 1838, vol. XXX, Third Report of the Inspectors of Prisons, pp. 120 et seq.

39 2 & 3 Vict. c. 39.

40 Chesterton, *Revelations of Prison Life*, vol. I, p. 316.

41 *P.P.* 1835, vol. XII, p. 477.

42 So thought the Rev. Kingsmill of Pen-

tonville after some years of experience. See *P.P.* 1854, vol. XXXIII, 'Report on the Discipline and Management of the Convict Prisons', p. 8.

43 Rev. J. Field, *Bodily and Spiritual Diseases Compared: A Sermon Preached Before the University of Oxford*, Oxford, 1850. p. 12.

44 Nihil, *Prison Discipline*, p. 35.

45 *Ibid.*, p. 37.

46 Quoted by Philip Collins in *Dickens and Crime*, 2nd edn, London, 1965, p. 162.

47 Burt, *The Results of the System*, p. 45.

48 *Ibid.*, pp. 48–9.

49 Elizabeth Melling, *Kentish Sources, VI: Crime and Punishment*, Maidstone, 1969, p. 270.

50 *P.P.* 1837, vol. XXXII, Second Report of the Inspectors of Prisons, pp. 32 et seq.; Demetz and Blouet, *Rapports*, 'De la Construction des Prisons', pp. 88 et seq. For Bullar's involvement see p. 91.

51 W.S. Inman, *Reports of the Committee of the House of Commons on Ventilation Warming and the Transmission of Sound*, London, 1836. This publication contained the deliberations of a 12 man committee under Benjamin Hawes, R.I.B.A., set up with particular reference to the design of a new House of Commons.

52 Demetz and Blouet, *Rapports*, p. 91.

53 *Ibid.*, pp. 89–90.

54 Six cells were afterwards built with less expensive types of cavity wall. See *P.P.* 1837, vol. XXXII, Second Report of Inspectors of Prisons, p. 38.

55 Haviland Papers, Somerset C.R.O., HV. 88, newspaper cutting on Berkshire Prison, Pennsylvania.

56 Burt, *The Results of the System*, Appendix V, pp. 271 et seq.

57 Henry Mayhew and John Binney, *The Criminal Prisons of London*, London, 1862, p. 163.

58 Demetz and Blouet, *Rapports*, p. 60.

59 *P.P.* 1835, vol. XII, p. 646.

60 It is perhaps of incidental interest that the Rev. Nihil, in *Prison Discipline* (1839) and R. Smith in *The Evils of the Silent and Separate Systems Removed*, London, 1838, urged the building of Bentham's Panopticon as the 'experimental' prison.

61 According to Max Grunhut the cell/ yards of Cherry Hill were copied in Belgium. See *Penal Reform*, Oxford, 1948, p. 60.

62 *P.P.* 1835, vol. XI, p. 169.

63 Ramon de la Sagra, *Atlas Carcelario*, Madrid, 1843, sect. II, plate VII.

64 *P.P.* 1847, vol. XXIX, Joshua Jebb, Second Report of the Surveyor General of Prisons, p. 17; and Sidney and Beatrice Webb, *English Prisons Under Local Government*, London, 1922, p. 51.

65 Demetz and Blouet, *Rapport*. p. 58.

66 *Ibid.*, p. 69.

67 *Ibid.*, pp. 85 et seq.

68 The word thermo-ventilation was applied to what would now be termed ducted air heating. The term was coined in 1777 by Adam Walker.

69 *P.P.* 1837, vol. XXXII, Second Report of the Inspectors of Prisons, p. 38.

70 London Patent Office, Red Abridgement on Ventilation.

71 Inman, *Reports . . . on Ventilation*, pp. 47 and 56—7.

72 Joshua Jebb, *Report on the Construction, Ventilation and Details of Pentonville Prison*, London, 1844, p. 267; and Islington Central Library, Cuttings on Pentonville, letter in the *Builder*, 8 Feb. 1845. Heather Tomlinson notes that poor ventilation was, nevertheless, a common complaint in many of the prisons built after Pentonville. See M.H. Tomlinson, 'Victorian Prisons', unpublished thesis, Bedford College, London, 1975, pp. 113—17, 140—1.

73 Haviland Papers, Somerset C.R.O., HV.

88, *The Public Ledger*, Pennsylvania, 1 Feb. 1850.

74 Burt, *The Results of the System*, p. 7.

75 Nihil, *Prison Discipline*, p. 75.

76 Field, *Bodily and Spiritual Diseases Compared*, p. 12.

77 Field, *The Advantages of the Separate System*, p. 115.

78 *P.P.* 1835, vol. XI, p. 139.

79 Nihil, *Prison Discipline*, p. 75.

80 *P.P.* 1834, vol. XLVI, Crawford Report, p. 378.

81 *Ibid.*

82 Burt, *Results of the System*, p. 280, from Lord Russell's circular of 15 Aug. 1837.

83 M. Morreau-Christophe, *Rapports sur les Prisons d'Angleterre, de l'Ecosse, de la Holand, de la Belgique et de la Suisse*, Paris, 1839, p. 49.

84 As quoted in Demetz and Blouet, *Rapports*, p. 41.

85 Tomlinson, 'Victorian Prisons', ch. 1.

86 Three months before Jebb's appointment Lord John Russell announced this prospect in his circular to local authorities of 15 Aug. 1837 (Burt, *Results of the System*).

87 *P.P.* 1837, vol. XXXII, Second Report of the Inspectors of Prisons, pp. 44 et seq.

88 Demetz and Blouet, *Rapports*, p. 69.

89 *P.P.* 1836, vol. XXXV, First Report of the Inspectors of Prisons for the Home District, plates 3—5 and pp. 101—2.

90 Demetz and Blouet, *Rapports*, pp. 9—11, 18—19, 54.

8. The Model Prison

1 J.T. Burt, *The Results of the System of Separate Confinement*, London, 1852, p. 45.

2 Joseph Adshead, *Prisons and Prisoners*, London, 1845, pp. 256—7.

3 *The Times*, 14 June 1841.

4 See above: the Millbank Penitentiary, pp. 244—50.

5 Joshua Jebb, *Report on the Construction, Ventilation and Details of Pentonville Prison*, London, 1844, p. 49.

6 *Ibid.*, p. 50.

7 *Sentinel*, 14 Jan. 1843.

8 Jebb, *Report on Pentonville*, Appendix on Costs of Construction.

9 Jebb, *Report on Pentonville*, p. 34.

10 Henry Mayhew and John Binney, *The Criminal Prisons of London*, London, 1862, p. 120.

11 *Illustrated London News*, 28 May 1864, p. 349.

12 For the Model Rules to go with Model Prisons see Home Office, *Regulations for Prisons in England and Wales*, London,

1843.

13 Jebb, *Report on Pentonville*, p. 15.

14 *Ibid.*, p. 28.

15 *Ibid.*, p. 18.

16 Mayhew and Binney, *The Criminal Prisons of London*, p. 135. For an illustration of trucks, trays and rollers see N.H. Julius, *England's Mustergefangniss in Pentonville*, Berlin, 1846, plate VIII.

17 Jebb, *Report on Pentonville*, p. 30.

18 Adshead, *Prisons and Prisoners*, p. 234.

19 Jebb, *Report on Pentonville*, p. 15.

20 *Ibid.*, p. 16.

21 Mayhew and Binney, *The Criminal Prisons of London*, p. 125.

22 Collins, Peter, *Changing Ideals in Modern Architecture, 1750–1950*, pp. 235 et seq.

23 In 1844 it was calculated — perhaps spuriously — that 8,000 cells were being constructed with thermo-ventilation. See, An Engineer, *Remarks on the Warming & Ventilation of Prisons and other Public Buildings*, London, 1844, p. 13.

24 M.H. Tomlinson, 'Victorian Prisons', unpublished thesis, Bedford College, London, 1975, Appendix D.

25 As in Alfred Waterhouse's three enormous prisons for males and females at Salford and Preston. See E. Chadwick, *Description of the Hundred of Salford Assize Courts*, Lancs. C.R.O., for illustrations of the interior.

26 C.L.R.O., Surveyor's Justice Plans, portfolio 1, plans 499, 500 and 653, for plant at Newgate.

27 Plans of Devizes House of Correction dated 1867, Wiltshire C.R.O.

28 The City Library and Museum at Hereford have photographs showing the conversion, taken in 1930 prior to the gaol's demolition.

29 *P.P.* 1847, vol. XXXIX, 'Second Report of the Surveyor General of Prisons', plates 20, 21.

30 *P.P.* 1854, vol. XXXIII, 'Report on the Discipline and Management of the Convict Prisons', p. 88:

31 Kenneth Clark, *The Gothic Revival*, Harmondsworth, 1964, pp. 114, 115.

32 James Murray's tracings of Barry's original Pentonville designs are contained in the Smaller Italian Atlas, R.I.B.A. Prints and Drawings.

33 Home Office, *Regulations for Prisons in England and Wales*, 1840.

34 Examination of Prison Discipline Taken Before a Committee of Magistrates, 9 May 1844, Essex C.R.O., QAG/p.19.

35 Essex C.R.O., Plans QAG/b.1/11.

36 Essex C.R.O., QAG/p.19., letter from Jebb, 6 Dec. 1843.

37 See also Eric Stockdale, *A Study of Bedford Prison 1660–1877*, Bedford, 1977, pp. 161 et seq. for Jebb's harrying of the Beds. County Surveyor, Frances Giles in 1848/9; and Tomlinson, 'Victorian Prisons', pp. 128 et seq. for a wealth of fascinating detail on Jebb's interventions.

38 William Hepworth Dixon, *The London Prisons*, London, 1850, pp. 364–8.

39 'Prisons and Architecture', *Building News*, vol. III (1857), p. 227.

40 Ministère de l'Interieur, *Instruction et Programme pour la Construction des Maisons d'Arret et de Justice*, Paris, 1841. See also Charles Gourlier, *Choix d'Edifices Publics*, Paris, 1825–50, vol. III, for prisons built on the *Instruction* models.

41 Rev. John Field. *The Advantages of the Separate System of Imprisonment*, London, 1846, pp. 108–9.

42 Model plans were included in Oscar's work on reform, *On Punishment and Prisons*, trans. from 2nd edn, London, 1842.

43 C. Krohne and R. Uber, *Die Strafanstalten und Gefangnisse in Preusen*, Berlin, 1901, plates 60–1.

44 Haviland Papers, Somerset C.R.O., HV. 88, cutting from the *North-American*, vol. VI, no. 1, 726 (14 Oct. 1844). The *Journal of Prison Discipline*, launched in 1845 by the Philadelphia Society for Alleviating the Miseries of Prisoners, was also international in scope.

45 N.K. Teeters and J.D. Shearer, *The Prison at Philadelphia: Cherry Hill*, N.Y., 1957, p. 227.

46 *P.P.* 1847, vol. XXIX, 'Second Report of the Inspectors of Prisons', pp. 27–8, a quote from the Rev. Charles Demme, in praise of Cherry Hill.

47 Peter Laurie, *Prison Discipline and Secondary Punishment: Remarks on the First Report of the Inspectors of*

Prisons, London, 1837, prefatory quote.

48 *Ibid.*, p. 9.

49 Islington Central Library, Pentonville File, *John Bull*, 2 Dec. 1843.

50 Mayhew and Binney, *The Criminal Prisons of London*, p. 105.

51 Burt, *The Results of the System*, p. 81.

52 *Ibid.*, p. 93; Daniel Nihil, *Prison Discipline in its Relation to Society and Individuals*, London, 1839, p. 78; Mayhew and Binney, *The Criminal Prisons of London*, pp. 103–4; Adshead, *Prisons and Prisoners*, p. 18.

53 Arthur Griffiths, *Memorials of Millbank*, London, 1875, vol. II, p. 34.

54 Dixon, *The London Prisons*, pp. 143–4.

55 Mayhew and Binney, *The Criminal Prisons of London*. p. 104.

56 Charles Dickens, *American Notes*, London, 1842, ch. VII.

57 *The Dispatch*, 21 Jan. 1844, edited letter from Mr Henry Dowell Griffiths, who held that the House of Commons 'no more represents the people of England than the people of Russia'.

58 Laurie, *Prison Discipline*, p. 31.

9. The uncoupling of architecture and reform

1 Peter Laurie, *Prison Discipline and Secondary Punishment*, London, 1837, p. 47. The local Justices were also roundly criticized by Edward Mullins for frittering away such large sums on their prison buildings: 'Within the last 50 years there has sprung up among the justices and their friends an irregular *mania* on the subject of criminal law.' See Mullins, *A Treatise on the Magistracy of England*, London, 1836, p. 76. According to the same author annual expenditure on prison buildings had risen from £92,000 in 1793 to £177,000 in 1833.

2 Henry Mayhew and John Binney, *The Criminal Prisons of London*, London, 1862, p. 169.

3 A concise but very informative account of the separate versus silent controversy can be found in Phillip Collins, *Dickens and Crime*, 2nd edn, London, 1965, chs. III, V and VI.

4 *P.P.* 1837, vol. XXXII, 'Second Report of the Inspectors of Prisons for the Home District', p. 65.

5 *P.P.* 1854, vol. XXXIII, p. 26.

6 The following deliberations are cited by Collins, *Dickens and Crime*, p. 78: 'The Committee . . . do not consider that the moral reformation of the offender holds the primary place in the prison system; that mere industrial employment without wages is a sufficient punishment for many crimes; that punishment in itself is morally prejudicial to the criminal and useless to society, or that it is desirable

to abolish both the crank and the tread wheel as soon as possible.'

7 Sir Edmund Du Cane, *The Punishment and Prevention of Crime*, London, 1885, pp. 1–2.

8 Orby Shipley, *The Purgatory of Prisoners*, London, 1857, pp. 19–20.

9 Joseph Adshead, who had energetically defended the separate system as a means of reformation in 1845, was, 12 years later, proposing that independent reformatories for juvenile criminals be built; see Adshead, *On Juvenile Criminals, Reformatories and the Means of Rendering the Perishing and Dangerous Classes Serviceable to the State*, Manchester, 1857.

10 Charles Gourlier, *Choix d'Edifices Publics*, Paris, 1825–50, vol. III, section 7, Edifices de Sûreté Publique, three plates.

11 Schools had, however, been considered as places of reformation before, and a similar rural style of construction had been employed by Fellenberg and other educationalists unconnected with the penal system; see W.A.C. Stewart and W.P. McCann, *The Educational Innovators: 1750–1880*, London, 1967, pp. 205–9, 216–18, 142–5.

12 The Chef de Famille occupied a room adjoining the dormitory and had powers of constant supervision, according to G.L. Chesterton visiting Mettray in 1855; see Chesterton, *Revelations of Prison Life*, 2nd edn, London, 1856,

vol. I, p. 245.

13 Enoch C. Wines, *The State of the Prisons and Child Saving Institutions of the World*, Cambridge, 1880, p. 343.

14 *Ibid.*, p. 224. Parkhurst, designed by Bullar, was not built on the family home principle but contained standard cellularized convict accommodation, although an 80 acre farm was kept under cultivation by the boys; see William Hepworth Dixon, *The London Prisons*, London, 1850, pp. 178–9.

15 Although perhaps not invariably so in earlier times. Sellin records that when Jan Van Hout visited the Amsterdam Rasphuis in 1597 he asked why the recalcitrant children of good parents were not kept separate from the worst and lowest vagabonds and pilferers. His guide told him that if anyone were to be improved by such separation it would be the vagabonds and pilferers and not the children; see Thorsten Sellin, *Pioneering in Penology*, Philadelphia, 1944, p. 62.

16 The S.I.P.D. – the full title of which was the Society for the Improvement of Prison Discipline and the Reformation of Young Offenders – approved of sending youths to gaol so long as it was sufficiently classified and well-managed. See p. 266.

17 G. de Beaumont and A. de Tocqueville, *On the Penitentiary System of the United States*, Introduction by F. Lieber, Philadelphia, 1833, p. xviii.

18 A. Demetz and A. Blouet, *Rapports sur les Penitenciers des Etats Unis*, Paris, 1837, p. 6.

19 A.N.W. Pugin, *Contrasts*, 2nd edn, London, 1841. Also added to the 2nd edition of *Contrasts* were the 'Con-

trasted Residences of the Poor' where the moralizing is all the more explicit for being depicted as a cartoon melodrama. The medieval poorhouse is distinguished by its charity, the nineteenth-century equivalent by its brutality.

20 Thomas Carlyle, *Latter Day Pamphlets no. 11*, 'Model Prisons', March 1850, pp. 10–11.

21 First coined by Francis Lieber in 1834, N.K. Teeters and J.D. Shearer, *The Prison at Philadelphia: Cherry Hill*, N.Y., 1957, p. 24.

22 I do not recollect ever reading the word in eighteenth-century literature on prison reform, although the *O.E.D.* dates its earliest use in that century.

23 See David de Giustino, *Conquest of Mind: Phrenology and Victorian Social Thought*, London, 1975, pp. 145–61. and J.P. Browne, *Phrenology and its Application to Education, Insanity and Prison Discipline*, London, 1869.

24 Chesterton, *Revelations of Prison Life*, vol. II, pp. 279–80.

25 Blake McKelvey, *American Prisons*, Chicago, 1936, pp. 26–7.

26 Leon Radzinowicz, *Ideology and Crime*, London, 1966, p. 46 lists Morel's theory of degeneracy, the physiognomists, the alienists and many others researching into the possibility of moral insanity and disorders of the criminal personality.

27 Du Cane, *The Punishment and Prevention of Crime*, p. 3, citing the opinion of a Professor Bain.

28 *Ibid.*, p. 2.

29 Arthur Griffiths, *The Secrets of the Prison House*, London, 1894, vol. I, p. 3.

30 Radzinowicz, *Ideology and Crime*, ch. 2, 'The Deterministic Position', esp. pp. 39–45.

10. Architecture limited and unlimited

1 David Rothman, *The Discovery of the Asylum*, Boston, 1971, pp. 152–3; Michel Foucault, *Discipline and Punish*, trans. Sheridan, London, 1975, pp. 144–5; Michael Ignatieff, *A Just Measure of Pain*, London, 1978, pp. 76, 106, and especially Dario Melossi and Massimo Pavarini, *The Prison and the*

Factory, London, 1981.

2 John Cornforth and John Fowler, *English Decoration in the Eighteenth Century*, London, 1974, chs. 2, 3; also Mark Girouard, *Life in the English Country House*, London, 1978, ch. 8.

3 Society for Improving the Condition of

the Labouring Classes, *Prospectus of the Society*, London, 1857, p. 1.

4 R. Evans., 'Il Contagio dell'Imoralita: Casa a Famiglia nella Londre dell'Ottocento', in Georges Teyssot and Paolo Morachiello (eds.), *Le Macchine Imperfette*, Rome, 1980, p. 269.

5 *Ibid.*, pp. 273—82.

6 H.M. Colvin, *Biographical Dictionary of British Architects*, London, 1978. Nearly all the material that follows has been gleaned from this indispensable source.

7 James Elmes, *Hints for the Improvement of Prisons*, London, 1817.

8 Colvin, *B.D.B.A.*

9 J. Mordaunt Crook, 'The Pre-Victorian Architect', *Architectural History, Journal of the Society of Architectural Historians of Great Britain*, vol. XII (1969), p. 66.

10 *Gentleman's Magazine*, vol. LXX (1800), p. 409.

11 *Gentleman's Magazine*, vol. LXXII (1801), pp. 697—8. Brown's proposal had been passed over by the magistrates who chose instead the 'ingenious' plan from George Byfield which was to become the first of a new generation of improved radial prisons. Brown too can lay modest claim to originality for his

was the first circular courtyard prison plan produced in this country.

12 Examples of this are the coved cornice around the inner court that presumably served to prevent escapes across the roof, and the applied pilasters around the outside of the prison wall.

13 *Gentleman's Magazine*, vol. LXXII (1801), p. 697.

14 Instead of doing as Ingleman did seven years later in the circular plan for Devizes House of Correction (Fig. 124), that is, placing the gaoler's and keepers' accommodation and the chapel in the centre, Brown displaced them to the edge, where they provided the one discontinuity in an otherwise unbroken ring of cells and arcades. Thus he was able to express their presence on the external facade as a conventional, symmetrical frontage focussed on the altar apse of the chapel, reverting once more to a visible demonstration of an order that was essentially emblematic. Nevertheless, remaining at the geometrical centre was the circular court 'communicating with all the others'.

15 *Gentleman's Magazine*, vol. LXX (1800), p. 409.

Index